CU00829731

Garlic and Oil

Garlic and Oil
Politics and Food in Italy

Carol Helstosky

Oxford • New York

English edition
First published in 2004 by
Berg
Editorial offices:
1st Floor, Angel Court, 81 St Clements Street, Oxford, OX4 1AW, UK
175 Fifth Avenue, New York, NY 10010, USA

© Carol Helstosky 2004

All rights reserved.
No part of this publication may be reproduced in any form
or by any means without the written permission of Berg.

Berg is the imprint of Oxford International Publishers Ltd.

Library of Congress Cataloguing-in-Publication Data
A catalogue record for this book is available from the Library of Congress.

British Library Cataloguing-in-Publication Data
A catalogue record for this book is available from the British Library.

ISBN 1 85973 890 7 (Cloth)

Typeset by Avocet Typeset, Chilton, Aylesbury, Bucks
Printed in the United Kingdom by Biddles Ltd, King's Lynn

www.bergpublishers.com

Contents

Acknowledgements

I am grateful to the institutions and organizations that offered generous financial support for the research and completion of this book. I received post-doctoral support from the National Endowment for the Humanities, through the American Academy in Rome, and the German Marshall Fund. Research for Chapters Two and Three was funded by the Fulbright Foundation, the American Historical Association, and Rutgers University, where I completed my doctoral dissertation.
I would also like to thank the archivists and staff at the Archivio Centrale dello Stato, Rome; the Biblioteca Nazionale, Rome; the Biblioteca Alessandrina, Rome; the Biblioteca di Storia Contemporanea, Rome; the Museo Criminologico, Rome; the Biblioteca Nazionale, Florence; and the librarians at the American Academy in Rome, the Ministero dell'Agricoltura, Rome, and Penrose Library at the University of Denver.

Several people have guided this project through completion and generously offered their time and advice in reading parts of this manuscript. I thank Victoria de Grazia, who shaped this project in its earliest stages. I am also grateful to Carole Counihan, Belinda Davis, John Davis, Donna Gabaccia, and Linda Reeder for reading the manuscript and supporting the project. However, all errors and omissions are the responsibility of the author.

This work has benefited from numerous conversations, in the United States and in Italy, with friends and colleagues in the field of history and elsewhere. My heartfelt thanks to colleagues at the University of Denver, to Nancy Bisaha, Paul Deslandes, Joanna Drell, Paul Garfinkel, Wendy Kaplan, Suzanne Kaufman, Giuseppe Lauricella, Laurel McSherry, Borden Painter, Livio Pestilli, Susan Pennybacker, and Scott Sandage. Thanks also to Zack Poppel, who provided research assistance at the last minute.

And last but not least, I'd like to thank my family. My husband Martin Gloege has provided unflagging support and sound editorial advice. My daughter, Helen Flannery Gloege, supplied some much-needed humor at the end of this project. This book is dedicated to my father, Edward V. Helstosky, and to the memory of my mother, Helen C. Helstosky. Her life and death taught me about the frailty of the physical body and the resilience of the human spirit.

Introduction

Italian food is everywhere we look: espresso bars, lavishly photographed cook-books, Italian cooking shows on television, and pizza delivered to our doorsteps. Despite our familiarity with Italian food, we know very little about its history. We understand that Italian cuisine is rich in regional diversity and has been influenced by culinary styles from North Africa, the Middle East, and western Europe. We also know that for much of Italy's recent history, popular diet consisted of simple dishes prepared with few ingredients and the predominance of grains and produce over meat and dairy products, the so-called Mediterranean diet. We are perhaps most familiar with pizza and pasta, the foundations of Italian cuisine, given that these dishes are consumed throughout the world. Global consumers may prepare these foods to fit their own circumstances, but they strive to maintain the authenticity of these foods by using tomatoes or garlic and olive oil in the preparation and presentation of these dishes. What is known today as Italian food is a recent creation, however, and bears little resemblance to the abstemious and even inadequate diet endured by much of the population of Italy in the nineteenth and twentieth centuries. In fact, only in the last several decades have Italian consumers actually begun to eat what the rest of the world recognizes today as Italian cuisine.

During the nineteenth century and throughout much of the twentieth century, popular diet in Italy consisted of either bread or polenta, consumed with a *compa-natico*, usually onions, peppers, garlic, sardines, anchovies, or oil. Pasta, legumes, wine, dairy products, and fresh produce were consumed less frequently while meat and alcohol were consumed only on special occasions. The content of the Italian diet is not surprising, if we consider that a rocky terrain covers much of the peninsula. The landscape is excellent for growing grapes and olives, but very few crops, including staple crops like wheat, rice, or corn, can flourish on such uneven soil. To a great degree, Italy's Mediterranean diet was the unfortunate consequence of environment, yet human activity shaped popular consumption habits as well. Although few people starved or fell seriously ill from malnutrition in the nineteenth and twentieth centuries, the majority of the Italian population did not consume a nutritionally adequate diet because of economic and political constraints on their behavior as consumers and eaters. Subsistence farming and local markets characterized Italian agriculture while a weak national economy limited consumer options, even for urban workers and members of the middle class. Successive governments – liberal, fascist, democratic – grappled with the question of state intervention to assist consumers, but oftentimes their actions had minimal or detrimental effects on popular food habits. Cultural influences such as the Catholic belief in renunciation reinforced existing habits of sobriety and abstemiousness. Thus, Italian consumers remained trapped in a post-subsistence economy for multiple reasons, unable to make the transition to a more varied and nutritious diet.

The question remains, however, as to why Italian food habits have changed so little over the course of the nation's history? This book argues that politics shaped Italian diet. From the declaration of the Kingdom of Italy in 1861 to the 'economic miracle' of the 1960s, successive Italian governments have confronted the problems associated with poor nutrition and a monotonous diet. Since the latter half of the nineteenth century, adequate nutrition and a decent standard of living were the building blocks of European liberal statecraft, especially in the context of the second industrial revolution and the new imperialism. Although Italy had imperial ambitions, the nation lacked both an empire and a developed industry and therefore lacked the resources to provide for the population. In the context of the twentieth century's cycles of war and reconstruction, liberal, fascist, and democratic governments were forced to act, to guarantee the productivity, development, or survival of the population. In Italy and elsewhere in Europe, food became a national resource to be managed in order to preserve order, health, and productivity.[1] Yet we know little about the impact of state intervention on consumer choice or the creation of national identities as defined through food habits and consumption practice. The purpose of this book is to chart how government interventions created and sustained new consumption situations for Italians. The choices consumers made – how much or how little food to consume as well as the kinds of foods that are available – all derive from contests of power. In the case of modern Italy, power must be analyzed in the political, and not just the economic and cultural, realms.

This book's focus on the role of politics and state intervention lends itself to thinking about Italian food as a national resource to be managed. Moreover, this book tells the story of how a selection of foods and dishes came to exemplify, however accurately, the consumption habits, history, and identity of a nation. My use of the term national may offend those who maintain that Italian food and the idea of a national cuisine are fictions. After all, Italian cuisine today is characterized by a dazzling degree of regional diversity. As one of the foremost experts on Italian food, Marcella Hazan, described Italian cuisine: 'the first useful thing to know about Italian cooking is that as such it doesn't actually exist.'[2] While there is much truth to Hazan's assertion, this book is a history of consumer habit and not an explanation of how regional variety in Italian cuisine came to be. I refer to terms like national cuisine, popular diet, and Italian consumption habits in order to emphasize how food and its consumption constituted a national concern throughout much of Italian history to a growing number of concerned experts, consumers, and politicians. Although Italians most often used the word *alimentazione* to refer to everything from food provisioning to the act of eating, I have opted instead to refer to cuisine, diet, and food habits. Cuisine encompasses the foods, dishes, and preparation techniques that, however accurately, came to characterize Italian cooking and food-consumption. Diet refers to the kinds of foods and nutrients Italians consumed, while food habits describes they ways in which consumers purchased and prepared food.

Although I refer to terms like national cuisine, I also recognize that there were significant differences in habit between people of various regions, classes, occupations, and sex. These distinctions served as a basis from which scientific experts argued for more intensive state intervention to even out food consumption levels within the nation. Nineteenth-century studies of dietary habits revealed that the overwhelming majority of Italians consumed what we term a pre-industrial diet based on the predominance of cereals, legumes, and fresh produce (when available), with meat and animal proteins consumed on special occasions. The first industrial boom in the early twentieth century brought with it the first documented improvements manifest in the increased preference for wheat flour and a slight rise in the consumption of animal proteins. Industrial workers and some peasants consumed meat at least once a week. Even minor changes like these lifted experts' hopes that the state would do more to assist consumers. It did not. Instead, local authorities took an active role in provisioning; for example, municipalities in northern Italy, in cooperation with socialists and workers' organizations, organized consumer cooperatives, regulated merchants, and sponsored soup kitchens to feed the poor.

The First World War marked the beginning of state intervention in consumer habits. Wartime ministers were reluctant to take action, but their policies made a dramatic impact on food habits. Italy was ill prepared for war and survived on allied loans and wheat shipments. This situation benefited consumers, who enjoyed cheap, subsidized bread and could afford to purchase foods like meat, milk, or fresh produce. Wheat bread and pasta became the foundation of diet for many Italians, replacing corn, chestnuts, and rice. Wartime events preoccupied governing liberals, who worried about the balance of payments and dependence on outside powers for subsistence. At the war's end, public debate about the bread subsidy indicated that state intervention brought Italy to a political crossroads: should the government continue to foot the bill for a higher standard of food consumption? Would consumers be forced to choose between the necessity of bread and the luxury of meat as bread prices adjusted to the market?

Participants in the debate referred to a national 'alimentary problem'(*il problema dell'alimentazione*) and much of the debate was framed by the question of what the state could do to diversify and therefore improve popular diet.[3] Ultimately, the decision by Prime Minister Giovanni Giolitti to pull the subsidy in 1921 in favor of economic growth over social reform undermined his liberal support base (socialists, conservatives, and nationalists were all dissatisfied with the handling of the bread subsidy crisis), paving the way for a fascist takeover. In part, liberal consensus collapsed over whether the government could simultaneously accommodate competing political interests and satisfy the expectations of the postwar consumer. The first experiment in state control ended inconclusively; the war changed the quality of the Italian diet but would the postwar power struggles improve or worsen consumer habits? The fascist experiment in controlling consumption habits would provide a dramatic contrast to liberalism's troubled history.

When Mussolini and the fascist party seized power in 1922, they set out to control every aspect of food consumption and to nationalize Italian cuisine, essentially by making all Italians consume less food. Mussolini also wanted to assume the role of benevolent provider for the nation and spared no effort to associate himself with images of abundance. Charitable provisioning comprised the kinder side to fascist food policies. Harsher food controls followed the revaluation of the lire (1926) and increased with the policy of autarky or economic self-sufficiency in the mid-1930s. Instead of worrying about balancing consumer interests with available resources, fascism denied the possibility of a more diverse or nutritious diet, opting instead to bring consumer habits more in line with its goal of economic self-sufficiency. Mussolini's government accomplished this directly (through propaganda campaigns, the manipulation of scientific data, and public spectacles promoting austere consumer practice) and indirectly (decisions involving foreign policy, agriculture, and trade).

Broadly speaking, fascism nationalized Italian cuisine by forcing its policies on an unwilling population. The regime touted the economic and nutritional benefits of the Mediterranean diet, reinforcing its social and political value at every opportunity. Consumers eager to sample imported foods were discouraged by propaganda, export reductions, and trade sanctions against Italy for the invasion of Ethiopia. Italian cuisine was unified, but at great cost. Mussolini grew more relentless in his pursuit of economic self-sufficiency, particularly as the nation moved closer to an alliance with Germany and military preparations for war. During the war, the Italian population suffered terrible privations as the regime failed to live up to its image of benevolent provider and grossly mismanaged wartime food policies. Italians received one of the lowest food rations (measured in caloric value) in Europe, while up to 70 percent of consumer food purchases during wartime were made on the black market. Italian consumers were left with no option but to accept the prescribed fascist diet. Indeed, one could argue that one of the most visceral ways Italians experienced fascism was through their empty stomachs.

Under fascism, Mussolini's quest for political prestige dramatically shaped foodways by forcing Italian consumers to revert to nineteenth-century habits. After the regime collapsed and immediate provisioning crises were solved, Italians returned to debating the problems confronting the nation. Not surprisingly, the nature of these problems changed from worrying about scarce resources and malnutrition to fending off Americanization and managing the diseases of affluence. Amazingly, the general contours of national cuisine changed very little, despite a massive economic boom and the enticements of European integration and Americanization. In the early years of the economic miracle, Italians experimented with eating more meat and consuming desserts and snacks, but the essential structure of meals, along with the ingredients of Italian dishes, remained the same. Studies of consumer habits reveal that Italians simply consumed more of the foods they had always consumed once their wages increased. The postwar era witnessed a revival of interest in regional traditions and festivals as well as a concerted defense of Italian food against outside influence. It is not surprising that recently, Slow Food, an international movement resisting globalization and standardized tastes, is headquartered in Italy, nor is it remarkable that Italy has resisted McDonald's franchises longer than its European counterparts.[4]

The shape of Italian food habits had its roots in political struggles to encourage some culinary practices and discourage others. What seems peculiar about the Italian case is the nation's self-conscious struggle to improve the dietary standards of the population and the intensity with which this struggle was discussed and debated by the entire population. There developed a number of longstanding and sometimes volatile debates about what food meant to diverse groups of Italians: housewives, doctors, industrialists, social reformers, farmers, and government ministers. Although the primary focus of this book is on the impact of politics on consumption habits, this is also a history of the creation of a public discourse about food and the shifting symbolic value of food for various populations of Italians. For scientific experts in the nineteenth century, inadequate diet represented all that went wrong with national unification. For nationalists in the post-First World War era, the nearly free distribution of bread underscored the profligacy and decadence of the liberal state. For citizens living under the German occupation of Italy (1943–45), complaints about food shortages expressed an acute sense of betrayal by Nazi allies and Mussolini's fascist regime. Thus, food remained a persistent problem not only for the State but for citizens as well.

Taking my cue from Roland Barthes, who insisted that 'information about food must be gathered wherever it can be found,' I have utilized a variety of sources throughout this book.[5] Chapter One defines the nature of the problem of food consumption in Italy by examining the history of popular diet from Unification to the First World War. Here I have turned to the most common sources on food habits – scientific and social scientific monographs and dietary inquiries – to trace the development of an emerging public discourse on food consumption as an urgent problem that unified *and* divided the nation. The writings of experts were particularly suggestive; scientists and social scientists were part of an emerging professional community that felt empowered to direct the future of young Italy. Another significant source for understanding the formation of national identity through food consumption were the vast numbers of Italians who left to find better lives. By so doing, Italian immigrants invented a national cuisine outside of Italy and created a worldwide demand for characteristically Italian foods.

Chapters Two, Three, and Four reveal the unfolding of state intervention through food policies and their impact on consumers in the First World War and fascist eras. Chapter Two concentrates exclusively on World War I and the immediate postwar years, describing how and why state intervention shaped national cuisine. Archival sources trace the history of and debates surrounding state intervention, while more descriptive sources (scientific and social-scientific monographs) delineate the unification of consumer desires during and after the war by describing significant changes in consumer habits. Chapter Two concludes with an examination of the debate over the 'alimentary problem' and a detailed account of the public's violent reactions to state reversals of policy. The next two chapters deal with the fascist era, charting the rise and fall of fascist food policies. In Chapter Three, I use a variety of sources – archival, cookbooks, periodical literature – to define the contours of state intervention in the years 1922–35 and to assess its impact on the Italian population. Chapter Four then analyzes the overt and unintentional consequences of fascism's policy of economic self-sufficiency as the nation moved toward empire, war, and military disaster. Archival evidence from the years 1935–45 underscores the severity of living conditions while scientific and social scientific evidence confirms the radicalization of fascist rhetoric regarding food and its relationship to the nation. Unlike many other fascist policies that failed to motivate Italians or achieve consensus, food policies had certain and lasting effects, measurable even after fascism's collapse.

Chapter Five assesses the impact of the fascist years by describing how national cuisine did *not* change all that dramatically, despite the enormous economic, demographic, and cultural transformations after the war. Studies of consumer trends after 1945 yielded mixed results in terms of dramatic change: while Italians consumed more meat and more food outside the home, their shopping habits remained mostly the same, despite a rising standard of living. In fact, the Mediterranean diet resisted the onslaught of consumer abundance, the economic miracle, European integration, and Americanization. This chapter uses these studies and the history of the postwar modernization of the food industry to argue that food habits forged in the earlier part of the century were difficult to discard, even after the state minimized its role in governing food habits. Finally, the book concludes with an epilogue on the legacy of Italian cuisine. Populations throughout the world find Italian food tremendously appealing; pasta and pizza are dishes with universal appeal. At the same time that Italian cuisine has gone global, Italians in recent years have confronted external and domestic threats to the foods they eat and the ways in which they prepare and eat them. As Italians rally to defend their food habits, they have discovered that politics still matter, at least in the sense that current controversies over fast-food, globalization, and genetically modified foods are all about contests of power.

The issues covered in this study are diverse: policy formation, consumerism, food habits, and the science of nutrition. It seems only fair, then, that some readers might ask what kind of history this is. In the most general sense, this is a history of food consumption in Italy that looks at how and why people eat the foods they do. This has been my primary and guiding interest throughout the research for and completion of the project. It is also a history of the Italian people that pays atten-tion to an overlooked aspect of their lives: the struggle to survive on very little. Admittedly, the history of a post-subsistence economy lacks the drama of a pre-industrial world where populations face starvation, or the spectacle of a world of mass consumption where consumer desires are fulfilled. Yet there is drama in the struggle to get by: mothers made superhuman efforts to provide for their families; fathers made anguished choices about whether to resort to charity or go without; doctors pleaded for state intervention to improve diet; cabinet ministers made diffi-cult financial decisions that affected thousands of families. All of these stories deserve to be told. Thus, this is a history that blends cultural and social history while recognizing the primacy of politics in Italian history.

The way that I have chosen to analyze politics is by privileging the role of the State. There is no doubt that government intervention or inactivity had a profound impact on popular consumption habits throughout unified Italy's history, particu-larly with regard to trade and agricultural policies. This was the case from liber-alism to fascism to a democratic republic, although the policies of the diverse regimes varied considerably. While it is certainly true that Italy's topography and climate dictated the types of foods produced within Italy, it is also true that liberal hesitancy and fascist adamancy limited what foods were available to Italians. There were of course many discussions about the role the State should play in terms of consumption habits and popular diet. This book highlights the differences between radical, liberal, and conservative viewpoints on the nature and limits of state intervention and whenever possible, I have tried to capture popular response to state intervention. It is perhaps important to bear in mind that explaining the evolution of consumer taste is a difficult enterprise. While state intervention no doubt influenced the choices people made, or imposed certain constraints on consumer behavior, its influence must be placed in proper context. While I argue that the State's role in shaping consumer habits was profound, I do not believe that politics and the State had complete control over food choices; environment, economics, and cultural influences are recognized throughout the book as being influential in shaping food habits.

The attention I have paid to influences on food habits orient this book toward the production of a consumer ethic in modern Italy. My intent is to problematize the notion of a consumer ethic, or at least suggest that there were many paths to mass consumption by using Italy as a case study. The Italian ethic of consumption was built upon constraints and limits; food habits, when measured by variety and nutritional value, sometimes regressed. Although I continually reference consumers and their attitudes toward food, it is not my intention to write a book about Italian consumers per se, as there have been several compelling histories of Italian food told from the consumer's point of view.[6]

Finally, this book is a hybrid of two relatively new fields of academic research: the history of consumerism and food studies. I am indebted to all who have contributed to the history of consumerism, a body of knowledge that has enriched our understanding of the arts of purchase, the market economy, individual and group identity, gender formation, and notions of popular sovereignty, the body, and desire. This book builds on earlier studies of the origins of the consumer revolution that traced how individuals and households came to understand themselves as consuming units, not only in terms of social identity but also as part of a larger strategy for economic survival.[7] The Italian case most clearly resonates with these analyses of eighteenth- and early nineteenth-century Europe, where consumer practice bridged survival and identity formation. I have also utilized the studies on twentieth-century Europe that explain how consumption reshaped traditional structures of governance and ideas about sovereignty, as states confronted military and economic catastrophes as well as political restructuring. Here, historians have focused their attention on two related issues: how women combined their roles as consumers with new political entitlements as citizens; and how forms of consumption as entitlements come to be used in political arguments about welfare, economic growth, neo-mercantilism, and bio-politics.[8] Certainly, the Italian wartime and fascist regimes, as modernizing forces for the twentieth century, had to contend with all of these issues.

This book seeks to expand the study of consumerism once again by focusing on the formation of a national ethic of consumption: a set of values, assumptions, and practices that bring a population together while consciously distinguishing that population as unique. The Italian ethic of consumption was not based on the expansion of desire or the abundance of goods. Rather, austerity, limited choices, and very real constraints dictated the shape and development of consumerism in Italy. These characteristics are not unique to Italy, as other nations struggled with issues of wartime shortages and nutritional standards, for example. However, the Italian case provides an alternative path to the world of mass consumption. Italy's differences are worth thinking about, inasmuch as they reflect the difficulties and challenges governments faced – and continue to face – when providing food to citizens.

In the historiography of consumerism there are few studies that make food consumption their central focus. Perhaps this is because studies of food consumption are now labeled part of food studies, an interdisciplinary movement analyzing the meaning of food historically and across cultures. Pioneers in the field like Sidney Mintz, Stephen Mennell, Jack Goody, and Hans Teuteberg argued that food habits should be viewed as communicative processes encompassing whole societies, with important distinctions to be made between economic classes or populations from diverse regions.[9] A recent boom in food studies has led to publications, conferences, and even academic departments dedicated to understanding the social and political relevance of food. A new generation of scholars looks beyond strictly economic or cultural interpretations of food's meaning by bringing together all public and private sites of interaction around food. Food and culinary practice represent regional, national, and oppositional identities; sophisticated food industries manufacture our desires and our (physiological) tastes; and in the United States, we pay tribute to the worst excesses of cultural construction by consuming completely artificial foods.[10] The field of food studies has been instrumental in refocusing our attention on the most common and mundane of all consumer goods, often overlooked but significant because it is, in the words of Arjun Appadurai, 'well-suited to bear the load of everyday social discourse.'[11]

By emphasizing themes like the social construction of food habits and the culture of gastronomy, food studies runs the risk of overlooking one of the most significant qualities attached to food and its consumption. Despite the rich symbolic world that food and eating represent, there is also an animal reality attached to food, as Sidney Mintz aptly describes 'only because most of us eat plentifully and frequently ... may we sometimes too easily forget the astonishing, at times even terrifying, importance of food and eating.'[12] Having enough of the right kinds of foods to eat cannot be underestimated because food links one's own body with the broader world, economic structures and individual choices, excess and necessity. Italy is no stranger to the astonishing and terrifying importance of food. Throughout much of the nation's history, so many individuals and groups struggled to have enough of the right kinds of foods to eat and many failed in that effort. In fact, it makes more sense to write, as some Italian historians have, the history of appetite rather than write about what Italians actually consumed.[13] This book explores how the struggle to survive and the social construction of a national cuisine are related. Certainly, this relationship explains the longstanding simplicity of Italian cuisine. It also explains how, throughout much of modern Italy's history, Italians discussed, worried, and boasted about food – precisely because they had so little of it to eat. Today, the link between Italian identity and food habits seems an unremarkable fact. We acknowledge and admire Italians for obsessing over food, yet there are historical reasons for this obsession that shaped both Italian identity and Italian cuisine.

–1–

Unification through Monotony, Italy 1861–1914[1]

In 1884, author Matilde Serao observed that in Naples, no act of charity was too insignificant among the *popolo minuto* of the city. Since the poor and working classes struggled to make ends meet, neighbor helped neighbor in any way possible:

> One woman dispenses charity in a most ingenious fashion. She herself is poor and eats only boiled maccheroni seasoned with a little bit of sharp cheese, but her neighbor, who is very poor, has only a few morsels of dry, hard bread to eat.
>
> The woman who is less poor gives her neighbor the water in which her maccheroni was cooked, a whitish liquid that is spilled onto the morsels of bread, making them softer and giving them at least a certain flavor of maccheroni.[1]

A difficult economy necessitated charity; it also shaped a cuisine of scarcity. In nineteenth-century Italy, family budgets were meager and stretched to their limits. Survival meant making do or going without. Food and food habits symbolized the overwhelming poverty that confronted the young nation-state. Peasant and worker alike consumed an unvarying diet based primarily on corn, rice, chestnuts, potatoes, legumes, a few greens, and perhaps an occasional glass of watered-down wine. As Serao's description indicates, there were crucial distinctions between those who were poor and those who were slightly less poor. Many Italians measured their sense of well-being and economic status by the kind of bread they ate, the quality of wine they drank, or how many handfuls of dried beans they had in the kitchen.[2]

The miserable quality of popular diet reflected the hardships Italians faced in the liberal era. National unification – the *Risorgimento* – sparked hope for civic and economic renewal but it also produced its share of disappointment. Unification delivered few economic changes; textile production and agriculture continued to provide the most jobs for citizens, and industrial development was limited to the northwestern regions. Although they were modest efforts, urbanization and industrialization further divided prosperous Italy from the agricultural regions, which suffered tremendously from the agricultural depression of the 1880s. Despite the fact that southern regions were officially part of the nation and were economically viable in terms of agricultural production, northern Italians often dismissed these areas as economic liabilities and hotbeds of brigandage and poverty. The efforts of politicians and intellectuals (the *meridionalisti*) to probe the causality of the southern problem led to few concrete proposals for economic change. Many Italians responded to hardship and unemployment by leaving the country: by 1920, nine million Italians resided outside of Italy. Another response to the poor economy was social conflict. Agricultural depression and the poor economic conditions of the 1890s generated sporadic violence, whether manifest in the insurrections of the Sicilian *fasci* in 1893–94 or in the food riots and strikes throughout the peninsula in 1898. With the absence of a strong and powerful middle class, social conflict often pitted the underclasses against law and order and was much more likely to be fought out in a city *piazza* rather than in the halls of Parliament.

Within this context of nation building and industrialization, food was an all-important topic of discussion, whether in the halls of Parliament or in city markets. Discussions about food consumption were also discussions about the challenges facing the young nation – in particular, how Italians were to come together in order to realize the goals of unification. The purpose of this chapter is to sketch out the many problems with, and debates about, food consumption in the nineteenth century. The public discourse on food consumption articulated a specific ethic of consumption. The Italian ethic of consumption stressed thrift and renunciation out of necessity. Housewives used a minimum of ingredients, stretched the food budget as far as they could, and used more expensive foods (cheese, meat, milk) sparingly if at all. The Italian ethic of consumption also emphasized regional diversity in food-consumption habits. Such diversity carried both positive connotations, as gourmands like Pellegrino Artusi scoured the peninsula to compile national cookbooks, and negative ones, as scientific experts debated the existence of two diets dividing the nation along north/south lines. Lastly, this ethic of consumption stressed only a few ingredients, in particular the foods that have since become characteristic of Italian cuisine: pasta, olive oil, tomatoes, and hard cheeses. Surprisingly, the demand for these ingredients was first generated outside of Italy by immigrants seeking to invent their own culinary traditions; consumer demand within Italy was simply too weak in the first decades after unification to sustain a developed food industry. Eventually, however, these foods would become popular within Italy over the course of the twentieth century.

For much of liberal Italy's history, the State was conspicuously absent when it came to taking action to improve the Italian diet. Successive governments limited intervention to sponsoring parliamentary inquiries into living conditions and legislating against food adulteration and fraud. This lack of involvement is not surprising, given the nature of the liberal state in the decades after unification. Prior to the civil unrest of the 1890s, liberal governments lacked a clear social agenda and social policies were little more than a jumble of ideas and good intentions.[3] Moreover, the Italian state was itself poverty-stricken; the lack of funds prevented state intervention in the areas of public health, education, and the civil service.[4] Precisely because of government inaction, public discussion of food consumption focused on the difficulty Italians had in making ends meet. The poor, rural laborers, and industrial workers all suffered from inadequate nutrition and a monotonous diet. The nation as a whole suffered from inadequate nutrition, measurable in the nation's low productivity as well as by emerging international scientific standards.[5] Thus, social reformers tied inadequate diet to low productivity at the same time as scientists defined what was good to eat from a nutritional point of view. Participants in the discussion grew concerned about the gap between Italy and the rest of the industrialized world and were convinced that if the state intervened in these matters, Italy would finally experience the economic and civic revival promised by the *Risorgimento*.

This chapter provides the context for state intervention in the twentieth century by sketching out the many problems with, and debates about, food consumption in the nineteenth century. Throughout the late nineteenth century, a growing number of individuals and groups came to see Italy's poor diet as an impediment to political and economic progress. Consequently, a growing number of experts advocated a more nutritious diet for the entire population – a national cuisine of sorts – as a political imperative. The first section analyzes the central contradiction in recorded observations of popular diet: despite the fact that the nation was unified by a monotonous and inadequate diet, there remained crucial distinctions in consumption patterns between classes and regions. By way of contrast, the next section details the unintended consequences of Italian emigration on food-consumption habits – specifically, the ways in which the Italian diaspora nationalized a food industry within Italy that catered to the Mediterranean diet. The chapter concludes by delineating the first significant changes in popular consumption brought on by industrialization. On the eve of the First World War, the quality of the Italian diet had improved slightly and extended to more segments of the population.

It is difficult to speak of a national diet or national food habits in the decades after the *Risorgimento* because food and its consumption were sources of division and conflict. This was the case even though the majority of Italians consumed a similar diet in terms of the variety of foods consumed and the number of calories ingested. There was conflict over the definition and purpose of an ideal diet, as well as the level of state responsibility to ensure that more Italians ate better. Liberal governments did not yet see the political utility of improved nutritional standards or a national cuisine. Subsequent generations of policy-makers would use food as a means to bring the nation together or to make the population more productive, but in the nineteenth century, the task of making ends meet was left to housewives and families. These efforts were not insignificant if we consider that, according to historian Vera Zamagni, 'in the first fifty years after Unification ... food and drink made up some two-thirds of the total consumption (both public and private).'[6] Certainly, food and drink were important to Italians but not in the way we might think; it was their absence or scarcity that made them so significant.

Unification through Monotony or a Tale of Two Diets?

The political unification of Italy, a top-down process involving only a small portion of the ruling elite, did not lead automatically to a greater sense of national identity. Prior to Prime Minister Francesco Crispi's domination of Italian politics (1887–96), left and right parties were disillusioned with the *Risorgimento* and debated whether Italians would ever become more patriotic and productive – in other words, whether Italians could be 'made' out of a disparate and disgruntled collection of citizens. The debate over the difficulty of 'making Italians' continues to this day, with historians analyzing the peculiarities of Italy's special path to nationhood. While revisionist historians acknowledge the *Risorgimento* was neither a failed revolution nor a potent symbol of Italian backwardness, there remains the vexed question of Italian identity, of when and how and if Italians were made.[7] While Italians may not have felt an allegiance to the nation-state, common experience linked seemingly disparate populations together within the realm of the everyday, the ordinary, the familial, and the private. The most immediate and visceral element linking Italians together in the liberal period was diet.[8] The one activity shared by the majority of citizens was the seemingly endless quest to fill one's stomach. The dominant food for many was bread; the quality and type of bread mattered. Among the rural classes, according to historian Roberto Vivarelli, 'one could speak of three distinct areas of consumption: that of wheat flour, that of corn meal, and that of chestnut flour.'[9] Wheat bread was still considered by many to be a luxury in the nineteenth century. A Piedmontese peasant woman recalled how her parents, struggling to make ends meet, subsisted mostly on potatoes and chestnuts. 'In that time it was rare to see someone with a loaf of bread ... you asked them, "Is someone sick in your household?"' [10] An inquiry into diet conducted by the Società Italiana di Antropologia ed Etnologia (Italian Society for Anthropology and Ethnology) between 1872 and 1878 found that in over 488 *comuni* in all regions of Italy, the majority of Italians consumed polenta, rice, pasta, or chestnuts. For the poor, wheat bread was as rare as meat.[11] More often than not, bread was made from rye, chestnut, or lentil flour. White bread made from refined wheat flour was unheard of in most areas; its consumption was associated with gentility and wealth. For example, in the southern region of Calabria, a *donna di pane bianco* was synonymous with a *Signora*, or genteel woman.[12]

Meat was also a rarity. Meat, often beef, was reserved for illness or special occasions, and even then, a small portion of meat functioned as a condiment to bread, pasta, or polenta. Contemporary reports vary, but the amount consumed – even during holidays – was meager, ranging from a half-kilogram to a kilogram for an entire family on holidays or special occasions. Wine consumption was minimal: nineteenth-century monographs noted the absence of alcoholism and declared popular consumption levels to be 'discrete.' Monotony in diet was a fact of life for peasants, industrial workers, and the poor who found themselves without steady work or with no work at all.[13] Among the middle classes, as well as urban and rural workers, bread and pasta were more commonplace. Yet the availability or affordability of these staples was not guaranteed for working populations. Violent protests erupted whenever milling taxes increased, in 1868 in central Italy, or when a bad harvest led to higher prices, as was the case in 1898 in major cities throughout the nation.

Travelers to Italy, whether making the Grand Tour or a religious pilgrimage, duly noted the paucity of provisions and the dubious quality of Italian cuisine. An 1858 Murray's *Guide for Southern Italy* advised tourists that in the more remote districts, they would be well advised to make their own meals, by asking the proprietor of their lodging place to purchase ham and eggs so they could concoct a decent omelet. Much later, Luigi Barzini observed that 'local cookery must indeed have been repulsive, if English amateur efforts were to be preferred to it.' Nathaniel Hawthorne expressed his acute distaste for Rome with gustatory metaphors, lamenting the food that left him 'sick at stomach of sour bread, sour wine, rancid butter, and bad cookery, needlessly bestowed on evil meats.'[14] Unlike today, one traveled to Italy for the antiquities, the art, the sunshine, and for divine inspiration...but not for the cuisine.

Descriptions of popular diet, whether found in social-science monographs or in travel writings, constantly emphasized the monotony and scarcity of foods available for consumption. The reality of not having enough to eat was also reflected in language and reinforced by common sayings about people and life. A *uomo di panza*, or 'man with a belly' meant someone who had triumphed over adversity to prosper and flourish. A *uomo grasso*, or 'fat man' was not obese but a man of importance. To 'swim in lasagna' or 'to invite someone over for pasta *and* meat' carried similar connotations of success, generosity, and happiness. Language also noted the prevalence of scarcity in everyday life. Meals were often described as consisting of only 'bread and appetite' (*pane e appetito*) or 'bread and a knife' (*pane e coltello*). In the region of Reggio Calabria, it was common practice to 'marry lunch and dinner' when times were tough. In the Veneto, the phrase 'hunger is the best accompaniment to any meal' echoed the same sentiment.[15] The land of plenty was little more than a dream deferred for many Italians. The only time that Italians ate plentifully was on holidays, when food brought people together. Italian physician Paolo Mantegazza observed that there was something about holidays that leveled differences between Italians. Observing a spring festival in Genzano (a small village outside Rome), he noted the absence of any conversation during the modest repast: 'all had acquired the precious right to eat anything they wanted, to eat all of it, and to drink copiously. This was the blessed wish of those who became rich for a day and did not think about tomorrow.'[16]

Italians did not face starvation or even severe malnutrition; they did, however, face the daunting challenge of providing enough food for family members. In the nineteenth century, at least half of the family budget went to purchase the staple food of polenta, bread, or pasta, along with a *companatico*, usually oil, onions, or other vegetables. In the regions of Abruzzo and Molise, for example, agricultural laborers spent half of their incomes on bread, oil, and salt.[17] Careful budgeting was important in cases where a penny or two made a significant difference in the quality of food one could eat. Matilde Serao's chronicle of daily life for the Neapolitan lower classes (*Ventre di Napoli*, 1884) described a world in which minute differences in food prices affected dietary choice. Those in possession of one *soldo* (a penny) could afford only prepared cold foods: a slice of pizza with some tomatoes, garlic, pepper, or oregano; a piece of bread served with chestnut broth for dipping; *panzarotti*, a mixture of fried artichoke and cabbage; or *scapece*, fried and seasoned zucchini and eggplant served on a piece of bread. With two *soldi*, one could afford a piece of boiled octopus, or snails in broth, or hot foods like *maccheroni*, served at the numerous *osterie*:

> in all the streets in the worker's neighborhoods there are *osterie* that have stoves set up out-of-doors. Here the *maccheroni* is always boiling and there are pans containing tomato sauce and mountains of grated cheese … the portions are small and the buyer fights with the owner because he wants a little more sauce, a little more cheese, and a little more *maccheroni*.[18]

Consumers who had more than two *soldi* to spend on food were free to shop for food at the market stalls: ingredients for fresh salads, or a generous portion of *soffritto*: pork cooked in tomatoes, oil, and peppers, served in slices, which, 'felt like dynamite in your mouth.'[19] According to Serao's calculations, a large family could eat well for a modest eight *soldi* per day, provided that their diet was mostly vegetarian. For eight *soldi* one could afford to make a fragrant *minestra* (stew) of chicory, cabbage and endive; or yellow pumpkin and fresh peppers; or young potatoes cooked in a rich tomato broth. A few extra coins meant more choices and access to fresh, wholesome ingredients to prepare meals at home. Serao noted that most of the people she observed seldom purchased fresh foods to make at home because they often lacked cooking facilities and the proper utensils.

The latter half of the nineteenth century constitutes the end of a long and steady decline in the quality and quantity of food consumed in Italy. How did popular consumption habits become so restricted? Historians have located the origins of this decline in the seventeenth century. Certainly there were similarities between the early modern period and the nineteenth century, at least in terms of household budget expenditures on food. Carlo Cipolla's economic history of pre-industrial Europe estimates 70–80 percent of the total household budget was spent on food consumption in Italy. This figure changed little if we consider that as late as the fascist era, it was not unusual for a social-scientific monograph to note that 75 percent of the household budget was spent on food.[20] Historian Maria Antonietta Visceglia's overview of consumption in the early modern era points to an increasing divergence in food-consumption patterns, between rich and poor and to a lesser extent between urban and rural populations, from the fifteenth century onward. One of the biggest markers of this divergence was the steady decrease in meat consumption for the popular classes. Thus it would appear that Italians consumed more meat in previous centuries than in the eighteenth or nineteenth centuries. This theory is supported by Emilio Sereni's work on dietary habits of Neapolitans, in which over the span of the sixteenth and seventeenth centuries popular diet went from one based on meat and vegetables to one based almost entirely on carbohydrates.[21] Visceglia's comparison of dietary studies from the seventeenth century indicates that at least among some populations there was a balanced and varied diet, including sugar, meat, fresh fruits and vegetables, although among agricultural laborers, diet consisted mostly of bread with an accompaniment of cheese or oil, along with a moderate amount of wine. Studies of the Italian early modern diet indicate a regression in consumer habits, with an increasingly greater divide between populations and a greater monotony of diet for the popular classes by the beginning of the nineteenth century.

There were many reasons for the paucity of diet in the nineteenth century. Although there was no major agricultural revolution in the nineteenth century, Italian agriculture was hardly backward. Vera Zamagni characterizes the problem of Italian poverty as a demographic one: the population was 'disproportionately large when compared to the potential of the land.'[22] Moreover, food was expensive because the production and distribution sectors were disorganized. An expensive and inadequate transportation system meant that farmers either sold locally or exported out of Italy. Consequently, the nation's food industry was slow to develop because of imbalanced markets and weak demand. The retail sector was also in disarray, food storage was underdeveloped, and the lack of available credit hindered farmers and small businessmen alike. The Italian government did not help matters. Food prices remained high because of a Byzantine system of direct and indirect taxes throughout the nation that meant higher retail prices for consumers and reduced profits for producers.[23]

According to Vera Zamagni's calculations for the years between 1886 and 1913, exports of wine, olive oil, and rice decreased while the export of pasta, flour, eggs, cheese, citrus fruit and fresh produce increased. Imports increased only for wheat, cereals, preserved fish, coffee, and tobacco.[24] Based on these figures, then, it would seem that the foods making diet less monotonous (eggs, cheese, fruits and vegetables) were leaving the country rather than being sold to and consumed by Italians. Lastly, it appears that the Italian government was reluctant to intervene in order to improve popular consumption habits. This is not to say that the State did nothing at all; the government commissioned inquiries into living standards, but did little in the areas of charity or economic reform. Government spending focused on central administration and maintaining order, and not on social services.

We know a great deal about popular diet in the nineteenth century because there were so many studies conducted and published on food consumption and family budgeting. Monographs on food-consumption levels first appeared in Italy in the latter half of the nineteenth century, following a more general trend of tabulating the living conditions of the laboring populations. In Italy, the trend was sparked in the 1870s by an increased recognition of, and interest in, the 'Social Question;' scientists, intellectuals, and politicians seized the moment as a time to fulfill the *Risorgimento*'s mission to 'make Italians' by addressing the social problems Italy faced.[25] Italian observers were affiliated either with left-reform organizations like the Società Umanitaria in Milan, or with university economics and statistics departments. Most social scientists working in the decades prior to the First World War were liberals or socialists. However, social-scientific investigation also met the approval of the Catholic Church, which supported the development of such endeavors with Pope Leo XIII's *Immortale Dei* (1885), an encyclical that decried abstract scientific justifications of liberal economics in favor of concrete findings about the standard of living.

Small-scale inquiries were often published in statistics or economics journals, as well as left-reform periodicals like *La riforma sociale*. The majority of these studies focused on small groups – a single family in some cases – for short periods of time in an effort to delineate regional and class variations in food-consumption habits. They did so by observing the physical health and stature of populations, noting the percentage of household budgets spent on food, and describing which kinds of food were eaten and in what amounts. The government also sponsored several large-scale inquiries in which diet played a considerable evaluative role. The sections on food consumption combine copious anecdotal evidence about eating habits with statistics on physical stature, morbidity and mortality rates, and economic indicators for the region under study. Italy's first major government-sponsored inquiry was the agricultural inquiry (*Inchiesta Agricoltura Jacini*), commissioned by Parliament in 1877.[26]

Scientific observers in Italy were part of a budding professional community with international ties to scientific communities in Germany, Great Britain, and the United States. Consequently, observers made much of the contrast between Italy and its more industrialized neighbors. Such comparisons often referred to the

Italian population as a backward and inadequate whole in need of repair and restoration. Thinking about the population in this way was one way of coming to terms with Italy's social question and the possible paths to social reform. Simply put, Italy needed a better diet in order to realize its full productive and intellectual potential. Frequently, inquiry committees and social scientists suggested agricultural reform as a means to improve national food habits. For example, the previously mentioned Jacini inquiry was a massive undertaking, carried out over eight years and resulting in fifteen published volumes of findings. The inquiry committee concluded that dire economic conditions in rural areas necessitated a revival of Italian agriculture. Only through agricultural reform would Italy realize the goals of an independent and unified state. Because of its ambitious recommendations, and because it criticized protectionism, the Jacini Inquest was forgotten soon after its publication.[27]

Thinking about the population as backward or inadequately provisioned in this way also distinguished Italian experts from those in other European nations. Working in the wake of industrialization and urbanization, French and English observers analyzed mental and physical fatigue and their manifestations of degeneration and neurasthenia as by-products of the modernizing process and as strictly urban phenomena.[28] There were only a handful of studies of fatigue in Italy (Angelo Mosso's *La fatica* in 1891 being the best known), because the scientific community did not conceptualize physical and moral degeneration as being relevant. While scientific experts agreed that Italian consumption habits were inferior to those in other countries, they disagreed as to which populations suffered from the worst diet in the nation. More often than not, divisions and gradations of habit were based on regional differences. Of secondary importance were class distinctions, although the majority of monographs and inquiries concentrated on the working classes exclusively.[29] What began as a description of a social problem turned into a regional contest that reflected all the persistent divisions of practice and opinion in unified Italy.

Despite the tensions and contradictions they contain, monographs and inquiries into living standards constitute the most important sources for finding out about consumption habits in Italy. They are not wholly accurate, given the difficulties observers had with obtaining and recording data. The value of these studies lies within how they described food consumption as a specific kind of historical and political problem.[30] Regional and class differences in food-consumption levels underscored the link between food and social inequality, for example. It would also be inaccurate to label the authors of these studies nutritionists. Although some experts were physiologists and were specifically concerned with the body's absorption of nutrients, most observers were interested in the social context of food consumption and used techniques and theories from the emerging fields of anthropology, physiology, and psychology. A growing number of people in a variety of academic disciplines offered commentary and observations about popular diet and consumption habits. It would be premature, however, to speak of a community of nutritionists.

Expert consensus maintained that the Italian population could not realize its full potential as a nation until the population consumed more food and different kinds of food. Many publications emphasized the link between inadequate diet and underdevelopment (physical, intellectual, and moral). Italy suffered from a nutritional and physical disadvantage, visible in physical stature and mental development. In 1890, an Italian positivist characterized 'the Italian as the most sober consumer in all of Europe. This sobriety is not a virtue but a sad necessity. In Italy, we not only eat less than those from other nations, we eat worse foods, of poor quality.'[31] Radical economist Francesco Nitti summarized his views on the Italian diet in 1894; 'the Italians, the Hungarians, the Poles, the Bohemians, (all) are used to a dietary regime that does not permit them to develop into a strong labor force … if they work at all it is in the less developed industries, those which require minimal energy.'[32] According to Nitti, Italy shared more in common with eastern European populations than with western European ones. Reinforcing this sense of inadequacy were the nutritional standards set by the international scientific community. Although there was no clear consensus as to what constituted adequate nutrition, German and American physiologists held to high levels of protein (between 100 and 130 grams per day) and fat (50–100 grams per day), that Italians couldn't possibly meet.[33] Italian experts recognized the relationship between protein, fats, and increased labor power, but they confronted a reality where urban workers and rural peasants consumed roughly half the amount of protein and fat recommended by international experts.[34]

Left and right agreed that the archetype of the under-developed Italian was the *contadino* (a general term for agricultural laborer who did not own land), characterized by his stoic acceptance of an inadequate diet and his physical and mental underdevelopment. In reform circles, politicians brought up *la questione contadina* in Parliament in order to address the plight of those whom conservative Sidney Sonnino described in 1880 as 'badly paid, poorly housed, malnourished, crushed by excessive labor under the most insalubrious working conditions.'[35] The health and welfare of the *contadini* were common governmental concerns, given that low agricultural productivity affected the national economy. Rural and urban economies were interdependent in the liberal era: peasants sometimes worked in factories and agricultural profits were invested in industry. Discussions regarding the *contadino* often implied more general, even national, concerns.

Studies of rural laborers all over Italy affirmed the relationship between poor diet and low productivity. Doctor Arsenio Brugnola of the University of Perugia went so far as to determine that, among the Umbrian peasants he studied, few received adequate caloric intake for maintaining even a minimal physical well-being:

We must therefore conclude that about one-third of these agricultural laborers eat enough to compensate for the physical labor performed, while the other two-thirds eat enough to remain on their feet or in a somewhat sedentary state, being worn down even by moderate labor – *These contadini fall prey to and are at the mercy of a kind of autofagy.*[36]

Social scientists Pietro Albertoni and Felice Rossi, writing on the *contadini* from Abruzzo in 1906, bemoaned the low intellect that resulted from environmental conditions: 'that which becomes apparent immediately in their physiognomy is the imprint of an appalling mental poverty. Gestures are without enthusiasm, the eye without expression, the mouth impassive and half-open, cheekbones protruding.'[37] Experts writing about food were fascinated by the *contadino's* primitive features and underdevelopment, and sought to define peasant underdevelopment by using evolutionary terms. Some experts maintained that inadequate diet and differences in health, intellect, and physical stature were proof of the arrested nature of the evolutionary development of the rural classes. Thus, Italy's agricultural – and by extension industrial – productivity remained stagnant. An 1893 study from Naples described how the lack of protein in Neapolitan diet 'is one of the main reasons why the Neapolitan population remains short in stature, with an emaciated look and a slight muscular build. Correlated with these (characteristics) are a deficit of energy and a tendency toward indolence.'[38] Anthropologist Alfredo Niceforo argued that the short stature and dark pigmentation of rural Italians were proof of a stalled evolutionary process. His 1907 study of the poor posited that malnutrition altered organic tissues and hence physiological and psychological development.[39]

Poor nutrition affected intellectual development as well. Dr. Maria Montessori, as a professor of hygiene at the Scuola Superiore Femminile in Rome, defined proper nutrition as one of four major environmental elements influencing intellect, along with housing conditions, the profession of the father, and how the child spent his/her spare time. Over half of the "non-intelligent" children in Montessori's sample group skipped a major meal (*colazione*) or ate only bread, while 76 percent of the children of average intelligence ate at least one balanced meal per day, often including meat.[40] The above-mentioned study on the *contadini* of Abruzzo included an intelligence test administered to each of the twenty-four subjects, who were asked questions regarding national politics and questions that tested abstract thought (What is the State? What are the stars?). The authors of the study recognized that diet was miserable; although the *contadini* engaged in strenuous labor, men consumed 2,746 calories per day and women, 2,204 calories. Corn meal comprised half of all total calories, dairy products were not consumed, and the only meat consumed was pork, at an average of eight kilograms per year per person. The authors concluded that inadequate nutrition caused physiological dysfunction and low intelligence levels.

Experts agreed that the majority of the population did not reach its full potential on corn meal and a few vegetables. Although some experts like Niceforo argued for a kind of biological and evolutionary determinism, most experts maintained that the State, not nature, controlled the pace of Italian development. Higher salaries and a booming economy could reverse years of poor nutrition and health. The problem of course was how to extract more labor power from a population of workers given the resources available to feed them. Francesco Nitti summarized Italy's quandary neatly in an 1894 article for *La Riforma Sociale*. Based on his reading of monographs from the 1870s and 1880s, Nitti argued that workers from the United States consumed the most nutritious diets because food was cheap there. In Italy, food was too expensive and workers did not earn enough. Because Italian workers could not afford adequate nutrition, the nation experienced a crisis in production related directly to inadequate labor power. At the crux of this problem was inadequate protein consumption. Nitti's comparison of social-science monographs revealed that Italian workers ate half the meat French workers did and one-quarter that of British workers. Nitti concluded by noting 'this deficit of protein will not kill them; but the population or group in question will slowly waste away or simply not develop.'[41] Italy remained trapped in a cycle of underproduction, poor health, and inadequate labor power.

Commentators like Nitti attempted to frame the problem of diet as a national one. However, they were torn between emphasizing the national dimensions of the problem and discussing differences in consumption habits between the various populations within Italy. The two most common dietary distinctions were based on regional and class differences. These two differences spoke most urgently to issues of social inequality in young Italy. Dietary differences between the northern and southern regions bespoke a tale of two diets, with observers claiming that popular diet from their region was the most deficient. To view the nation in terms of north/south difference was a common way to understand political and economic problems of the post-*Risorgimento* era. From the mid-1860s onward, numerous intellectuals and politicians devoted their energies to understanding the 'Southern Problem' using statistics and studies that established the existence of two Italies.[42] Food was one of the most obvious and tangible ways to illustrate the difference in lifestyle in the two regions, and descriptions of physical bodies underscored physical difference and its implications of physical and moral inferiority. The contrast drawn between northern and southern habits remained a constant throughout the nineteenth century. The authors of an 1863 study of Neapolitan diet observed that while southerners suffered from inadequate nutrition, northern workers, 'who eat big plates of polenta and hard cheese, enjoy florid and robust health, and are tirelessly resistant to fatigue.'[43] Sidney Sonnino's 1876 observations of diet in Sicily later argued the exact opposite: 'the Sicilian peasant eats bread made of grain and, except for extreme cases, nourishes himself sufficiently, while the Lombard peasant eats nothing but corn and suffers physiological hunger, even when his stomach is full.'[44] A study of the Sardinian peasant diet published in 1906 demonstrated the strength and longevity of regional comparisons by concluding that '… the peasants in northern Italy eat polenta, minestra, anchovies, lard, chestnut flour in the winter; during the summer there is tuna in oil, cheese, watermelon, greens and fruits. The *contadino* from Sassari eats only bread, which is of decent quality because it is made at home by the housewife, but this is not sufficient to satisfy hunger.'[45]

Northern observers often lamented the scourge of pellagra (a disease caused by niacin deficiency) in regions where corn consumption was high: Piedmont, Lombardy, the Veneto, and Emilia.[46] Those experts who maintained that the northern diet was inferior to the southern diet were concerned about the digestion and assimilation of nutrients. This was a common concern and object of study for Italian physiologists in the nineteenth century.[47] Corn was not as easily digested as wheat; those who consumed mostly polenta suffered from imperfect digestion and malnutrition. Southern observers were more concerned about the lack of protein in the southern diet. According to Alfredo Niceforo's study of 1901, southern Italians consumed only half the meat that northern Italians did.[48] A diet lacking in protein led to a stunted population, lacking physical strength and mental acuity. Regional distinctions amounted to a regional 'contest' for which diet was more deficient in terms of quantity consumed or nutrients in the foods, with each observer claiming his or her population to be worse off in terms of food consumption levels and therefore, more worthy of state assistance through economic reform, education, and medical assistance.

Despite their intentions, however, experts could not square their pleas for regional exceptionalism with the overall inadequacy of diet throughout Italy. Alfredo Niceforo's 1901 study, *Italiani del nord e Italiani del sud* posited the existence of 'Two Italies,' manifest most obviously in everyday life by eating habits, because 'the north of Italy is a more developed civilization than the south of Italy because – among other reasons – northern Italians eat *more* and *better* than southern Italians.'[49] Southern Italians in various occupations – farmers, soldiers, and students – ate less meat, eggs, cereals, and legumes than did their northern counterparts. Despite his painstaking efforts to use social-scientific monographs to prove the validity of regional difference, Niceforo continually emphasized how most Italians failed to eat enough of the proper foods. Thus, Niceforo's carefully drawn distinctions between northern and southern Italians were mirrored on a broader European canvas on which, 'populations that eat better are also the ones that work more and produce more.'[50] For Niceforo, the most significant dietary difference between northern and southern Italians was the fact that southerners consumed a mostly vegetarian diet while northerners consumed more animal-based proteins, such as meat, eggs, and other dairy products.[51] Dietary differences were literally imprinted on the bodies of Italians. Niceforo's analysis of physical-examination records of military conscripts found that the further south one traveled, the more one found a greater height differential between classes. Two diets led to two different physical types, manifest in the rich and the poor, or the north and the south.[52]

Niceforo never determined whether Italy's two diets were inevitable. Whereas Niceforo concluded that economic differences accounted for underdevelopment and inferiority, he ultimately subsumed his observations under a racial paradigm in that years of economic disadvantage became part of the evolutionary makeup of southern Italians. The tension implied here is specific to the study of food consumption. Food represents the workings of the market and social inequality, but it also becomes a physical part of the body. Niceforo and others understood this, although most experts who commented on dietary habits stopped short of declaring that the physical and mental inferiority of a given population was inevitable. Such a conclusion did not fit their positivist leanings and belief in reform. Poor diet was linked to poor economic conditions and the debate over regional differences in consumption habits was also a debate over the allocation of economic resources. Certainly, regional differences in economic development were significant ones, but did they tell the whole story? Scientific and social scientific experts were also concerned about differences between socio-economic classes.

Many of the small-scale studies carried out in the late nineteenth century underscored the persistence of two diets corresponding with class divisions. Class meant almost exclusively the lower classes: the urban and rural working class as well as the poor. Studies concentrated on anecdotal evidence regarding the quality of diet as well as family spending patterns. Gina Lombroso's 1896 study of workers in a Turin suburb estimated that the average family of six members, earning 3.40[th]lire per day, spent 2.63[th]lire per day on food. Diet, Lombroso judged, was adequate; workers consumed meat and other animal proteins but not on a daily basis. She also found that many families purchased sugar, coffee, and tobacco, despite costly taxes.[53] Workers were not well off, however. Lombroso noted with concern that the family accumulated little or no savings for emergencies.

In rural Italy, observers concentrated on the diet of day laborers and sharecroppers, who consumed bread with some kind of condiment (*companatico*), usually an onion, pepper, or on rare occasion, a piece of cheese or a bit of salted fish. More complex meals were also inadequate, as one description of popular diet in Lombardy detailed:

> ... corn meal, poorly cooked, clammy and rancid, and *minestra* into which the poorest
> quality foods are added – if not actually noxious, rice and pasta of the worst quality,
> old and spoiled legumes, vegetables which haven't been washed, a bit of oil and rancid

lard or fat – here is the *minestra* prepared for the sharecroppers who work in the countryside, here is the meager meal for a man who labors on Lombardy's land.[54]

There were vital distinctions made between the food habits of different types of
agricultural laborers. The Jacini Inquiry found that in Umbria, better-off rural
families dined on salted cornmeal *focaccia*, supplemented by beans, legumes, rice,
pork fat, vegetables, and potatoes. Poorer families ate the same cornmeal bread,
but they either consumed it by itself, or with an accompaniment of onions or potatoes.[55]

Even in industrializing regions like Lombardy and Piedmont, which were relatively prosperous by the late nineteenth century, class disparities in consumption
patterns were common. Historian Renato Allio's study of late nineteenth-century
diet in Piedmont indicates that industrial workers had the worst diets in this region.
Institutional feeding in hospitals and orphanages often provided more protein and
a greater variety of foods than was found in the diet of the industrial working
classes.[56] The only time workers received their fill of meat was during annual
banquets sponsored by mutual-aid societies (Società di mutuo soccorso), when
workers would feast on a pound of veal and a pound of bread each, plus roast lamb,
pasta, cheese, and wine.[57] Workers and others living in cities faced higher prices
because of taxes on basic goods like flour, meat, oil, sugar, and salt. Workers paid
a heavy burden in taxes for basic necessities given that there were no luxury or
gradual taxes in Italy. It was not unusual, for example, for a family in the nineteenth century to pay almost 10 percent of its annual income on food taxes alone.[58]
Given that taxes appeared to many as both unfair and illogical, it is no wonder that
customs duties on food were commonly referred to as the 'duty on hunger'
throughout the nineteenth century.

To contrast the spending habits of workers and peasants to those of the middle
classes is a difficult task; there were few published studies of middle-class diet. A
1910 study of five middle-class families in Foggia (Apulia) indicated that the families spent 38–60 percent of their annual income on food, a figure that is high for
an industrializing middle class. Nonetheless, middle-class families were able to
accumulate savings; they spent a small percentage of their budgets on leisure
activities and educational materials, and they were able to consume foods like
coffee, sugar, tobacco, and liquor on a daily basis. One family of seven from the
study consumed a daily average of 2.5 kilograms of bread, a kilogram of meat, a
kilogram of pasta, eggs, milk, fruit, cheese, coffee, sugar, oil, wine, and *rosolio*, a
liqueur.[59] Nonetheless, what little we know about the spending habits of the
middle classes stands in sharp contrast to the budgets of workers and peasants.
Middle-class families averaging three to five members spent three to four times
what peasant families of five to seven members spent on food.[60] It was not unusual
for a middle-class housewife to allocate two lire per day on meat for her family.

Peasant housewives spent a total of between 1 and 2 lire, per day, to feed the entire family.[61]

Whether focused on region or class, monographs, articles, and inquiries paid a significant amount of attention to dietary difference. These differences aggravated the difficulty of 'making Italians' and threatened to sap the young nation of labor power. They also underscored the need for a political solution to the problem of diet. Angelo Mosso, a physiologist from Turin, in his 1891 work, *La fatica* (*Fatigue*), expressed the concerns of a growing number of scientific experts when he registered his utter disbelief upon viewing military conscripts assembled for medical inspection: 'there was in front of me a row of naked young men: some were dark and thin and between these were others who were large, pale, and white, like they were of another race. They were the poor and the rich.'[62] In nineteenth-century Italy, there were two races of Italians just as there were two diets for the population. Scientific and social scientific experts agreed that a more varied and nutritious diet would do much to remedy divisions between region and class.

What could this community of experts do to accomplish this goal? When experts advocated agricultural modernization, the abolition of protectionism, or the reduction of taxes, their arguments and findings were ignored by conservatives in Parliament (as the example of the Jacini Inquiry proves). Moreover, physiologists, anthropologists, and other experts encountered institutional difficulties in pursuing their work. The study of nutrition as a laboratory science was not as extensive in Italy as it was in Germany or in the United States, two countries where theories of calories, nutrients, and average-man coefficients were tested and promoted. In Italy, physiological institutes (which existed at larger universities) devoted time and money to studying the science of physiology as it related to the biological processes of digestion. The government also funded some scientific research. The Ministry of Agriculture, for example, supported the Società Italiana per lo Studio della Alimentazione (Italian Society for the Study of Alimentation), which studied the biological composition of foodstuffs and public-health issues regarding nutrition. However, the society was short-lived; funding was cut after two years and the society folded.[63] Experts on food consumption tended to be affiliated with departments of anthropology, economics, and statistics. Moreover, there were very few laboratory-oriented analyses of Italian foods; Italian scientists were much more interested in the social context of dietary inadequacy and the link between consumption habits and physical and intellectual development. Proving this link was a tricky enterprise as there was no consensus that environment or biology caused underdevelopment. The science of hygiene, which would have bolstered the tenuous links between environment and health, focused instead on risk factors like water supply and overcrowding as related to diseases like cholera, typhus, and tuberculosis.[64]

Experts struggled to make the connection between underdevelopment and poor nutrition compelling enough for the government to take action. In scientific discourse, food represented all that was wrong with the nation: class and regional differences strained the fragile bonds of nationhood; uneven industrialization aggravated existing differences and kept standards of living low. Likewise, expert observers noted all that was wrong with the nation's food supply: the distributional sector was uncoordinated, agricultural production could be improved, taxes were too harsh, and the public needed to be educated about nutrition (a common lament was that Italians assuaged their hunger [*saziarsi*] but they did not nourish themselves properly [*nutrirsi*]). Yet the medical establishment within Italy was fragmented and politically weak. Scientific thinking was more likely to find its way into socialist reform circles than into government policy. Indeed, in many areas of intervention regarding public health, the government was reluctant to intervene. Experts provided a blueprint for later interventions in suggesting everything from state-sponsored charity to a radical redistribution of income as means to improve national health and productivity. Their work pointed to an emerging consensus that popular diet constituted a pressing national problem, to be resolved through more intensive government intervention.

Building a National Cuisine from Without

The reality of social divisions in Italy based on food-consumption habits was a stark one. Scientific experts wanted to build a nation by improving the quality of diet, but they were unable to achieve their goals without state intervention. They argued for the political relevance of deep divisions in food habits within Italy. At the same time, however, other communities and individuals used food to bring Italians together. Although it is now popular to discuss Italian cuisine as a collection of distinct regional cuisine, gourmand Pellegrino Artusi codified, classified, and created a national cuisine in his famous cookbook, *The Science of Cooking and the Art of Eating Well* (*La scienza in cucina e l'arte di mangiar bene*, 1891). Still considered to be the classic text of Italian culinary literature, Artusi's book was crafted for a newly emerging middle class that was to be trained properly in the necessary skills of food preparation and taste. Historian Piero Camporesi situated the homogenizing influence of Artusi's work within the 1890s, the decade of the *Rerum Novarum*, the birth of the Italian Socialist Party, as well as the incipient years of industrialization. Camporesi asserts it was in these years that the 'infinite regional peculiarities' of custom, tradition, culture, and practice 'rendered the unity of Italians mythic and futuristic.'[65] Artusi's impact – to bring Italians together through a shared language about food preparation and a shared practice of food consumption – would take years to develop, but his formula of middle-class sobriety, simplicity of presentation, and attention to regional difference proved to be the right formula for a national cuisine. Artusi remained popular through the First World War, fascism and afterward.

Numerous editions of his cookbook can be found in Italian bookstores even today.

In the first few decades after its publication, Artusi's *La scienza in cucina* reached only a limited audience of middle-class readers (a total of 52,000 copies were sold between 1891 and 1910). A broader effort to homogenize the national diet was the unintended consequence of the great out-migration of Italians to the rest of Europe and the Americas. These waves of migration had both direct and indirect impact on the food available within Italy. Relatedly, immigrant remittances and the decrease in competition for jobs within Italy meant the living standard improved over the course of the early twentieth century. And, as Italians began to leave the peninsula for greater economic opportunities in the Americas and elsewhere, they sought to recreate familiar dishes. This led to a growing body of consumers for Italian products (dried pasta, canned tomatoes, and olive oil), which in turn greatly aided the development of certain food industries within Italy. Only after substantial numbers of Italians abroad began consuming these foods did domestic production furnish more products for Italians at home. Ironically, it was because of the 'imagined communities' outside Italy that the food industry inside Italy produced the goods that became the foundations of Italian cuisine. Like Artusi's cookbook, the Italian diaspora gave greater definition or clarity to what constituted Italian cuisine because both delineated what was desirable to eat in ways that were not linked directly to the science of nutrition.

The relationship between the budding nationalization of food habits on the Italian peninsula and the Italian diaspora at the turn of the century warrants careful consideration. How did these two cultural and economic itineraries come together? It is obvious that many Italians left the peninsula to find work and bread. Hasia Diner's recent history of US immigrant foodways argues that Italians came to the United States for hard work, high salaries, and plentiful food.[66] High salaries were attractive incentives. Citizens from all regions of Italy could make over ten times the annual salary of a prosperous northern Italian farming family. The pull was irresistible; by 1920, about one-quarter of Italy's resident population lived outside Italy (9 million persons).[67] Italian immigrants chose a variety of living and working arrangements; return migration from countries like the United States and Argentina was the rule, not the exception. Immigrants accumulated significant savings in their new environments and sent much of it to family back in Italy. The impact of remittances increased the standard of living in both northern and southern Italy, although it did not, as many had hoped, lead to a national economic renaissance.[68] Whether they chose to stay in their new communities for a short period of time or to lay down permanent roots, many Italian immigrants appeared reluctant at first to alter their food habits. There were, however, immediate changes in immigrant eating patterns because of the increased availability and affordability of food. Thus, immigrants enjoyed more meat, more dairy products, more fresh fruits and vegetables.

Curiously, adequate and even extra income did not always translate into a dramatic change in eating habits for Italian immigrants; immigrants simply purchased *more* of the foods they were used to eating, rather than purchasing foods that were unfamiliar or seen as characteristically American, Brazilian, or German. The available evidence for understanding the relationship between immigration and the nationalization of cuisine is somewhat sparse. However, there was a connection between the rise of an external market for certain characteristically Italian foods (pasta, canned tomatoes, olive oil, hard cheeses) and the growth of an industry within Italy to supply these goods. Existing historiography on dietary change and Italian immigration focuses on *foodways*, the activities and culture surrounding food as they relate to one's identity. Historians have demonstrated that the experience of most Italians – that is, resistance to dramatic dietary changes – played a critical role in the forging of an immigrant identity. In the United States, for example, Italian immigrants fit into historian Donna Gabaccia's definition of 'culinary conservatives,' in that they desired to produce familiar dishes and foods in a new environment.[69] Recent immigrants solidified new consumption practices at home through business practices as food merchants and entrepreneurs, and via social channels like friendly societies and clubs. To many immigrants, the foods they consumed in their new homes embodied success, family, and community. What seems less clear is the impact that the activities of immigrants had on cultural practice and national identity back in Italy. In a recent book on the history of pasta and pizza, Franco La Cecla argued that the global popularization of these foods began with the widespread diaspora of southern Italians at the turn of the century. La Cecla posits that Italian immigrants, in affirming their ethnic identities through the consumption of pasta and pizza, homogenized Italian culinary practice in far-flung communities, ultimately exporting these practices to the rest of the world.[70]

Upon moving to cities in North and South America, as well as northern Europe, immigrants first experienced culinary change through the introduction of meat into daily diet. Calabrians, who moved to cities in North America, Brazil, and Argentina, gave up primarily vegetarian diets in favor of an *alimentazione mista*, or a mixed diet. Workers in the *fazendas* near Sao Paolo and agricultural laborers in Argentina consumed wheat bread, polenta, rice, potatoes, beans, fresh vegetables grown on small plots, pork, lard, a bit of beef, and some chicken, according to diplomatic and social-scientific observers.[71] The main reasons for such variety in diet were higher wages and cheaper food prices. Meat was available to all workers on a daily basis; only during times of inflation were workers on fixed salaries unable to afford meat. Calabrian immigrants in US cities reported similar dietary changes. Even unskilled laborers in cities like New York and Pittsburgh managed to eat well. '*La vita qui è a buon mercato*' according to one inspector for the Italian government's Commission on Emigration, regarding the situation of immigrants in Texas in 1904. Food prices were low even when jobs were difficult to find; Italian workers were almost always able to afford wheat flour, meat, and sugar.

Life in the United States was seen as a modern-day land of plenty, as evidenced by one observation of Italian-Americans in San Francisco in 1911:

> In the streets of the Italian neighborhoods on Friday evenings you can see hundreds of chickens displayed in the store windows. By Saturday, demand for the chickens has outstripped supply. Their homes are always amply stocked: two or three boxes of *maccheroni*, flour, wine, salami and pepperoni hang from the ceiling. This is true for every family of the healthy and employed working-class.[72]

Even the poorest immigrants in the Americas had enough to eat, as immigrants' memoirs, testimonies, and letters indicate. Yet recent immigrants did not purchase a variety of new foods indiscriminately. In the United States, Italian immigrants were a resourceful lot; they grew fresh vegetables in whatever space was available to them and canned the results of each harvest. Despite the occasional pressure from social workers or factory managers exerted on Italian-Americans to 'Americanize' their foodways, they chose to consume familiar foods. One southern Italian immigrant recalled that upon her father's death in 1915, her family was visited by a group of social workers, who deposited several mysterious boxes with the family, presumably as gifts. Only years later did the family realize that the unopened boxes contained breakfast cereals, familiar to Americans but alien and undesirable to Italians.[73] Simone Cinotto's analysis of Italian immigrants in New York City during the interwar period indicates that parents held on to traditions, exerting control over younger generations to maintain and preserve foodways.[74]

Similarly, immigrants from northern Italy experienced dietary improvement, but the path to such improvements varied slightly from that of southern Italians. Historian Paola Corti's study of the food habits of Piedmontese immigrants suggests different experiences followed from different itineraries. Male workers who moved temporarily to Switzerland and Germany often turned to institutional soup kitchens as the most convenient and economic method of feeding themselves. There they found a great variety of foods at reasonable prices, even wine and alcohol, leading many observers to note a tendency toward alcohol abuse in the Italian communities of northern Europe. The biggest changes in dietary practice for the Piedmontese workers were to be found in the Americas. Again, memoirs, letters, and oral histories indicate universal surprise regarding the availability and cheapness of a wide variety of foods. A letter from a Venetian peasant in 1888 describes a new life where 'everyone from the richest to the poorest enjoys meat, bread and *minestra* every day.' In Buenos Aires in 1898, a Piedmontese printer, his wife, and child consumed 200 grams of meat and 500 grams of bread, per person daily, for a cost of only 40 cents per day.[75]

Food constituted an important reference point for Italian immigrants, whether they were concentrated in boarding houses, neighborhoods, or communities. Food was one means by which Italians in a strange environment could come together. In other words, food, its preparation and consumption, became powerful ingredients for forging a specifically Italian identity abroad. Today, when definitions of ethnicity are bound up so intimately with questions of identity, this seems an unremarkable occurrence. Yet Italian immigrants were particularly creative in reinventing cuisine. The immigrant diet was almost always better in terms of nutritional quality and the quantity and variety of foods consumed. Moreover, Italian immigrants used food for social purposes, a habit in distinct contrast to populations back in Italy. In the nineteenth century, Italians may have come together on feast days and other special holidays, but every other day, peasant and worker consumed foods hurriedly and usually alone. The ritual of shared home-cooked meals simply did not exist for the majority of the population back in Italy. Thus, food and acts of consumption became ways to reproduce an identity not quite rooted in experience, but perhaps rooted in how previous experience should have been. Indeed, this is still the case today, at least in the United States, where nostalgia for authentic Italian cuisine goes hand in hand with memories of grandmother's kitchen and the family table. Such memories are now contrasted to the hurried horrors of American life, of canned spaghetti and microwaved pizza. These memories, of course, constitute an imagined tradition regarding life back in Italy and reflect a nostalgia for Italian food habits as they were Americanized after Italians left Italy.

The foodways of Italian immigrants generated a repository of memory regarding how diet should have been for Italians back home. These same foodways also reflected new consumption practices, in the sense that Italians abroad were able to purchase and consume more food than previously was imaginable. American markets for goods like olive oil, dried pasta, hard cheese, and canned tomatoes were well established by the outbreak of the First World War. These external markets reinforced the growing strength of these industries, stimulating production and profits. Ultimately, then, it was the force of external markets that made foods like pasta and canned tomatoes into mass-produced goods consumed by Italians as well as by recent immigrants. Ironically, it was because of immigration that several of the major staples of the Italian diet became popularized and homogenized throughout Italy.

Pasta was already consumed in southern Italy and had been a mass-produced food in the city of Naples by the eighteenth century, mostly because it was highly portable and could be stored for long periods of time.[76] Pasta production was artisanal until the late nineteenth century, when the industry mechanized because of two important inventions: the motorized *semolatrice*, able to sort and sift wheat, invented in 1878; and the *impastatrice*, a mechanical kneading machine, invented in 1882. Several plants began shipping dried pasta to the United States by the turn of the century. The firm of Torre Anunziata, which operated fifty-four plants and employed approximately 10,000 people, began exporting products to the United States by 1880, under the brand names Napoli Bella and Vesuvio. By 1900, De Cecco dried pasta was available in markets in New York City. By the turn of the century, numerous Italian immigrants set up dried pasta factories in the United States, including the Fouluds plant set up in 1890 and chef Ettore Boiardi, who moved to the United States in 1910, cooking first in New York City before moving to Cleveland. In Cleveland, Boiardi experimented with canning cooked spaghetti in sauce, a confection which later took on the more familiar brand-name of Chef Boy-Ar-Dee canned pasta.[77]

Italian migration boosted the development of other food industries within Italy as well. Vegetable canning plants, which had modest beginnings in the regions of Campania and Emilia in the latter half of the nineteenth century, increased rapidly. By the end of the First World War, there were 600 processing plants, employing a total of 20,000 persons, the majority of whom were female workers, employed as seasonal laborers. The most popular products on foreign markets were tomato conserves; there were approximately 140 plants operating by 1925, producing over one million quintals of processed tomatoes per year (one quintal equals 220.46 pounds). Almost two-thirds of the goods produced, an estimated 700,000 quintals per year by 1922, were exported to markets in the Americas and throughout the rest of Europe. The most dramatic increases in export transpired in the years prior to the war and again in the latter half of the 1920s. The production of prepared meats such as *salami*, *mortadella*, and *prosciutto* increased by the turn of the century and exports of these products, particularly those made with pork, climbed steadily throughout the first three decades of the twentieth century. During the fascist period, the regime allowed for continued exports of these products, despite its strident rhetoric of economic self-sufficiency, no doubt because foreign markets were extremely profitable.[78]

Clearly, the outmigration of Italians at the turn of the century had some effect on the making of a national cuisine through the creation of external markets for foods we now associate with Italian cuisine. Since so many immigrants were southern Italian in origin, the largest markets created were for dried pasta and canned tomatoes, goods that at the turn of the century had not yet become staples for Italians, given their prohibitive cost.[79] As industries like Cirio canned tomatoes and De Cecco pasta developed, they were able to produce foods at cheaper prices, making these goods available to more and more Italians. Admittedly this was a slow process, as many Italian food industries continued to rely upon foreign markets for the majority of their sales until after the Second World War. Yet, the food habits of Italian immigrant communities warrant consideration because those who left Italy had more money to spend on food.[80] Immigrants chose to consume more of what they could not eat back in Italy, thereby reinforcing culinary and dietary norms, exporting them back to Italy via industry and repatriation. Eventually, the staples of the Italian diet – pizza and pasta – became global in their appeal as simple and satisfying meals. Ironically, then, it was only through the process of Italians leaving Italy and thus desiring to reproduce their cuisine, that certain staples of the Italian diet were nationalized.

Toward a National Cuisine

The first noticeable and significant changes in food-consumption levels in Italy were recorded at the end of the nineteenth century. The period from the 1890s until the First World War has often been characterized as one of improvement for both the economic and physiological health of the nation. Italy's industrial revolution raised living standards while hospital reform and an active municipal socialism assisted the poor through charity and improved health care. The era of Prime Minister Giovanni Giolitti (1901–14) meant optimism and economic success for Italy, measurable in popular health statistics. According to historian Vera Zamagni, the average life span of Italians rose from thirty years in 1860 to forty-seven years in 1910, while the mortality rate dropped from 31 to 14.7 per thousand in that same time-span and the infant mortality rate decreased from 223 to 138 per thousand. Despite such marked improvements in national health, many families still existed near subsistence levels, whether they were peasants or members of the growing industrial working classes.[81] Riccardo Bachi, who chronicled food-consumption patterns during the First World War, observed that the working classes enjoyed a better diet in these years, although the percentage of the family salary spent on food was still 50–80 percent.[82] Disparities between regions were still evident, however. A 1908 inquiry into meat production and consumption in cities of more than 10,000 residents (conducted by the Ministero dell'Interno, Direzione Generale di Sanità) revealed major differences between northern and southern cities. Consumption of meat ranged from the highest level of 52.9 kilograms per year, per person, in Milan to the lowest level of 3.3 kilograms per person, per year, in the Sicilian city of Trapani. The average was 36.7 kilograms per person, per year, which amounts to slightly more than one-hundred grams of meat per person on a daily basis.[83] Nonetheless, there were significant changes in consumption practice during the period of industrialization and well into Giolittian Italy; the terms of measurement, however, must be adjusted to fit the peculiarities of Italy's path to dietary improvement.

Dietary change in this period was reflected most clearly in the national parliamentary inquiry known as the Faina Inquiry (1907–10) which focused on the living conditions of the southern and Sicilian *contadini*.[84] The most significant change was the increased preference for wheat flour over flour made of corn, rye, barley, or chestnuts. The situation of the rural classes in Calabria was typical: they consumed 'more grain and less corn; by now, bread made with chestnuts or beans is no more than a memory; meat, cheese, salted fish, etc., frequently appear on the *contadino*'s table.'[85] The standard of living for most peasants was not high enough to allow for the consumption of meat or dairy products on a daily or more frequent basis. Meat was still a rarity in the south, as evidenced by one peasant's claim never to have seen meat. Another replied that he saw meat, but it was usually attached to a dead animal and was therefore inedible. Another replied that peasants in Calabria ate meat every two or three years, 'only when they go to vote.'[86]

For central and northern Italians, there were changes in consumption habits as well. A 1906 study of the peasants in Umbria found slow but steady improvement. Polenta, which for years constituted the basis of popular diet, was replaced by the more nutritious *minestra* (soup, stew, or pasta). Cornmeal bread replaced bread made from a mixture of bran, sorghum, and bean flour, and in the spring and summer, peasants could afford wheat bread.[87] Some of the most detailed studies of budgeting and food preparation for this period were done for urban populations in the north and central regions, most notably, the work of Domenico Orano for Rome. Orano's 1912 analysis of food consumption in the working-class neighborhood of Testaccio described the particulars of how Roman families were able to eat a wide variety of foods including meat. Breakfast was always coffee or coffee substitute (toasted orzo or chickpeas) with milk and bread, with a small percentage of families eating meat or cheese with bread or chestnuts and bread. Lunch or the main meal of the day was a *minestra* – pasta and/or potatoes, rice and potatoes, or pasta with cabbage, usually served in a sauce made with tomatoes, onions, and lard (a characteristic ingredient of Roman cooking). Sometimes families consumed legumes – lentils or beans – prepared with onions, garlic, and lard, or sautéed with potatoes, tomatoes, and lard, a mixture commonly referred to as *sugo finto*, or 'pretend sauce,' because no meat was used in preparation. Only a few families consumed meat on a regular basis. Dinner for most families consisted of bread with *companatico*, salad, fried polenta, or leftovers from lunch, accompanied by wine or coffee with milk. Popular diet, however, fell short of Orano's expectations. Inadequate nutrition contributed to the 'physical and moral disorganization of the worker's family ... hundreds of families eat a *minestra* composed of lard, canned tomatoes, seasoning and pasta for both lunch and dinner.'[88] Although Orano did not recognize it as such, the substitution of *minestra* for bread, along with the use of canned tomatoes, indicated significant changes in consumption habits for workers.

There is no doubt that by the early twentieth century, there were more foods available to Italian consumers. Outmigration greatly facilitated the rise of a modern food industry; immigrant communities in the Americas became major consumers of canned goods, dried pasta, dried meats, and liquors. Markets for Cirio canned tomatoes and Buitoni pasta expanded at the turn of the century; Maggi meat extracts rivaled its German competitor Leibig for Italian customers while Perugina chocolates rivaled competitors Nestlé and Suchard. In the region of Piedmont, local *rosolio* distilleries became industrial concerns, producing brand names like Cinzano, Martini, and Riccadonna. This development stood in sharp contrast to the state of the food industry at the time of national unification. Because only one-fifth of the population lived in urban centers of 20,000 or more in 1860, small-scale artisanal production and the *piccola bottega* predominated. Production of foods was limited to grain milling, oil and wine production, and cheesemaking.

As historian Francesco Chiapparino's work on the Italian food industry demonstrates, the liberalization of inter-regional trade and trade with other countries was a significant factor in facilitating the large-scale production of processed food. The Cirio canned-tomato company had opened a large processing plant as early as 1856 in Turin; Caffarel chocolates in Turin created and exported *gianduiotti*, little milk-chocolate confections, in 1867; the Barilla dried-pasta company opened its first plant in Parma in 1877; Buitoni dried pasta, in existence since 1827, increased production in the 1880s with a new plant in San Sepulcro in Arezzo; by the turn of the century, industrial liquor production took off in Milan (Branca) and Trieste (Stock); and, in 1907, Perugina chocolates opened its first factory.[89] We must be careful, however, not to exaggerate the significance of these trends. The major food industries numbered in the tens instead of the hundreds and were situated primarily in the northern and central regions of the nation. In comparison to other European countries, Italy's food industry was limited. For example, Italy's imports of cocoa for the year 1904 amounted to only 10,000 quintals, most of which was used by the chocolate industry. Italian import levels were dwarfed by those of Germany (300,000 quintals), Great Britain (200,000), or France (220,000).[90] The national market for non-essential processed foods was small, tied closely to the standard of living, and limited to the northern regions, where small firms faced stiff competition from food industries in Switzerland, France, and Austria.

There is also much evidence to suggest that after the turn of the century, political parties became more active in improving the affordability and nutritional quality of the Italian diet. The Italian cooperative movement, founded by members of the Democratic Party in 1886 as the National League of Cooperative Societies, underwent a significant transformation by the eve of the First World War. Increased participation by the Socialist Party in the National League led to its expansion; the League was subdivided into other associations and unions with headquarters in most major cities. By 1915, there were 7,420 cooperative societies throughout the country, this number would almost triple over the course of the war.[91] The Italian

Socialist Party also participated in establishing commissions to investigate the high cost of living (*rincaro dei viveri*) in urban areas. These committees focused on taxation and the retail sector as possible points of state intervention to assist and protect consumers. In Venice, for example, the municipal commission spent three years examining the price of fish, seafood, fruits, vegetables, dairy products, meat, and fodder. The commission concluded that local taxes priced foods out of the reach of working-class Venetians. Fish, seafood, and produce were then exported to other regions because of weak local demand. To remedy this situation, the commission urged the municipality to reduce local taxes, organize consumer cooperatives, and monitor retail prices through a permanent committee. The case of Venice was typical in that municipal governments across Italy began to experiment with controlling prices and regulating local markets. In many instances, an active local Socialist Party urged municipal governments to become more involved in guaranteeing the availability of inexpensive and nutritious food. The national government would have a minimal role, stepping in only in cases of emergency, as was the case during the disturbances of 1898, when the government implemented the Royal Decree of 4 May 1898 (Number 276), which gave local government the right to fix prices temporarily.

Local authorities, charities, and worker societies also became involved with implementing soup kitchens (the *cucina popolare* or *cucina economica*). Kitchens were popular in the northern regions where pellagra was prevalent. Pellagra is caused by the absence of niacin in an exclusively corn-based diet, common in the nineteenth century in regions like the Veneto, Piedmont, and Lombardy. The disease causes disturbances of the digestive and nervous systems, as well as skin rashes (oddly shaped reddish marks). In acute cases, the disease led to delusions and depression, sometimes resulting in suicide. Recorded cases of pellagra reached their peak in Italy in the year 1881, with an estimated 104,000 documented cases. This number decreased to 46,984 by 1904 and 33,861 in 1910.[92] The national government took limited action against the disease in 1902 by banning the sale of under-ripe or rotten corn and forcing local authorities to take responsibility for the worst cases in their district.

Although pellagra affected mostly peasants, northern urban governments took action to assist those urban workers with the disease. In the regions of the Veneto, Piedmont, Lombardy, and Friuli, soup kitchens offered well-balanced meals, including meat, for as little as ten cents. The first kitchens were set up in Turin, beginning in the 1880s; Milan followed suit in the 1890s. Later, soup kitchens were set up in Naples and Rome in order to feed the indigent. The kitchens attracted numerous customers in urban areas, where workers could stop by on their way home from work to pick up a meal or eat there. They were less successful in rural areas and in the southern regions, where charity was inadequate and carried a certain stigma. A delegate from the Faina Inquiry noted that in Sicily

sometimes public charity intervenes, although it is never enough. There are food distributions or soup kitchens, either free of cost or at minimal prices. But the *contadino* is
ashamed to resort to these. He furtively sends one of his children, or goes at night-
time.[93]

Although they were effective in containing pellagra in the north, soup kitchens
were not all that popular prior to the First World War. Consumers disliked the institutional setting and preferred charity in the form of food distribution or subsidies
for staple foods. In liberal Italy, charity remained at home. Charity still carried
with it a certain social stigma, and in some areas of Italy, citizens resented the
Catholic Church's paternalistic control over charity.

Although more and more people were drawn into public debates about food and
its consumption at the beginning of the twentieth century, these discussions transpired within distinct communities. Scientific experts, local authorities, socialists,
and consumers all grappled with the distance between material, quotidian reality
and the new possibilities afforded by greater consumer cooperation and local food
controls, or scientific standards of proper nutrition. Sometimes, changes in dietary
practice came from unexpected sources or were very indirect in causation, as was
the case with the rise of food industries supplying goods for Italian immigrants.
By the eve of the First World War, public discussion about food appeared to be a
confusing and fractured debate over what should be done and for whom. The only
consensus was that popular consumption habits could still stand improvement,
even after the first wave of industrialization swept over Italy.

This slippage between what was recorded and what was anticipated for popular
diet demonstrates the political nature of food consumption in the newly-unified
state. This slippage also underscores the inactivity of the successive liberal governments. The national government continued to have an indirect effect on the cost
and availability of foods, but improvements in diet at the beginning of the twentieth century would be the result of industrialization and outmigration. Left
reformers and some scientific experts criticized the lack of state intervention,
particularly in times of inflation when the need for retail modernization and tax
reform was more urgent. The absence of direct controls under liberalism would
also be criticized later by the fascist regime as a glaring example of liberalism's
'do-nothing' approach to the welfare of the population. Indeed, it was largely up to
citizens themselves to change their living conditions, either by leaving or by
protesting. The dietary changes of the early twentieth century – the substitution of
wheat flour for corn, the increased consumption of produce and dairy products, a
more widespread use of luxury foods like sugar, coffee, and even tobacco – were
significant ones, even though consumption practices were still austere.

The First World War changed everything. The war is often considered a water-
shed in the history of European food consumption because European governments

became more involved in controlling prices and providing food. The wartime experience of Italy lay somewhere between that of Germany, where dramatic shortages caused protest and food riots; and England, where consumers experienced few inconveniences on account of available supplies from the colonies. In Italy, popular diet actually improved over the course of the war because the government imported and subsidized wheat, thereby bringing down the price of the staple of bread. State intervention introduced new controls over food supply and distribution, while agreements between citizen and state empowered Italian consumers. To some degree, then, a greater leveling out of diet occurred during the war, but this process only served to make Italian citizens more adamant about sustaining the momentum for dietary improvement. This suggests that conflict over food during the First World War focused on political questions regarding who could eat what kinds of foods, and less on material issues regarding whether or not everyone had enough to eat. The discussions regarding what people *should* eat versus what they ate, so germane to nineteenth-century liberal debates, would be intensified and further complicated by the introduction of the State in the quest to improve the quantity and quality of the Italian diet.

–2–

The Great War and the Rise of State Intervention, Italy 1915–22

The First World War shook the foundations of European culture and politics. The war also transformed the nature of state intervention, as governments had to sustain military and civilian populations for the war's duration. Food was a critical resource, to be managed through active government intervention in the form of food policies. Thus, the First World War was 'not only a war of steel and gold, but a war of bread and potatoes,' according to historian Avner Offer.[1] Liberal governments abandoned their laissez-faire attitudes toward state control in favor of coordinating and regulating food production, distribution, and consumption. The most common features of wartime food policies were agricultural production campaigns, controlling consumption through rationing, regulating the balance of trade, and fixing prices. For Italians, the need to increase industrial production – desirable to nineteenth-century experts and politicians – became a national emergency in the context of war.

Italians experienced the war differently from their counterparts in Great Britain, France, or Germany. Italy entered the war on 24 May 1915, after breaking its diplomatic ties with Germany and Austria-Hungary in order to obtain territories on Italy's alpine frontier and on the Adriatic.[2] The majority of Italians were never enthusiastic about fighting the war; only a few ardent nationalists expressed strident patriotism; and the battlefront was removed from everyday life. All of this is not to say that Italy's experience of the war was insignificant. The days of 'Radiant May' (May 1915) brought interventionists and nationalists in direct confrontation with socialists, presaging the difficulties the liberal regime would face in terms of containing partisan conflict after the war. The Italian front was the most difficult in Europe: a 400–mile line snaking through steep hills and high mountains. Military defeats (including the humiliating rout at Caporetto in October of 1917) tested the nation's mettle, but Italy responded by turning the military situation around to wind up on offensive territory by the end of the war in November of 1918.

It has been difficult for Italian historians to evaluate the war as a distinct experience for Italians. Indeed, *La Grande Guerra* has been neatly framed between the *belle époque* of the Giolittian era (1901–14) and the decades of Benito Mussolini's

rule (1922–45). The First World War sits awkwardly in between two more significant eras, and it is difficult to analyze the war without seeing the looming shadow
of fascism on the horizon. Although it is debatable as to whether the wartime experience 'nationalized' the masses in Italy, one thing was certain: the political crises
of the postwar era, combined with a deepening economic crisis, paved the way for
a conservative reaction to the liberal government's failure to control inflation and
political opposition. Everyday life and the transformation of social relations were
critical factors in this turn to authoritarianism. However, Italian historians have
considered the social context of the war only recently. In particular, they have
examined the wartime experiences of industrial workers and peasants on both
fronts, as well as the importance of memory and cultural commemorations of
nationalism and war.[3] Still, we know very little about the fabric of everyday life for
Italian citizens during the war. Food consumption receives passing mention in
histories of the war and many authors tend to repeat the findings of contemporary
accounts of wartime consumption.[4] Contemporary accounts of wartime consumption argued that the war was a dietary modernizer because Italians consumed a
more nutritious and varied diet during the war than in previous decades.[5] There is
no doubt that the war improved popular diet. Consumers were able to buy more
food and higher-quality goods because of full employment and higher wages.
During and after the war, politicians, scientists, and, consumers debated whether
the State should continue to finance consumption and the standard of living.[6]
Consumers vigorously supported continued intervention and protested when they
saw their standard of living – and eating – decline.

This chapter supports the argument that state intervention during and immediately after the war substantially improved people's eating habits. Wartime intervention solidified and extended the dietary changes that occurred in the late
Giolittian period: namely, the trends toward consuming wheat bread as well as a
greater variety of foods. The government's preoccupation with wheat supplies
ensured that more Italians consumed wheat bread as a dietary staple. State subsidies made bread inexpensive and consequently, more Italians could afford to
purchase items like pasta, olive oil, wine, and even meat. State intervention
extended and homogenized certain eating practices, thereby solidifying the foundations of Italian cuisine. This chapter chronicles the transformation of popular
diet and examines both official and popular reactions to wartime food policies. The
first two sections of the chapter provide an overview of state intervention, from
early voluntary measures to the institution of a complex wartime bureaucracy.
Whereas the liberal state was reluctant to govern or control aspects of everyday
life, consumers and local governments continually pushed for more intensive
action, even when the State could not afford it. Food still represented what was
wrong with Italy, but during the war, discussions about food consumption reflected
the conflict between consumers and the State over the price and availability of

food. Consumption habits and expectations were 'nationalized' in the sense that Italians became accustomed to goods like wheat bread, olive oil, canned tomatoes, and pasta. When the government failed to control prices or threatened to pull subsidies, consumers protested because they did not want to give up their wartime gains. Although wartime policies were considered experiments in state control, they changed the composition of Italian cuisine by making some foods more available and affordable.

Early Interventions

Even before Italy entered the war in May of 1915, there were problems with food supplies. The closing of the Bosporus and Dardenelles straits at the end of 1914 curtailed Italy's imports of grain from Russia and Romania, leading to sporadic shortages. Throughout the winter and into the spring of 1915, local prefects sent telegrams to the Minister of Interior, describing how little grain was available and asking for advice or free grain. The Ministry responded by encouraging prefects to form voluntary grain consortia, local organizations of grain producers, importers, and merchants. The grain consortia were supposed to regulate prices, keep track of existing grain supplies, and procure additional grain supplies if necessary.[7] On 26 January 1915, the Ministry of Agriculture, Industry, and Commerce was placed in charge of a new organization known as the Ufficio Temporaneo per l'Approvvigionamento del Grano (Temporary Office for Grain Provisioning), more commonly known as UTAG.[8]

Maintaining the nation's wheat supplies was of the utmost importance because wheat had partially replaced other grains in the years prior to the war and became a staple of the Italian diet during the war. Wheat-flour imports increased over 9,000 percent from 1914 to 1918, reflecting the use of wheat for military and civilian provisioning.[9] After the war, Giorgio Mortara, professor of statistics at University of Milan, estimated that grain consumption for Italy increased from sixty-three million to sixty-nine million quintals per year; domestic production averaged forty-five-million quintals per year during the war (one quintal equals 220.46 pounds or 100 kilograms).[10] Thus, the government had to worry about a twenty-five million-quintal deficit in grain supplies, to be made up through imports, improving agricultural yields, and the conservation of existing stocks. However, agricultural production schemes were limited to providing fertilizers and educating farmers about rationalized farming methods.[11] Efforts to conserve existing stocks met with widespread resistance. Through UTAG, the government sought new sources in the United States, Australia, Canada, and Argentina.

Despite all this activity, sporadic grain shortages and higher bread prices preoccupied consumers throughout the winter of 1915. Large protests were first mounted in Caltanisetta (Sicily) in early January, with thousands demonstrating in the streets. By the end of the month, citizens throughout the province of Catania boarded grain ships and tried to take wheat by force. They also threatened to loot bakeries. By mid-February, protests and violence spread north to Livorno, Bari, Florence, and Arezzo; by March, prefects from Chieti, Ferrara, Bologna, Brescia, Milan, Perugia, and Udine all reported civil disorder, noting in some cases that the *carabinieri* had to be called in to protect grain supplies.[12] These protests, coming before Italy's entry into the war, the halting of emigration, and the commencement of military provisioning, constituted a very widespread public declaration of citizens' desire for cheap grain. These disturbances also tested the capabilities of local leaders, who were forced to bridge the gap between consumer demand and government-mediated supplies. Although Parliament debated grain prices in February of 1915, the national government did little about the situation, and public unrest remained a local matter.

In response to consumer protests, prefects instituted a fixed price or *calmiere*, set by municipal authorities, for flour and bread. These early experiments in asserting local authority over food policies brought varied results. The mayor of Ancona, after accepting a price increase of ten lire per quintal for grain on 15 March, immediately dropped the price of grain when confronted by hundreds of protesting women and children. In other locales, fixing prices meant balancing the interests of consumers with those of merchants. The municipal council of Chiari, in Brescia, instituted a fixed price for grain on 23 March. Bakers threatened to strike, whereupon consumers took to the streets again in protest. After a week, bakers still refused to accept the newly mandated price of fifty cents per loaf, an amount that was five cents below what they had requested. Bakeries shut down on 29 March. Ultimately, the municipal council purchased bread from the nearby city of Milan, undercutting the bakers, who were forced to accept the price and resume operations.[13] Throughout the spring and summer of 1915, local authorities preserved order by fixing prices, posting these legal price limits in public places, and enforcing merchant compliance.

Initially, the national government shied away from implementing a central policy to distribute or fix the price of grain. Instead the government emphasized the need to conserve existing supplies. This was to be done mostly through the control of the bread-making and milling industries, to ensure that wheat was not wasted on the production of highly refined flour and white bread. These efforts by the Ministry of Interior angered merchants, consumers, and local officials. A Royal Decree Law of 7 March 1915 mandated the production and sale of *tipo unico* bread, coarse bread made with flour containing at least 80 percent of the wheat milled. Presumably, bakers were to sell only *tipo unico* and thus consumers were limited to purchasing one kind of bread. Although the Ministry of Interior's Department of Public Health (Ministero dell'Interno, Direzione Generale di Sanità) stressed obedience to the *tipo unico* laws, the law was difficult for prefects and mayors to enforce, given the lack of manpower to inspect bakeries, shops, and restaurants. Occasionally, restaurants and bakers caught selling white bread were reported to local officials and/or denounced in the newspapers. Enforcement was particularly difficult in urban areas where consumers were used to eating white bread and were more reluctant to give it up in favor of coarse, dark bread.

Retail merchants vehemently opposed the *tipo unico* law. The National Federation of Workers in the Bread-Making Industry requested that the *tipo unico* law be rescinded because coarse bread was 'unhealthy' for Italians. Ultimately, however, lack of enforcement of the *tipo unico* laws meant the production and sale of white bread continued. Violations were widespread and prefects complained that any effective enforcement of the law would push their budgets to breaking. Government ministers blamed prefects for inadequate vigilance, as indicated by a memorandum from the Ministry of Agriculture to the Ministry of Interior (25 August 1916), 'in many areas local authorities tolerate bread-making with white flour, (they are) unable to comprehend the amount of energy and activity necessary to impede each violation of the vigilance orders.'[14] The *tipo unico* law, as a means of conserving existing grain stocks, was ineffective because it presumed full cooperation from commercial interests and consumers. At this early stage in the war, neither bakers nor consumers were prepared to make such sacrifices.

The government also tried to conserve existing food supplies by instituting export bans and keeping a close watch on food supplies within Italy.[15] There is no doubt, however, that the most successful instrument of early wartime food policy was price fixing. By the spring of 1916, most grains, pasta, flour, and sugar were subject to fixed prices across the nation, although local authorities had the ultimate responsibility for prices. Local control worked well in cities like Rome and Milan, where municipal governments reacted quickly and forcefully to avert possible price increases.[16] In cities and towns where authorities had little experience controlling prices, confusion reigned. Throughout the summer and fall of 1915, bakers and butchers shut down their stores in response to the attempts by local authorities to institute fixed prices. Consumers were outraged by these shutdowns and local authorities were helpless in the face of consumer/merchant conflicts. In the town of Chiàvari, near Genoa, bakers went on strike after the price of bread was lowered from 55 to 50 cents per loaf. In response to the rumors that bakers left their shops in order to take a holiday, citizens staged violent demonstrations. According to the prefect of Genoa, a crowd comprised mostly of women 'flung themselves at all the bakeries and shops where bread is sold, breaking down the doors and destroying everything inside.' Public confrontations continued during the period 4–17 July, until eighty soldiers and thirty *carabinieri* restored order. Finally, the town's bakers relented and accepted the 5-cent price decrease.[17] In the town of Cattolica Eracléa, in Sicily, a crowd of 400 demonstrated against price increases for grain on 24 July. They injured several police and broke the windows of the municipal building. In

Monterchi, near Arezzo, 500 people demonstrated, scuffled with *carabinieri* (one protester died after being shot when a revolver went off accidentally), and petitioned the mayor for greater citizen representation in fixing prices.[18]

Citizens took to the streets all over Italy to protest higher bread prices. These protests targeted municipal authorities and requested greater consumer representation in local provisioning matters. Mayors responded to these disturbances by encouraging citizen participation and forming special committees to set fair prices and to inform the public about price policies. Citizens took an active interest in this new role. Perhaps the best example of civic participation in price controls was in the city of Bologna, where members of political parties (Anarchist, Socialist, Republican, and Mazzinian parties), and labor-union representatives met to establish a committee *"per la difesa del pane"* (for the defense of bread) in February 1915. Citizen representatives not only assisted in the implementation of the *calmiere*, but they also launched a publicity campaign to keep food supplies within the province and demanded the immediate abolition of all taxes on food items. Noting the national government's reluctance to control prices, the committee urged greater public participation in keeping inexpensive food within the city, for 'during these sad hours, the people, with their indefatigable energy, must allow for the deficiencies in the laws and in the men who administer them.'[19] During the first year of the war, price fixing was a very effective policy. The prices of basic food items such as bread, pasta, lard, flour, oil, and milk increased by a national average of only 20–25 percent during the entire year of 1915.[20] Citizen participation in local price committees meant increased scrutiny over the slightest increase in prices. Early and vigorous municipal action set the tone for the duration of the war, as national policies tended to follow local initiative.

A More Complex System of Control

The year 1915 witnessed numerous confrontations over the price and availability of bread. While consumers and local officials clashed over these matters, the national government took no direct action, preferring instead to adopt voluntary and temporary measures in 1915–16. The events of 1917 forced the national government to act. Italy was devastated by submarine warfare, having lost the highest percentage of food stocks in the summer of 1917, and having no large merchant marine to procure substitutions.[21] Shortages led to civil discontent, eclipsing in the August 1917 riots in Turin, which left fifty dead, 200 injured, and over 900 arrested. A few months later, Italian troops were humiliated at the Battle of Caporetto. These events led to more intensive interventions and Italy's participation in inter-allied provisioning efforts.

Ultimately, allied loans alleviated Italy's provisioning crisis, but inter-allied cooperation reminded Italians of where their diet stood compared to that of other

European nations. The Scientific Food Committee of the Inter-Allied Scientific Commission, for example, declared in March 1918 'that the requirements of the average man of seventy kilogram body weight doing eight hours average physical work in a climate such as England's or France's is to be considered as 3,300 calories as purchased.'[22] A 10 percent margin was allowed for domestic spoilage or waste, for a total of 3,000 calories consumed, per day. According to national averages devised by the Scientific Food Committee, Italy was the only allied country that fell short of the minimum caloric requirements. Italy was also last in terms of the percentage of calories derived from animal origin: 12 percent compared to 27 percent in France and 36 percent in Great Britain.[23] If meat consumption guaranteed strength and courage as the Scientific Food Committee maintained, Italian troops and civilians faced an uphill struggle simply to guarantee compliance with minimal nutritional requirements.

This struggle was most apparent in the area of military provisioning.[24] At the beginning of the war, scientific experts optimistically devised theoretical dietary scales for efficient military performance. In June 1915, Filippo Rho, the Medical General for the Royal Navy, requested that soldiers receive at least 3,500 calories per day. This ration included 375 grams of meat, a figure unheard of for most civilians, but certainly a modest amount in comparison with that of French soldiers, who received 500 grams of meat per day, and that of British soldiers, who received 700 grams per day.[25] Rho recognized Italy's limited resources and stressed moderate protein intake, but social reformers and hygienists contested even this modest proposal, decrying what they deemed an "excessive" amount of animal foods consumed. Angelo Pugliese of the left-reform Società Umanitaria warned that meat and dairy stocks would be quickly depleted under Rho's plan; Italy simply did not have the resources to support a military diet heavy in proteins and fats.[26]

Certainly Rho's recommendations revealed the shortcomings of Italy's productive capacities in wartime; the Italian government had to import over 936,000 quintals of frozen meat per year in order to supply the military. Rations remained at 2,794 calories per day for territorial troops and 3,013 calories for mobilized soldiers. These rations were reduced again in late 1916, and the meat ration averaged 290 grams per soldier for the course of the war.[27] Italian soldiers consumed less meat than French or German soldiers, but they consumed considerably more meat than Italians on the homefront. Statistical averages indicate that civilian meat consumption during the war ranged from a low of 44 grams per person per day in Catania to a high of 157 grams per day in Milan.[28] The ongoing controversy over military meat rations reflected the prewar scientific association between meat and labor power; it also called into question the vast disparities within the national population, in this case military versus civilian, measured by one's access to meat and other animal products. Indeed, in a nation of limited resources, the controversy over military rations pitted civilian against soldier. The nation's Office of

Propaganda to Discipline Consumption repeatedly asked citizens to voluntarily reduce meat consumption by at least 30 grams per day so that soldiers would have enough meat to eat. Even this small reduction would have done little to address the shortage. The Italian Socialist Party responded to these requests by complaining that the volume of food consumed by soldiers was more than double their peace-time rations and therefore should be adequate for combat.[29]

Military provisioning often generated more anxiety than good faith. Historian Assunta Trova's work on military provisioning depicts a constantly deteriorating situation in which military officials were forced to request more food for their troops.[30] The amount of meat, bread, and coffee rations fluctuated; substitutions like frozen meat or hard tack were frequent. Italian prisoners of war suffered the most, subsisting on an average of less than 1,000 calories per day. Daily diet in the Austrian and German camps consisted mostly of orzo coffee, cabbage soup, and bread or potatoes. The fact that the Italian government did little to supplement these meager rations angered prisoners, who remembered how French prisoners 'would receive bread or canned meat from their government each week while we, with our plates in hand, would ask them for some of their food.'[31]

The military's provisioning crises exposed the inadequacies of the Italian food industry. For example, there were only two factories where canned goods were produced specifically for the military; a few private factories were contracted out for the war's duration.[32] Critics of military provisioning believed the reduction in rations in late 1916 led to the military disaster at Caporetto (24 October 1917), which resulted in 10,000 dead, 30,000 injured, 400,000 deserted and 300,000 prisoners of war. The rout demonstrated not only the weakness of the Italian high command, but also the failure of will and nerve of the average Italian soldier. The Caporetto disaster sparked fierce debate within the Italian scientific community regarding the relationship between proper nutrition and military performance. Italian scientists were already on the defensive, considering that members of Inter-Allied Scientific Commission thought Italy's military provisioning to be physiologically unsound (and perhaps psychologically unsound as well, as reductions might have led to a loss of courage and resistance).[33] Rations were increased after Caporetto and by the end of the war, soldiers received almost 3,300 calories per day, considered by physiologists to be adequate for moderate labor, but not enough for the strenuous work of combat, where 4,000 calories per day was recommended.[34] Even the modest concessions after Caporetto literally drained the military's storehouses. By the end of the war, storehouses maintained only a few days' supply of goods like lard, meat, and cereals. Soldiers complained during and after the war that a complex bureaucracy hindered an efficient distribution of foods.[35] While Italian soldiers' rations fell far short of those of their allied counterparts, many soldiers were able to consume foods they seldom received at home: meat, coffee, tobacco, sugar, and liquor (provided to alpine troops). Benito Mussolini's wartime memoirs recalled adequate and even abundant rations on the Austrian front: 'Liquids – a cup of coffee, a little wine, and a little grappa. Solids – a piece of cheese and half a can of meat. Almost all one wants of good bread.'[36]

Despite these setbacks and shortages, military provisioning was not surrounded in as much controversy as civilian provisioning. Put simply, Italian consumers wanted more food because they could afford to purchase more goods with higher wages and full employment. As the war dragged on, the needs of civilians and the military strained Italy's productive capacities. In order to centralize food policies, Parliament formed the Commissariato Generale di Consumi Alimentari (General Commissariat for Food Consumption) in January of 1917, under the Ministry of the Interior. Socialist Luigi Canepa was put in charge of the Commissariat. Canepa took immediate action to conserve existing wheat stocks by mandating an even coarser type of *tipo unico* bread. The American Consul in Florence noted that the bread was 'dark, sour, unattractive and having a bad taste, provoking intestinal irritation, above the limits of toleration.'[37] The decree was rescinded after popular protest. Undaunted, Canepa moved to conserve supplies of other foods, urging in May of 1917 that prefects ration meat, fat, sugar, flour, and even bread. Various towns tried to ration these goods, but most local authorities were reluctant to ration a necessity like bread for fear of public reprisals.[38] Throughout the summer of 1917, Canepa's Commissariat was deluged with urgent telegrams and letters from prefects and mayors, complaining of bread shortages and requesting essential supplies for hungry citizens.[39] Canepa's response, issued in a circular of 11 September 1917, urged the adoption of bread rationing, but ultimately left it up to prefects and mayors to decide the best course of action.[40] Such ambivalence did not sit well with local authorities weary of managing provisioning crises on their own.

Critics from all points on the political spectrum criticized Canepa for his measures to conserve existing food stocks. Merchants objected to his efforts to regularize national food distribution through grain consortia, cooperatives, and provisioning warehouses. Commercial interests regarded his proposal for national coordination as an instrument of bureaucratic and authoritarian control over commerce.[41] As a Socialist, Canepa envisioned the proliferation of consumer cooperatives and other alternatives to retail distribution, but he hoped that voluntary initiatives would accomplish this goal. Canepa's Commissariat failed to impede the growth of the black market or to control price hikes, however. When large protests erupted in Milan (May 1917) and Turin (August 1917), spurred by food shortages and complaints of high prices, protesters sacked stores and bakeries, clashing with police and soldiers. The national government could no longer ignore popular protest and was forced to reorganize its provisioning policies. Parliament elevated Canepa's Commissariat into a Ministry and urged mandatory rationing for cereals. Laws passed in September allowed prefects to alter rationing systems in accordance with their own particular circumstances and needs.[42] Several weeks after the Turin riots, Italian troops were defeated at Caporetto. In the aftermath of Caporetto, industrialist Silvio Crespi replaced Canepa as the undersecretary for provisioning and consumption. Crespi, who was especially nervous that food shortages would bring about revolution, attacked the problem of distribution more systematically than did his predecessor.[43] Mandatory rationing was extended to meat, sugar, fats, and oils; the manufacture of sweets was prohibited; and heavier penalties were inflicted on hoarders and profiteers.

As Director of Provisioning, Crespi aggressively pursued the importation of food from Italy's allies, turning away from Canepa's policies of conservation toward a policy of acquisition. Because the grain harvest of 1917 fell short of official projections by eleven million quintals, Crespi was determined to make up the difference through allied loans. He then launched a campaign to talk to the international press and to the Inter-Allied Commissions in Paris through the fall and winter of 1917, to emphasize the point that Italians did not have enough to eat.[44] Crespi was right to be concerned about food shortages. Throughout the fall of 1917, local authorities from Genoa to Palermo noted public dissatisfaction with high prices, sporadic shortages, and the irregular distribution of goods.

The events of 1917 underscored the need for increased state intervention to procure and guarantee an efficient distribution of food throughout the nation. The press called for a vigorous national campaign against speculation, hoarding, and the black market as prices rose steadily throughout the autumn of 1917.[45] Left politicians called for the national support of consumer cooperatives as a remedy to high prices; everywhere the government's level of activity and commitment was called into question. Much of the criticism leveled against the government had to do with the unintended effects of policies. Umberto Ricci, one of the most outspoken critics of wartime food policies, argued that state intervention unintentionally privileged rural populations. City-dwellers could obtain only low-quality bread, made of 'various and mysterious' ingredients, whereas in the countryside, farm laborers had access to quality white flour.[46] Critics also maintained that price controls had the unintended consequences of helping the rich save money on items like bread and pasta. Some proposed two prices for *tipo unico* bread: one for the wealthy and one for the poor.[47] Some local authorities attempted to regulate the production of different kinds of bread at varying prices. These efforts ran afoul of the national *tipo unico* laws and generated little cooperation from bakers, who chose to produce high-quality expensive bread rather than coarser types. Rationing only aggravated this situation, particularly in areas where shortages were frequent. In Milan, for example, rationing limited the quantities of bread, pasta, flour, and rice for the urban poor but provided them with ration cards for foods that they could not afford, like olive oil, butter, sugar, and cheese.[48] Fixed prices, requisitioning, and subsidies all had unintended effects, sharpening social distinctions between populations in Italy and recasting the 'tale of two diets' during wartime. Once again, food (or the absence of food) came to represent inequalities as well as the means to remedy them.

Crespi's efforts to obtain more grain from the Allies paid off. By the summer of 1918, Italy had been granted 'most favored nation' status and the Allies provided the nation with almost twice as much wheat in 1918 as they did in 1917.[49] Although Crespi made heroic efforts to increase grain imports, distribution problems plagued the nation, leading to temporary grain shortages in some areas in the year 1918. Even cities with efficient municipal provisioning boards, such as Rome, experienced temporary grain shortages, which led to rowdy assaults on bakers. Prefects were sometimes at their wits' end in trying to calm public unrest, regulate commerce, and negotiate with national authorities for promised supplies. The public often took to the streets in protest. Minor disturbances and work stoppages occurred throughout the nation, with the largest demonstrations and strikes taking place in Ferrara, Florence, Genoa, Girgenti, Grosseto, Livorno, Lucca, Mantua, Milan, Naples, Pisa, and Rome.[50] For the most part, local authorities waited out sporadic shortages and distributional problems. Meanwhile, the Ministry of the Interior told prefects that the national government was in serious debt; circulars warned prefects of an alarming situation with no immediate relief in sight. Prefects were advised to do anything within their power to reduce consumption levels further. However, they had no legal means of enforcing austerity on their populations and could only urge citizens to cut back on food purchases voluntarily.[51]

By the war's end in November of 1918, there were sporadic shortages, yet citizens were not in danger of starvation or malnutrition. Despite the many criticisms leveled at the wartime governments for their inept handling of food policies, the Ministry for Provisioning and Consumption prevented any severe shortage or crisis. This fact was cold comfort to consumers and merchants, who constantly protested the policies implemented by local authorities. More often than not, the national government was content to let local officials take charge of volatile situations. Indeed, as the history of wartime intervention has demonstrated, most of the protests and legislation took place on the local level. We must be careful, however, not to dismiss the role of the national government in wartime food policies. Silvio Crespi doggedly pursued the most significant intervention to improve popular diet: procuring more wheat from the allies. During the war, cheap and available bread sustained the nation's labor force. Simply put, increased imports, controlled prices, and full employment meant that Italians could afford more food and a higher-quality diet. Total wheat imports increased 900 percent over the course of the war.[52] In particular, urban populations had access to more food, at cheaper prices. A study by the Office of Labor of the forty-two most populated municipalities found a significant increase in the quantity of food purchased, per individual. Statistician Mario Balestrieri's study of the war years maintained that during the war, consumers ate more nutritious foods at cheaper prices. These foods included wheat bread, fresh fruits and vegetables, and animal proteins in the form of dairy products and meat. Balestrieri found that most consumers were willing to pay more per caloric unit of food after the war (1919–21) even when prices rose astronomically.[53]

Total food imports increased from 19 percent of all goods imported in 1913, to 32 percent of goods imported in 1922, including more wheat from the United States and Canada. US State Department statistics calculated that per capita consumption of wheat in Italy increased by eighteen kilograms per year between 1913 and 1921, while the consumption of wheat alternatives such as corn, rice, potatoes, and chestnuts decreased steadily in the same period of time.[54] Given that the government maintained wheat prices at artificially low prices, more consumers could afford wheat bread. Economist Luigi Einaudi noted that consumers preferred the taste of wheat bread to that of bread made from rice or other cereals, even if they had to pay more for it.[55] Statisticians also noted the increased consumption of pork, beef, eggs, milk, and cheese in both rural and urban areas. Imports and subsidies extended and cemented prewar consumption trends toward more wheat bread and more animal proteins. Unfortunately, there were only a few small-scale studies of consumer habits conducted during the war and most of these focused on the province and city of Milan.[56] The Società Umanitaria's Angelo Pugliese completed the most detailed studies of consumer habits. His work on the Milanese working class showed a steady upward climb in the consumption of basic foodstuffs like bread, grain, potatoes, and milk from the period just prior to the war through the first two years of the war. Although meat consumption declined from 138.31 grams per day in 1913 to 88.2 grams per day in 1917, Pugliese concluded that diet improved overall because of increased consumption of bread, rice, and corn meal, all of which were offered at subsidized prices.[57]

Subsidized prices allowed many wartime consumers to purchase non-nutritious items such as alcohol, coffee, and tobacco. In Milan, the Chamber of Commerce found that the volume of tobacco consumed almost doubled over the course of the war while spending quadrupled. Consumers preferred the finer, more expensive tobacco, and the Chamber observed that the highest expenditures (in terms of monetary value) on tobacco were in the city's poorest neighborhoods. Tobacco was not the only luxury item in high demand in Milan. Angelo Pugliese reported a rapid rise in alcohol consumption among industrial workers, especially among women and adolescents.[58] To what extent did trends in Milan mirror those throughout the nation? Certainly Milan's level of spending on non-necessity goods was higher than that found in other cities.[59] However there is evidence to suggest that the rest of the nation followed trends in Milan. The consumption of alcoholic beverages (excluding wine) in the nation doubled over the course of the war, despite a tax increase of roughly 25 percent per year. The tax on coffee increased ten times over between 1915 and 1924, but this did not affect consumption, which increased twelve times over in volume in this same period.[60] Likewise, consumers learned to appreciate sugar, so much so that many refused surrogates like saccharine during the times sugar was scarce. Luigi Einaudi noted how even agricultural laborers manifested an 'invincible repugnance' to saccharine.[61] Consumers found it difficult to return to prewar consumption habits at the war's end, opting instead to pay higher prices and more taxes to secure the goods they desired.

The increased consumption of non-necessity items fostered fears about the so-called irrationality of consumption among scientific professionals, who worried that consumers would opt for non-nutritious and expensive foods despite the availability of lower-priced and more nutritious items.[62] Italian scientists had hoped to actively reshape consumption habits in a rational manner. Thus, they hoped consumers would purchase more meat, dairy products, and vegetables instead of wine, sugar, and tobacco. This preoccupation with stimulants reflects the tensions inherent in scientific thought about the Italian diet. On the one hand, wartime conditions opened doors to an expansion of popular diet and improved nutrition while, at the same time, they allowed for the possibility of increased consumption of non-nutritious or even deleterious items. The fear that Italians would succumb to what was termed *il sensualismo alimentare* was perhaps exaggerated.[63] The war sped up changes that were already prevalent in prewar Italy; consumers were not limited to the tastes of necessity and could choose the foods they desired. Given that scientists advocated the most rational approach to diet and that government officials stressed a disciplined consumption, it appeared that few experts were happy with wartime and postwar consumption habits.[64] Concern about the irrationality of consumption demonstrated a self-consciousness about dietary improvement and a desire for the state to control and rationalize consumption habits. In the postwar years, however, ministries had to address the mounting public debt by balancing the interests of social reformers with those of conservatives who prioritized the nation's financial health over higher levels of consumption. Fiscal accountability won out over social reform, but not without serious political consequences for the liberal state.

The Unification of Desire

After the armistice of 3 November and the cessation of hostilities the next day, Silvio Crespi noted the irony of the situation at the war's end, in which 'victory gave us an enormous population to provision; a population lacking in every resource and for whom we must now provide everything.'[65] New and recovered territories meant more people to feed: people who were poorly nourished during the last months of the war. Reports from invaded territories graphically described the illnesses caused by malnutrition. In the northern provinces of Belluno, Treviso,

Udine, and Venezia, citizens subsisted on an average of one hundred grams of flour per day, supplemented by whatever they could find in the fields or obtain by barter.[66] War requisitioning depleted existing food stocks, leading to cases of extreme malnutrition, hunger edema, and disease. For northern Italy, severe conditions peaked in the winter of 1918 before improving. In the south, some prefects complained that the distribution of food was still disorganized and inadequate, straining the limits of public tolerance.[67] However, these were regional pockets of concern. Despite the urgent situation in the recovered territories, food shortages were not chronic nor did they endanger the health of the population throughout the rest of Italy. Many Italians expected to buy more food at lower prices, subscribing to what experts often termed 'the psychology of the postwar era.' Although the country averted malnutrition, rising expectations for the postwar period created new concerns about food, the standard of living, and popular welfare.

Government intervention improved the quantity and quality of the foods consumed by many Italians, yet food policies created an onerous debt for the government to manage, especially in the context of postwar inflation. Several times in the postwar era, most notably in the cost-of-living riots of 1919 and during the nation's bread-subsidy crisis, consumers demanded continued intervention to guarantee the wartime standard of living. In other words, the war had solidified the contours of popular food habits and unified consumer desire for more foods of higher quality. Yet postwar liberal governments could not continue to satisfy consumers without destroying the financial stability of the state. The national problem of food consumption now appeared to be an impossible dilemma for anyone to solve.

Historians have divided Italy's postwar years into periods of revolution and reaction. The *biennio rosso* (red biennium) of 1918–20 witnessed dislocating inflation and mass agitation, including strikes, riots, and the widespread sacking of stores. Old loyalties disintegrated along with any identification with liberal authority. The ensuing crisis of legitimacy only fanned the flames of discontent engendered by the popular disillusionment with the peace and the behavior of Ministers Vittorio Emanuele Orlando and Sidney Sonnino at Versailles. A number of Italians were inspired by the October 1917 revolution in Russia and looked to the radical redistribution of wealth as a solution to the nation's problems.[68] The next two years have been viewed as reactions to the revolutionary phase, with the occupation of the factories in northern cities (September 1920) marking the transition between the two stages. The number of mass actions declined dramatically, while the deepening economic crisis combined with the ongoing political crisis encouraged a more conservative orientation for liberalism and paved the way for fascism's seizure of power. Many historians have suggested that the postwar crisis faced by Italy was nothing new. Rather, the war had only partially suppressed existing societal divisions and, after the war, these divisions were felt with full force.[69] Yet the urgency of the economic situation was new indeed. State spending and debt soared at the war's end: state expenses went from 2.5 billion lire in 1913–14 to 30.9 billion lire in 1918–19, while the falling value of the lira and the heavy demand for scarce consumer goods led to crushing inflation by 1919. To cushion the harsh effects of the economic crisis, the liberal state took on even more debt in subsidizing coal for industry and bread for consumers.

Spiraling inflation coincided with the demobilization of wartime controls, thereby aggravating an already critical situation. For consumers, the rapid increase in food prices destroyed household budgets. The Municipal Office of Statistics for Milan reported a steady increase in spending on food for a typical working-class family of four. In 1918, families spent an average of 68.42[th]lire per week on food. This amount increased to 107.18[th]lire per week in 1919 and 189.76[th]lire in 1920, more than doubling over the course of two years.[70] Industrial wage levels did not keep pace with increasing prices, rising from 11.60[th]lire per day average in 1918 to 16.69[th]lire in 1920. Postwar economic instability was rooted in monetary inflation and buoyed by the shocks of demobilization. Popular anxiety over the price/wage imbalance, combined with a growing sense of consumer entitlement (from the small but certain shifts in consumption habits), resulted in a series of riots, looting, and violent confrontations across the nation in July 1919. Months before the riots of 1919, prefects and mayors reported widespread fear that retailers were ignoring fixed prices. In response, the Ministry of Interior issued a circular in May 1919, requesting that all prefects crack down on abuses with 'constant vigilance and repression' in order to prevent *vivace agitazione*.[71] Prefectoral responses reported few serious infractions of the law by merchants, yet consumers feared price controls might be lifted too quickly.

The cost-of-living riots began in the first week of July and continued for several days. Unrest began in central Italy on 2 July in the town of Imola (near Bologna), when a general strike led to the sacking of food and clothing shops. Police arrived and the ensuing scuffle with citizens left six dead and dozens injured. The next day, rioting broke out in Florence, the city that suffered the most extensive damage and had the highest number of citizens arrested for looting: 404 shops were sacked and an estimated 6.5 million lire worth of goods were stolen, an astonishing amount if we consider that the next highest financial loss for a city was in Milan, with 800,000 lire worth of goods stolen. The rioting and looting spread quickly across the peninsula, through Tuscany and up to Milan, as well as southward to Naples and Palermo. Disturbances peaked between 4 and 8 July, and stopped by 14 July. Rioters inflicted damage almost exclusively on retail shops, although in cities where *carabinieri* were called in, violent confrontations led to the death of several dozen citizens throughout the nation.[72] Prefectoral reports indicate that the majority of shops sacked were not bakeries or flour mills, but wine shops, groceries, butchers, shoe stores, cloth shops, and consumer cooperatives. The typical pattern was for citizens to loot a few bakeries and mills, but to concentrate on taking more expensive items like canned foods, soap, wine, cheese, cloth, and leather goods. Losses in Vicenza (Veneto) were typical: there the prefect reported losing over 95,000 lire worth of pastries, liquor, and wine. All that was recovered were six bottles of wine, a few sacks of sugar, and a case of liquor.[73]

In order to prevent looting, local authorities, often in cooperation with merchants, requisitioned goods and sold them at fixed and reduced prices, sometimes by as much as 50 percent.[74] Prime Minister Francesco Nitti was clearly annoyed by such deep price cuts; his initial response was to encourage local authorities to 'reinforce existing fixed prices…any other measure that maintains or imposes prices below that of the legal limit is lacking in any just foundation and … puts the consumer in grave danger.'[75] Nitti feared that at some point in the near future, the United States and Britain would cut off aid to Italy. Drastic price cuts that encouraged consumption and hoarding had no place in Nitti's plan to consume less for the purpose of conserving existing stocks for the future. On 6 July, the Ministerial Council (Consiglio dei Ministri) issued an official decree to all prefects, instructing them in the proper course of legal action during the riots (D.L. 1141). Prefects were told to stabilize the *calmiere* as soon as possible; to institute severe penalties for anyone selling goods above fixed prices; and to decrease prices immediately on all frozen and preserved meat, oils, and dried legumes. The government encouraged cooperatives to sell goods at slightly lower prices than the market rate, but it warned against dramatic reductions of 40 or 50 percent. A Decree Law of 24 July (D.L. 1455) secured 50 million lire in loans for consumer cooperatives in order to cushion the price decreases and to facilitate provisioning. Lastly, the *carabinieri* and the *guardia di finanza* attempted to retrieve stolen goods and to return them to merchants, but most of the food was consumed. On average, merchants received less than one-third the amount stolen from them.

The riots highlighted the new political prominence of the standard of living. Certainly the war had a complex effect on living standards. Because of low requisitioning prices and price controls, many Italians were able to purchase foods that previously they could not afford. One study of the working classes during the war found that postwar demands for salary increases were directly linked to a decreasing capacity to consume foods such as meat and dairy products. Workers who had become used to certain foods wanted to continue eating them.[76] Wartime inflation, which was kept under partial control by state intervention, slowly eroded the purchasing power of industrial, clerical, and agricultural workers. In the riots of 1919, the Italian people defined their minimal standard of living. What consumers could no longer afford would be taken by force, in an effort to pressure authorities to decrease prices. In the aftermath of the riots, the most pressing issues were questions of whether or not, and to what extent, the state should continue to assume responsibility for improving the standard of living for the majority of the population.

The question on everyone's mind was who was going to foot the bill for the rise of mass consumption in Italy? In the months before the riots, both industrial and commercial interests suggested possible paths for state intervention in the context of postwar inflation. The General Confederation of Italian Industry suggested that the government sell off existing stocks of food at reasonable prices to alleviate the effects of inflation. The Confederation also urged the government to adopt more stringent vigilance over speculation and private commerce and to encourage the growth of the consumer cooperative movement. Finally, in order to educate consumers about how prices are determined, the government should require a national price policy whereby consumers would be told which portion of the price went to the producers and which portion went to retail middlemen.[77] These suggestions were clearly antagonistic toward commercial interests. By focusing on the retail sector's responsibility for the high cost of living, industrialists deflected any blame away from themselves. Prices, not wages, they argued, were the most significant factors of the high cost of living (*caroviveri*).[78]

Commercial interests vehemently disagreed. In May of 1919, the National Confederation of the Association of Merchants and Retailers supported a gradual return to free commercial practice, requesting that the provincial export ban be lifted. Price increases, the Confederation declared, were due to greedy producers, not retailers, who 'many times...have had to limit their already scarce earnings.' Moreover, prices were fixed, not on a sound economic basis of production costs, but according to negotiations between local authorities and consumers.[79] In the spring of 1919, the Confederation was not openly antagonistic toward state control, stressing instead the need for cooperation between the government and merchants in the dismantling of food policies. Thus, the political views of merchants were primarily defensive; in the aftermath of the standard-of-living riots, however, retailers adopted a more offensive strategy that culminated in the widespread strikes of bread-makers and merchants in 1920. In the postwar period, popular agitation for political (subsidized) prices among the salaried classes went hand in hand with agitation for salary increases. Industrialists were intent on heeding calls for increased production, thereby funneling more lire into financing national economic growth, not labor costs. If industrialists were unwilling to increase salaries, then should the State continue to subsidize the price of necessary food items like bread? These concerns exploded with full political force during the national debate over the dismantling of the bread subsidy.

By July 1919, the Italian treasury contributed an average of 200 million lire each month to maintain the price of bread at eighty cents per kilogram, a price that amounted to only half the cost of production. The reasons for the subsidy were two-fold: inflation had cut into the purchasing power of Italians while the consumption of wheat bread continued to rise. Economist Giorgio Mortara estimated that the consumption of wheat increased from sixty-three to sixty-nine million quintals per year throughout the course of the war. Domestic production could not meet these demands. In 1919, for example, forty million quintals of wheat were harvested, which meant the government had to import almost 23 million quintals of grain.[80] The state imported grain at 230 lire per quintal. However, the total cost of food subsidies is impossible to determine with any degree of accuracy because of the confused records-keeping by the grain consortia. Historian Douglas Forsyth estimates that during the ministries of Francesco Nitti and Giovanni Giolitti, bread subsidies may have accounted for half the state deficit.[81] Citizens recognized cheap bread as a right for workers in exchange for their cooperation in the war effort, whereas the government saw cheap bread as a massive drain on the budget.[82]

But such a fiscal burden was onerous, if not impossible, to sustain. Economists and politicians suggested numerous ways to alleviate the subsidy crisis, the most popular measure being the institution of two prices for two qualities of bread, but this suggestion was soon buried by socialist critics who argued that the poor would be constrained to buying the cheaper coarse bread.[83] Most political parties agreed that the bread subsidy was a fiscal burden that could no longer be maintained at the expense of the country's economic growth. However, disagreements over resolving the bread-subsidy crisis reflected a more widespread political dissatis-faction with Nitti's handling of the postwar economic transition. Historian Charles Maier summarized the partisan nature of Nitti's crisis aptly: 'deficits fed an infla-tion that contributed to widespread agitation and turmoil. While special commit-tees worked on progressive reforms that would tax dividends and war profits, the right looked only at the costly bread subsidy as an unjustified social luxury.'[84] Socialist and Communist Parties maintained that cheap bread was a necessity; moderates and conservatives labeled their parliamentary tactics as obstructionist. Nitti's success hinged upon whether his ministry could implement a national program of austerity. According to the political right, the adoption of such an austerity campaign would redefine liberal food policy by cutting the bread subsidy and returning the country to a free market as soon as possible. Nitti was already in trouble: his price cuts antagonized businessmen and industry while his austerity maxims irritated consumers.

In March 1920, the Chamber of Deputies voted to keep the political price of bread. The left was jubilant. The left newspaper *Avanti!* praised the decision as a strike in favor of the working classes, already hard hit by wartime sacrifice and postwar inflation. Socialists supported the Chamber's plan to adopt a progressive income tax and a luxury tax to remedy the state's financial burden and narrow the growing margin of consumer habit between rich and poor.[85] By June, however, a workable plan seemed impossible; no amount of tax increases could begin to make up for the seven billion lire per year deficit caused by the bread subsidy. Prime

Minister Nitti attempted to raise the price of bread by decree, from eighty cents to one and a half lire per kilogram. The decree instructed employers to provide family wage supplements to workers (funded by taxation) or raise wages by twenty-five cents per worker per day. On 6 June, Nitti's Ministry fell on a bill submitted to the Chamber of Deputies calling for the eventual but total abolition of the bread subsidy. Socialists objected that Nitti had pledged to consult the Chamber before taking further action on the price of bread. It now appeared that Nitti was removing the subsidy with a vague promise of increased wages. Riots broke out in Milan and Bari; on 9 June, Nitti announced his resignation. Nitti's fall signaled the beginning of the end for the Italian left. By the end of 1920, left parties were in retreat everywhere and conservative order was restored.

According to Nitti's memoirs, his decision to abolish the bread subsidy was the result of meetings with executives from the Banca Commerciale, who insisted that drastic measures were necessary to restore domestic and international confidence in Italy's public finances. The bankers promised to convince their industrial clients to raise wages if Nitti moved to abolish the bread subsidy. According to Nitti, the same bankers then betrayed him by convincing deputies to vote against the proposal.[86] Even if industrialists raised wages by the amount Nitti requested, it was unlikely that working-class families could have adjusted to higher bread prices. Economist Alessandro Schiavi, working with data from the city of Milan, calculated that for a working-class family of five, spending for bread and pasta amounted to 10.16[th]lire per week (with bread at 0.83[th]lire and pasta at 1.26[th]lire per kilogram). Applying the newly suggested price for bread at 1.50[th]lire per kilogram and pasta at 2.30[th]lire per kilogram, the family needed an additional 8.26[th]lire per week. A 25 cent raise per person per day would not cover the increased expenditure on food once the subsidy was abolished.[87] Nitti's decision, coming soon after the cost-of-living riots, was badly timed. The summer and fall of 1920 witnessed rapid inflation, according to statistics kept by the municipalities of Rome, Milan, and Florence. Consumers were paying over 600 percent of what they used to pay for staple foods in 1914.[88] Surely, consumers reasoned, cheap bread was not too much to ask from the government.

It was not until February 1921 that Marcello Soleri, Undersecretary for Provisioning under Giovanni Giolitti's postwar ministry (from 15 June 1920 to 4 July 1921), tackled the bread subsidy issue. This time, political timing was on the government's side. The left was demoralized by an industrial recession, the inconclusive occupation of the factories, and the spread of rural fascism, and therefore offered little resistance to the eventual abolition of the subsidy. For fiscal conservatives, the political price of bread stood for the 'fundamental unsoundness of postwar concessions to the left.'[89] Giolitti himself had become increasingly resentful of the left's uncooperative attitude. Socialists used obstructive tactics in Parliament to block Giolitti's plan for abolishing the subsidy but were ultimately unsuccessful. Economic timing also mattered: the price of wheat on international markets fell to 150 lire per quintal in mid-1921 and again to 125 lire by the end of the year. And within Italy, the largest wheat crop in recent memory was harvested in 1920–21: over 52.2 million quintals compared to an average harvest of 38.5 million quintals during the war years.

Soleri moved to abolish the bread subsidy in stages, beginning in early 1921, by increasing the price of bread to 90 cents per kilogram. Soleri determined that this price still fell below bread prices in other European countries. In France, for example, bread sold for the equivalent of 2.90[th]lire.[90] To cover the cost of the subsidies, Giolitti approved a rigorous luxury tax on goods like perfume, jewelry, and liquors. The tariff on tobacco was raised, as was the tax on yearly incomes of over 10,000 lire.[91] Grain sales were deregulated and the only subsidies that remained were the monetary bonuses paid to farmers with high yields. When Ivanoe Bonomi assumed the Prime Ministry in July 1921, he was able to eliminate the bread subsidy altogether by the beginning of 1922. The elimination of the bread subsidy was only possible when the militant days of the *biennio rosso* were over.

Political timing was on Giolitti's side, but the bread subsidy was not eliminated without difficulty. From December 1920 through the summer of 1921, sporadic protests erupted in Palermo, Naples, and Rome. These protests were overwhelmingly working-class in nature. Citizens complained about the high price of bread and asked for social justice. As one poster from Rome asked, 'why does the government talk of the necessity of absolute sacrifice among the people in order to revive the national economy when it gives three million lire to the metallurgic industry!'[92] On the municipal level, prefects encountered resistance from the commercial bread-making sector. Proprietors and workers in bakeries and flour mills, constrained by the *tipo unico* laws and desirous of higher profits from the sale of other goods, agitated for the repeal of fixed prices, the abolition of *tipo unico* bread, and increased autonomy from state intervention. A series of work stoppages and strikes by bakers and millers swept through Italy in the summer of 1920 and continued sporadically through the early months of 1921. Aggravating the bakery strikes were temporary shortages of bread and flour in some areas. The situation in many cities was tense, as workers threatened to strike in order to protest the cost of living. Increasing wholesale prices, coupled with shrinking retail profit margins, strained labor relations between bakery owners and workers. Bakery workers supported increased retail prices, as they wanted higher salaries to keep pace with the cost of living. These demands were difficult ones for proprietors, who could not raise salaries unless their profit margin increased. Local authorities worked hard to negotiate labor settlements and keep the price of bread down.

The last word on the postwar crises came from the newly formed Fascist Party. In June of 1921, the National Fascist Party (PNF) in Rome staged demonstrations and handed out leaflets stressing the need for greater public vigilance over the retail sector. Any consumer who felt that he or she was charged too much should report to the local fascist *squadristi*, who would then manage the situation. Retailers were warned to watch prices. Fascist squads also marched down Rome's Via Condotti on 17 June in order to make sure goods sold at local merchants were nationally produced.[93] It would seem that one political party was willing to intervene forcefully to control prices, but were the fascists capable of achieving lasting effects through bullying? 'Can they protect the price of every last chicken?' wondered Ugo Trevisanto, president of Venice's Chamber of Commerce, or would there be terrible consequences of shortage and high prices in fascism's wake? Merchants warned that in the long term, this solution was impractical, 'it is absurd to think one could overcome economic difficulties with brute force.'[94]

Public protest against inflation and the abolition of the bread subsidy demonstrated that Italian consumers desired to protect gains in their living standard. These protests gave voice to citizens' dissatisfaction with the government's response to inflation. They also demonstrate that Italians had *something* to protect: changes in consumer habits that brought new tastes and expectations to the dinner table. During the war, wheat bread was cheap and available. As a consequence of government imports, and later subsidies, more Italians enjoyed wheat bread as their dietary staple. Because bread was inexpensive, consumers could afford dairy products, wine, coffee, sugar, prepared foods, and even meat. When postwar inflation cut into their purchasing power and the government demobilized, Italians took what they felt was rightfully theirs. The riots and protests of the postwar period not only demonstrated intense political instability in the face of economic crises; they reflected a unification of consumer desire and expectation based on the transformation of diet during the war. The government facilitated the transformation of consumption habits and thus expectations. The question before consumers, scientists, and parliamentarians was how to protect these new habits from economic instability. By our standards, these changes in consumption habits hardly seem dramatic, yet they threatened to bring down liberal statesmen who tried to balance the needs of Italy's citizens with the needs of Italy in the postwar world.

The Dietary Crossroads

Government officials and scientific experts were well aware that popular diet had improved during the war. Italy was at a crossroads: poised at the brink of good health and high productivity while the financial interests of the state beckoned policy-makers to pull back from public spending. In the postwar period, a great number of books, pamphlets, and articles grappled with the so-called problem of food consumption in Italy.[95] This problem was laid out succinctly in a 1918 article by Filippo Virgilii addressing the needs of agricultural production after the war,

'… in every corner of Italy groups of farmers and agricultural workers think about the formidable dilemma of whether to produce meat or bread; if one wants bread, one cannot have meat because livestock must be used to work the land.'[96] Simply put, Italy alone could not produce enough food to feed its citizens. Proposed solutions to Italy's dilemma included increasing imports, thoroughly modernizing the distribution sector, and boosting agricultural production. Modernizing the food-storage and transportation systems garnered much attention after the war, as evidenced by a remarkable increase in published materials about frozen foods, rationalized distribution mechanisms, and modern storage systems. However, the most popular solution to the problem of consumption was to increase agricultural production. Producing more was a viable alternative to consuming less, given that wartime subsidies and price controls only strained the national budget to the point of breaking. Production schemes were not all that easy to implement, however. Improving grain yields necessitated more money in the form of higher prices paid to farmers and expenditures on fertilizers and farm implements. And there was only so much the country could do, given Italy's rocky terrain. According to prewar agricultural experts, grain yield per hectare could be improved within certain limits. Before the war, European countries averaged 18 quintals of wheat per hectare while Italy averaged only ten. Experts were sure that production could at least reach eighteen quintals per hectare and some felt that Italy could triple prewar yields.[97] However, choosing wheat production canceled out the possibility of raising livestock, given the scarcity of available grazing land.[98]

Italy's difficulties reflected a larger tension created by the war. The nation constantly struggled with limited resources, balancing civilian and military concerns throughout the course of the war. Yet, as a result of imports and allied loans, the standard of living increased for much of the population. The tension between consumer expectations and economic realities was partially resolved during and after the war by the government's reliance upon external assistance through loans and imports. When social reformers, scientific experts, and politicians attempted to solve Italy's postwar difficulties, they focused more on domestic production and modernization schemes, rather than maintaining or increasing imports. Such a strategy was short-sighted, given the decrease in worldwide wheat prices after the war, for example. Conservatives and nationalists feared Italy's growing dependence on external powers. Socialists were more ambivalent about this dependence yet they stood by domestic plans to increase and rationalize food production. Thus, the political mindset was such that many endorsed a domestic solution to Italy's problem of food availability. After 1922, the fascist regime would elaborate on and codify this solution by privileging economic self-sufficiency and import reductions.

The war lent new urgency and meaning to the prospect of dividing food up more equitably between civilian and military populations. The war also lent new urgency to furthering hygienic practice through nutritional education for the sake of building labor power and disciplining consumption.[99] Wartime liberal regimes were reluctant to become involved with such intimate details of everyday life, and thus attempted to intervene only minimally. While this strategy worked in the early stages of the war, the latter half of the war and the postwar crises demanded immediate and dramatic action. Postwar liberal regimes found it impossible to satisfy everyone with minimal intervention. The situation had much to do with the loss of liberal authority in the face of sharp partisan politics and fascist violence. Certainly the collective wartime experience of Italians had much to do with creating this liberal conundrum. Several histories of the war have viewed the event as a 'collective trauma' for the population, not necessarily because of the impact of total war on everday life, but in terms of general loss of faith in laissez-faire politics and a frustration with the impotence of collective revolt in the face of economic turmoil and political crisis.[100] Was there indeed a way that Italians could have bettered their collective condition? Mass actions in the face of inflation proved inconclusive and the state's lukewarm response to the crisis in living standards discouraged citizens even more. What, then, was to be done?

Mussolini and his cohort believed they had the remedy to this collective trauma. With regard to food issues, the fascist regime would step in and resolve the problem of consumption quickly and definitively. Presumably, old liberal conundrums mattered little, given that fascism, once in power, did not have to rely on popular approval; yet this is perhaps an exaggerated characterization of fascism-as-regime. In fact, popular approval mattered a great deal in the early years of fascism, when Mussolini's power was still not secured. Early fascist food policies resembled liberal policies, given that citizens had not forgotten the traumas of the wartime and postwar years and expected the government to protect food supplies and guarantee fair prices. Later, the regime would take a much bolder stance with regard to food supplies, promising complete economic self-sufficiency for the nation. The experience of the First World War, however, made a profound impact on fascist ministers, who intervened heavily around grain issues and price controls. Thus the war's relevance to the unfolding of fascist policies was based not only on the transformation of past habits but also on the future direction for food policies as they related to demographic strength and economic stability.

–3–

The Cooking of Consent, Italy 1922–35

The fascist regime of Benito Mussolini sought to revolutionize state control over food consumption. Lorenzo La Via, the foremost authority on fascist food policy, defined this revolution as an intensive commitment to food and its consumption. Whereas liberal regimes controlled prices and provided food in times of civil unrest, the fascist regime used food to promote public order, popular health, and social equality.[1] These were ambitious goals, to be sure, but La Via was correct in asserting food's power as both political symbol and tool under fascism. Fascism's stated goals were to improve national health and productivity; to obtain statistical and scientific knowledge about the food habits and nutritional status of the entire population; and to make the nation more self-sufficient. The regime used food as a kind of glue to hold populations together and bind them to the regime, not just through thrift and sacrifice but through the everyday tasks of preparing and purchasing food. Admittedly, the political stakes were lower in the early years of fascism than they were during the First World War. Italians were no longer storming the mayor's residence. Rather, citizens were to think *with* and *through* food about their duties and obligations to the fascist state.

Writing in 1937, La Via had not yet seen the end results of fascist food policies and therefore did not understand how the regime failed to live up to its lofty promises. The foundation of fascist food policies was the goal of complete self-sufficiency; food became one way to assert Italy's independence in an increasingly interdependent world market. Still fresh in everyone's mind was the chaos of the postwar period, fueled by Italy's mounting debt and growing dependence on the allied powers. The regime's approach to achieving self-sufficiency was heavy-handed. Quite simply, the government shut down possibilities for the further expansion for export markets, discouraged consumers from purchasing non-Italian goods, and started a campaign to increase domestic wheat production. The logic behind this strategy was that if less food were available to Italians, consumption habits would shift accordingly. In order to subordinate consumption habits to the needs of the State, the fascist regime worked on a broad canvas: they utilized scientific expertise, influenced housewives through domestic economy literature, and conducted propaganda campaigns promoting only those foods produced in Italy. The ideal fascist diet was based on carbohydrates, not animal proteins, and supplemented by fresh produce, legumes, olive oil, citrus fruit, and wine. Thus, fascism reinforced already existing consumption patterns but tied them to political allegiance and national identity.

The connection between austerity and Italian strength of character had been made previously by nationalists prior to the First World War; Mussolini intensified this connection, elevating the practices of renunciation and thrift to the status of national virtues.[2] As he explained in 1933, 'from the very start Fascism set up an austere way of life. It made no demagogic appeal to the masses, held out to them no promises of good times ahead. It preached duties not rights; hard work and sacrifice, not facile triumphs.'[3] Sober consumption habits reflected the fascist way of life and softened the impact of fascism's form of economic 'shock therapy.' Mussolini himself saw the nation's backward status as an asset to a lean economic program that eschewed consumerist abundance: 'fortunately the Italian people has not yet accustomed itself to eat many times a day, and possessing a modest level of living, it feels deficiency and suffering less.'[4] Fascism revered sober consumption habits for their political utility.

Those familiar with the history and ideology of Italian fascism recognize the contradictions and unrealistic posturing so reminiscent of Mussolini's reign. There was, for example, a clear contradiction between emphasizing renunciation and attempting to use food as an emblem of the regime's benevolence, an effort that presumes at least some notion of abundance or consumer satisfaction. It was also unrealistic for Mussolini and his ministers to assume they could shape popular food habits in accordance with their own prescribed economic goals *after* Italy had entered the world market and made tentative steps into the world of mass consumption. Historians of Italian fascism have found it frustrating and fascinating to categorize and explain the workings of the regime. This is partly because Mussolini and his followers privileged action over ideology and deeds over words. As a consequence there is substantial room left open for the interpretation of goals and intent, specifically with regard to policies. After fascism's brutal demise, historians have analyzed its role as a modernizing force in unified Italy's history, and its degree of authoritarian control and its ability to generate popular consent. More recently, historians inspired by the historiography of German Nazism have examined fascist racial policies to determine the intent and direction of an explicitly fascist version of racism.[5] This chapter and the next contribute to the ongoing debate about the regime's intentions for, and implementations of, official policy to monitor and control the Italian population. This chapter argues that for much of the 1920s, fascist food policies were not all that distinctive from liberal ones; their impact, moreover, was minimal, given the relative stability of the economy. However, the intent behind such policies – self-sufficiency, or autarky – remained a constant throughout Mussolini's rule, intensifying throughout the 1930s until consumers felt the full force of autarky at home, in the kitchen, on their dinner plates.

There is no doubt that fascism had significant impact on Italian life and politics in the twentieth century, given that it was the longest-running regime of that century (1922–45). Italians experienced fascist rule in stages, in accordance with Mussolini's shifting goals and strategies. After an initial period of economic uncertainty and the crackdown on opposition (1922–25), the standard of living remained adequate and Italy even managed to avoid the worst excesses of the worldwide economic depression. This is not to say that the 1920s and early 1930s were prosperous. The regime constantly meddled with wage and price levels after shutting down any possible channels for protest or recourse (such as trade unions or independent professional organizations). Moreover, the regime dealt with rising unemployment with a system of internal passports and domestic surveillance. However, there were few protests until after the Italian invasion of Ethiopia (3 October 1935), an event that was simultaneously the zenith of Mussolini's popularity and the beginning of his political downfall. Mussolini's goal of launching a great Italian empire led to the Ethiopian invasion and eventually to an alliance with Adolf Hitler (the Pact of Steel was signed in May 1939), pushing the nation closer to war and straining the nation's dwindling resources. Because of Mussolini's shortsightedness and foolish bravado, the Italian population suffered severe privations and shortages during the Second World War. In terms of everyday life and popular response to fascism, the two decades of fascist rule were distinct, with the relatively calm years of the 1920s giving way to hardship and rising opposition from the mid-1930s through the war.

Fascism's impact on Italian food habits was twofold. Economic policies limited the amount and type of food available while propaganda on all fronts created new ways of thinking about food and the nation. The first section of this chapter explains the unfolding of fascist food policies and how they compared to those of liberal governments. Policies for the 1920s focused almost exclusively on price controls for the sake of maintaining public order, an activity reminiscent of wartime governments. Where fascism differed from its liberal predecessors lay within the regime's intensive campaign against retailers as the primary cause of high food prices. The next section examines the origins of fascism's policy of self-sufficiency by discussing which foods and habits the regime endorsed and, ultimately, how the regime promoted the Mediterranean diet as the most appropriate one for the Italian population and the Italian state. Finally, the chapter explains the content and nature of the 'cooking of consent' as it was detailed in domestic economy literature and social scientific surveys. The cooking of consent was a highly politicized way of thinking about food that resurrected previous ideas and debates about consumption habits. What was miserable and inadequate in the nineteenth century became healthful and patriotic under fascism. Through this process of pastiche, however, the fascist regime created something new. Fascism halted the process of dietary improvement and diversification, freezing consumption practice in place to best suit the needs of the authoritarian state. Politics actively and intensively shaped the national cuisine.

The Fascist Difference

Fascism's mechanisms of intervention – production incentives, price controls, and charity – were similar to liberal ones. Where the two political systems differed lay within the scope and intent of food policies. Whereas liberal governments shied away from becoming involved in provisioning matters, the fascist government attempted to control *too much*. From the fixing of prices of meals on trains to regulations on the type and strength of lighting in cafés, the regime tried to govern even minute details of food consumption. This obsessive focus on food, its availability, distribution, and consumption led to a highly bureaucratized system of controls that surpassed liberal interventions. Secondly, the fascist regime consciously embraced the symbolic role of food as it related to popular health and well-being. Mussolini himself was acutely aware of the political value of food. Food was the most visceral connection between government and population, and was crucial to bolstering his reputation as provider for the people. Images of food saturated the press, whether as photos of a bare-chested Mussolini threshing wheat or the public distribution of food baskets to the poor on the holiday of Epiphany (*Befana*).

For the period 1922–35, there were two distinct stages of fascist intervention in food issues. The first stage corresponded to the first four years of fascist rule and consisted mainly of price controls intended to quiet consumers. Intervention in this area was limited in scope, yet it was during these years that the early contours of fascist food politics were sketched out. In 1925, Mussolini launched the Battle for Grain, an agricultural production program that constituted the first plank in the regime's plan for economic self-sufficiency. The second phase of intervention began with the revaluation of the lira in 1926 and continued through the economic crisis of 1931–34. The revaluation of the lire sparked a more vigorous effort on the part of the government to bring retail prices more into line with dropping wholesale prices. The Discipline of Commerce campaign led to more centralized price policies and the increased harassment of retail merchants. By the late 1920s, the regime enlisted the assistance of scientific experts and domestic economists for a Discipline of Consumption campaign, an effort to achieve greater self-sufficiency with regard to food supplies. The regime made a radical departure from previous liberal policies by prioritizing self-sufficiency above other issues like the population's health or increasing labor productivity through proper nutrition. Italians were encouraged to think about the consumption of certain foods in relation to the economic health of the nation, through the promotion of domestic produce in propaganda and in the form of food celebrations.

In the first years of fascist rule, the regime mostly reacted to consumer complaints generated by inflation. Only a few months after the fascists assumed power, in January of 1923, Giuseppe Di Cagno, a citizen of Bari and 'a true fascist in mind and heart,' asked Mussolini to crack down on merchants who 'sold their merchandise at prices so exaggeratedly high that it is enough to make you pull your hair out in despair.'[6] Variations on this theme fill the archival records of the Ministry of Interior for the early years of fascist rule. Salaries had kept pace with the cost of living throughout most of 1922, but fell behind starting in 1923 and continued falling throughout 1924 (see Table 3.1).[7] Mussolini inherited a situation in which food-consumption patterns had shifted while the dismantling of wartime policies, combined with inflation, led to higher prices. Outraged by high prices, consumers expected the government to crack down on merchants. It is not surprising that consumers focused on retail merchants; the cooperative movement had all but disappeared, attacked physically by fascists and politically by liberals, who lashed out at cooperatives for living off the state in wartime.

Meanwhile local governments openly debated the causes of and solutions to high prices. In 1924, for example, the Association of Italian Communes (comprised of current and former directors of the wartime provisioning boards, prefects and former wartime municipal administrators) organized a national congress on provisioning to assess current problems and suggest a plan for future action.[8] Members of the Congress agreed that the persistence of high prices was due to the survival of disorganized food retail and processing industries. A major policy goal for the fascist regime, the Congress explained, should be the implementation of a modern system for food production, transportation, and refrigeration of foods like frozen meat, bread, vegetables, and dairy products.[9] The Congress recognized that modernization would be costly and therefore did not answer the question of who would foot the bill. Clearly some form of government intervention would have been necessary, considering that a single oven (producing over 8 quintals of bread per day) cost an excess of 30,000 lire, a sum far beyond what a baker or small businessman could afford.

Other studies of the food distribution system in Italy agreed that it needed an overhaul. A 1924 study conducted by the Rome Chamber of Commerce, under the

Table 3.1 Numerical Indices, 1913–1924
(1913–14=100)

	Cost of Living	*Salaries*
1922 January	503	515
1923 January	495	480
1924 January	517	474
1924 December	580	485

Giorgio Mortara, *Prospettive economiche, 1925*

direction of the Ministry of the National Economy, found wildly divergent food prices in cities throughout the country. Prices for fresh produce were higher in cities like Naples and Rome than in Milan or Turin, a curious fact considering the proximity of agricultural production to central and southern cities. In the region of Campania, for example, up to 25 percent of the total cost of fresh fruit and vegetables was absorbed by various indirect costs charged by intermediaries. This was the case largely because southern cities lacked municipal markets where goods could be sold directly to consumers.[10] The Chamber of Commerce declared the market system throughout Italy to be primitive and chaotic. Whereas merchants requested government assistance to bring down intermediary costs, Rome's Chamber of Labor joined consumers in requesting that alternative systems of distribution, such as consumer cooperatives, be encouraged.[11]

The fascist regime approached high prices and the state of the retail sector cautiously. Early on, Alberto De Stefani, Minister of Finance, vowed fascist action in the retail sector to reorganize markets, standardize prices, and reduce the number of intermediaries between the wholesale and retail sectors. Yet the national Union of Chambers of Commerce noted how retail prices failed to drop in accordance with wholesale prices. In fact, retail prices increased over the course of 1923, despite De Stefani's promise of vigilance.[12] It still fell to local authorities to control the cost of living. The fixed price or *calmiere* was the preferred tool of prefects and other local authorities, although fixed prices often led to protest. The prefect of Turin reported that when he attempted to lower the price of bread by 10 cents per kilogram in response to decreasing flour prices, he met with vehement protest from the retail bakers' association, which insisted that the *calmiere* be abolished altogether. The prefect of Milan abolished fixed prices in fall of 1924, requesting that bakers post the price and weight of bread for public inspection. After an initial price hike of 10–20 cents per kilogram, consumer protest wore off and business resumed. Requests from bakers to abolish fixed bread prices were common, prompting a major strike in Naples and the threat of strikes elsewhere throughout the winter of 1923–24. Bakers requested a just price for bread to be determined by an impartial provisioning commission. Merchants complained that the dismantling of wartime price controls did not happen fast enough, and in some areas, fixed prices prevailed, despite the fact that the war was over. Why were merchants singled out? asked the merchants of Benevento, a city near Naples. 'Who among us has become rich or maintains a lifestyle more luxuriant or comfortable than that of any other modest family?' Elsewhere, consumers felt unprotected and wondered whether the fascist regime would resolve the cost-of-living crisis. An association of Florentine consumers complained that local government conspired with dishonest merchants, leaving consumers to fend for themselves.[13]

The national government was forced to take action in 1925 when a poor wheat crop drove up the price of bread. The Ministry of the National Economy refused to subsidize a political price for bread but recognized that something had to be done to guarantee cheap bread for those who needed it. The Ministry increased the milling tax, so that those who could afford to buy white bread paid more for it. The Ministry also organized provincial bread commissions, consisting of the prefect, union representatives, and representatives from baking and milling interests.[14] Bread prices increased from just under 2 lire per kilogram for *pane comune* in January to over 2.5 lire by July. Higher prices led to consumer protest, especially in areas where bakers chose to produce more of the expensive white bread in the hopes of increasing their profits. Prefects were ordered to keep prices down and ensure that bakers continued to produce *pane comune*. The scope of public unrest in 1925 underscored the regime's fragility, especially in the wake of the Matteotti assassination (June 1924) and Mussolini's acceptance of blame for all past fascist actions (3 January 1925).[15] Public disturbances occurred mostly in the south, but protests occurred as far north as Como. The largest demonstrations took place in Naples, where women and children took to the streets, metallurgic workers threatened to strike, and bakers staged 24 hour walk-outs. On 21 February 1925, Minister of Interior Luigi Federzoni warned all prefects of possible subversive activities; opposition parties could be mobilizing public sentiment against the regime by complaining about the price of bread. Months later, Mussolini dismissed this consumer unrest while speaking to a crowd in Pesaro about the regime's monetary policies: 'There are pessimists who say that things cost more than before; there are the uncontentable individuals who think that from now on we can eat without paying.'[16] As Mussolini gained more confidence in the wake of the Matteotti incident, he frequently dismissed complaining consumers as unpatriotic.

The year 1925 also marked the end of laissez-faire agricultural economics and the return of the corn laws, including the restoration of the duty on imported grain (Royal Decree 24 July 1925). Bread prices held steady at 2.50–2.70[th]lire per kilogram, but merchants, bakers, and millers worried about the effects of the tariffs on prices. Minister of the Interior Federzoni and Minister of the National Economy Giuseppe Belluzzo agreed that the national system of bread production needed improvement. Perhaps, Belluzzo suggested, local governments could assist the bread-making industry by replacing outdated equipment; the replacement of human labor with machines would bring down prices.[17] The Ministers asked Provincial Bread Committees and Central Market Committees to assist and discipline the bread-making industry. However, more discipline than assistance was meted out to bakers. Threats of strikes by 'anti-government bakers' were quelled by fascist threats of violence, but fascist thugs could do little to stem the tide of public grumbling. The prefect of Rome reported much ill-humor among the working classes on account of increased prices for bread and pasta: 'there has been a constant and audible grumbling, coarse phrases and vague threats against the government.'[18] The regime was particularly sensitive about public grumbling that linked the price of food with *malgoverno*. The legitimacy of fascist rule was in doubt given recent political events. Popular discontent about bread was more than simply an annoyance; it threatened the regime's recent consolidation of power. The regime attempted to respond to the situation but was instead characterized by indecision and a reluctance to wrest control away from local authorities. Indeed, the fact that municipal authorities continued to adopt or eliminate controlled prices suggests that the power of local initiative still carried over from the liberal period.

With the revaluation of the lira in 1926, the regime attacked food prices more systematically. Mussolini ordered the revaluation of the lira, from 153 to 90 lire per British pound sterling, for political, not economic, reasons. Revaluation led to a tighter regulation of the labor market (in order to cut production costs), while enormous public expenditures on investment projects, such as integral land reclamation, called for control over wages, prices, and profits. In the wake of state-mandated wage cuts, wholesale prices were reduced so as to keep the cost of living at an acceptable level. When retail prices failed to drop in accordance with wholesale prices, the fascist regime attempted to discipline the retail sector, bullying retail merchants into lowering prices and passing legislation to stem the growth of the retail sector. Thus, the Discipline of Commerce campaign (1926) sought to promote greater social equality through consumption by targeting retailers. The campaign played up the symbolic benevolence of a regime that took on the role of protecting consumers against retailers. The regime called upon the Fascist Confederation of Italian Merchants (which, at 300,000 members, was one of the largest of the employers' confederations) to improve retail practice in the interest of the consumer.

Over the course of the spring and summer of 1926, prefects reported few problems with prices; the bread *calmiere* was not needed or it was fixed with the consent of bakers and retailers. High prices still weighed heavily on the minds of Ministers Belluzzo and Federzoni, both of whom asked prefects to keep them apprised of price increases. As Minister of the National Economy, Belluzzo felt an obligation to keep prices low. His goal was to return the Italian retail sector to its prewar state, prior to the boom in retail shops of the 1920s. Excess competition and a proliferation of shops made for a highly disorganized market and therefore, Belluzzo reasoned, the numbers of stores in urban areas had to be reduced. This line of argument was nothing new; local chambers of commerce had long advocated a reduction in the numbers of stores primarily as a defense against the new shops cutting into the profit margins of existing ones.[19] Both Federzoni and Belluzzo hoped that this more stringent disciplining of merchants and consumers would solve the problem of high prices, but they were wrong. Retail prices failed to keep pace with dropping wholesale prices and in 1927 the government reinstated the *calmiere*.[20] Later, local control was abrogated in favor of stricter controls by prefects and the central government. The Minister of the National Economy was worried that in some places, price controls were too vigorous and this discouraged agricultural production or encouraged some farmers to export their goods out of a particular area.

The question of how to bring retail prices in line with wholesale prices led to much study and speculation in the fascist years about the phenomenon of price viscosity, or the slippage between the two price levels. The regime chose to blame retailers for this slippage, but economists pointed to taxation and a disorganized retail sector as the major causes of high prices. In 1930, expert on price viscosity Giacomo Veronese estimated that a working-class family of five in Milan paid 24.15[th]lire out of a weekly food budget of 146.15[th]lire in order to cover the costs of distribution. This amounted to almost twenty percent of the total food budget, a figure that was slightly higher than those in other European nations.[21] American economist Henry Miller's analysis of Italian economic writing revealed that heavy consumption taxes, especially for luxury goods such as sugar and coffee, effectively blocked the impact of price reductions. Indeed, articles from *Il commercio* found that Italian families in major cities paid between 500 and 1,000 lire per year in food and luxury-good taxes. Economists and retail interests often advocated the reduction or abolition of local taxes as the best solution to remedy high prices.[22] Locally, chambers of commerce made it clear that greater state intervention was needed to improve transportation, reduce taxes, subsidize the construction of food-storage systems, and rationalize the retail food sector.[23]

Not surprisingly, the regime consistently focused on the retail sector, in particular the numbers of shopkeepers, as the cause of price viscosity. This had been a standard fascist complaint since 1923, when Minister of Commerce and Industry Cesare Rossi railed against the proliferation of retail shops for keeping food prices artificially high. But if the number of retail merchants increased after the First World War, so had the population; the proportion of shopkeepers to consumers was on par with that of other European countries and did not appear to create unusually high prices.[24] Yet the regime clung to the Discipline of Commerce campaign and followed debates about price viscosity because these efforts represented the regime as being on the side of the consumers, when in reality, the government continued to collect taxes from the sale of non-necessity items like tobacco, coffee, liquor, beer, and sugar, all of which experienced dramatic increases in consumption in the postwar era. Tax revenues from the sale of tobacco, for example, increased fifteen times over between 1915 and 1924.[25] As a result of fascist bullying (carried out by the municipal police, the Ministry of Finance, and the market police), price reductions of 5–19 percent were common. Meanwhile, shopkeepers' salaries decreased, from 16.12[th]lire per day in 1930 to 13.89[th]lire per day in 1935, indicating where some of the costs were cut.[26]

Although consumers complained about high prices almost constantly throughout the 1920s, they suffered few privations or shortages. Statistician Lorenzo Spina from the Istituto Centrale di Statistica (ISTAT) estimated that the number of calories available, per person, steadily increased under fascism, from 3,080 calories during the First World War to a high of 3,477 calories in 1930. ISTAT's Benedetto Barberi came to a similar conclusion: a high of 3,400–3,500 calories was available, per person, by the mid-1920s and this continued until 1930. Scientific experts employed by the regime claimed that living standards improved under fascism. The Commissione per lo Studio dei Problemi dell'Alimentazione (the Committee for the Study of Alimentary Problems, hereafter referred to as the Food Committee) was founded in 1928 as a subcommittee of the fascist-founded Consiglio Nazionale delle Ricerche (National Research Council) or CNR. One of the first major projects of the CNR's Food Committee was an ambitious study of the habits of over 10,000 subjects in seven provinces. Guido Galeotti, supervisor of the inquiry, and Filippo Bottazzi, the president of the Food Committee, reported adequate caloric intake for the majority of Italians, although the inquiry revealed pockets of undernutrition in southern Italy. Despite numerous press releases indicating a favorable view of living conditions in Italy, the published findings of the studies still pointed to significant dietary differences between class and region. The study found vast differences between the classes in southern regions, where the working classes lagged behind the middle classes in terms of protein and fat intake. However, in the northern regions, the gap between classes was barely noticeable. Regional differences in food consumption still existed. Residents in Bolzano consumed twice as much fat as those living in Salerno. Northern Italians consumed twice as many eggs and three times the volume of dairy products as did southern Italians. Southern Italians consumed 50 percent more bread and slightly more fresh and dried legumes than did their northern counterparts.[27]

Smaller-scale studies of consumption also indicated that regional differences persisted, even in the prosperous 1920s. A 1925 study of Italian meat consumption, conducted by the Milan Chamber of Commerce, found wildly variable rates of consumption throughout the peninsula. Citizens from the northern region of Piedmont consumed 14.5 kilograms of beef per year while those in the southern region of Basilicata consumed only 1.59 kilograms in a year. Other statistical studies found that meat consumption was higher for urban residents. In major cities, meat was both available and affordable. Peasants only consumed meat when they could afford to; slight increases in salaries often led to slight increases in meat consumption.[28] Small-scale studies also indicated that class-based distinctions in diet persisted. In Sicily, the middle classes consumed adequate amounts of proteins and their diet was judged 'varied and complete.' By contrast, agricultural workers ate only bread for breakfast, and for lunch consumed a simple *minestra* of rice or legumes, supplemented by a slice of bread and an occasional glass of wine.[29]

Scientific and social-scientific research sponsored by the fascist regime did not delve into class and regional differences in food-consumption habits, opting instead to look at the Italian population – and their nutritional needs – in the aggregate. According to historian Domenico Preti, tracing the actual development of material life conditions under fascism was an endeavor closely bound up with the problem of racial integrity, that is, understanding the strength, capabilities, and potential of the Italian race.[30] This was very much reflected in the work that the CNR's Food Committee undertook: massive studies of dietary habits from 1929 forward, which always charted satisfactory nutritional standards and dietary practice for the entire population. Disparities between region and class were glossed over in favor of breaking down the population by average-man coefficients and emphasizing the total numbers of calories consumed, instead of breaking foods down into nutrients. The 1929 inquiry, for example, reconfigured the population into average-man coefficients and found that the Italian population finally met minimum international nutritional standards.[31] Individual physiologists and social scientists may have worried about whether two diets persisted under fascism, but the Food Committee did not. Another type of statistical study that became increasingly popular under fascism was the quantification of food availability (*disponibilità*) for the nation as a whole. As these efforts were part of the national drive toward self-sufficiency, they are therefore analyzed in greater detail in the next chapter. Nonetheless, their popularity underscores the new national priorities of state-sponsored scientific research.

Reformers still maintained that there was room for dietary improvement. A 1923 study of consumption habits by Milan's Chamber of Labor found that workers and peasants needed more proteins and fats in order to work more efficiently and productively. Giuseppe Galletti, of the statistical office of the Chamber, calculated that a worker needed at least 7.08[th]lire per day in order to meet what he considered to be minimal nutritional requirements set by the Inter-Allied Scientific Commission during the First World War (109 grams of protein, 80 grams of fat, 527 grams of carbohydrates, and 3,308 calories).[32] A single worker would be able to afford this type of diet, but a family dependent on one worker's wage would not. Agricultural wages hovered between 12 and 14 lire per day throughout the 1920s but dropped to only 10 lire per day in 1931. Industrial workers fared slightly better. Statistics from 1925 show an average wage of 16.62[th]lire per day, with a low of 8 lire per day for female silk spinners and a high of 27 lire per day for male workers in the automobile industry.[33] After 1930, economic conditions worsened. Rising unemployment meant the institution of a shorter workweek (*il Sabato fascista*) for industrial workers, and salary increases failed to keep pace with increasing prices. Although there was no dramatic downturn in consumer habits throughout much of the fascist era, consumption levels stagnated, as personal consumption increased by only 6 percent between 1923 and 1939.[34]

Throughout the 1920s, fascist food policies consisted primarily of controlling prices. In the early years, consumers, local officials, and retail interests asked for state intervention to lower the cost of food, although officials and retailers also urged the state to modernize the food-distribution sector. Initially, the regime's response was tepid, corresponding to its uncertain hold on power. As Mussolini gained confidence, price controls lost their voluntary and temporary qualities in favor of becoming permanent planks for fascist economic policy. Moreover, as fascism continued to garner political support, the regime rejected plans for retail modernization in favor of the Discipline of Commerce campaign, which attempted to manage intermediary costs by turning back the clock to the prewar period. This was hardly the modernization plan that some officials and retail interests anticipated. Nonetheless, the history of price controls highlights fascism's initial timidity as well as its ability to use food issues (in this case the cost of food) to divide and conquer. Price controls were an attempt to promote the regime as a consumer advocate. Little was done to reduce the intermediary costs that had real impact on people's spending habits, and price controls were little more than a short-term fix to a series of enduring problems within the distributive sector. Despite much propaganda distinguishing fascist policies from liberal ones, there was little difference between the two political systems, at least not in terms of their handling of consumer protests against the cost of living.

The Nationalization of Cuisine

By the late 1920s, the regime vigorously promoted the foods that made Italy more self-sufficient. The major campaigns were for Italians to eat more rice, grapes, and citrus fruits and reduce their consumption of imported foods such as wheat. Fascist ministers attempted to channel consumption habits for the sake of maintaining civil order; they remembered how recently the price and availability of bread brought down Nitti's prime ministry. The fascist solution to potential wheat shortage was the conservation of wheat stocks through the management of consumption. In fact, fascism subordinated consumer habits to economic goals and strategies. The regime regarded everyday habits as a resource to be managed in order to avoid financial pressures or crushing debt. Foods like wheat were critical to the functioning of the nation. Mussolini's plan to eliminate wheat imports was unrealistic, but he persevered in implementing a discipline of consumption campaign to conserve the nation's wheat stocks.Because the regime sought to channel and limit consumption habits, it had to sell the benefits of a diet that would not strain the nation's budget. The late 1920s marked the beginning of state-conducted food campaigns. In particular, the regime turned to scientific and medical professionals to bring consumption habits in line with the productive capacities of the nation. Scientists affiliated with the National Research Council's (CNR) Food Committee published frequent reports on the nutritional value of domestic produce in the pages of the *Quaderni della nutrizione*. The regime also placed advertisements and articles in trade periodicals like *Il giornale del commercio*, *L'alimentazione italiana*, and *La voce del consumatore*, to encourage retailers to sell only domestically produced food.

Fascist ministers were acutely aware of the political significance of cheap, plentiful bread. Fascist agricultural policies focused on *granarizzazione*, or heavy state intervention around wheat production, often at the expense of other agricultural crops. The foundation for this campaign was the Battle for Grain, launched in 1925. The regime also implemented high tariffs and extended credit to wheat farmers. The reasons for these interventions were obvious: wheat imports rose steadily, doubling in volume from the period 1905–24. Whereas in 1918 imported wheat comprised 8 percent of the total monetary value of goods imported, by 1922 this amount increased to over 19 percent.[35] The poor domestic wheat crop in 1924 merely aggravated the trade deficit and increased anxiety over dependence on foreign supplies. In post-First World War Europe, Italy was not alone in thinking that wheat was critical to national stability. The consumption of wheat products had become a significant indicator of an improved living standard. During the interwar period, Germany launched a Battle for Wheat Production, Great Britain passed the Wheat Act of 1932 to secure a national defense stock, and France's *Office du blé* coordinated wheat production and storage.[36]

In launching the Battle for Grain on 14 June 1925, Mussolini promised that the regime would liberate the population from the 'slavery' of foreign bread, a task Italy's rulers had tried to accomplish for centuries. Mussolini adopted a two-pronged approach, consisting of a production campaign and a consumer propaganda initiative urging Italians to think of wheat as a precious commodity. The Duce's oft-quoted poem, 'Love Bread,' praised the simplicity of the nation's needs and warned citizens not to waste this precious food,

Love Bread,
Heart of the home,
Perfume of the table,
Joy of the hearth.
Honor Bread,
Glory of the fields,
Fragrance of the earth,
Feast of life.[37]

Mussolini himself never missed a chance to associate himself with wheat or bread production. The press frequently depicted him as the first peasant of Italy, and every year at harvest time he would assist the peasants with threshing, take his pay slip for an hour's work, then join the locals for a simple meal *al fresco*.[38]

For all the importance attached to its launch, the Battle for Grain was an ill-timed venture. In 1925, world grain prices were declining, but this mattered little to Mussolini, who was determined to slow down Italian imports. There was, more-over, nothing unique about the regime's agricultural policies: the emphasis on self-sufficiency in food supplies and high protective tariffs were standard European responses to the economic crises of the interwar period. Italy remained consistent in its intense support for such policies, however, even to its detriment.[39] This intense focus on wheat took postwar agricultural development in a new direction. Prior to the Battle for Grain, the first attempts to examine agricultural productivity and suggest initiatives came from Arrigo Serpieri, who as undersecretary of agriculture in 1923 advocated the increased production of all crops along with the protection of small landholders and tenant farmers through land-reclamation programs. Local initiatives through provincial provisioning consortia and traveling agricultural experts attempted to boost the production of various crops through educational efforts. Wheat and grapes were among the nation's most profitable crops; high yields encouraged farmers to adopt wheat cultivation over the period 1910–22.[40] Farmers also found the low cost of labor and rigid consumer demand for wheat to be attractive incentives. By the outbreak of the Second World War, 35 percent of the peninsula's total area for food crops (not including rocky or hilly terrain for grapes, olives, and fruit) was dedicated to wheat production. Corn production decreased while rice- and potato-production levels remained stable. Because wheat cultivation took precedence over more labor- and land-intensive farming, livestock and dairy production also decreased.[41]

In the end, the Battle for Grain was a costly mistake. The Royal Institute for International Affairs in London estimated that the Battle for Grain cost Italy 225,570,000 lire between the years 1925 and 1929, given the international wheat surplus and a turn of exchange in Italy's favor.[42] Mussolini anticipated that wheat production would reach an average of 80–100 million quintals per year. According to statistics furnished by the regime, the harvest reached the antici-pated goal only in the years 1933 and 1937. Meanwhile, wheat imports dropped steadily: from an average of 22.2 million quintals per year in the period 1922–28, to only 4.7 million quintals in 1937. Statistics demonstrated that yields per hectare increased, but this depended largely on geography. The northern and central regions experienced a 50 percent increase while the south and the islands lagged behind with only a 20–30 percent increase in yield. The Battle for Grain proved that Italy could reduce its dependence on foreign wheat over a period of two decades, but the campaign could not provide more wheat at cheaper prices for Italian consumers. According to statistician Benedetto Barberi's analysis of food availability in Italy, the average amount of wheat available, per person, decreased between the decade 1921–30 (178.5 kilograms per person) and 1931–40 (164.4 kilograms per person).[43]

Because the Battle for Grain could not completely replace the volume of wheat imported into Italy, the regime had to devise ways of conserving domestic wheat stocks and reducing imports. One campaign urged Italians to consume only whole wheat bread because it stretched wheat supplies. The campaign for whole wheat bread attacked the production of refined white bread, 'insipid because of the taste of the undercooked parts, indigestible, and endowed with only a few hours of shelf life.'[44] Nutritionists criticized white bread for causing malnutrition, nervous disorders, decreased blood alkaline, a predisposition to tuberculosis, pellagra, cavities, beriberi, peptic disturbances in children, and exhaustion among adults.[45] Patriotic and sensible Italians preferred whole wheat bread or *pane integrale* because it stayed fresh longer, satisfied hunger, and gave more strength to the laborer. In one of the stranger moments of the campaign, scientist Giuseppe Tallarico (parliamentary deputy and member of CNR's Food Committee) alleged that whole wheat bread boosted fertility levels among men and women. Later on, scientists and journalists linked whole wheat bread to higher levels of civilization and culture.[46]

The regime did its part to promote the consumption of *pane integrale*. The *Festa del pane* was instituted in 1929 and celebrated in mid-April of each year. Bakers and members of the local fascist party handed out sandwiches and distributed pamphlets about the nutritional value of bread. The festival never garnered much enthusiasm and was celebrated only sporadically, if at all, in most regions. Commercial bread-making interests were enlisted to promote the production and sale of whole-grain breads with the formation of the Federazione Nazionale Fascista dei Panificatori (Fascist National Federation of Bread-makers), although not without some tension. Obviously bread-makers had a vested interest in making white bread because it sold at a higher price. Individuals from the CNR's Food Committee conducted inquiries into bread production in various regions in order to determine where it could be more rationalized or mechanized.[47] Despite this flurry of scientific, political, and commercial activity, consumers expressed only lukewarm interest in whole wheat bread, preferring white bread instead.

Italians continued to associate whole wheat or home-made bread with a monotonous and inadequate diet; this was especially the case for rural Italy. An inquiry conducted by INEA (the Istituto Nazionale di Economia Agraria) for the period 1928–37 determined that among rural Italians, the foundation of diet was coarse wheat bread, whether eaten alone, with onions or peppers, or as the main ingredient for a *minestra di pane*:

> Every evening the housewife makes two or three panfuls of *minestra* with dried beans and black cabbage: she cuts the bread into thin, thin slices, fitting them into a pan and then, a half-hour before serving dinner, she skims the broth from the pot in which the cabbage and beans have been boiling, and then pours the boiling liquid over the bread. When the bread is soaked through, she calls the family to the table.[48]

The unrelieved monotony of bread and *companatico* was common among rural populations. Author Ignazio Silone recalled how peasants consumed, 'in the morning a piece of corn bread with an onion; at mid-day another big piece of the same bread with raw peppers, flavored with oil and salt; in the evening, an abundant *minestra* made with beans and potatoes.'[49] Carlo Levi's *Christ Stopped at Eboli* also noted how the peasants of Basilicata ate 'plain bread the whole year around, spiced occasionally with a carefully crushed raw tomato, or a little garlic and oil, or a Spanish pepper.'[50] Agricultural workers consumed as much as 900 grams of bread per day, but seldom touched meat, dairy products, or eggs, preferring to sell whatever they could produce rather than consuming it. Given that some rural laborers spent as much as 70 percent of their income on bread alone (according to the INEA study), fascist insistence on the conservation of bread appeared unreasonable and short-sighted.[51]

Fascist ministers were not the only ones interested in conserving wheat. In 1932, Futurist leader Filippo Tommaso Marinetti published *The Futurist Cookbook* (*La cucina futurista*) as a proposal to take Italian food into the modern, technological age, to adopt 'a total renewal of food and cooking' for the nation.[52] The centerpiece of the 'Manifesto of Futurist Cooking,' and its most controversial point called for the abolition of pasta, 'an absurd gastronomic religion' that drained Italians of their energy, creativity, and intelligence. In place of pasta, Futurists counseled, should be appetizing food sculptures and innovative dishes. The weight and volume of the food consumed was not nearly as important as the complete sensory experience of eating the meal itself. Thus, food sculptures and odd food combinations (meat prepared with cologne or mussels served with vanilla creme) heightened the tactile and sensory experience of the meal. Eventually, Futurists hoped, Italian citizens would rely solely on vitamin pills and other supplements furnished by the State, eating food only for the value of the aesthetic or tactile experience. To the Futurists, presentation and form outweighed substance and volume. Pasta, as a filling carbohydrate, represented an excess of volume. The Futurist battle against pasta attracted a fair amount of curiosity and attention. Articles in newspapers and culinary periodicals like *La cucina italiana* reported on scientific debates about the nutritional value of pasta and sitings of Marinetti himself devouring huge plates of spaghetti. Futurists defended themselves by citing scientific evidence that pasta was more difficult to digest than other foods, particularly when the consumer swallowed the pasta whole instead of chewing it. The campaign against pasta also picked up on fascist political imperatives; the abolition of pasta would free Italy from wheat imports.

Marinetti and the Futurists were thinking along aesthetic lines when they called for pasta's abolition. Greedy diners slurping up their 'biquotidian pyramid' of pasta looked grotesque, backward, and un-Italian when measured against the Futurist vision of the modern Italian man. As one reformed *pastasciuttist* described to Marinetti, 'We should also liberate ourselves from pasta, which is also a form of slavery. It puffs out our cheeks like grotesque masks on a fountain, it stuffs our gullets as if we were Christmas turkeys, it ties up our insides with its flabby strings; it nails us to the chair, gorged and stupefied, apoplectic and gasping, with that sensation of uselessness which, depending on the individual, brings pleasure or shame.'[53] According to Marinetti and his supporters, surrendering oneself so completely to any food was a shameful act; perpetual surrender made generations of Italians listless and dispassionate. The Futurist antidote for pasta addiction came in the form of the 'get up to date dinner' which consisted of rice, boiled then fried in butter, compressed inside little balls of raw lettuce, sprinkled with grappa and served on a puree of fresh tomatoes and boiled potatoes. The campaign to abolish pasta was intended to shock Italians out of their passéist habits and outlook. Futurists staged outrageous banquets and circulated rumors about who consumed large plates of spaghetti and why. Yet the connection Futurists drew between food consumption and national pride resonated with ideas circulating in the political atmosphere of fascism.

While Mussolini and his followers never went so far as to propose the abolition of pasta, they avidly supported the consumption of rice as a substitute for pasta. Magazines and newspapers reported that Italians consumed a yearly average of only 6 kilograms of rice per person.[54] The reasons for such low levels of consumption were many: southern Italians were not accustomed to eating rice and many Italians were given rice during the First World War as a bread substitute. There was, then, a popular prejudice against rice in central and southern Italy, as it was associated with wartime deprivation, a low standard of living, and inferior nutrition. In order to combat popular prejudice, the Ente Nazionale Risi (National Rice Board) was founded in 1928 to extend propaganda encouraging rice consumption.[55] Bringing rice to the people was one way to overcome popular prejudice against rice. The Rice Board launched rice-lorries (*autotreni*), traveling kitchens that prepared and distributed rice. In their inaugural year (1932), the lorries covered a total of 30,000 kilometers throughout the southern regions and Sicily, distributing thousands of free samples and hundreds of thousands of recipe pamphlets to southern Italians. There was also a 'National Day for Rice Propaganda' first instituted in February 1928 and consisting of free rice distributions to the needy by the local fascist federation of merchants. On the production side, the Fascist Confederation of Agricultural Workers published studies and pamphlets celebrating the work of female rice harvesters. Depictions of young, single, healthy women in rice fields established rice production as a kind of national service that women could perform for the State.[56] Such depictions allayed any suspicions about young single women working in the fields by linking the feminine with service to the nation. The reasons for promoting the consumption of whole wheat bread and rice were obvious: the increased consumption of domestically produced foods eased Italy's balance of payments and fostered greater economic independence. Moreover, whole wheat bread and rice were considered acceptable protein substitutes; increased consumption would lessen the pressure to build up the nation's livestock industry.

The most concerted effort to increase consumption of a particular food was reserved for grapes. Here the regime recognized the importance of small-scale wine production to local economies. Arturo Marescalchi, wine merchant, parliamentary deputy, and loyal fascist supporter, undertook a campaign to educate hoteliers, managers of worker caféterias, and proprietors of cafés about wine. The Gruppo Nazionale Fascista dell'Industria dei Liquori (The National Fascist Group of Liquor Industries) sponsored Italy's *Autotreno del Vino*, which moved from city to city, dispensing free samples and educating the public about the country's regional wines.[57] Largely because of Marescalchi's efforts during the fascist era, there was a proliferation of books, pamphlets, and studies detailing the biological and social benefits of wine consumption. At best, wine consumption was 'normalized' under fascism. Officially, however, the regime was reluctant to promote a beverage that could be associated with alcoholism, social disorder, and decreased productivity. The National Festival of the Grape was first celebrated in 1929 as a way to support viticulture without endorsing wine consumption.

The Festival of the Grape took place during the grape harvest at the end of September and combined colorful folkloric costumes and floats with free grape distributions by the local women's fascist organization (*Fasci Femminili*), evening concerts, and lectures. The Ministry of the Interior required all prefects to report the details and success of the day's events directly to the Minister. What began as a loose-knit localized event grew more coordinated and bureaucratized with each year. Nationally, a committee under the supervision of the Ministry of Forestry and Agriculture organized the celebration of the annual festival. Local committees consisted of the mayor, a representative of the clergy, and members of pertinent commercial and agricultural interests. The national committee circulated copious memos to local groups, standardizing every detail of the festival from the proper extension of store hours to the kind of paper used to wrap grapes for distribution. The Festival of the Grape generated a great deal of popular enthusiasm. In some locales the Festival took the place of the local *sagra* or harvest festival; in others, citizens participated in colorful, elaborate parades complete with floats and various forms of entertainment. Telegrams from local prefects, along with newspaper and magazine accounts, suggest that Italians avidly participated, despite the absence of free wine.

By encouraging the consumption of some foods over others, the fascist regime took an active role in shaping the national cuisine. Italians were supposed to feel pride in certain Italian foods by celebrating them with special events. Italians were also supposed to think of the nation when selecting foods at the market or corner grocery shop. However, consumers were reluctant to abandon white bread or red meat once they had become accustomed to consuming these foods regularly. The First World War and the 'roaring twenties' introduced mostly middle-class Italians to new foods and habits; could whole wheat bread and grape juice compete with hot dogs and cocktail parties? It is difficult to assess the impact of fascist policies only in the short term, given other factors such as food prices, consumer trends, established traditions, and household budgets. As the next section details, however, there is much evidence indicating that many Italians struggled to balance their preferences and needs with the dictates of government policies. There was a tremendous boom in domestic-economy literature in the 1920s, as women devised methods to juggle household budgets, family desires, and political imperatives. Social-scientific studies and government inquiries into consumer habits indicated that people did adjust to political circumstances by moderating their food intake. The various ways in which Italians transformed political imperatives into everyday practice constituted a 'cooking of consent', or a new way of thinking about the relationship between food, the nation, and fascism.

The Cooking of Consent

So many histories of fascism have dealt with the issues of consent and resistance that it is impossible to make a neat analysis of levels of popular support for fascist policies. With regard to food consumption, the issue of consent is particularly problematic. By the late 1930s and throughout the Second World War, consumers had little choice about food shortages, the expansion of the black market, and wartime rationing. It would be foolish, then, to think of consumers during the latter part of fascist rule as having options outside of protesting ineffective wartime food policies and the Nazi exploitation of Italian food supplies (which, as the next chapter details, consumers did). However, there is evidence to suggest that, early on in the fascist regime, Italian consumers tried to work within the limits set by the drive toward self-sufficiency, while seeking to satisfy their own desires as well as the dictates of regional and class identities.

This juggling act was particularly visible within the ranks of middle-class consumers, who were essentially 'created' by the convergence of fascist economic policies and the rise of mass consumption in Italy.[58] Although fascism is known for creating a petty bourgeois bureaucracy existing on *mille lire al mese* (a thousand lire a month), this process must not be exaggerated. Automobiles and consumer durables were rare among middle-class families. By the outbreak of the Second World War, there were an estimated 268 refrigerators, 120,000 electric oven/stoves, and 148 washing machines in the entire country.[59] Conditions in the nation's kitchens were rudimentary at best. Government inquiries in the 1930s estimated that only 66 percent of habitations surveyed had running water, 76 percent had electricity, and 12 percent had bath and hygienic facilities.[60] Smaller mass-produced household items – irons, machines for boiling water, coffee makers – were more popular than consumer durables. Consumer purchases for the lower middle classes and the working classes tended to be small but affordable: movie tickets, cigarettes, or a meal outside the home in a humble *trattoria*. Although the Italian middle classes had few problems getting by, their spending habits were far from excessive. Mass consumption may have held out the possibilities of dramatically new consumption situations, but everyday practice, especially with regard to buying food and preparing meals, was not at all dramatic.

In fact, Italian cuisine under fascism was quite bland. Although there was a tremendous boom in domestic and culinary literature in Italy in the 1920s, the cookbooks and manuals published between the wars were not oriented toward *haute cuisine*, at least in terms of style and content.[61] As one book warned, 'This is not a gourmet's book. Here one can find advice for how to prepare a good broth, flavorful *minestre*, a roast, a sauté, fried foods, stewed fruit or marmalade, aromatic coffee, a cup of tea or hot chocolate … contained within these little things there is a great deal.'[62] This type of cuisine, simply prepared with few ingredients, was adopted and maintained by the middle and lower middle classes in Italy, so much so that historian Piero Meldini has labeled it the 'cooking of consent,' implying of course that middle-class food habits at least accommodated fascism's economic and political imperatives.[63]

I use the term 'cooking of consent' here to tease out the implications of Meldini's analysis. More specifically, what does the boom in culinary literature tell us about Italian cuisine under fascism and what does the 'cooking of consent' tell us about the position of the middle classes under increased fascist pressure on household budgets and spending habits? The 1920s witnessed a dramatic increase in publication of cookbooks, culinary magazines like *La cucina italiana*, and household rationalization manuals. The history of Italian culinary literature stretches back to the Renaissance, but it would not be until 1891, with the publication of Pellegrino Artusi's *La scienza in cucina e l'arte di mangiar bene*, that Italian cuisine was codified and explained for a middle-class readership. Artusi paid close attention to regional variation in cuisine, he equipped his readers with much technical instruction in preparation, and he stressed the rules of hygiene.[64] Fascist-era authors paid attention to all these issues, instructing housewives in the ways of budgeting, food preparation, hygiene, and manners. Many of the classic dishes and traditions now associated with middle-class propriety were heavily promoted by domestic literature in the 1920s: the *merenda* or child's snack, the hearty soups and stews known as *minestre*, humble meat dishes that stretched the food budget, and simple desserts like pudding or fruit compote.

In addition to defining the middle class, recipes and advice from culinary literature enabled housewives to adapt to the political circumstances and economic conditions of fascism. Tips on budgeting and cutting costs were particularly important, considering the constant anxiety over food prices throughout the 1920s. Domestic experts kept female readers informed of the latest national policies as well as food prices in major urban markets. The right recipe or tip also meant the difference between eating and eating well for women anxious to define their families' social status or to make a good impression on guests (*fare bella figura*). Thus, the 'cooking of consent' became a way of thinking about food preparation that furthered the interests of the fragile middle class, despite increased fascist pressure to consume less food and only certain kinds of foods. Although several domestic experts were open supporters of the fascist regime (for example, Delia and Umberto Notari, founders and editors of the famous culinary magazine *La cucina italiana*) and nearly all cookbooks made at least some positive reference to fascist campaigns, it is difficult to define culinary literature solely by its support for fascism. Rather, domestic literature taught women how to survive life under fascism by getting around some of the regime's admonitions and policies, presumably through the arts of substitution or careful shopping. Domestic economists did this by combining old and new ideas about food consumption, whether drawing upon the ethics of thrift and renunciation in order to cope with fixed wages and rising prices under fascism, or incorporating the rules of nutrition into a daily menu plan for the family. Thus, the cooking of consent also provides us with a road map to understanding the cultural and political meanings of food in the 1920s and how these meanings came together to shape Italian cuisine.

As outlined by domestic-economy literature, the ideal Italian diet consisted primarily of grains, cereals, fresh fruit, and vegetables, with little meat or other animal proteins. Vegetables and raw foods were particularly important for a healthy diet because they contained vitamins and minerals (elements discovered by physiologists during the First World War and popularized in the postwar period). The culinary periodical *La cucina italiana* contained a regular section titled *La cucina vegetariana* while Zia Carolina's *Cucina pratica* contained at least 32 recipes for vegetable soups and stews. The daily use of vegetables in the family's diet constituted a modern approach to cooking. According to many domestic economists, the inclusion of raw vegetables facilitated digestion and thinned one's blood. *Casa e lavoro*, the household rationalization magazine, frequently showcased raw vegetables and fruits because they maximized nutritional value and saved cooking time for the housewife, such that 'the preparation of dishes is a pleasure, not a torment.' Fruit was particularly important in light of the regime's campaign to promote grape and citrus consumption. Even a high-end culinary periodical like *La cucina italiana* carried features on popularizing the consumption of relatively inexpensive foods for their readers: 'There are snobs who accuse oranges of being a vulgar and popular fruit, but vitamins and nutrients know no class boundaries and therefore should be consumed by all.'[65]

If cookbooks enthusiastically endorsed fruits and vegetables, they were considerably less sanguine about meat consumption. Cookbook authors warned that meat was a stimulant and therefore individuals should not consume more than 100 grams per day. Authors suggested substitutions to save money and improve health. Fernanda Momigliano's *Vivere bene in tempi difficili* (Living Well in Difficult Times) suggested substituting meat broth for meat dishes, as 'the best aperitif' to stimulate the appetite and combat fatigue.[66] For housewives, the question of whether or not to decrease meat consumption depended on whether the family could afford meat at all. Meat marked one's economic standing in a country where the majority of the population consumed meat only on Sundays or holidays. Because daily meat consumption was an indicator of economic well-being, domestic-economy literature balanced the rules of nutrition with the middle-class imperative of *fare bella figura*. Weekly meal plans downplayed the importance of meat as a dietary mainstay, but included suggestions for substitution. One book counseled that a plate of polenta or pasta, garnished with cheese and butter and served with a glass of milk, contained as much protein as, if not more than, a meat-based meal. Other books advised that if one meal contained meat, the second meal of the day should not, but should be based on cheese, eggs, or milk.[67] Most books and magazines suggested viable substitutes for meat or ways to stretch a small portion of meat into a meal. For the lower middle classes, a popular meat dish under fascism was *la polpa*, a meat loaf made from ground meat and whatever else was on hand: a bit of lard, a few carrots, or a small piece of *prosciutto*. When meat was included in the daily menu, it absorbed a significant portion of the household budget. A 1932 cookbook that budgeted meals for a family of four tried to keep costs per day down to 7 or 8 lire. Meat purchases constituted more than half the daily budget, then, with 800 grams of frozen meat selling for 4 lire and a whole chicken for a Sunday meal selling for 11 lire (the total cost for Sunday was 15.55 lire).[68] Cookbooks advised readers to use meat sparingly, well before the worsening economic conditions of the mid-1930s. The cooking of consent suggested a diet composed mostly of cereals, whether in the form of bread, pasta, polenta, or *minestra*.

The classic dish promoted in domestic economy literature was the *minestra*; simple and inexpensive, it was defined by one author as 'a dish that keeps the population healthy and strong and demonstrates our fairly simple way of life.' The *minestra* was the first course for either lunch or dinner, whether prepared as soup or stew (*in brodo*) or dry (*asciutta*) as in pasta with sauce. Domestic literature featured many recipes for *minestra* because it was cheap, easy to prepare, and versatile. Nationalism heightened this enthusiasm. Polenta, for example, was hailed as 'a frugal and healthy dish, always welcomed with pleasure.'[69] Such an endorsement was a far cry from nineteenth-century descriptions of polenta as the cause of misery and pellagra. Domestic economists with some understanding of nutrition found *minestra* to be nutritionally complete; a plate of pasta garnished with butter and cheese furnished enough protein and fat for even a robust worker. The addition of fruit and a plate of salad provided the necessary vitamins and minerals.[70] Pasta dishes were particularly popular because they had a second life as leftovers, whether made into a gratin, a *fritatta* (a kind of omelet), or a *fritelle* (fried in a paste of flour, milk, and egg yolks). Rice was also versatile as it could be shaped into croquets, covered in sauce, or steamed in a mold. *Minestra* lived again as a *rimasto* (left overs) as long as one had a few simple ingredients on hand.

Such enthusiasm for the Italian *minestra* reflected a broader emphasis in domestic literature on what was characteristically Italian in terms of cuisine. Soups, stews, and pasta fulfilled the tenets of simplicity and thrift. Domestic literature delineated an ethic of consumption that emphasized savings and renunciation over spending and acquisition. Domestic economy was defined as the 'science of small and humble things;' readers were reminded of how 'savings is the fruit of the patient activity of vigilance and renunciation.' Food must be simply prepared; a good wife must be careful not to ruin her family's health by overindulging them. Here, savings and consumption were not seen as antithetical; rather, the two activities went hand in hand. Cookbooks and magazines devoted ample attention to the *piatti di magro*, or Lenten dishes which could be served on weekdays: salted cod, rice croquets, cauliflower in sauce, omelets, fried fish, artichokes and mushrooms, snacks of milk and bread for the children.[71] Patriotic imperatives to save predated the regime's official savings campaigns accompanying the invasion of Ethiopia. Women were told to think that if there were eight million families in Italy and if each family saved a crust of bread or an ounce of meat, these amounts would lead to thousands of tons of food saved per year.[72] Even though every cookbook featured a section on entertaining guests, many of the 'exquisite dishes' (*piatti squisiti*) made the most of a few simple ingredients. True extravagance came with entertaining guests. Menu plans included several meat courses and elaborate desserts that required refrigeration or freezing. Domestic experts recognized that expensive and elaborate preparations were for guests only; the family was supposed to be content with a hearty *minestra*, a salad, and fresh fruit.

As reflected in the literature of domestic economy, sobriety became the hallmark of middle-class life under fascism. This was especially true with regard to household budgeting, a task that made the difference between living and living well. Advice manuals and periodicals reflected an intense concentration on little things and small gestures, indicating that in a low-wage, low-consumption economy like Italy's, small renunciations of food could lead to accumulated savings. The middle class of the 1920s was defined by income; domestic-economy literature estimated that the comfortable middle classes earned between 1,300 and 1,500 lire per month for a family of five. Out of this income, between two-fifths and one-third should be spent on food. Fernanda Momigliano's *Vivere bene in tempi difficili* used a case study of a white-collar Milanese family in 1931 (insurance company executive, wife, and two children, ages five and six) with a monthly income of 1,300 lire per month. The expenditure of 500 lire per month on food (38.5 percent of the monthly income) suggests no extravagance, only bourgeois sobriety. Daily expenditures on meat, chicken, or fish averaged 4–5 lire, while 2–5 lire were spent on eggs or cheese. (Only cheaper cheeses like *gorgonzola* or *stracchino* were purchased.) Added to these amounts was the invariable sum of 32.5 lire per week spent on bread, milk, coffee, sugar, and oil, a sum that amounted to 26.12 percent of the total food budget. Extravagance came in the form of treats like stewed prunes or chocolate pudding. There was little money left over for extravagant dinners, wines, or liquor. There were, however, three courses for lunch and dinner, meat, and a variety of animal-based proteins served every day.

By way of comparison, Momigliano used a case study of a bricklayer and his family (wife and a 10-year-old child) to demonstrate working-class budgeting. The bricklayer earned 720 lire per month out of which 420 lire, or 58 percent of the total income, was spent on food. Spending on meat, eggs, and cheese amounted to 3–5 lire per day; meat was served at least once a day. In addition, a weekly sum of 37.10 lire was spent on bread, milk, sugar, coffee, and wine.[73] Class distinctions were illustrated in the components and structure of the meals: the middle-class family ate meat twice a day and enjoyed a minimum of three courses for both lunch and dinner. The two families ate similar foods, however. Like the insurance executive's family, the bricklayer's family consumed drab dishes like stewed prunes and polenta. According to Momigliano's budget studies, then, class distinctions rested on the quantity of foods consumed.

Domestic literature also explored the regional diversity of cuisine. Zia Carolina's *Cucina pratica* listed a full range of regional specialties like *maccheroni alla napoletana, pasta col pesto alla genovese, risotto alla milanese*, along with a few international specialties like Irish potato soup and English pudding. Ada Boni's *Il talismano della felicità* also brought together regional specialties; minestra, salted cod, sardines, tripe, eggplant, and peppers were prepared according to regional styles. Cookbooks and magazines were not the only sources promoting culinary regionalism. In 1931, the Touring Club Italiano's first *Guida gastronomica* demonstrated a growing awareness of regional dishes and wines that tourists might like to sample: the *bagna cauda* and *agnelotti* of Piedmont, the risotto with saffron and *ossobuco* of Lombardy, the steak and stuffed *cannelloni* of Tuscany, tripe and pasta *amatriciana* of Lazio, and the *zèppole* and grilled *scamorza* of Campania.[74] Fascist-era literature stressed the positive attributes of regional diversity in culinary styles and characteristic dishes. Travel writers and domestic economists stand in marked contrast, then, to the nineteenth-century social scientists who viewed regional differences as a source of shame, not pride.

Hand in hand with a pride in regional cuisine were warnings to revere all that was characteristically Italian in terms of foods and methods of preparation. Even before the official fascist campaign of autarky and imperatives to 'buy Italian,' cookbook authors like the household rationalization specialist Dr. Maria Diez Gasca wrote that Italians 'must eliminate all that is rare and exotic,' in purchasing and preparing food.[75] The periodical *La cucina italiana*, subtitled *Il giornale per le famiglie e per i buongustai* (*The Journal of Gastronomy for Families and Gourmands*), carried a regular feature called *la cucina folkloristica* introducing readers to regional cooking practices through an ethnographic exploration of food preparation, local produce, and celebrations. Other articles supported Italian cuisine as national heritage: 'Down with Gastronomic Cosmopolitanism' or 'Out with the Barbarians,' proposed the elimination of English cooking terms such as lunch, toast, grill-room, and picnic.[76] Enthusiasm for culinary nationalism ebbed and flowed. When F.T. Marinetti proposed in the *Futurist Cookbook* of 1932 that Italian terms replace all foreign culinary words, only certain words caught on: the Italian word *tramezzino* became a popular term for sandwich, but Italians found the word *polibibite* too difficult a substitute for the word cocktail.

Most cookbook authors attempted to instill national pride in Italian cuisine by promoting it as the most simple and healthful in all of Europe or compared to North American trends. German cuisine was too heavy, British food was often smothered in mustard, and as for American cuisine, 'true housewives don't exist in this turbulent country; the modern women there improvise meals with the help of the most disparate collection of canned goods.'[77] Italian domestic economists admired the American household-rationalization movement, however. Lidia Morelli, the main proponent of domestic rationalization in Italy, wrote extensively on the topics of domestic architecture and streamlining kitchen construction for optimum efficiency.[78] In Morelli's eyes, the United States was a paragon of hygiene: every kitchen maintained a hospital-like cleanliness with colorful linoleum and sparkling appliances with easy-to-clean surfaces. Rationalized cooking in Italy meant conserving money wherever possible, avoiding luxury items like coffee, tea, or alcohol, and recycling even scraps of food like potato peels (which could be burned, pulverized, and used as cockroach deterrent). In terms of daily menus, rationalized cooking meant that meals were far from extravagant. Lidia Morelli's menu plans estimated that one could feed a family of four for 10–13 lire per day; meals consisted of potatoes, bread, cabbage, and pasta, with tripe, lard, entrails, and eggs constituting the bulk of dietary animal proteins. The more technological and consumption-oriented aspects of household rationalization were beyond reach for many middle-class readers. Women who dreamed of electric ovens and gleaming countertops had to content themselves with turning fruit peels into vinegar or starting a home rabbit-raising venture.[79]

There is much evidence to suggest, however, that middle-class women played some role in the creation of the cooking of consent. It would be foolish to presume that women who made an inexpensive polenta did so because of their allegiance to Mussolini; but the cooking of consent was not about blind patriotism. Instead, it was a process of rehabilitation, synthesis, and adaptation that shaped a coherent idea about what was 'good to eat' according to cultural and political circumstance. Middle-class housewives at least considered the ramifications of fascism when it came to budgeting and preparing food for their families. Reader participation in recipe contests (sponsored by magazines and food manufactures) suggests that women struggled to provide something extra or special for their families while keeping within the family budget. One 1936 contest attracted over 3,000 contestants, all proposing innovative ways to use canned tomatoes. Tomatoes were stewed in *marsala* wine, slathered in cream sauce, ground up in meatballs or lasagne; one of the more innovative recipes used tomato paste to glue together 'pretend birds in a nest,' veal-and-bacon birds in fried vegetable and potato nests.[80] Whenever Mussolini launched a new campaign to celebrate Italian food, the magazine *La cucina italiana* solicited reader input through contests or letters to the editor. Readers devised the tastiest Italian sandwich, the best way to use rice or leftover bread, and once Italy invaded Ethiopia, the best *pranzo sanzionista*:

- minestra with rice and stewed pumpkin
- scrambled eggs with cheese
- spinach
- spinach tortellini
- chestnut cakes[81]

Middle-class housewives also took seriously the cultural imperative to make a good impression on their neighbors; domestic literature offered plenty of advice and tips in support of their efforts. Susanna Agnelli, who grew up in a comfortable middle-class family, recalled how her mother took great pains to ensure that family members enjoyed meals and snacks that were appropriate to their economic status. This meant that Agnelli always had a sandwich of white bread, chicken, and butter for her *merenda*.[82]

The cooking of consent was a somewhat eclectic process whereby housewives and domestic experts discussed how to prepare food to fit fascist prescriptions. Much of the cooking of consent focused on how to provide for one's family in a low-wage, low-consumption economy. Women's work consisted of finding the best possible way to work with these policies or, when these policies became onerous, to protect and cushion the family from the harsher realities of life under fascism. As the prosperous 1920s gave way to the lean 1930s, the cooking of consent became even more important to family survival. Tips on 'cooking with little' gave way to 'cooking with nothing,' as food supplies dwindled and prices crept up.

Thus, the full impact of the cooking of consent can only be measured over a longer time frame, encompassing the difficult economic conditions of empire and war.

Throughout the 1920s, consumers did not fare poorly. They maintained consumption levels from the wartime and postwar years while securing a powerful psychological sense of satisfaction that price levels would be controlled and numerous goods would be available for purchase. This sense of security was about to end. Once Mussolini invaded Ethiopia, more and more Italians experienced a declining standard of living. The conquest of Ethiopia failed to provide Italians with additional food supplies, acting instead as a drain on the national economy. The League of Nations' economic sanctions against Italy for the invasion had no immediate effect on consumer habits. Rather, Mussolini's insistence that imports be dramatically reduced was much more significant a factor in reducing food availability. Ultimately, the difficulties and inconveniences generated by autarky would pale in comparison to the problems generated by Italy's alliance with Nazi Germany and involvement in the Second World War. By comparison, then, the years of fascist consent were relatively peaceful ones as far as provisioning crises were concerned. However, the foundations for a more strident food politics – one that emphasized greater self-sufficiency, minimal nutritional requirements, and stricter consumer discipline – were already apparent in early fascist interventions around food issues.

—4—

Austerity and Decline, Italy 1935–45

In the last weeks of September 1935, citizens across Italy celebrated the sixth annual National Festival of the Grape with 'vibrant enthusiasm' and 'unanimous consent' as reported by the press. The largest and most popular celebration was in Rome, where the city's Dopolavoro Club (the fascist leisure organization) and the Provincial Association of Farmworkers and Merchants sponsored a parade, the highlight of the festival. The winner of the prize for best float that year was a group of cannons festooned with grapes and manned by fascist blackshirts. The crowds cheered as the blackshirts flung bunches of grapes to nearby spectators. The winning float stood in stark contrast to the rest of the floats, which recreated ancient Rome or displayed young women in folkloric costumes. The float's celebration of the link between food and militarization was prescient, however. Several days later, on 3 October 1935, Mussolini sent troops to Ethiopia, beginning what was to be a decade of military aggression and civilian discontent in Italy.[1] By December 1935, over 400,000 soldiers were in Ethiopia, and another 250,000 joined them in the winter of 1936. The Italian forces fought ruthlessly, using mustard gas and terror to subdue Ethiopian soldiers and civilians. When Mussolini proclaimed victory and an Italian empire on 9 May 1936, his gamble paid off. Land-hungry Italians pinned their hopes on a new empire while the nation celebrated a much-needed affirmation of fascist strength and determination. These benefits came at a cost. The military venture drained the national budget and distorted Italy's balance of trade. (African colonies took up one-quarter of Italy's exports after 1936.) The League of Nations attempted to punish Italian aggression by boycotting Italian goods (from 18 November 1935 to 4 July 1936). Italy's former allies turned definitively against Mussolini, whose isolation and military pretensions pushed him toward an alliance with Adolf Hitler.

The Ethiopian invasion radicalized fascist food policies. Although the invasion had little immediate impact, Italians noticed a steady decline in their standard of living that did not end until the postwar reconstruction era. After the relatively calm decade of the 1920s, the period 1935–45 stands in sharp contrast in terms of food shortages, high prices, and consumer deprivation. Consumer complaints and elevated prices during the Ethiopian war gave way to food shortages, non-existent rations, and a thriving black market during the Second World War. Italians were deprived of even staple foods like bread, flour, pasta, and corn meal during the war, and civilians experienced severe shortages and malnutrition in the last two years of the war. As a result of Mussolini's new military orientation, the political significance of food shifted: from representing a benevolent political regime to linking a determined regime and an obedient citizenry during wartime. Official propaganda made much of the regime's efforts in the area of agricultural production; scientists offered their expertise to determine how Italy could survive a trade embargo or war; and consumers were advised to tighten their belts in support of the nation. Recommendations to save a few grams of food here and there gave way to a national austerity program. Mussolini's foreign policies aggravated an already tense situation, and by the outbreak of the Second World War, policy solutions to food shortages were late in coming and poorly planned. Unlike in the First World War, Italy did not have access to cheap wheat supplies. Instead, Mussolini's ally, Nazi Germany, drained Italy of both manpower and food. By the war's end, Italians received one of the lowest per diem rations in Europe, and 70 percent of all food purchases were made on the black market. Fascist Italy chose guns over butter, and after 1935 this decision had significant impact on Italian diet.

It is not surprising that Italy's military ventures contributed to a lower standard of living among the population. What is surprising is the fact that this dramatic decline was the result of a coherent and purposeful food policy formulated well before Italy entered the Second World War. In devising and implementing this policy, Mussolini's regime constantly reduced the amount of food available even when the political stakes were high. Yet consumers were assured over and over again that the nation would not starve as long as citizens were prepared to make small sacrifices. These small sacrifices were anything but insignificant when, as a result of sanctions, food imports were cut by almost one-third within a year. (Food exports decreased by only 7 percent.) Whether measured by propaganda, recipes, high prices, or consumer complaints, food consumption became one of the most important economic activities for the nation.[2]

Food also became linked to national survival. Scientists from the National Research Council (the Consiglio Nazionale delle Ricerche or CNR) determined the minimal nutritional needs of the nation in order to survive a lengthy war. These statistical studies were part of a larger effort to scrutinize and redefine the Italian population according to its labor power and minimum consumption needs to supply that labor power. In other words, as Italy strode toward imperialism, an alliance with Nazi Germany, and total war, Mussolini grew more insistent that the population become stronger, fitter, and more productive. Rather than provide the food necessary for increased productivity, strength, or health, the fascist regime tried to limit the amount of food available to Italians. During the Second World War, fascist food policies were characterized by sheer callousness and bungling. The regime treated both food supplies and the population as expendable resources to be managed or bargained away for the sake of military expediency. Ultimately, fascism failed to make good on any of its promises of benevolence or independence, thereby depriving the Italian people of the foods they came to expect and, ultimately, the foods that kept them alive.

Over the course of this tumultuous decade, food came to represent all that was wrong with Italian fascism. This chapter tells the little-known story of what happened. The first section explains how the Ethiopian invasion led to a more severe austerity program and what austerity meant for the average Italian consumer. Ethiopia raised hopes across the nation that more food could be grown in Italy's empire, but ultimately, the conflict failed to benefit Italian consumers. The next section details this heightened austerity campaign and links it to fascism's vision of the Italian population as an expendable resource. Austerity was more than just a propaganda campaign; it had become a whole way of life. However, Italians only grudgingly accepted their new fate, and scientific experts began to ask whether fascism could provide even the minimal nutritional needs for the population. The next section chronicles the history of food policies during the war and after 1943, under allied occupation and Mussolini's Social Republic (RSI). Everywhere, Italians struggled to survive on very little. The final section of this chapter evaluates the impact of fascist food policy by situating it within the broader context of fascist ideology regarding racial health and the Italian population. The history of food consumption between 1935 and 1945 tells us a great deal about Mussolini's intentions for the Italian people, especially in the context of Italy's alliance with Nazi Germany. Although fascism's crimes and offenses pale in comparison with those of Nazi Germany, the history of food consumption exposes the more calculating and authoritarian side of fascism, a side that is often difficult to evaluate in the context of military and political disaster.

The Ethiopian Invasion

When Mussolini invaded Ethiopia, the press devoted ample coverage to food issues, especially after the League of Nations called for trade sanctions against Italy. Reporters turned to Sabato Visco, the director of the National Institute of Physiology at the University of Rome, for his expert opinion on whether Italy could survive economic sanctions in the wake of the Ethiopian invasion. Visco calculated that Italy would not suffer from the war or sanctions. Based on data from the CNR's 1929 dietary inquiry (see Chapter 3), there would be 3,000 calories, 100 grams of protein, and 70 grams of fat available, per day, for every Italian. Although Visco noted that animal proteins might be in short supply if the war dragged on, he repeatedly assured Italian consumers that there was no need for worry or concern.[3] 'Women of Italy,' screamed the headline from *La cucina italiana*, 'man your kitchens!' Readers were told that the eyes of the world were focused on Italy, and that populations used to eating all the time could not understand that for Italians, sanctions meant few sacrifices: 'these are small sacrifices, because we are a moderate, frugal people who use our heads more than our stomachs.'[4] Later, editors changed the magazine's masthead from 'The Journal of Gastronomy for Families and Gourmands' to 'The Journal for Italian Families and Women: for the Resistance and Victory of Economic Independence.'

Fascist propaganda used the war and sanctions to praise the Italian population for its presumed willingness to adopt more austere habits. Economic sanctions against Italy had little impact on the nation. Oil imports were untouched, for example, and even though food imports were cut by one-third within a year after the invasion, consumers complained only sporadically about food availability, focusing their protests instead on high prices and low wages. Food continued to leave Italy, even for the nation's avowed enemies.[5] Despite this lack of serious material impact, the Ethiopian invasion set the stage for more serious deprivations during the Second World War, in that the regime failed to learn anything about the management of food supplies.

During and after Ethiopia, the regime continued to focus on price controls in order to calm Italian consumers. In fact, price controls became the primary means to check inflation by the mid-1930s. Prior to the invasion, food prices rose steadily throughout 1934 and increased sharply between January and November of 1935 as the nation prepared for war. The regime renewed its efforts to control prices as early as April 1934 and asked prefects to lower prices for all food staples by at least 10 percent.[6] In June, party secretary Achille Starace sent orders to all provincial secretaries to enforce new prices and maintain the cost of living. Meanwhile, Intersyndical Price Committees issued maximum price lists for twenty-one staple foods (including bread, wheat and corn flour, pasta, rice, meats, eggs, lard, cheese, butter, coffee, and milk), with several more items added to the list in 1936. Maximum price lists were supposed to be updated, issued, and posted every fifteen days. However, these price lists were ineffective and failed to assuage consumer anxiety. Consumers in the cities of Rome, Genoa, Palermo, Verona, and Como complained that the listed prices were often higher than those that merchants posted. Thus, some merchants regarded the maximum price lists as minimum price lists for goods, and raised their prices accordingly. The year 1935 also marked a period of greater austerity after imports were reduced in February, in response to the nation's declining gold reserves. 'Meatless days' were decreed for Tuesdays and Wednesdays; no oxen, pork, or poultry were sold in markets or shops. However, these measures did little to quiet consumer complaints. In September 1935, the party secretary from Milan reported low public spirits throughout the city because 'salary increases are found to be disproportionately smaller than the increases in the cost of living, which tend to increase with each passing day.'[7]

This renewed emphasis on price controls required support from retailers, and fascist propaganda emphasized merchant compliance and shopkeepers' enthusiasm for the Ethiopian conflict. *Il giornale del commercio*, for example, reported that on the evening of the invasion, Roman merchants and their families marched proudly from the Ponte Cavour to the Castel Sant'Angelo near St. Peter's, where they listened attentively to Mussolini's speech. Throughout the night, merchants kept their shop lights blazing to demonstrate support for the war, adding to the *brio ed animazione* of the Roman street scene that evening.[8] Propaganda could not mask the fact that the Discipline of Commerce campaign and other economic policies had decimated retail profits for merchants. Price-control enforcement varied between cities. In 1935, for example, the price of milk was 57 lire per hectoliter in Bologna while the same amount sold for 110 lire in Naples. However, Italy's closed economy afforded effective control over prices. Henry Miller's contemporary study of price controls in Italy found that wholesale prices in Italy increased only 23.8 percent in the period 1936–38 while in France, prices increased by 33.2 percent for the same time period. Yet there were some dramatic price increases – most notably for fresh meat, cheese, and lard – during the years of the invasion and sanctions.[9] The regime clung stubbornly to price controls because they were the most immediate, and visible, means of calming consumer anxiety. The strategy of selling commodities at lowest possible cost survived the years following the Ethiopian invasion because merchants were already broken by the Discipline of Commerce campaign. After Italy entered the Second World War, however, price controls proved to be ineffectual.

The least successful area of fascist food policy continued to be agricultural production. The Ethiopian invasion resurrected the question of whether Italy could produce enough food for its population. Increasing food production was necessary given the nation's balance of trade.[10] Yet all that the regime could offer was the Battle for Grain. There is no doubt that the Battle for Grain decreased Italy's financial dependency on wheat imports: by 1936, Italy spent only 15 percent of what it had spent on wheat in 1924.[11] By the middle of the 1930s, however, more and more critics questioned the wisdom of this production strategy. Italian economists and agricultural experts maintained that specialization in export crops (olives, grapes, citrus) should be the main focus of agricultural policy. Specialized production meant intensive amounts of labor by small family-run farms. Small producers were poorly organized and politically weak, and therefore the regime never considered such a plan.[12] There is no doubt that pumping funds and organizational skill into Italy's food-export industry would have produced significant results. Italy was a world leader in fruit and wine production prior to the First World War, but fell behind countries like France and Spain during the fascist era.

Indeed, the Battle for Grain, the revaluation of the lira, and the worldwide economic depression weakened Italy's food export industry. Moreover, currency revaluation, tariff policies, and the scarcity of credit meant only the largest producers of export crops could survive. In the absence of state protection, exports dropped steadily throughout the 1930s. Critics of the regime complained about the government's reluctance to protect typical Italian food products such as wine and cheese. Critics also noted the irony of a situation in which fascist propaganda advocated the increased consumption of fresh fruits, vegetables, fish, and wine at the very same time as the production of these foods was unprofitable.[13] The production and availability of fresh and dried fruit, vegetables, citrus, and tomatoes declined in the period 1925–35; the production of livestock decreased as well, given that it was less profitable than wheat and, according to the fascist regime, an inefficient use of land.[14] Wheat replaced animal-fodder crops and the regime kept meat prices low, even though the regime openly admitted (at the First National Convention for Increasing Agricultural Production in 1936) that Italian production of meat and fish were entirely deficient.[15] Per capita meat consumption dropped from 18.8 kilograms per year in the period 1926–30 to 14.5 kilograms per person in the year 1937. The consumption of more expensive meats such as beef and pork declined more than the consumption of fish, chicken, and organ meat.[16] A decade of *granarizzazione* distorted the productive potential of the nation and failed to provide adequate food supplies to consumers.

Despite these failures at home, the invasion of Ethiopia led to ambitious production schemes for the empire. The National Research Council's (Consiglio Nazionale delle Ricerche or CNR) Agricultural Committee sent experts to Somalia, Eritrea, and Ethiopia to examine the productive potential of the land and to determine whether familiar foods could be grown in Africa.[17] Originally, experts planned to turn the colonies into Italy's breadbasket, but they also evaluated the possibility of other crops to be grown there. Bananas, peanuts, sesame seeds, and hibiscus flowers (for an herbal tea called *karkadè*, an autarkic substitute for coffee) were crops considered acceptable for Italian tastes back home and were exported back to Italy. Although a few experiments with growing crops like corn, wheat, rice, coffee, and tobacco were successful, the colonies did not become Italy's granary, given the lack of manpower and resources. In fact, the invasion and attempted colonization of Ethiopia actually aggravated Italy's food-supply problems, as the area never became self-sufficient in food supplies and the settlers there had to be fed with food imported from Italy.[18]

It was the Duce's invasion of Ethiopia, and not the economic crisis of the early 1930s, that had the greatest impact on food-consumption levels in Italy. As charted by statisticians at the time, the period from 1929 to 1932 witnessed few changes in food availability. After 1932, however, there was a continuous decline in the quantity of food available, with a particularly sharp drop in the availability of some foods (legumes, cereals, vegetables, fruit, pork, lard, coffee, and wine) during the years of the invasion.[19] High prices compounded the difficulties caused by shortage. According to the Fascist Party (PNF) reports on the political and economic situation in the provinces, consumers initially blamed rising prices on retail speculation. There were also doubts that the government had done enough to remedy the problem. The Ethiopian invasion was not devastating to consumers, but increasing numbers found it more difficult to make ends meet. Families with numerous children, an unemployed breadwinner, sick or disabled members, were desperate enough to ask Mussolini or his family members for help. Most letters complained about living on as little as 200 or 250 lire per month with a family to support. Requests for assistance reflected the difficult circumstances of many large families.[20]

It appeared that more and more Italians discovered a clear contradiction between the regime's pressure on families to increase their numbers and the lack of social-welfare programs to support large families in need. Indeed, there was a rise in charitable works over the course of the fascist period. Even before Italy invaded Ethiopia, fascist charities (in particular the *Ente Opere Assistenziali*) dispensed over 3 million meals per day through soup kitchens across the nation.[21] Generally, the regime increased the administration of charity through the Fascist Party and the Fascist Women's Auxiliaries, solidifying what David Horn referred to as a shift in the 'locus of assistance,' from hospital and philanthropic organizations toward Party activity in neighborhoods and private homes.[22] These more private forms of charity coexisted with the public spectacle of food distributions: the *Befana fascista* (during which special food packets were distributed to children), winter food assistance, and the food giveaways to the needy on special food 'holidays', such as the festival of the grape. The number of well-publicized food distributions support historian Simona Colarizi's contention that fascist charity functioned more successfully as a public-relations maneuver than as an effort to alleviate poverty.[23]

Foreign observers were unimpressed with Italy's economic situation. Henry Miller's *Price Control in Fascist Italy* concluded by noting the situation after the invasion, sanctions, and currency devaluation:

> In January, 1938 bread was selling at an average of 1.77 lire per chilogram ... eggs were selling at 41 cents a dozen, cheese at 32 cents per pound, butter at 40 cents per pound, olive oil at 40 cents per litre and milk at 6.4 cents per litre. These are not low prices for a country with an average industrial wage of 11 cents per hour.[24]

Consumer complaints only increased as the nation moved closer to an alliance with Nazi Germany and the Second World War. Reports from the Fascist Party files indicate that in many cities, consumer reaction to the high cost of living shifted away from blaming local merchants and speculators to blaming the regime for not intervening vigorously enough to bring prices down. These reports highlight the failure of fascist food policies to be proactive in terms of controlling prices and guaranteeing more foods for purchase. Although the regime failed to satisfy consumer demand, it was far from inactive when it came to food issues. The regime stepped up scientific research into nutrition and intensified propaganda efforts to promote the proper Italian diet. By doing so, the regime also furthered the ongoing discussion about the relationship between food and the nation. This time, however, the debate shifted focus as the proper Italian diet was linked more firmly to ideas about demographic strength and military might.

Although the invasion and subsequent sanctions may have brought Italians closer together, they raised unsettling questions about the nation's economic stability and food availability should Italy be involved in a lengthier conflict. Prior to the invasion, international opinion questioned the viability of fascist political economy in light of decreasing imports, a dwindling gold reserve, and a mounting debt from Mussolini's large-scale public works programs. Italian consumers survived the invasion and sanctions with only minor price increases and temporary shortages, but the conflict drained the nation's budget and military reserve. Moreover, bureaucrats failed to use the Ethiopian conflict as practice for surviving a more devastating conflict. Despite all the propaganda devoted to austerity, the nation was ill prepared to survive the deprivations of the Second World War. The regime failed to innovate, relying instead upon the liberal solutions from the First World War: price controls, attempts to conserve food, and rationing as a last resort. There were distinct differences between the two world wars, however, given that during the Second World War the government lacked organization, timing, and access to cheap food supplies.

Austerity as a Way of Life

Clearly, the regime could have done more to increase agricultural productivity or transform the balance of trade, but Mussolini chose to pursue an aggressive foreign policy without much thought to Italy's domestic situation. During the Ethiopian war, it was up to consumers to tighten their belts and eat less, so that Italy's military objectives could be achieved. Thus the period after 1935 witnessed an explosion of propaganda urging consumers to adopt austerity as a way of life. Austerity was crucial to make fascist food policies work in the absence of a greater variety of food available, more generous wages, or adequate social-welfare provisions. The ideal diet consisted only of domestic produce: bread, cereals, tomatoes, citrus, and vegetables to be consumed daily; oils and fats, fresh and dried fruit, milk, and sugar to be consumed several times per week; and dried legumes, eggs, meat, cheese, and fish to be consumed only two or three times per week. Although the majority of Italians did not consume a particularly extravagant diet, the regime decided that further restrictions were necessary. For much of Italy's history, this austere diet signified immiseration; after 1935 it became a symbol of national resistance.

As early as 1931, the regime instituted a Day of Saving (*La giornata del risparmio*) to remind consumers that no form of thrift was too insignificant or undignified. To celebrate the Day of Saving, the Dopolavoro (the fascist worker's leisure agency) organized exhibits about savings and waste to call attention to what was thrown out in Italian kitchens. Recycling bones or coffee grounds conserved the nation's food supplies.[25] Ideally, sanctions built national morality and enabled citizens to help the nation's balance of trade by reducing imports. Ferrucio Lantini, Undersecretary of Corporations, asserted that if each Italian saved five grams of meat per day, the country could then cut meat imports by almost three-quarters (an amount totaling 750,000 quintals of meat per year). Lantini argued that physiologically, Italians required less fat and protein than other populations did, and therefore, such sacrifices would cause only minimal discomfort.[26] Elsewhere, readers were reminded that Mussolini himself consumed an austere diet, yet he was industrious, agile, and sharp-witted. Historian Luisa Passerini's readings of Mussolini's biographies noted that his abstemious habits and rigorous self-discipline were well publicized and contributed to his image as a handsome physical specimen. Mussolini never consumed coffee, alcohol, or tobacco. In the morning, he drank a cup of warm milk; at 2 p.m., he ate a small steak, omelet, or boiled fish accompanied by boiled vegetables; at 10 p.m., he had a piece of fruit and another glass of milk. Once or twice a month, he would fast for a day, drinking nothing but sugar water.[27]

Although anecdotes about Mussolini framed austerity in a masculine light, the intended audience for propaganda on savings was women, the most likely candidates to control waste in the kitchen. According to Rina Peloggio of the Fascist Women's Auxiliary of Novara, 'Housewives can make a big contribution in resolving the problem of autarky, as they can contribute much to the fight against waste.'[28] The motive behind domestic economy went from saving a few extra lire here and there to ensuring family survival in the face of worsening economic conditions. Cookbooks issued during the late 1930s emphasized cooking with lots of domestic produce: fresh vegetables, polenta, legumes, and the ubiquitous *minestra*. There were few recipes for dishes with meat, fats, or oil, except where substitutions were suggested. Lina Ferrini's *Economia in cucina senza sacrificio a tavola* (*Economy in the Kitchen without Sacrifice at the Table*), published in 1939, provided a hundred daily menus for a family of five while keeping to a budget of 20 lire per day. Ferrini's menu plans provided for either 120 grams of meat or 200 grams of fish per person per day, along with 150 grams of pasta. The meals were simple ones, consisting of three courses: the appetizer, the main dish, and dessert. Breakfast was always bread with coffee and/or milk. A sample lunch consisted of toast with chopped hardboiled eggs and tomatoes, mixed boiled meats, and cocoa pudding; dinner was pea soup, cold seasoned cauliflower, and a rice mold garnished with cooked fruit. Housewives were instructed to use eggs and organ meat (everything from spleens to pig's ears) in order to stretch the meat budget and guarantee sufficient protein for the family diet. When fish was served, it was inexpensive and stretched out with pasta, as in *spaghetti al sugo delle sarde* or *al sugo d'acciughe* or *con le vongole* (spaghetti with sardine or anchovy sauce, or served with clams). [29]

The recipes from Ferrini's book emphasized simplicity of preparation and ingredients. Yet, the majority of consumers – on account of the First World War and the prosperous 1920s – had become accustomed to consuming sugar, meat, liquor, coffee, and tobacco. Would fresh fruit, chicory coffee, and pig's ears satisfy them? Fascist propaganda heralded the period of sanctions as a return to simpler times, presumably the days before the First World War, although the regime distorted the significance of Italy's past, as few consumers actually desired to return to nineteenth-century eating habits. It was left to Italian women, then, to resolve the contradictions of life under fascism: one, how to cut back on so-called luxury items that became necessity items to most families, and two, how to resist the siren call of mass consumption as an essentially imported social practice and yet invent a distinctly Italian way of promoting leisure, elegance, and good taste.

The 'cooking of consent,' as a way of strategizing about food preparation under fascism, became even more important in the context of Ethiopia and sanctions. Lidia Morelli's *Le massaie contro le sanzioni* (*Housewives against Sanctions*, 1935) instructed women on how to survive sanctions while still preserving a sense of elegance in the home and a sense of personal beauty and fashion. A perfect example of 'autarkic elegance' was advice on how to use the lemon, a characteristically Italian fruit, to be used as astringent, dentifrice, skin softener, anti-dandruff shampoo, disinfectant, and, when mixed with bicarbonate of soda, a cure for indigestion. According to Morelli, women who possessed the ability to use ordinary items creatively would not have to make annoying sacrifices. However, the recipes for family meals hardly seem elegant: fried rice with beans, bread soup, potatoes prepared in multiple ways, tomatoes stuffed with ground nuts, and *pasticcio povera donna* (poor woman's pâté): made with 150 grams of pig's liver, 100 grams of sausage, two eggs, and 50 grams of grated cheese.[30]

The fascist regime also enlisted the aid of scientific experts to defend austere consumption levels as sound nutritional practice. The scientific discourse on food consumption shifted from approaching diet as a social question to be resolved through steady economic progress to a greater emphasis on the nutritional value of domestic produce. This shift in thinking followed the acceptance of nutrition as a science, but it also played into the fascist logic of drawing attention away from the structural issues causing low living standards toward a scientific reevaluation of adequate consumption levels. These evaluations were published everywhere, from professional journals such as *Quaderni della nutrizione* to popular scientific periodicals like *Sapere* and culinary magazines like *La cucina italiana* and *L'alimentazione italiana*. Consumers were told that the diet of average Italians was sufficient in nutrients. Filippo Bottazzi, president of CNR's Food Committee, claimed Italians consumed, on average, 108 grams of protein, 71 grams of fat, and 537 grams of carbohydrates per day, although this would appear to be a generous estimate.[31] CNR physiologists would recommend calorie levels as low as 2,500 calories per day for a person engaged in moderate labor. This stood in sharp contrast to the British Medical Association's Nutrition Committee which, in 1932, recommended 3,400 calories per day for a person performing sedentary work.[32] By 1937, Italian scientists like anthropologist and criminologist Alfredo Niceforo, who bemoaned the inadequate diet of Italians in the nineteenth century, began to question the utility of international nutritional standards. Comparing statistics on diet from the region of Puglia to average-man statistics set by American physiologist Graham Lusk, Niceforo observed that at no point between 1900 and 1937 did a majority of families measure up to these standards. He then suggested dropping the daily protein requirement for Italians to 90 grams per day (as opposed to 118), fats to 40 grams (from 56), carbohydrates to 450 (from 500) and daily caloric intake to 3,000 (instead of 3,300). These new recommendations, Niceforo reasoned, were more suited to Italian circumstance.[33]

Many scientific and medical professionals ran up against the contradiction between what fascism could provide for consumers and what an international community of experts defined as nutritionally adequate. While Alfredo Niceforo rejected international recommendations, other experts like Carlo Foà (a physiology professor at the University of Milan) tried to reconcile scientific recommendations with food available under fascism. Foà recognized, for example, that his recommendation of 3,000 calories and at least 100 grams of protein per day could not be furnished with Italian meat-production levels. Foà then suggested that Italians raise chickens and rabbits in their backyards. To make up for deficiencies in fat consumption, Foà proposed that farmers plant more soy, peanut, and sesame crops to supply the nation's nutritional needs while the upper classes restrict their consumption of butter, so that the lower classes could consume more. Although Foà frowned upon excess wine consumption, he noted that this was the one product Italy produced in abundance. Again Foà compromised by declaring that wine consumption was beneficial up to a point, as long as the effects of wine did not cancel out the nutritional value of foods consumed.[34] Foà's work clearly demonstrated how the effort to reconcile fascist policy with international science was difficult, if not impossible, to accomplish under sanctions.

Italian scientists were particularly concerned about inadequate protein consumption. In autumn 1937, the Reale Accademia d'Italia (Royal Italian Academy) sponsored an international conference in Rome on the current status of nutritional research. CNR Food Committee president Filippo Bottazzi's opening address spoke more to the Italian case than to the international situation. Although Bottazzi mentioned that more physiologists recommend lower protein consumption (provided that at least one-third of daily protein intake came from

animal sources), he spoke out against dramatic reductions of these recommendations. 'It is all well and good to know the minimum energy-giving levels needed
for civilian rations' in case of war, Bottazzi warned, 'but restrictions of any kind
cannot be but temporary and they cannot constitute normal consumption
levels.'[35] Bottazzi sounded the alarm regarding the regime's desire for more
drastic reductions in consumption. As the 1930s wore on, more scientists questioned the impact of fascist policies on popular nutrition levels. Even non-
scientists understood what was happening. A 1938 article in *The Economist*
observed, 'Food self-sufficiency is nowhere measured in accordance with scientific standards of nutrition.'[36]

Studies of dietary habits within Italy revealed persistent divisions between
segments of the population. Vera Cao-Pinna's analysis of middle-class families in
Cagliari (Sardegna), published in 1935, found class differentials in consumption
habits in southern Italy and the islands. Members of the middle classes consumed
more nutrients than did members of the artisan classes, including a daily average
of 70 additional grams of fat and 44 additional grams of protein.[37] Unfortunately,
detailed, small-scale monographs such as this one were rare during the fascist era,
so our understanding of class differentials in consumption can only be incomplete.
What little we have is revealing. A 1928 study by statistician Ugo Giusti on food
consumption in various cities throughout Italy pointed to striking disparities in
consumption patterns between north and south. The greatest disparities were to be
found in meat consumption, with residents in Milan consuming 62 kilograms of
meat per year versus residents in Palermo, who ate only 17 kilograms per year.[38]
A study of 744 working-class families sponsored by the Fascist Confederation of
Industrial Workers found that caloric intake for workers ranged from 3,335 calories per day in Genoa to 2,786 calories per day in Naples.[39] Differences in
consumption applied not only to meat but also to non-staple foods like sugar,
liquor, and canned goods.

From the descriptions of food consumption patterns in the late nineteenth
century to those of the fascist era, scientists altered their way of thinking about
nutritional standards. Recommended levels of calories, proteins, fats, and carbohydrates began to reflect actual consumption patterns rather than define idealized
goals for the population to meet. What accounted for this shift was an understanding that the majority of Italians would not meet international scientific
recommendations despite the prosperous 1920s, and certainly not in the wake of
the Ethiopian invasion and sanctions. Although ideas about the role of nutrition in
national life changed over time, there was continuity in scientific thought that
linked consumption habits to levels of national progress. Members of the CNR's
Food Committee may have debated the wisdom and the purpose of fascist food
policies, but they shared with the regime the understanding that popular diet was
linked to Italy's reputation. An increasing number of scientists examined, or at

least made reference to, consumption habits as the measure of Italian civilization or *Italianità*. Thus, it was not unusual for scientists to express an interest in cuisine and domestic economy. As Angelo Pugliese concluded in his study on the relationship between food consumption and social progress: 'The desire for a more appetizing and delicate cuisine contributes significantly to the development of a higher, more comfortable standard of living, representing a population's transition to higher levels of civilization, wealth, and social welfare.'[40]

Pugliese was not alone in thinking about how food represented the nation in cultural terms. The heightened sense of nationalism that accompanied the period of sanctions led to a discovery of Italy's culinary history. Several books published at this time proudly explained the origins of Italian cuisine, explaining the roots of *minestra*, rice, or *maccheroni*. These works also described in detail the rich regional diversity of cuisine, from the Piedmontese *bagna cauda* to *risotto allo zafferano* from Lombardy; from the *canelloni ripieni* in Tuscany to *spaghetti all'amatriciana* in Lazio.[41] Tourists and other non-Italian observers also began to notice Italy's diverse regional cuisine. Henry Aimes Abot's *Eating My Way Through Italy*, published on the eve of the Second World War, found that some regional specialties, like Tuscan *minestrone* or Roman *fettuccine* with cheese and butter, had become standard menu offerings around the nation.[42] This increased emphasis on Italian cuisine is not surprising, if we consider that the 1930s were a decade of heightened nationalism within Italy. This pride went hand in hand with an anxiety that Italian cuisine might lose its Italian-ness under the pernicious influence of Americanization or Anglicization. Gourmands feared that wholesome Italian dishes would be replaced with insipid white bread, frozen meat, and boiled chicken.[43]

During the period of the Ethiopian invasion and sanctions, food consumption symbolized the resistance of the entire nation. Ultimately, this way of thinking about food overruled any scientific criticisms that popular diet was becoming less varied and less nutritious. The regime's propaganda, recipes, and speeches defined what was characteristically Italian by discussing which foods *should* be eaten and why. The criteria for the ideal diet had shifted. In the late nineteenth century, and during the First World War, scientific experts and other interested parties advocated a popular diet to increase individual health and productivity, which in turn would contribute to the overall economic development of the nation. By the mid-1930s, the fascist regime had shifted the debate to discussing food in the context of patriotism and demographic strength. Moreover, fascist propaganda increasingly defined the Italian diet by what was *not* available or acceptable for consumption. The regime's defenders saw austerity as a necessary discipline, as one book on sanctions described it: 'this discipline imposes a certain parsimony that is a tradition for our race and makes dietary choices easier.'[44] Under fascism, abstemious habits became part of the Italian character. Of course, fascist rhetoric denied consumer choice in the matter. But one thing was certain: austerity had become a way of life for many Italians.

The War

Since the Ethiopian invasion, fascist Italy and Nazi Germany had come closer together diplomatically (although Mussolini and Hitler did not share much in common in terms of their military strategies for imperial domination). Germany began to export much-needed coal to Italy in the midst of international sanctions. Both Germany and Italy sent volunteers and war material to Franco's forces during the Spanish Civil War. Soon thereafter, Mussolini was speaking of a Rome-Berlin Axis. By 1938, German officials visited Italy with some regularity and Hitler made his historic visit to Rome, Florence, and Naples in May of that year. The relationship between the two leaders was, at times, ambiguously defined. Although Mussolini attempted to curry favor with the Nazi regime by implementing anti-Semitic legislation (starting in September 1938), he viewed his alliance with Hitler as a tool to further his own desires for Mediterranean dominance.[45] When Germany invaded Poland on 1 September 1939, Italy declared non-belligerence. The *Duce's* original plan was to launch a parallel war, but not until the nation was prepared, perhaps in several years' time (1942 was the anticipated date). However, Mussolini and his Foreign Minister, Galeazzo Ciano, misunderstood Hitler's intentions. When war broke out, the bellicose Mussolini was prevented from becoming involved immediately: the armed forces were completely unprepared and undersupplied; the country's industrial base and supply of skilled labor were small; the public was not enthusiastic; and the king was vehemently opposed to war. There is little evidence to suggest that food supply influenced Mussolini's decision to proclaim non-belligerence, but it certainly should have been a factor. Fascist food policies did little to increase food production, and the nation had nothing stored away in case of war.

The economic pressures exerted by the Ethiopian invasion and sanctions demanded greater flexibility with respect to procuring and distributing food. However, the regime became *more*, not less, rigid in its efforts to centralize controls and coordinate propaganda. How then would Italy meet the demands of another world war? Could Italy survive? Foreign observers were skeptical. In 1938, *The Economist* observed that 'it may be fair to add that by careful storage and a sharp tightening of their belts the Italian people might scrape through for a short time. But the war would have to be short.'[46] Italians in charge of food policies understood this as well. Vittorio Ronchi, the Director of Provisioning, and Giuseppe Tassinari, Minister of Agriculture, hoped for a short conflict so that rationing could be limited to bread, meat, and sugar. Ronchi later recalled that their anticipation of a brief conflict accounted in part for the disorganized nature of food controls during the war.[47]

Italian consumers had already tightened their belts prior to 1939. Since 1937, the government mandated the sale of very coarse *tipo unico* bread. *The Economist* observed that throughout 1938, commercially baked bread contained significant portions of rice, corn, bran, and other flours, rumored to be as high as 30 percent of the bread's content, although the Italian press disputed this allegation.[48] Consumers may have been prepared for worsening conditions, but the government was not. One of the key criticisms leveled at the Italian government was that they waited too long to implement rationing and other controls; there were no controls in place as of September 1939. When the war broke out, Italy frantically imported wheat from Hungary and Yugoslavia. Meanwhile, Nazi officials, including Agricultural Minister Walter Darrè, toured Italy, and evaluated Italian food production for possible export to Germany.[49] Ugo Angellili, editor of *L'alimentazione italiana*, cautioned readers not to panic; 'daily existence in Italy is normal: under the vigilant and omnipresent watch of the *Duce*, the nation's activities are exemplary.' Angellili's words echoed those of Mussolini who, in his speech on the wheat harvest of 1940, declared that 'while the rest of the world is distraught, the majority of our peasants provide an example of serenity and discipline, as always, more than ever and more so than anyone else.'[50] Propaganda from the period of sanctions resurfaced, stressing the sober and parsimonious nature of Italians. Doctors and other experts recommended the increased consumption of fresh fruits and vegetables, the reduction of fat and oil consumption, and the substitution of rice for wheat and dairy products for meat.[51]

By the spring of 1940, Germany's quick and decisive victories convinced Mussolini that there would be few risks in joining the war, which Italy did officially on 10 June. The Decree Law of 21 May 1940, for the organization of the nation for war, gave the government full authority to requisition goods, discipline consumption, ban food exports, and organize provincial committees to oversee food policies. The delegation of authority was diffuse. Civilian and military rationing fell under the control of the Ministry of Agriculture and Forestry (Servizio degli approvvigionamenti per l'alimentazione nazionale); all aspects of food distribution and retail sales fell under the Ministry of Corporations (Servizio della distribuzione dei generi alimentari e del controllo degli stabilimenti dell'industria alimentare); and these two services were supervised by the Ministry of the Interior (Ufficio di collegamento tra detti servizi). Locally, provincial organizations known as SEPRAL (Sezione provinciale dell'alimentazione) oversaw all aspects of food control. Unlike the highly effective provincial committees of the First World War, SEPRAL committees were too large for decisive or rapid action.

Archival evidence indicates that very early on in the war, there were some complaints about shortages and high prices for coffee, liquor, and sugar, but there were few complaints about food prices or food availability.[52] By the end of 1940, however, it was clear that the war would not be short, quick, or victorious for Italy.

As part of his parallel war, Mussolini invaded Greece at the end of October (28 October 1940), a move that ended in humiliation: a Greek counteroffensive pushed Italian troops back to Albania in the winter of 1940–41, and ultimately, German troops invaded and forced Greece to surrender in April 1941. As the Greek invasion dragged on, tighter controls and more decisive action were needed. The government responded with a tripartite plan to control prices, stockpile, and ration if necessary. Not much thought was given to stimulating agricultural production. This was a critical error, considering Italy's options for food imports were so limited. In fact, agricultural yields declined by 25 percent from 1938 to 1943, and production was at 63 percent of its prewar capacity by 1945. Mussolini's Battle for Grain fell into complete disarray during the war. Although in northern Italy grain yields held steady at a high rate of production (20 quintals per hectare) until 1942, in central Italy wheat yields dropped from 14.2 to 12.4 quintals per hectare, and in the south, yields dropped from 10.6 to 6.9 quintals.[53]

Rationing was introduced relatively late and, in early 1940, covered only coffee and sugar. By October 1940, rationing was extended to oils and fats and by the end of the year, to rice and pasta. Bread was not rationed until 1 October 1941, and shortages of bread and flour comprised a major headache throughout the war.[54] Later, in 1942, the bread ration was reduced to only 150 grams per day, with 250 grams available for certain workers. Rations for meat, oil, butter, and fat were reduced throughout late 1942 and into 1943. Each time foods were placed on the ration list, fascist organizations appealed to the Direzione Generale dell'Alimentazione (General Office for Food Provisioning), requesting additional quantities of bread, pasta, cornmeal, or legumes for their constituencies. The National Federation of Street Vendors requested additional rations for vendors who had to carry lots of goods or push heavy carts for hours on end; the Fascist Confederation of Industrial Workers asked for additional food for workers who made rayon fabric (the working environment was very humid, causing heat stress and fatigue); and the Fascist Confederation of Merchants requested extra rations for bread makers because their work was important to the war effort.[55]

Price controls, the foundation of fascist food policies, were poorly implemented during the war and prices skyrocketed. In Rome, for example, the price of flour increased from 40 to 120 lire per kilogram during the first few days of the war. Given that the daily bread ration reached a low of 100 grams per day in some areas, the black market for bread and other foods was inevitable. The first months of the war generated consumer panic. Many citizens remembered the shortages from the First World War. Members of the working class were used to going without certain items like coffee or liquor, but middle-class Italians became anxious and hoarded food as soon as Italy declared war. Perhaps the most spectacular reported case of early hoarding involved a Milanese accountant and his family, caught by police for sequestering food in the summer of 1940. A search of their apartment led to the discovery of a cache of goods in the walls: 111 kilograms of olive oil, 109 kilograms of rice, 45 kilograms of sugar, 38 kilograms of pasta, 54 kilograms of laundry soap, and, incredibly, 5,700 kilograms of coffee. The family claimed that they purchased the food in small amounts since February of that year. The prefect of Milan reported that the accountant denied any wrongdoing at his trial: 'When asked to justify his actions, he declared that he simply intended to have food on reserve and that he accomplished this through legal means, as he remembered the difficulty of provisioning and the long lines in front of the stores during the Great War.' His explanation was not convincing enough, however; the trial ended with a guilty verdict and the accountant was sentenced to the *confino*.[56]

In 1941, food shortages became commonplace and Italy became increasingly dependent on Nazi Germany. Italy's balance of trade shifted from an import balance in 1940 to an export balance in 1941–42, with more agricultural produce heading for Germany. Initially, the regime attempted to deal with shortages and other problems by reorganizing provisioning services (Decree Law of 24 April 1941, no. 385): the Ministry of Agriculture assumed most provisioning responsibilities and SEPRAL was re-organized. In the summer and fall of 1940, consumers continued to hoard food; whatever was not rationed disappeared quickly from store shelves, even at outrageously high prices.[57] Prefects complained to Vittorio Ronchi, the General Director for Provisioning, that price controls were nearly impossible to enforce, especially among bakers and millers. Ronchi himself toured the country throughout the winter of 1940–41, noting serious defects in the national food-distribution network. He found the city of Naples to be in a state of *grande miseria* in March 1941 and regretted that the fascist regime did not do more to assist populations in need *prior* to the war.[58] Provisioning was particularly problematic for southern Italy, even in the early years of the war. There were chronic shortages of bread, flour, and other cereals; agricultural production continued to decline; and the prices of non-rationed goods were out of reach for the poor and the working class.

Food shortages and high prices plagued the northern and central regions of Italy as well. Censored letters from the years 1941–42 revealed strong discontent in northern cities like Genoa and Milan. Consumers complained bitterly about food shortages, the black market, and the inefficiency of food-distribution mechanisms. Initially, citizens vilified local fascist officials for their privileged and unsavory relationships with speculators and black marketeers. As food supplies grew scarce and rations decreased, more and more citizens blamed the regime and Mussolini. The regime's response to these complaints was to keep a close watch over the population. In the fall of 1941, the Ministry of Interior instructed police chiefs, mayors, and prefects to report all activities and complaints. Simona Colarizi's examination of the documents from the Ministry's division of Public Security reveals widespread discontent because of insufficient supplies of staples like bread, flour, and oil. Local authorities constantly reported the actions of exasperated consumers who protested daily in front of fascist party headquarters, municipal buildings, and mayoral residences.[59]

In November of 1941, Hitler finally agreed to Mussolini's request to send Italian troops to the eastern front. Mussolini's parallel war had been a dismal failure. Italy's war against Greece had to be finished off by the German army and, in the winter of 1940–41, a British counteroffensive chipped away at Italian forces in North and East Africa. In order to save face, Mussolini pushed to commit Italian troops to Operation Barbarossa. The Italian army then assembled 220,000 men to send to the eastern front. In the wake of Italy's military failures, including the rout of the Italian army on the eastern front, Germany dropped all pretense of an axis alliance and began to dictate policy to Mussolini and his cabinet. Military losses or victories were of secondary importance for many Italian consumers. As a government informer from Milan reported in June 1942, 'Morale remains the same. The recent military victories, even taken together, have not improved it. It seems that the increase in the bread ration, if only by a few grams, has had more of an impact than the recent military victories. The dominant topic of discussion is always food.'[60]

By the time of the allied invasion of Sicily (10 July 1943), even the most privileged classes in Italy were suffering. 'Hunger had barreled its way into our daily lives,' author Rosetta Loy recalled of that summer spent at the vacation resort of Brusson.[61] In the wake of the allied invasion, on 24 July, the Fascist Grand Council voted to oust Mussolini by requesting he give up command of the armed forces. The next day, King Victor Emanuel III dismissed Mussolini; he was arrested and then imprisoned, but liberated by Nazis on 12 September. Thereafter, Italy was divided literally, as two occupations forces fought for control of the peninsula. The nation was also divided ideologically, between the fascist Italian Social Republic (RSI) and the anti-fascist forces of the Resistance.

The fascist regime's efforts to reorganize food provisioning under the Ministry of Agriculture in 1941 failed to make provisioning more efficient. It appeared that the General Office for Food Provisioning made too many promises to consumers that it could not keep. Moreover, the Office attempted to control even the minute aspects of provisioning, down to regulating how much broken-up pasta was to be rationed for the nation's guide dogs.[62] The utter lack of coordination and communication between regional, provincial, and national authorities hindered food distribution. A Byzantine code for food regulations only complicated matters. In the fall of 1943, German occupation forces were surprised at the number of laws and ordinances regarding food supply. There were, for example, 21 laws as well as 156 ministerial decrees dealing with meat alone![63] After Mussolini's dismissal, arrest, and restoration to power, food policies were again reorganized. In Mussolini's Italian Social Republic, food policies fell under the guidance of the

Ministry of Agriculture and local authority. In the liberated areas, the Alto Commissariato dell'Alimentazione (High Commissariat for Food Provisioning) took over for the defunct General Office.

As the Second World War dragged on, agricultural production and food transport became the most serious problems in both parts of the divided nation. Domestically produced foods like vegetables, olive oil, legumes, potatoes, and fats were in short supply throughout the peninsula, and from 1942 on, farmers continually evaded laws regarding wholesale price controls and requisitioning.[64] Italy continued to import wheat from countries like Romania, but the nation could not import enough to prevent major shortages of bread and flour. By the spring of 1944, in cities like Rome where bread was scarce, the bread ration was reduced from 150 to 100 grams per day. All cities experienced skyrocketing prices; rich and poor alike had to resort to the black market to survive. The government, and later Italy's occupiers, did little to curb black-market activities.[65] Although strict laws against black-market activity were passed (in February of 1944, black marketeers were threatened with the death penalty), there was little enforcement. The entire city of Milan, for example, employed only twenty agents to investigate and prosecute any infractions of food regulations.[66]

Italian consumers became desperate. Ration tickets did not ensure adequate supplies of foods, and by 1943 it was widespread practice for consumers to use ration tickets intended for future months in order to get bread. The quality of available food was also a major concern. Rationed bread tasted terrible. As one consumer complained, 'The bread functions as a laxative. You shouldn't eat it unless you want to lose weight.' Other consumers swore that bakers used wood pulp to stretch out bread supplies. Bakers frequently substituted chickpea flour and corn meal for wheat flour so as to reserve the best wheat flour to make black-market bread. Rationed pasta also tasted terrible. Consumers everywhere, even in southern Italy, substituted rice for pasta whenever they could.[67] The few cookbook authors publishing during the war attempted to replicate Italian favorites with only a few ingredients: bechamel sauce (*balsamella*) without butter and little milk; mayonnaise made from flour, water, and egg whites; *pastina* (little pasta bits) in broth without the *pastina*. The names of the various dishes suggest that Italian women went from 'cooking with little' to 'cooking with nothing:' *torta autarchica*; *polpettine di finta carne* (meatballs made with pretend meat); and *polpettine fatte di nulla* (meatballs made of nothing).[68] Cookbooks celebrated humble foods like onions, zucchini, carrots, oranges, and of course, the *polpettine*, which could be fashioned out of breadcrumbs, egg whites, grated cheese, anything *but* meat.

The difficulty of 'cooking with nothing' during wartime was compounded by the trials women endured in trying to find food for their families. Oral histories from Pesaro recounted how women were always on the move, looking for enough food so that their families might 'be able to eat a piece of fruit, or have two or three extra beans, or a bit of grain ground up for coffee.' Pasta was made of water, flour, and sea salt: 'without any sauce or seasoning, it tasted like pap.' One woman recalled eating mostly pears for an entire month: boiled pears for lunch and roasted pears for dinner. Other women resorted to stealing from farmer's crops in the surrounding countryside.[69] Women were still responsible, then, for the little things (*piccole cose*) to ensure family survival, but now the location of this daily struggle changed. No longer were women scrimping and saving within the private space of the home and kitchen to ensure their families' comfort. Rather, these activities had become public in the face of war and the struggle for mere survival. Norman Lewis, a British Intelligence Officer stationed in Naples, recalled how in October 1943, he witnessed children prying limpets off rocks in the bay. These limpets, along with whatever else they might find, 'if boiled long enough could be expected to add some faint, fishy flavour to a broth produced from any edible odds and ends ... Nothing, absolutely nothing that can be tackled by the human digestive system is wasted in Naples.'[70]

There were few scientific or social-scientific studies of the Italian diet conducted during wartime, but the few published studies reveal that no segment of the population was untouched by scarcity and deprivation. Pier Paolo Luzzatto-Fegiz, director of the Institute of Statistics at the University of Trieste, noted that the nutritional value of the middle-class diet declined significantly, reaching working-class levels; even wealthy families consumed a less nutritious diet in wartime. According to Luzzatto-Fegiz's survey, families and individuals not engaged in agricultural production suffered the most: roughly 40 percent of those polled by the University of Trieste's Statistics Department reported suffering hunger 'in the full physiological sense of the word.' Interviews with citizens all over Italy revealed bitter complaints from state employees and pensioners who had no money for food. State employees often called in sick to work because of illness and other problems associated with hunger, while most of the people interviewed described days when they felt tired, listless, and unable to concentrate. Almost every person interviewed reported losing weight during the war – between three and ten kilograms – and many took up smoking as a means of quelling hunger pangs.[71]

Rural workers may have had access to more food, but oral histories, memoirs, and contemporary anecdotes underscore, time and again, an overwhelming hunger in the countryside. Even early on in the war (1941), rice harvesters from Mantua could not work because of the lack of important staples such as corn meal, oil, and lard. Their daily diet, 'an insufficient quantity of bread, with marmalade, dried figs or cheese,' was hardly enough to compensate for ten hours of strenuous labor.[72] Overall, however, urban consumers suffered more from the inadequacies of Italy's food provisioning policies. Little was done to control rising prices or the increase in black-market activities. In 1943, Luzzatto-Fegiz, in work based on family budgets from the city of Trieste and its environs, estimated that families spent 40 percent of their food budget on black-market items. Between 1929 and 1943, salaries remained the same or increased slightly. Meanwhile, black market prices increased twelve-fold in the same time period.[73] On the black market, bread sold for 40 lire per kilogram, a kilogram of pasta cost 60 lire, and oil was priced between 180 and 300 lire per liter.[74] Across Italy, the owners of restaurants and hotels flouted rationing laws; everything was available for the right price. Patrons paid as much as 40 lire for a plate of pasta and 25 lire for a liter of wine. Given that the weekly wage for factory worker averaged 200 lire (230–240 lire per week at the Mirafiori plant in Turin, for example), these prices put many foods, even staples, out of the reach of many Italians.[75]

Yet the black market thrived in Italy. One of the largest black markets was in the city of Rome. The city maintained a special status under wartime, when German troops poured in to secure the capital after the King and Marshal Badoglio, head of the new government, negotiated an armistice with US General Eisenhower (announced 8 September 1943). Until the allied forces liberated Rome on 4 June 1944, the city remained vulnerable to Nazi aggression. As a result of the city's occupied status, industry shut down in and around the city and unemployment skyrocketed. The lower middle classes – schoolteachers, state employees, and pensioners – were reduced to seeking charity and frequenting soup kitchens.[76] Food that was officially available through ration cards averaged about 1670 calories per day and contained an average of 7 grams of protein (instead of the 60 grams of protein per day recommended by the National Research Council). However, most Romans could not obtain rationed food; the black market absorbed much of the food that was supposed to be rationed. Allied occupation forces estimated that by July 1944, almost three-quarters of food available in Rome was available only on the black market, compared to 22.6 percent on the free market and only 3.4 percent on the rationed market.[77]

The black market absorbed people as well as food, from large food manufacturers such as Alibrandi, Pompei, and Buitoni to small shopkeepers, hotel owners, and restaurateurs. Black-market meat sold for as high as 320 lire per kilogram while coffee sold for up to 3,000 lire per kilogram. Other goods sold for more than official prices. For example, lard, officially listed at 45 lire per kilogram, sold at 400 lire per kilogram. A can of condensed milk went for 120 lire while chocolate fetched a black-market price of 1,000 lire per kilogram (see Table 4.1).

Despite the fact that prices quadrupled between 1943 and 1944, black-market activity only increased, particularly in the working-class neighborhoods of Rome such as Piazza Vittoria and Trastevere. Activity increased despite the fact that in 1939, the fascist regime mandated two years in prison for anyone caught buying or selling. Authorities certainly knew the extent of clandestine activity in Rome. The Ministry of the Interior's Ispettorato Generale di Pubblica Sicurezza (General Inspectorate of Public Security) tracked black-market activities by intercepting

Table 4.1 Black market prices in Rome, average for 1943–45

Item	Black Market Price	Official Price
Sugar	230 lire/kg.	25 lire/kilogram
Lard	400 lire/g.	45 lire/kg.
Butter	600 lire/kg.	47.50 lire/kg.
Eggs	13 lire each	9 lire each
Condensed Milk	120 lire/can	17 lire/can
Chocolate	1000 lire/kg.	200 lire/kg

Figures on prices are from ACS, Pubblica Sicurezza, Ispettorato Generale di Pubblica Sicurezza, Servizi Annonari, b. 17.

phone calls, mostly in hotels, *pensiones*, and eating establishments. What the transcripts of the tapped conversations reveal is that anything and everything was available at a price. One transcript of a conversation between an unknown woman and Rosina, the proprietress of *Pensione Boz*, is typical:

Rosina: I have some beautiful meat, extremely rare, veal.
Signora: How much?
Rosina: 170 [lire].
Signora: How much do you have?
Rosina: Whatever you want.

Other transcripts reveal how much food was available in Rome's restaurants. One young man told his fiancée of a lunch where he had spaghetti, veal cutlet, beef and potatoes, cheese and wine in March 1944.[78] Other transcripts detailed how the various fascist organizations patronized the black market in order to acquire food for their members; how women deplored sending their children to school hungry; and how the sick and elderly were forced to resort to the black market even though stores were supposed to reserve goods like eggs, milk, marmalade, and oil for them. Rome's black market was acknowledged, ignored, and sometimes even encouraged by Italian authorities, German occupiers, and later, Allied occupation forces. Indeed the black market was too large a problem for any one authority to solve.

By 1944, the entire system of food provisioning – in both liberated territories and in the Italian Social Republic – had broken down. In the Italian Social Republic (RSI), the Ministry of Agriculture was supposed to supervise the various provinces, yet the Minister of Agriculture lamented an 'absolute breakdown between center and periphery ... each province goes its own way.' Prices were a case in point. It was virtually impossible to maintain controlled prices throughout the RSI; instead, prices fluctuated wildly between Bologna and Milan, for example, and were the source of continued controversy throughout 1944.[79] In the fall of 1943, German occupation forces insisted that the RSI implement political prices for food in order to control inflation. The Minister of Agriculture Edoardo Moroni responded that such gestures would only be symbolic ones, given that the control of prices was entirely beyond the scope of authorities and therefore, 'to talk about prices at this moment is purely delusional, given that many shops have no food in stock and that the black market has, unfortunately, exploded.'[80] Nonetheless, German occupiers constantly pressured the RSI's Price Commission (Commissario Nazionale dei Prezzi) to adjust food prices in accordance with 1943 levels, not based on market values or production costs. This would be difficult, German Ambassador Rudolf von Rahn noted in April 1944, but he reminded Mussolini and his ministers that 'in total war one cannot, unfortunately, avoid difficulties.' Indeed, difficult decisions had to be made. The Commission refused to make them, however, believing the German position to be too rigid. Mussolini responded to the Ambassador's request by maintaining a hard line: producers need financial incentives to produce. Therefore, reasonable increases in agricultural prices were absolutely necessary to avoid shortages and curtail black-market activities.[81] This difference of opinion illustrates well the regime's reluctance to stray from its liberal leanings by implementing more authoritarian controls, even in the midst of the war.

The German occupation forces had few illusions about the Italian situation. Their memorandums indicated that they could not eliminate the black market, 'given the Latin mentality', and their correspondence blamed a disorganized Italian bureaucracy for the severe shortages. German correspondence frequently adopted a moral tone by lamenting that Italians brought these difficulties on themselves through their ineptitude and inaction. For example, the Head of Police for Security Services for Italy, Brigade Führer S.S. Harster, observed that Italians seemed quite indifferent to food shortages, having gotten used to them over the course of the war. Those Italians willing to work for the Nazi war machine should be allowed to eat, but 'those who don't work will go without food.'[82]

German frustration was justified to an extent, as high prices continued to spark consumer discontent through the summer and fall of 1944. Local price committees were unable to guarantee the availability of bread, given that bakers refused to sell loaves at mandated prices, opting instead for clandestine sales on the black market. These committees, as they were organized in the RSI, proved unwieldy. Members included the prefect, mayor, provincial agricultural inspector, and police chief, plus representatives from the provincial economic council, and local shops and farms. Given the diverse range of interests represented on these committees, price controls were difficult to implement. The local price committees for the region of Piedmont simply gave up by the end of 1944, citing difficulties with prices and transportation. As reported by the Commissariato Staordinario del Governo per il Piemonte (Governing Commissariat for Piedmont), the situation in Turin had become unbearable. Bread rations could be guaranteed only for a few days, pasta rations had not been distributed in over four months, meat rations were available perhaps once a month, and no one recalled seeing fresh vegetables for at least several months. Further, according to the Commissariat, any efforts to check inflation and implement price controls 'generates quibbling about the social policies of the Italian Social Republic and can lead to seditious activities, and none of this can be prevented because we lack an adequate police force.'[83] Within this desperate situation, however, there was some hope that the provisioning situation could be improved. Numerous organizations and committees forwarded ideas and proposals to Mussolini, suggesting how the nationalization of food controls might be implemented. Proposals for nationalization were, of course, in keeping with the new ideological foundation of Mussolini's Social Republic. Among the many proposals were plans to requisition all retail establishments, implement large cooperatives, and nationalize food transport.[84]

Obviously these suggestions were too little, too late. The fascist regime's concentration on propaganda and price controls, at the expense of boosting agricultural production, failed to address wartime circumstances. Even Agricultural Minister Moroni acknowledged these missed opportunities by lamenting an unbalanced food policy that favored propaganda and retail control over boosting production. Throughout 1944, the RSI made requests to prefects and local authorities to keep a close eye on distribution and carefully obey all current provisioning laws, but there was no mention of agricultural production. The Ministry of Agriculture, in a confidential 15-page memorandum regarding provisioning (sent to provincial heads) was extraordinarily specific about cracking down on the black market, but vague in terms of an overall plan for national survival. The best the Ministry could offer in terms of a policy direction were references to creating a favorable psychological state in the Social Republic. The technical aspects of provisioning problems were ignored.[85] It would appear, then, that the Ministry of Agriculture had no other options or ideas left.

High prices and shortage continued to plague the regional leaders of the RSI until the demise of the government after Mussolini's death and the surrender of German forces in Italy to the Allied armies (27–29 April 1945). In the province of Milan, for example, reports from December of 1944 complained of having no flour for making rationed bread. Hard cheese substituted for meat rations, and citizens were supposed to receive only 75 rationed grams of fat *per month*. Mayors from the region were helpless to assist citizens. The most they could do was to write to the regional leader, requesting immediate relief. The situation improved slightly by February 1945 in that citizens were able to obtain rationed bread, but almost every other kind of food was available only on the black market.[86] In the provinces of Milan, Alessandria, and Como, the black market absorbed more food and participants. Any meat available in these provinces was sold on the black market. Non-municipal soup kitchens and cafeterias sold requisitioned food at black-market prices rather than distributing it to needy citizens. And, as late as March 1945, regional leaders complained that the intransigence of farmers and the lack of transportation prevented food distribution.[87] The desperation conveyed by the regional reports is hardly surprising. Mussolini's Italian Social Republic was but a shadow of the fascist regime and was largely under the control of the Third Reich. As the next section details, Italians under German occupation were treated more like enemies than allies, and the food situation in Italy resembled that of occupied areas in eastern Europe.

In the areas of Italy liberated by the Allies, conditions were not significantly better. Communication between local SEPRAL directors and the High Commissariat for Food Provisioning (Alto Commissariato dell'Alimentazione) highlight many of the same problems endured by Italians in the RSI. Typical was a March 1944 monthly report from the SEPRAL director in Agrigento: '... prices have reached exaggerated figures. The intense, clandestine export of food on other parts of the island have left this province almost entirely deprived of grain, oil, fats, cheese, legumes, fresh meat, salted fish, dried fruit, etcetera, etcetera.'[88] Help from the Allied forces was desperately needed yet excruciatingly slow. Journalist Alan Moorehead remembered the shock experienced by Allied forces upon their entry into Naples on 1 October, 1943: 'hunger governed all ... What we are witnessing in fact was the moral collapse of a people. They had no pride any more, or dignity. The animal struggle for existence governed everything. Food. That was the only thing that mattered.'[89] Historian David Ellwood, in his history of the Allied advance in Italy, argues that the social problem of hunger was beyond the scope of what any of the Allied forces had expected or anticipated. The enormity of the problem bogged down the Allied advance; plans for provisioning such vast numbers of people were not a part of Allied strategy. Even with the institution of the Allied Military Government (AMGOT), food shortages persisted; Paolo De Marco's study of occupied Naples points to ongoing difficulties in the south, caused in part by inefficient Allied provisioning strategies. Complicating the struggle to provision Italians was the black market. In Naples, an estimated 60 percent of the total tonnage devoted to relief efforts found its way into the black market.[90]

The Commissariat did little to control the black market, opting instead to regulate rationing. The Commissariat became heavily involved with administering additional rations to those segments of the population involved with rebuilding the nation. Additional rations validated one's contribution to the war and postwar efforts. As of February 1944, all workers involved in heavy labor received an extra 175 grams of bread per day, when available. A few months later, in July, extra rations were extended to some public servants – public security agents, prison guards, forest rangers, and firemen – as well as the sick and hospitalized. These groups received an additional bread ration, plus 550 grams of pasta per week, and an additional amount of milk, sugar, dried legumes, canned meat, or olive oil, depending on what was available.[91] Later, in January 1945, SEPRAL's provincial supply office decreed that in towns and cities of more than 10,000 inhabitants, certain foods (powdered soup, dried legumes, and canned meat) could be distributed. However, the amounts distributed were negligible, averaging a mere 100 grams *per month* per person. Additional rations, no matter how meager, were possible largely because of external assistance, first through the Allied occupation forces and then at the war's end (1945–46), through the United Nations Relief and Rehabilitation Administration (UNRRA). The United Nations decided to assist Italy in September of 1944. Later, a formal accord between Italy and the United Nations (DLL 19 March 1945, no. 79) guaranteed 50 million dollars' worth of goods and services. Members of UNRRA worked with the Provincial Assistance Committees in liberated areas through 1946, providing much-needed nutritional assistance to Italians, especially children. (An estimated two million rations per day were distributed to Italian children in 1945–46.)[92]

It would appear from the experience of the Second World War that the fascist regime learned very little from Italy's experience of the First World War. From the very beginning of the conflict, food controls were disorganized and poorly coordinated. Price controls, which were so successful in fascism's early reign, were not strictly enforced and therefore prices, and the black market, ballooned. Instead, the fascist wartime government relied too heavily on rationing. Years of slighting agricultural production cost the regime dearly. Thus, the Battle for Grain failed to provide Italians with enough bread; agricultural production in Italy dropped from 8.18 million tons in 1938 to 6.51 million tons in 1943.[93] Virtually no consideration was given to issues of nutrition and health during the war. Years of scientific research and mountains of propaganda dissolved in the context of wartime exigencies. As General Director for Provisioning Vittorio Ronchi later explained, 'The nutritional aspects of food consumption, fundamental for health, should have been considered in normal times ... but now it was too late and we had to concentrate on what was possible given the extreme state of penury in which we found ourselves.'[94]

Consumers certainly noticed the regime's failures in this critical aspect of wartime policy. During the Second World War, consumers resorted to the same pattern of protest as they did during the First World War, although the scale and stakes had shifted. Subjects of Pier Paolo Luzzatto-Fegiz's study of food consumption spoke of a continual frustration with local government and the fascist regime. Citizens were angry with the privileged members of the Fascist Party who always received the best cuts of meat or the largest loaves of bread while civilians had to wait in line for hours to buy very little. They viewed local enforcement officials as busybodies with no right to enforce laws against clandestine activity. A Bolognese pensioner's story was typical: 'The other day I was on the tram. An agent stopped a woman carrying a suitcase. The woman was bringing a kilogram of flour and a few eggs to her son, a soldier. A passenger intervened, saying, "Leave this woman alone and go and visit the homes of the prefect and the other bigwigs. There you'll find plenty of food. Tell them I sent you." The agent got off without saying a word.'[95]

The failure of fascist food policies to provide for the population led to consumer deprivation on a massive scale during the war. Inadequate nutrition and low levels of consumption affected more than popular health: they slowed wartime production, bogged down the Allied advance across the peninsula, and demonstrated to Italians that the regime could not provide even for their minimal needs. This last point is crucial. The regime hoped to build consensus for its policies regarding food consumption, by forging a bond between citizen and state through the everyday activities surrounding food. Delays and mistakes in wartime policy severed this fragile bond completely. The failures and contradictions in fascist policy would have us believe that the regime was, at best, uninterested in food consumption and at worst, completely inept when it came to provisioning. Either characterization questions the totalizing nature or intent of fascism as a political system. Such questions about fascism have been asked before. Since Mussolini's seizure of power, fascism has been criticized by some for failing to build popular consent, and subsequent generations of historians have echoed these criticisms. Furthermore, historians have pointed to so many structural problems and contradictions within the mechanisms of fascist power that the label 'totalitarian' seems entirely inappropriate and the label 'authoritarian' open to debate. Yet, if we understand food policies only in terms of what they failed to do, we have missed an important aspect of fascist rule. Tracing the implications of all of these discussions, projects, and policies concerning food sheds new light on the regime's intentions toward the Italian population. If we consider all the activities surrounding food within the context of fascist demographic and racial politics, a different picture of fascism emerges in which food consumption plays a critical, and revealing, role.

The Impact of Fascism

Fascist policies borrowed heavily from liberal predecessors, popular consent was broadly based but superficial, and ultimately, fascist Italy became a pale imitation of the more ruthless dictatorship in Germany. Indeed, histories that concentrate on the contradictions of fascist ideology or Mussolini's opportunism have downplayed the more authoritarian aspects of fascist rule. Cruel or severe policies, such as the deportation of Italian Jews, were depicted as imports, adopted so that Mussolini could gain Hitler's approval. Seldom have Italians, or Mussolini, been depicted as anti-Semitic or racist.[96] Evaluating fascism's authoritarian nature solely in terms of anti-Semitism, however, misses a significant aspect of fascist rule: the ways in which certain policies in the aggregate shaped a specific vision of the population and society.[97] Understanding the history of food policy helps to adequately characterize the unique nature of fascist rule over society. As we have seen, fascist food policy was comprised of agricultural policies, price controls, and propaganda campaigns to control consumers. But in the broader scheme of fascist politics, issues of food supply and consumption were related to questions of Italian demography and race. Most obviously, there were professional relationships between scientists on CNR's Food Committee and those scientists working for the Office of Demography and Race. Physiologists and statisticians from CNR and ISTAT (the Central Institute for Statistics) devoted a great deal of time and energy to calculating the absolute minimum nutritional requirements for Italians and the availability of food for the nation in case of war. Thus food supply and the population became resources to be managed in the face of crisis. Yet, as fascist Italy and Nazi Germany cemented their alliance, food as a resource came to symbolize Italy's racial inferiority and lower status in both biological and political terms: Nazi occupation forces expropriated both food supplies and human labor as Italy's status declined.

There is no question that in fascist Italy, questions of demography and race were intertwined. Because there was never a rapid or massive influx of outsiders into Italy, there was never any fear of non-Italians that assumed racialized dimensions. Scientists looking for the origins of a pure Italian race found a mixture of peoples from Europe, North Africa, and the Middle East. Racial theory in the 1920s defined Italy as a 'proletarian' nation, with a population that was particularly good at reproducing and spreading itself all over the world. This was an inclusive vision of race, readily taken up by nationalists and fascists because it could be channeled into imperial ambitions. In other words, this unique vision of race served to bolster fascist pronatalist and imperialist leanings.[98] Italy's population was perhaps the most important natural resource that the country possessed. Thus, fascist Italy's racial concerns had more to do with issues of demography and resource management rather than the discovery of a pure Italian race.

Mussolini turned his attention to demography when he launched the Battle for Numbers in 1927 to convince the population to reproduce more, despite the fact that Italy already had a high birthrate, third in Europe after Romania and Spain. Nonetheless, the Battle for Numbers combined financial incentives for more children and improved maternity care with repressive measures against birth control and financial burdens on those who did not marry and reproduce. Given Italy's high birthrate and given the regime's support for decreased food imports, the Battle for Numbers makes little sense. Why would a nation want to increase the population and decrease food imports at the same time? Quite simply, the regime thought of the Italian population as a resource to be managed and ultimately exploited by the state. In light of fascist population policy, fascist food policy takes on a new meaning. In order to make the regime's population policies work, Italians were going to have to eat less. It comes as no surprise, then, that scientific experts employed by the regime to study food consumption were also very much interested in questions of demography and race.

Several members of the CNR's Food Committee were also part of the Central Office for Demography and Race, or as it was more commonly known, Demorazza. These experts include the Food Committee's president Filippo Bottazzi, Livio Livi (Professor of Statistics at the University of Florence), and Sabato Visco (Professor of Physiology at the University of Rome). Sabato Visco became particularly involved in questions of food and race. He presided over the National Nutrition Institute (Istituto Nazionale della Nutrizione) at the University of Rome, and in 1938 launched the periodical *Autarchia alimentare*, which blended scientific research with updates on government food policy. Visco dedicated much of his time to calculating Italy's consumption needs and productive capacity.[99] Visco worried about the physical effects of protein underconsumption, but he ultimately concluded that protein and other dietary deficiencies in Italy were relative and did not contribute significantly to racial degeneration. Scientists like Filippo Bottazzi were interested in the link between food consumption and the demographic problem insofar as statistics and the science of nutrition could contribute to understanding how to manage the Italian population. Bottazzi frequently requested assistance from Corrado Gini, Mussolini's demographic expert, to study the links between nutrition and Italy's birthrate.[100] Several scientists tried to link food consumption with the notion of a specifically Italian racial identity, but with little conviction.[101] Perhaps the best-known scientist who explored the connection between food and race was Giuseppe Tallarico, parliamentary deputy and member of the CNR's Food Committee. Tallarico published extensively on the connection between wheat bread and fertility, postulating that the wheat germ found in whole wheat bread somehow aided human fertility. Because his work supported the consumption of whole wheat bread, Tallarico's publications were often cited in fascist propaganda.[102] Scientists may have failed to make concrete connections between food consumption and racial identity, but this did not mean that ideas about race had little impact on the scientific profession of nutrition. Jewish scientists who dedicated their careers to food consumption were expelled from or left their university posts after Italy passed a series of anti-Semitic laws beginning in 1938.[103]

The links between heightened race consciousness and food consumption were tentative ones at best. Ideas about food consumption and proper nutrition were more concretely related to demographic concerns like female fertility and infant mortality rates. Scientific inquiries into food consumption habits and statistical calculations of food availability were perhaps the most significant scientific contributions to fascism's goal of managing the population. In anticipation of economic sanctions and war, statistical studies of national nutritional needs and food availability predicted the population's ability to survive on very little. Prior to the rise of fascism, there were few national surveys of food availability.[104] Under fascism, determining what and how much Italians ate became a major statistical enterprise. Mussolini himself was obsessed with statistics and ISTAT was created in 1926 to begin to address the needs of the nation. Lorenzo Spina and Benedetto Barberi, both of ISTAT, compiled the most comprehensive surveys of food availability for the fascist period. Spina's work compared consumption levels of prewar years (1910–14) to those of the early fascist period (1926–30) and the years of the worldwide economic depression (1928–32). His work determined that the total volume of food consumed increased little in this period, but the proportions of food consumed changed over time. Italians consumed more fresh vegetables, meat, and fish in the 1920s. Barberi's work, which charted the availability of basic foods between 1910 and 1942, confirmed Spina's findings. Barberi found significant increases in the consumption of wheat, milk, sugar, and meat over a 30-year span. Both Spina and Barberi found nutritional levels to be adequate for the 1920s and early 1930s, and both were optimistic about Italy's continued progress in the area of popular-consumption levels.[105] Thus, both statisticians linked improved food consumption levels to fascism's economic success.

Once Italy invaded Ethiopia, scientists like Sabato Visco wrote about caloric availability in much less optimistic terms, using data from Barberi and Spina to determine the minimal physiological needs of the nation so that Italians could survive a trade embargo.[106] Carlo Foà, director of the Physiological Institute at University of Milan, confirmed the relevance of nutrition to national survival by implying that food supplies – broken down into vitamins, minerals, and calories – could be rationed on a national scale.[107] At the outbreak of the Second World War, the National Biology Institute (Istituto Nazionale di Biologia) attempted to determine national needs for wartime production, using the CNR national inquiry from 1929 as their database for consumption habits. The report recommended additional rations of milk and meat for war workers but recognized that these would be difficult to furnish, given the nation's productive capacities.[108] The Institute's report demonstrated the increasing importance of nutrition in the discussion of food and national life. Although scientists were frequently optimistic about the nation's prospects for surviving a trade embargo or war, their constant references to absolute minimum nutritional requirements indicated that they were at least aware of the difficulties Italy would face.

Statisticians and physiologists were keenly interested in food availability as a way to manage the Italian population in wartime. Mussolini and his cabinet also were interested in these issues. Early on in the war, Mussolini was apprised of crop yields while the Ministry of Agriculture kept a census for harvests of potatoes, legumes, and vegetables.[109] By 1941, Italy's wheat imports (coming mostly from Romania) were reduced dramatically from those of the previous two years. Mussolini's alliance with Hitler meant Italy had even fewer options for importing food than it did during the period of sanctions. Italy's economic and military situation made the nation ever more dependent on Germany for war material, but what could Italy offer in return? Food and labor were the most obvious answers. After all, the population was Italy's only valuable resource. The fascist regime attempted to manage the two resources but ceded control over them to Germany. The Nazi regime took full advantage of Italy's economic and military situation, using racial ideology to support the exploitation of its ally.[110] Food supplies were a particularly sensitive issue, in that the Nazi expropriation of foods from Italians reinforced Italy's inferior status.

Even before the Nazi occupation of Italy in 1943, Italian citizens and food were exported to Germany. Before Italy entered the war, Italians were recruited to work in German industry and agriculture. By June 1942, an estimated 300,000 Italians were working in Germany, although by May 1943, this number fell to 230,000 at the request of Mussolini, who wanted laborers to return home to work for Italy's benefit. Italy had to pay for the repatriation of these workers, but after Mussolini's fall in July 1943, the repatriation process stopped. Some Italian civilians were sent by the SS to Germany to work, and Italian soldiers interned in Germany were put to work while private firms continued to advertise for help in the Italian press. The actual numbers of Italians who worked in Germany fell far short of German expectations of 1.5 million Italians by 1944. Nonetheless, the way that workers were treated by the Third Reich indicated that the value of Italy's population declined along with Italy's military and economic status.[111]

Italy's alliance with Germany had a measurable impact on the health and well-being of the population. Italian workers in Germany received meager rations, consisting mostly of cabbage, carrots, potatoes, and in rare cases, supplemental rations of wine, canned tomatoes, and *parmigiano* cheese. The quality of the food left much to be desired, and the quantity was considerably less than promised. Italian miners, for example, were assured a daily *minestra*, but they complained about constant shortages of pasta, oil, and cheese. In addition, workers received 40 grams of butter and a half-kilogram of bread per day, a kilogram of meat per week, and 900 grams of sugar a month. These paltry amounts, miners complained, were not enough for them to do their jobs adequately.[112] During the German occupation of Italy, all Italians who worked for the German *Wehrmacht* were granted extra rations. Workers received special cards that enabled them to purchase items like an extra kilogram of sugar in certain stores, depending of course on availability.[113] This practice did little to lessen the impact of the black market, and oftentimes shopkeepers did not accept the preferential cards. Within Italy, citizens protested the distribution of food to German occupiers and the export of goods to Germany. Letters to Mussolini expressed disbelief and outrage that the government and merchants would even consider provisioning Germans. One letter to Mussolini from an anonymous Roman worker (dated 27 April 1944) questioned why butchers in Rome favored Germans by giving them choice cuts of meat and leaving nothing for Italians?[114]

Prior to the war, in 1939–40, almost half of Italian exports were sent to Germany. In exchange for primary materials such as coal, 10 percent of Italy's annual wheat yield (6,500,000 quintals) was exported to Germany in 1942, and this amount increased throughout the war.[115] As a result of the Pact of Steel, Italy supplied Germany with rice, tobacco, cheese, fruits, and vegetables while Germany provided no food for Italy. German occupation forces only aggravated the situation. A teacher from Abruzzo noted how the German occupation force 'intercepted everything and sent it to Germany while avoiding the law. They have sent back egg yolks in large bottles (they probably threw away the egg whites). In Abruzzo, someone found an entire ham in the pack of a fallen German soldier. The population is irritated by the exportation of goods to Germany, "they are eating away at Italy" (they say).'[116] Citizens also complained that German soldiers bought up baskets and cartons of food at local marketplaces, procured the whitest bread and the finest pasta, and did not seem at all deprived or hungry. Numerous letters sent to Mussolini described the indignities of German occupation with incredulity, as one letter from a group of Milanese war veterans described: 'In Milan the life of a worker's or public servant's family is very difficult because of food shortages and high prices. After the German occupation, all the food that Milan normally receives has disappeared ... the citizens have never, ever thought that the German people, friends and allies, would treat Italians in the same manner that they treat their enemies ... why are the Germans allowed to requisition everything to our detriment?'[117]

As food disappeared across the Italian border, the population faced increasingly severe shortages. Although it is difficult to determine with any degree of certainty how much Italians consumed, given the lack of statistical studies during the war, ISTAT figures confirm that in the years prior to the war (1936–39), the availability of food declined consistently. In terms of nutritional level of popular diet, Italy lagged behind other European nations (Great Britain, France, Germany, Holland, Spain, Yugoslavia, and Bulgaria) in terms of caloric intake and the consumption of fats, oils, and milk. In terms of caloric availability, ISTAT traced an average decline from 2,652 calories per day in 1936, to 1,733 calories per day in 1945.[118] By 1944, in Nazi-occupied Italy, bread was unavailable for days in many cities and fat rations dropped to 20 grams *per month* in some rural areas. Civilians suffered the most. As the head of the province of Milan reported in February 1945, the availability of goods was totally insufficient because of transportation problems.

The 'small quantities of food that have arrived are enough for the armed forces, and for worker's caféterias and cooperatives. There is almost nothing left over for any civilian who does not frequent one of these caféterias or cooperatives.'[119] Minister of Agriculture Edoardo Moroni repeatedly voiced these concerns to Mussolini throughout 1944 and 1945, begging the *Duce* to request at least a half-million quintals of cereal and 300 transport trucks from Germany so that cities could be adequately provisioned for the year 1944. As seen in his correspondence, Moroni was bitter about Italy's subordinate position to Germany. He complained that every time Italy received a small amount of cereal from Germany or Hungary, they had to send rice, corn, cheese, or sugar to Germany. Meanwhile, he reminded Mussolini, German soldiers received a meat ration of 750 grams per week.[120]

Mussolini failed to act on any requests and Moroni became increasingly frustrated in his role as the Minister of Agriculture and the director of provisioning. Moroni also complained to Mussolini about German demands on his Ministry – specifically, German requests for data and information throughout the summer of 1944. Germans dictated their own rationing rules to Moroni, stipulating extra rations for categories such as workers who refused to strike and doctors who treated a certain number of patients per month. All of this struck Moroni as ridiculous, given that most cities had enough bread available for only the next twenty-four hours. Moreover, Moroni wondered, how could Germans believe that '50 grams of bread here and there would silence the political demands of workers?' Moroni found the German distrust of Italians to be humiliating and frustrating, given that initially, Italians were promised German assistance with provisioning.[121] Indeed, Italians were in a difficult situation. Trade between the two countries was clearly advantageous to Germany, and the German occupation forces worked to direct the Italian economy to ensure continued access to Italian supplies.

The combination of policy failures and German exploitation spelled disaster for Italy. Per capita rationing levels in Italy were among the lowest in all of Europe, comparable to occupied Poland's during the war (see Table 4.2). Based on these figures, fascist Italy fell into the category of occupied territory rather than political ally of Nazi Germany. Certainly, German occupiers had only contempt for Italians during the war. Germans in charge of conscripted Italian labor repeatedly noted

Table 4.2 Calories available per capita, through rationed foods:

	1941	1942	1943	1944
Italy	1010	950	990	1065
Germany	1990	1750	1980	1930
Poland	850	1070	855	1200

Shepard B. Clough, *The Economic History of Modern Italy*, p. 278.

124 · *Garlic and Oil*

that Italian workers were not as useful as workers from other countries.[122] Josef
Goebbels asserted that Italy never wanted to be a great power: 'Old Hindenburg
was right when he said of Mussolini that even he would never be able to make
anything but Italians out of Italians.'[123] Mussolini himself shared this contempt,
given that his much hoped-for transformation of the Italian population had not
transpired. Mussolini was disappointed in Italy's military performance in Ethiopia
(he disliked the open fraternizing between Italians and Ethiopians), and he
despised the intellectual and middle classes, who were rotten with 'cowardice,
laziness (and) love of the quiet life.'[124] During the brief life of the Italian Social
Republic, Mussolini became even more determined to reignite the fascist revolution, to transform what he called the 'inferior category ... physically and mentally
below par, blind, lame, toothless, feeble-minded, shirkers, people lacking in some
quality.'[125] This frustration with the Italian character, characterized as it was by
racial terminology, opened the door for German exploitation.

Thus, over the course of the decade from 1935 to 1945, Mussolini gambled
away the Italian population so that he could fight his parallel war in the
Mediterranean. The key to understanding the peculiar nature of fascist racial politics lies with the situation endured by the civilian population. Italians were
deprived of the necessities for maintaining even a minimal standard of living. The
regime's population policies made it perfectly clear that Mussolini and his ministers saw the Italian population as a strategic asset. In the context of total war, this
asset became an expendable resource. The regime's preoccupation with food availability, while not the determining factor of this racism, certainly enables us to see
how control over life processes facilitated a way of thinking about populations that
ultimately can be termed racist. It is perhaps difficult to characterize this political
behavior as racist, given the current meanings attached to race and race hatreds.
Racism, however, seems a more apt label than populationism because of its historical contingency. Although the ultimate goal of these policies and ideas was to
control and manipulate the population, words like *razza* and *stirpe* were used as
purposeful scientific terms. These words implied the cultivation or improvement of
the Italian population from *within*. When the Italian population repeatedly failed
to rise to Mussolini's expectations, it became, in his eyes, an expendable resource
for military gain through strategic alliance with Hitler.

The developing lines of food policies confirm this new direction in population
policy: the regime's policy of national austerity trumped all other plans for
improving the health of the population through a more nutritious diet. Although
Italian fascism never assumed the genocidal racism of German Nazism, its population policies must be considered as unique aspects of fascist rule. In other words,
population policies, in conjunction with food policies and racial policies, constitute a particular vision of fascist statecraft that warrants careful consideration out
from under the shadow of Nazi racism or wartime exigencies. As we have seen,

Mussolini's drive toward self-sufficiency, as misguided as it was, was a consistent force throughout the regime's existence, and had considerable impact on consumption habits and popular health. Food's increased political significance, and its decreased availability, enable us to better define fascist authoritarianism.

Conclusion

Although the fascist regime promoted and engendered myriad discussions about food and everyday life, its ultimate success turned on this question of whether or not the regime could satisfy consumer demands and needs. Fascist policies failed for a number of reasons. The most obvious reason was the regime's neglect of agricultural production while pursuing a policy of restricted imports. Moreover, the regime failed to protect Italian consumers despite numerous policies that were supposed to satisfy them. For example, early wartime policies favored the control of retail food distribution with the express intent of appeasing consumer anxiety. By the end of the war, however, the regime refused to adopt political prices for food staples and could not provide even minimal sustenance through rationing. German occupiers saw the glaring deficiencies of fascist policy very clearly. German Ambassador Rudolf Von Rahn commented in correspondence of April 1944 that Italian salaries and prices were completely out of step with those in the rest of Europe. Moreover, Italians failed to see that economic self-sufficiency 'has become an absolutely impossible economic structure.'[126] Under fascism, food and its consumption were supposed to tie individuals firmly to the destiny of the nation. Here the regime succeeded admirably, given that near starvation followed in the wake of fascism's political and military defeat.

Obviously, fascism's failure to provide enough food for the Italian population did not mean that the fascist regime had little impact on Italian food habits and the national cuisine. Fascism's impact was both negative and positive. The negative impact is easier to determine from the contents of this chapter; Italians faced near starvation because of the regime's calculated policies that prioritized self-sufficiency over health. The positive impact is perhaps more difficult to discern based on the wartime experience alone, and must therefore, be seen in the context of postwar developments in the Italian popular diet. By constantly evoking the necessity of austerity and restraint, fascist propaganda turned these qualities into positive attributes of *Italianità*. Although scientists and domestic economists may have criticized the regime for failing to provide enough food, they chose to work within the consumption limits set by fascism, adjusting nutritional recommendations or recipe ingredients to suit economic circumstance. Thus, the predominance of grains and produce over meat and fats; the simplicity of preparation technique; and the pride in regional cooking became the foundations of Italian cooking in the 1920s and 1930s.

After the Second World War ended, Italians were only too happy to break with fascism, which represented hardship, but the food habits formed earlier on in the fascist years lingered. The immediate postwar years (1945–46) were the most difficult ones, and even in the early 1950s many Italians wondered if they would ever get enough to eat. As much as (the lack of) food symbolized popular grievances, food also represented the desire for a new beginning and later, the discovery of a national cuisine. However, dreams of plenty were deferred until Italy's economic reconstruction. In 1957, Italy's participation in the world market flooded the country with goods while the nation's economic miracle provided consumers with full employment, jobs, and growing discretionary incomes. At last, the average number of calories and nutrients consumed, per person, exceeded international scientific standards. Surprisingly, such dramatic improvements in living standards did not lead automatically to dramatic changes in the types of foods consumed. Rather, Italian consumers chose to eat more of the foods they had always consumed, with a few minor changes in consumption practice. For example, Italians may have purchased more processed foods and American goods like Coca-Cola and McDonald's hamburgers, but the Italian diet proved remarkably resistant to dramatic change. What accounted for this lack of change? Certainly, old habits learned during periods of scarcity in the 1930s and 1940s partially explain this phenomenon. How Italians chose to appropriate and accommodate the imperative to save is significant because certain habits became deeply embedded in cultural practice and were therefore difficult to discard. As the next chapter will argue, economic change alone does not explain Italian food habits; political and cultural influences continued to shape the contemporary Italian diet as a social practice resistant to dramatic change.

–5–

The Challenge of Abundance: Italy 1945–1960

The Second World War may have exposed all the shortcomings of the fascist regime, but the pressing needs of reconstruction left little time or resources for delving into past mistakes. The Alto Commissariato dell'Alimentazione (High Commissariat for Food Provisioning) struggled to provide food for millions of needy citizens in the face of dismal harvests, rising unemployment, rampant inflation, and social unrest.[1] Fortunately, the allied occupation forces were more cooperative than their German predecessors had been, but the Commissariat was unable to contain the nation's material crisis until well into the 1950s. Prefects complained bitterly about the lack of food while individuals, organizations, and communities petitioned the Commissariat for assistance.[2] Local food shortages, combined with inflation and unemployment, aggravated a dire situation in the first few years after the war. Social-scientific surveys indicated that in 1947, Roman citizens subsisted on an average of less than 2,000 calories per day.[3] By 1952, however, Italians consumed as much food as they did prior to the war (1938), and by the mid-1950s, they experienced dramatic reversals in their living standards. Household expenditure on food dropped below 50 percent of families' annual incomes; food imports increased dramatically, accounting for one-third of all the nation's imports; and Italians tried new foods like Coca-Cola and Ritz crackers. The pace of economic change was staggering. Italy went from an agricultural to an industrial to a post-industrial society in the span of a few decades.[4] The high standard of living created by Italy's economic revival meant that, for the first time, the majority of Italians had the freedom to choose what they wanted to eat. At last, Italians entered the land of plenty.

Initially Italians experimented with their newfound consumer freedoms. Cocktails, thick steaks, and complicated desserts were all the rage in Italian restaurants and middle-class homes in the 1950s. Consumption habits flexed to incorporate this new prosperity but, ultimately, they changed little in terms of the kinds of foods consumed and popular food habits. Housewives still made a hearty *minestra* to satisfy their families. Consumers purchased more of the foods they consumed prior to the war but did not alter the content or structure of their daily meals. The Italian food industry reinforced existing habits by concentrating on producing and marketing the foods characteristic of the Mediterranean diet: pasta, olive oil, tomatoes, wine, and bread. Renunciation and thrift were upheld as national values even in the midst of abundance. Regional differences in food preparation were impor-tant to understanding the nation's cuisine. And despite trade liberalization and the threat of Americanization, Italian food habits remained largely impervious to outside influences.

The decades after the Second World War provided Italians with ample opportu-nity to act out their fantasies of abundance by adopting new trends and attitudes about food and its consumption. Italians chose an eclectic approach to consumer abundance, combining past traditions of austerity with newfound consumer free-doms. Consumers purchased and ate more meat, but they likely prepared the meat according to a recipe from Ada Boni's *Il talismano della felicità* (1925) or even Pellegrino Artusi's *La scienza in cucina e l'arte di mangiar bene* (1891). In part, this eclecticism was a response to rapid economic change or what some might define as a process of modernization. Yet this chapter argues that the national cuisine forged in the decades after the war is about more than resistance to rapid change, although resistance and nostalgia certainly influenced ways of thinking about food. Rather, this chapter argues that contemporary Italian food habits were the product of ways of thinking *about* food that were conditioned in part by the political circumstances of the past. Indeed, the cumulative effect of state interven-tion throughout the twentieth century reinforced a cuisine of scarcity. Thus, a generation of Italians tended to see postwar possibilities through the lens of fascist and wartime austerity. Moreover, Italians thought *through* food about changes in family, work, and leisure structures in the years of postwar affluence. After 1945, Italians drew their inspiration from familiar habits and foods, adjusting them accordingly to the new circumstances of abundance.

The eclecticism Italians maintained toward matters of food consumption mirrored a political and cultural eclecticism that characterized the postwar period. After the war, cold-war politics replaced fascist dictatorship with the powerful Christian Democratic Party dominating national politics for several decades after defeating the Communist Party in 1948. Dramatic economic changes fueled by Marshall Plan funds (two billion dollars between 1943 and 1947) and, later, European economic integration spurred hope for a better life for more Italians. The period between 1951 and 1967 witnessed Italy's largest labor migration in history, with over 2.5 million rural Italians leaving for cities in Italy and elsewhere in western Europe. Rural Italy became significantly less important: agricultural employment dropped from 8 to 2 million over the course of fifty years while agri-cultural production comprised only 5 percent of the Gross Domestic Product by 1990.[5] Italians experienced social change through the continuing class struggle, the battle for women's rights, and the widening gap between generations, all of which suggested divided allegiances along new lines.

After discarding the fascist past, Italians sought political and cultural paradigms more in sync with their new lifestyles and habits. There was, for example, a great deal of enthusiasm for American goods and American style, but some were reluctant to embrace a lifestyle so heavily endorsed and promoted by the Christian Democrats as a model for national and global development. Although the left (in particular the Communist Party) established a credible legacy of anti-fascism, the Soviet lifestyle was hardly a viable alternative to a world of television programs, consumer durables, and gleaming kitchen appliances. Skepticism about either lifestyle produced eclecticism among Italians who, for example, purchased cheap paperbacks of Marxist literature and frequented Hollywood movies. In many respects, postwar prosperity was a very deliberate process. Consumer culture was one way to reconcile the competing layers that constituted and challenged Italian identity in a new world.[6]

Postwar food habits reflected a similar combination of impulses, desires, and sensibilities. This chapter explains postwar food habits by discussing how Italians made the transition between the austere past and their current conditions of abundance. As expected, the Italian state played a significant role in facilitating this transition, but it did so indirectly, opting to liberalize trade as one way to even out inequalities in consumption habits. After Italy joined the European Economic Community in 1957, food imports became second only to oil imports. Although its role was greatly diminished in the aftermath of fascism, the government monitored food-consumption habits as a measure of democracy's success. Trade liberalization and high wages sparked a change in consumption patterns, but curiously, the change was not all that dramatic, at least not because Italians purchased new types of foods. In fact, Italian consumers purchased more of the foods they had always consumed – bread, pasta, oil, wine, and fresh produce – and they prepared them in familiar ways. Meanwhile, domestic and international scientific opinion noticed and approved of the Mediterranean Diet in the 1960s. Although Italy maintained a homogenous consumption practice largely immune to outside influence, fear of dramatic change fed nostalgia for the simple foods of Italy's past. In fact, the discovery of Italian cuisine happened first in Italy, with a growing interest in the nation's regional heritage and artisanal food production. This discovery of Italian cuisine eventually spread in popularity around the globe, but in Italy, nostalgia for an imagined past was politicized as a national form of resistance to social and political change. Given Italy's history of an uneven and unpredictable economy, it is not surprising that political and cultural influences continued to shape consumption patterns even after the economy improved so remarkably.

The State's New Concerns

The new Italian government distinguished itself from the fascist regime in every conceivable way regarding food issues. Fascism left no legacy to the postwar government in terms of food policies. Food still held great symbolic value, but social equality and health replaced nationalism and self-sufficiency as key governmental concerns. Certainly the most immediate postwar concern was to ensure that millions of needy Italians had enough food to survive and perform the work required of them. Unlike the liberal regimes of the post-First World War era, the government took up the task without hesitation. The experience of providing for so many in need and the new orientation toward social equality meant that early on, the government took up the study of food consumption habits as important markers of the nation's economic and social progress. After 1945, the government sponsored numerous surveys of living standards in order to evaluate popular nutritional levels. Analyzing the persistence of Italy's two diets was crucial to building a more secure postwar democracy. Observers found that the tale of two diets continued primarily along regional lines. The rapidly developing economy did not benefit all citizens equally, although the postwar governments tried to ensure greater access to more food for all Italians.

By rejecting the fascist past and embracing trade liberalization, the government pushed the nation in dramatic new directions. On the one hand, more Italians ate better. Improved food habits became a significant barometer of social equality and economic success in Italy. Consequently, pockets of poverty and misery were all the more noticeable. On the other hand, the government's policy of trade liberalization resurrected old nationalist fears and anxieties that touched upon the relationship between food habits and national identity. Would Italians embrace American (or French or German or British) foods? Would food preparation change in response to changes in the types and amount of foods available for purchase? State intervention did more than prevent starvation after the war. Interventions changed lifestyles and attitudes toward food and eating. The postwar state played less of a direct role in people's lives but it was no less significant a role.

It is difficult to speak of a coherent postwar food policy because so much of the official activity between 1945 and 1950 consisted of responding to provisioning crises and shortages as they happened. The Alto Commissariato dell'Alimentazione (High Commissariat for Food Provisioning) was simply overwhelmed by requests for additional food supplies to prevent starvation or malnutrition. In addition, citizens, organizations, and communities asked the state for favors or special rationing status. To cite but a few examples: in 1948 a group of nuclear physicists from the Valle d'Aosta requested additional fats and sugars so they could adapt to high altitudes; Italy's surviving Jewish communities requested additional supplies of flour to make Passover matzo; and the Italian Society of Dog Lovers requested broken rice to feed their purebred dogs. Requests for extra food reflected the desire of many to get back to normal as well as the hope of launching the new, more consumerist-oriented Italy. For example, prefects and hoteliers from northern regions requested additional rations and supplies so tourists could have decent meals. Often, the Commissariat had few resources to furnish these requests and forwarded them to the appropriate SEPRAL office.[7] Meanwhile, SEPRAL offices struggled to manage these requests, supply adequate food to institutions (hospitals, anti-tuberculosis clinics, and hospices for the elderly), and attend to local crises.

The impact of official intervention (local and national) was measurable in terms of what did *not* happen. Italians did not experience severe malnutrition after the war, thanks largely to a local and private provisioning network that fed millions of hungry Italians through soup kitchens, school lunch programs, and factory canteens. The most successful provisioning organizations were the Enti Comunali di Assistenza or ECA (Comunal Assistance Boards), which ran the *cucine popolari*, soup kitchens where food was distributed free or at cost. In addition, the ECA distributed money, food parcels, clothing, and medicine. Controlled by the state and organized by individual *comuni*, the ECA provided help to millions of citizens after the war. Even as late as 1959, an estimated 4.3 million people across the nation still received assistance that year from a local board.[8] On the national level, the Commissariat provided food packages for the unemployed, the disabled, and pensioners. These packets consisted of pasta, rice, sugar, and cornmeal (in the north) or beans (in the south). Occasionally, additional packets of dried soup mix or dried vegetables were distributed.[9] Non-Italian relief organizations also provided assistance. UNRRA (the United Nations Relief and Rehabilitation Administration) negotiated a series of accords with Italy in 1945, appropriating over US$50 million to help the needy and to assist Italian children. The International Refugee Organization fed the thousands of Croats, Slavs, and Orthodox Russians in the northern and central regions of the country, many of whom later emigrated to Argentina, Venezuela, Canada, and South Africa.[10]

Many Italians purchased food and meals in factory canteens, public dining halls, company stores, and consumer cooperatives. The Catholic Church (through the Pontificia Opera di Assistenza, or POA), local SEPRAL offices, and private corporations organized and implemented most of these ventures. Some institutions provided cheap or free food for the poor. The POA's *refettori del Papa* (the Pope's dining halls), for example, provided free food during the winter months for the indigent. Meals at soup kitchens left much to be desired in this climate of postwar austerity. Giorgio Almirante, leader of the post-fascist Movimento Sociale Italiano, recalled eating 'a *minestra* with a few pieces of pasta or some kernels of rice; one quarter – I said one quarter – of a hardboiled egg with a leaf – I said a leaf – of salad and a small roll.'[11] An increasing number of institutions supplied middle-class Italians (especially government employees) with low-cost meals and snacks. These canteens were more successful in northern Italy than in the south, where efforts to feed workers were disorganized and improperly funded. After the war, an estimated two to three million workers ate lunch in factory canteens.[12] Canteen meals were popular among workers because they were substantial, consisting of a pasta or soup course followed by a second course of cheese, eggs, or meat. The availability of canteen lunches stretched family budgets; the heartiest eaters were properly provisioned at work for minimal cost.

Collective feedings were not new to Italians, but in the past these efforts had met with limited success because citizens preferred to consume food at home. Partly as a result of numerous efforts made by the fascist regime and partly out of necessity during wartime, these forms of 'dining out' became more accepted social practice after 1945. As Giuseppe Aliberti, parliamentary senator and historian of medicine at the University of Rome commented, 'The war – started a welfare movement that, in the postwar period, became widespread through the construction of canteens, which represented great progress in terms of food consumption for the masses.'[13] Aliberti spoke of progress in the nutritional sense. Workers and schoolchildren received between 40 and 100 grams of protein per day from institutional meals and snacks. Children's food programs also showed promising results in terms of promoting childhood development and growth. The Catholic Church's summer camps provided children with a diet of 3000 calories per day, including 84–115 grams of protein, depending on height and weight. The city of Milan fed schoolchildren supplemental snacks of between 700 and 1,400 calories. The National Nutrition Institute (Istituto Nazionale della Nutrizione) carefully studied these initiatives and found that they contributed dramatically to good health and steady development among children, so much so that many studies concluded that postwar feedings might possibly reverse the effects of wartime malnutrition among children.[14]

These institutional feedings meant that millions of Italians became more accustomed to eating outside the home, whether in canteens, caféterias, and later, bars and cafés. Food represented changing social custom inasmuch as it represented a broader vision of popular welfare in the new Italy. Political parties were acutely aware of the significance of this symbolism. Left and right parties maintained social clubs, distributed food to the needy, and participated in discussions about state policy and nutrition. The relationship between food and party politics was nothing new: since Unification, local politicians bought votes with packets of pasta or cuts of meat. After 1945, the Christian Democratic Party promoted its ability to put food on Italy's tables, with the assistance of the United States. A poster from the infamous 1948 contest between Christian Democrat Alcide De Gasperi and Communist Palmiro Togliatti made the campaign's stakes perfectly clear, stating: 'Don't think that with Togliatti's speeches you'll be able to flavour your *pastasciutta*. All intelligent people will vote for De Gasperi because he's obtained free from America the flour for your spaghetti as well as the sauce to go with it.'[15] Food was still a potent barometer of political stability and social progress, and the Christian Democrats were content to live with aid from the United States. Their election slogan, *Pane, pasta, e lavoro* (Bread, pasta, and work) could be written on walls without the party's affiliation; voters readily understood the connection between cheap bread and Christian Democracy.[16]

Food consumption also represented a more equitable Italy and a vision of future prosperity. Indeed, the language of social justice permeated public debates about and inquiries into food-consumption levels. The vast majority of government and private inquiries into living standards focused on this issue by returning to regional and class differences in food consumption. Gone were the studies that assembled data based on average-man coefficients or the national availability of food. After the war, the Italian Republic recognized its new responsibility to promote equality, as the 1951–52 Parliamentary inquiry on poverty proposed: 'Still, Italy could appear to be a country without unemployment, but does it also appear, at the same time, to be prosperous? We believe we would answer this in the negative for the simple fact that the actual level of our population's average salary is much less than those from other economically developed nations to support any other conclusion.'[17] Nutritional levels became one way to measure whether the Republic delivered its promise of freedom and dignity for all citizens. This progressive vision was evident in the explosion of inquiries during this period, and in the government's efforts to address long-standing dietary deficiencies among populations of schoolchildren, southerners, and prisoners. Here, a few extra grams of sugar or meat were significant in that they brought health and dignity to the consumer.[18] Inquiries were conducted by governmental institutions such as the Istituto Centrale di Statistica (ISTAT), the Istituto Nazionale di Economia Agraria (INEA), and the Istituto Nazionale della Nutrizione (National Nutrition Institute), or through hospitals and university clinics.[19] Although scientific experts had made the connection between diet, mortality levels, and productivity since the nineteenth century, it was not until after the Second World War that the Italian government made a concerted effort to study this connection as a remediable problem.

Scientific inquiries and monographs focused on the impact of Italy's economic change both in terms of persistent dietary differences within Italy as well as the country's nutritional status in comparison to other industrialized nations.[20] Shortly after the war's end, in 1951, the Italian Parliament launched several inquiries into unemployment and poverty, and ISTAT supplied much of the statistical information regarding food consumption. For the poor, the unemployed, or those living on fixed incomes, postwar recovery was a long and grueling process. The results shocked many Italians, given that living conditions in the south in the 1950s were not much better than in the days of the Jacini inquiry of 1877. The 1951 inquiry found that poor and some working-class Italians did not consume meat or wine, except on holidays. Some of the poorest families in Southern Italy devoted almost three-quarters (73 percent) of their income to food, a figure reminiscent of nineteenth-century data on living standards.[21] Although a substantial number of individuals did not consume meat or wine on a regular basis (38.2 percent consumed meat on special occasions, 28.7 percent consumed wine on special occasions), the new diet of the poor contained substantial amounts of sugar and fat. Almost 20 percent of those surveyed consumed more than 40 grams of sugar daily, while fat consumption averaged 40 grams per day.[22]

The Inquiry Commission speculated that the poor consumed sugar and fat because these foods were cheap and livened up an otherwise drab diet. This new habit was a complete reversal of earlier times, when the poor assuaged their hunger with bread and little else. Members of the middle and upper classes consumed more meat and dairy products than members of the lower classes did. All classes consumed foods like sugar, coffee, produce, and wheat products.[23] The 1951 inquiry determined that although the middle and lower middle classes consumed fewer calories than did members of the working classes (including agricultural laborers), they consumed more meat and other animal proteins. Thus, the quality of diet was distinct from the quantity of food consumed. The data from the survey of 1,026 families in Grassano (Basilicata) is telling: agricultural day laborers consumed upwards of 3,200 calories per day, but consumed only 3 or 4 grams of animal protein, whereas state employees consumed only 2,500 calories, but consumed 16 grams of animal protein per day.[24]

Dietary differences between classes were sharper in the southern regions. In fact, north/south differences became more significant than class differences after the war, at least in terms of the scientific attention they received. The implementation of welfare and public-health programs (such as the spraying of DDT in swampy areas to eradicate malaria) combined with mass emigration out of the south led to improvements in public health and mortality levels there. It should be noted, however, that such improvements were relative to the situation in the north.[25] The Parliamentary Inquiry of 1951 found that southern regions and the islands lagged behind the northern and central regions in terms of total calories, animal proteins, and fats consumed (see Table 5.1).[26] The Inquiry Commission noted that in Abruzzo and Molise, 'The diet of the majority of this population consists of bread that is baked, sometimes in primitive ovens, in quantities sufficient for an entire week. This bread is made with a mixture of wheat and potato flour in order to conserve wheat.' And in observing rural Sardinians, 'Their innate sobriety and traditional frugality make their poor state of health physically tolerable.'[27]

Inquiries throughout the 1950s found that southern Italy lagged behind the north in terms of the amount of wine, sugar, and meat consumed. Many southern Italians reported consuming meat on Sundays (*carne della domenica*) or not at all.[28] One study by the National Nutrition Institute conducted in 1956 contrasted a high of 3,760 calories per day consumed in Modena (Emilia-Romagna) with a caloric low of 2,385 consumed in Cassino (southern Lazio). Citizens of Cassino consumed half the protein (and one-sixth the amount of animal proteins) of the *Modenese*.[29]

Table 5.1 Calories and Nutrients Consumed, 1951

	North	Center	South	Islands
Calories	2,657	2,642	2,273	2,138
Animal Proteins (gr.)	29	21	9	8
Fats (gr.)	74	71	47	42

Vol. 1 *Relazione Generale*, p. 91, Table 40.

ISTAT's inquiry into urban and suburban consumption patterns in 1953–54 revealed that while the gap between the northern and central regions had closed, the south and the islands still lagged behind in meat, milk, sugar, and beverage consumption.[30] Danilo Dolci's personal research into living conditions in 1950s Palermo found numerous respondents who survived by gathering snails, eels, wild herbs, and frogs from the surrounding countryside. One young man recalled how his neighbor's children went begging for the water used for boiling pasta; for the poor of Naples, little had changed since Matilde Serao chronicled their habits in 1884.[31] However, Dolci's efforts to draw attention to the plight of the poor (he also went on hunger strikes) reminds us of a long trajectory of left-reform concern with the diet of the poor and the working classes, stretching back to the days of *La Critica Sociale* and the Società Umanitaria.

Certainly, government officials were concerned about differentials in regional consumption patterns, living standards, and purchasing power. Domenico Miraglia, the General Director of the Alto Commissariato in 1951, cited a survey of regional capitals to emphasize regional differences: citizens in Lombardy consumed an average of 30.15 kilograms of meat per year whereas Sicilians consumed an average of 9.6 kilograms; citizens from Liguria consumed 21.1 kilograms of sugar per year while those in Basilicata consumed a mere 1.8 kilograms. Although Miraglia acknowledged that Italy was 'a land of bread and pasta,' he argued that such differences in consumption levels demonstrated a clear need for some form of state intervention. Miraglia recommended improving distribution, provisioning for the neediest Italians, and intensifying agricultural production schemes.[32]

The gap between north and south closed somewhat in the 1960s. An ISTAT survey of 1963–64 determined that in terms of nutrients consumed, southern Italians lagged behind northern Italians by only 4 grams of protein and 12 grams of fat per day. In terms of variety and cost of food, however, northern Italians continued to outspend, and out-eat, southern Italians, spending more money on food (especially animal proteins and beverages), although this sum occupied a smaller percentage of their annual incomes.[33] A study of fertility among Sicilian women in 1966 found that nutritional levels were inadequate for half the families studied. Only 20 percent of the families consumed meat daily while the majority

(40 percent of the families) consumed meat once or twice a month.[34] Another study from the mid-1960s found that instances of grave malnutrition were rare, but latent or sub-clinical malnutrition persisted, especially in southern Italy.[35] A 1967 study of over 94,000 children found that 'there are still geographic areas where there is clinical malnutrition. Along general lines, rural citizens are more malnour-ished than urban ones, and the communities on the periphery of the central-south regions are more malnourished than those in northern regions.'[36] More recent statistical analyses of consumption habits have reinforced the findings of postwar social scientists. For example, Carmela D'Apice's study of Italian consumption patterns traces persistent regional differences in food-consumption habits. Northern Italians spent more money than southern Italians on food and consumed more meat, milk, cheese, fruit, sugar, and fats. Southern Italians consumed more carbohydrates, fish, and dried legumes than northern Italians did. These differ-ences continued throughout the 1970s, although the caloric gap between north and south closed almost completely by the end of that decade (2,672 calories per day for the north and 2,644 calories for the south).[37]

In the midst of plenty, regional contrasts in food habits seemed all the more noticeable: pockets of poverty and malnutrition contradicted the newly created image of Italy as a society of *benessere*. The majority of social-science inquiries emphasized Italy's status as a nation still divided by consumption habits, even though many Italians were eating better than they did during the war. The slow pace of reform – particularly in the areas of housing, public transportation, and distribution mechanisms – aggravated postwar hardships among the poor and the working classes. What, if anything, was to be done to ensure that *all* Italians ate adequately? The persistence of poverty and malnutrition became a politically contentious issue after reconstruction. Left parties continually criticized the ruling Christian Democratic party for merely providing charity at Christmastime (*'la democrazia cristiana fa la parte della buona befana'*) and not attacking poverty more systematically.[38] The left pushed for the modernization of the food industry, the protection of Italian agriculture, and lower food taxes as ways to equalize consumption habits. The Christian Democratic Party deflected these criticisms about its economic policies by pointing to Italy's high living standards as repre-sentative of dramatic economic progress. Italy had reason to be optimistic, the Christian Democrats maintained, as years of forced sobriety and Malthusian worries gave way to new lifestyles, a smaller population, and high levels of personal consumption. The Christian Democratic orientation toward diplomatic and economic integration meant that Italy joined the European Economic Community (with the signing of the Treaty of Rome in 1957) with little hesitation. Trade liberalization had significant impact on popular consumption habits. As the next section details, some of the most dramatic shifts in food consumption occurred after Italy embraced new markets.

As part of this new economic orientation, Italy developed several profitable and specialized industries (metallurgy, chemical production, and small consumer goods) for export. Agricultural production also branched into specialization for export in the areas of wine, citrus, and olive production. There was no more official talk of meeting all the nation's needs with domestic production. After 1945, the Italian government explicitly rejected the fascist past in terms of food policy.[39] This rejection of autarky went hand in hand with the ruling Christian Democrats' orientation toward a distinctly American model for economic development that prioritized high levels of consumption, industrial specialization, and open markets. Despite the weak nature of Italian agricultural policy in the postwar era, food production doubled between 1950 and 1970, as yields per hectare increased dramatically, especially with regard to wheat crops and, to a lesser extent, grape crops and livestock production.[40] Italy exported goods like wine while importing nearly half of its meat requirements. In the case of crops like citrus, tomatoes, and other fresh produce, state intervention had little impact. The shortage of rural labor, when combined with protectionist measures, meant that certain crops with the potential to sell on the foreign markets languished instead (as was the case with sugar-beet crops).

Generally, the Italian government had little interest in developing agriculture. State intervention confronted rural poverty in order to preserve political order, but the direction of the national economy had little to do with agricultural production. By 1977, the State handed responsibility for agriculture over to regional governments. The new role of the state was oriented toward the needs of an industrial (and later, a post-industrial) society. After meeting the immediate needs of reconstruction, the Alto Commissariato dell'Alimentazione (High Commissariat for Food Provisioning) coordinated the availability of food with consumer needs and organized internal markets so as to ensure a more adequate regional distribution of food. The Commissariat also vowed to fight fraud and adulteration within the food industry while supporting nutritional research and consumer-education efforts through institutions like the National Nutrition Institute. These tasks were seen as critical to the implementation of a modern food policy that balanced the needs of consumers with a rapidly developing economy.[41] Policy goals changed little over the course of the 1950s. In 1961, Domenico Miraglia, the Director of Provisioning, promised to coordinate production and imports with internal demand and to lower food prices. He also coordinated food distribution by preventing regional shortages, cracking down on fraud, and promoting technology within the food industry.[42] As food imports and consumption levels increased throughout the 1950s, the nation no longer viewed itself as one in need of intense assistance either from the Italian government or from foreign powers. Increasing salaries and reductions in food prices allowed nearly everybody to eat more food. At last, Italians entered the land of plenty.

The Land of Plenty

Italians struggled to come to terms with life in the new Italy, be it through participation in cold-war politics, the new consumerism, or any of the budding social movements. Not surprisingly, many Italians turned to food as a way to connect to the past and test out new possibilities in the era of economic transformation. There was, for example, a revival of interest in Pellegrino Artusi's recipes from the nineteenth century and a newfound fascination with cocktail parties and elaborate dinners for guests. After the initial provisioning crises of the postwar era, Italy's economic miracle provided consumers with more choice in terms of purchasing and preparation. Material constraints on diet eased considerably after Italy joined the European Economic Community and food imports swelled the market. High wages made dining out a more common occurrence while the rapid growth of the Italian food industry after 1945 offered a variety of prepared and preserved foods. Cultural constraints, however, were not as flexible, as many chose to continue purchasing familiar foods and maintaining established ways of preparing and presenting meals. This was the case despite the fact that Italians could now afford to purchase different kinds of foods. Italians may have entered the land of plenty, but it was strictly on their own terms.

A look at the statistical record of consumption habits illustrates the nature of these changes in consumption patterns. The most dramatic changes in consumption occurred in the late 1950s and reflected a steady improvement in living standards. Food-consumption levels followed the more general contours of the economic miracle, which reached its peak between the years 1958 and 1963.[43] The consumption of corn – the hallmark of poverty – decreased from an average of 22 kilograms per year in 1951–55 to only 7.7 kilograms by 1965–69. The consumption of tomatoes, citrus fruits, beef, veal, and poultry doubled and the consumption of coffee and sugar tripled over the course of the 1950s while the national average percentage of household income spent on food decreased from 43 to 37 percent (see Table 5.2).[44] For the first time, national demand for goods like meat, beverages (coffee, tea, and cocoa), and fats outpaced supply.

The most noticeable trend was that Italians ate more meat: beef, fish, rabbit, and chicken. Chicken became a dietary mainstay even after Italians could afford more expensive types of meat; domestic meat production more than doubled over the course of the 1950s.[45] Italians purchased meat despite its increasing cost. Although the price of meat rose over 280 percent between 1951 and 1970 (compared to a price increase of only 41 percent for cereals in the same time period), consumers simply allocated more of their food budget for meat, from 17.6 percent in 1951 to 27.1 percent by 1970.[46] When the cost of living increased (as it did in 1962–65), consumers substituted pork for more expensive beef and ate chicken when they could not afford pork.[47] Because salary increases outpaced the

Table 5.2 Foods Consumed by Italians after 1945

	1951–55	*1965–69*	*1971–73*	*1981–83*	*1992*
Corn	22.2	7.7	7.5	—	—
Tomatoes	19.6	40.1	41.5	49.8	57.7
Vegetables	72.9	107	91.5	108	101.7
Fresh Fruit	44.1	75	78.5	75	119.5
Citrus	11.9	25.6	33.2	33.1	50.8
Beef	8.2	21	25.4	25.2	25.9
Pork	3.8	8.5	12.5	21.6	28.8
Sugar	14.5	25.5	29.4	29.3	26.9

Vera Zamagni's calculations (based on various sources) in kilograms per year. Vera Zamagni, 'L'evoluzione dei consumi fra tradizione e innovazione,' in Alberto Capatti *et al.*, *Storia d'Italia*, Annali 13: *L'alimentazione* (Turin: Einaudi, 1998), p. 189.

cost of living between 1960 and 1975, however, most consumers did not need to make dramatic sacrifices in order to continue eating meat.[48] Although meat-consumption levels doubled between 1940 and 1970, the change only appears dramatic if we consider that meat consumption levels were so low prior to the Second World War. Moreover, the contours of the Mediterranean diet held firm. According to ISTAT figures, Italians consumed an average of 54.2 kilograms of meat in the year 1970, compared to 339 kilograms of fruit and vegetables or 185.6 kilograms of bread and pasta.[49] Scientific studies of popular diet revealed that increased meat consumption led to higher levels of fat consumption after the war, but total protein consumption actually decreased slightly.[50] Even though they could afford to do so, Italian consumers did not rush to consume a high-fat, high-protein diet, opting instead to maintain the nutritional balance in favor of carbo-hydrates and vegetable proteins (in the form of pasta, bread, and fresh produce).

Advice about what to eat urged a restraint very much in sync with previously established consumption habits. Popular books on nutrition and diet recommended an individual consumption level of 60–70 grams of protein, 50–70 grams of fat, 400–600 grams of carbohydrates, and 2,000–3,500 calories per day. Nutritionists still advocated a mixed diet (*alimentazione mista*) in order to ensure an adequate supply of vitamins and minerals. As the scientific community confronted the dietary changes brought on by economic change, they assessed the medical and social value of new habits and foods for consumers. Instead of worrying about the lure of '*il sensualismo alimentare*,' the Italian scientific community expressed a new confidence in the Italian diet, bolstered in part by growing international scien-tific support for a high carbohydrate, low-fat and low-protein diet.

This support took over a decade to materialize. In 1951, an EEC study of diet in western Europe ranked Italy and Greece among the lowest in the average consumption of meat, fats, milk, sugar, and potatoes. Italians consumed an average of 2,400 calories daily, the lowest in western Europe. (By way of comparison, Americans consumed an average of 3,800 calories per day, according to the same study.)[51] Immediately after the war, the international scientific community still evaluated the relationship between food and health based on the volume of food and nutrients consumed. More was better, especially more protein and fat. In the 1960s, however, an increasing number of scientists supported the guidelines set by the Food and Nutrition Board of the United States' National Research Council: 2,400 calories (for moderate labor), 70 grams of protein, and 90 grams of fat. These new recommendations reflected changes in labor and leisure patterns, as more people moved into white-collar work and a sedentary lifestyle. Moreover, as the international scientific community examined the problem of world hunger (with the formation of the United Nation's Food and Agriculture Organization [FAO], among other organizations), support for a maximum of calories and protein made less sense, given that 70 percent of the world's population consumed fewer than 2,400 calories a day. As further study elaborated the differences between the haves and the have-nots, scientific thinking about diet's impact on health shifted away from thinking about food in terms of the volume consumed and toward examining food's relationship to diseases and prevention.

Epidemiological studies from FAO and other organizations revealed which populations in the world lived longer and were less prone to developing diet-related diseases. Throughout the 1950s and 1960s, researchers focused on the traditional diets of the southern regions of the Western world, in particular Greece, Italy, Spain, Portugal, and southern France. The Italian diet in particular received a great deal of scientific and popular attention after the publication of Drs. Ancel and Margaret Keys' *Eat Well and Stay Well* in the United States in 1959. The Keys argued that a diet high in carbohydrates and low in protein and fat could prevent obesity and heart disease. They recommended simple Italian dishes like vegetable soup, risotto, polenta, salads, and wholegrain wheat bread. Meat consumption was limited to dishes that mixed small amounts of meat with other ingredients like vegetables or pasta.[52] After the publication of *Eat Well and Stay Well*, the Mediterranean Diet became a familiar term among scientists and consumers alike, although the health benefits of this diet were, and continue to be, debated.

Italian scientists and domestic economists advocated a simple diet. Cookbooks and popular nutrition books still counseled that the most nutritious foods were dried legumes, pasta, rice, bread, milk, and fresh produce. Authors recommended that legumes and vegetable proteins make up about two-thirds of the total protein consumed, with meat and animal sources accounting for one-third of total protein.[53] Cookbooks published immediately after the war reflected the maxim that one eats to live and doesn't live to eat (*si deve mangiare per vivere, non vivere per mangiare*). Recipes for dishes like lettuce soup, pasta with tomatoes and lard, and semolina pudding demonstrated that the ethic of cooking with little was still a necessity after the war.[54] Even the high-end culinary magazine *La cucina italiana* made few changes in its format or recipe offerings throughout the 1950s. Meals were still structured around a simple *minestra* followed by a main dish like meatballs or organ meat, salad, cheese, and fresh fruit or pudding. Indeed, the essential structure of the Italian meal changed little from previous decades. Women's advice books still counseled simple fare along with plenty of room-temperature liquids to facilitate digestion: 'the first meal should consist of milk with either coffee or chocolate with bread or *biscotti*, butter, marmalade or honey, cheese, fresh or stewed fruit, or cold meat. Lunch should consist of a *minestra*, meat, fish or eggs with a side dish of raw or cooked vegetables, dessert or fruit. Dinner should consist of soup, a plate of boiled or stewed meat or fish with a side dish of salad or cooked vegetables, dessert or fruit.'[55] Meal plans from cookbooks and culinary magazines resonated with suggestions from the fascist era. Culinary experts warned chefs for restaurants and *trattorie* to keep dishes simple and use only natural seasonings in order to preserve the Italian habit of simplicity.[56] Although culinary literature made reference to other cuisine and offered recipes for non-Italian foods, it did not embrace foreign cuisine or elaborate preparations. More subtle changes governed Italian foodways instead.

Chief among the changes was the increased availability and desirability of snack foods. The *merenda* was already an important snack for schoolchildren, but more Italians paused for a *spuntino*, a small snack (ice cream, crackers, or potato chips) consumed purely for pleasure outside the home. Beginning in the 1950s, the food industry developed and promoted snack foods for sale in cafés, bars, and mom-and-pop grocery stores. Throughout the 1950s the number of bars and cafés increased, indicating that Italians were getting used to the idea of consuming coffee, ice cream and other treats outside of the formal meal structure.[57] Sweets became particularly popular as snacks or desserts. Ready-made ice cream treats from Algida and Motta were available in bars and grocery stores while the diffusion of refrigerators made possible elaborate frozen and chilled desserts like *semifreddo* or *gelatina*. Perhaps the most popular sweet was Nutella, a chocolate-hazelnut spread. Nutella became a national institution after the war, as Italians acquired more money to spend on sweets. Originally, Nutella was conceived and marketed by the Ferrero chocolate company as a snack for children. A snack of Nutella transformed the more traditional *merenda* of bread and chocolate. Nutella was a creamy spread and thus, children had to consume both the bread and the chocolate, instead of throwing the bread away, as they sometimes did. Thus, chocolate functioned not as a treat but as a food (*alimento*) because it was consumed along with bread. After the war, even in the poorest villages in Southern Italy, children could go to the local store, bread in hand, for their *spalmata* of Supercrema or Cremalba (the official name of Nutella was not used until 1963); a light smear went for as little as five lire, a more generous portion cost 10 lire.

What started as a childhood tradition grew into a national trend. The spread was sold in reusable glass containers that became household fixtures and collectors' items. Print advertisements and television programs like *Carosello* encouraged consumers to try Nutella, and once they were hooked, consumers could redeem proofs of purchase for items like small toys, backpacks, and jackets. A recent history of Nutella argued that the food embodies a certain paradox. On the one hand, Nutella is a decadent chocolate spread. (One is tempted to consume it straight from the jar using a spoon or one's fingers.) Yet it was promoted as a nourishing food for children and it is packaged in reusable containers so as to lessen consumer guilt about its decadent nature.[58] Indeed, the history of the marketing of Nutella in part explains the peculiar history of Italy's entrance into a culture of abundance. Luxury goods like Nutella had to be introduced carefully to consumers. In the wake of the economic miracle, Italians had more money to spend on non-necessity items, but these items had to serve some other purpose.

The example of Nutella illustrates the extent to which the Italian food industry shaped consumer habit by emphasizing food's practical qualities. Italian food industries evolved in the postwar era to meet consumer demand. During the interwar period, food industries exported their products in order to make a profit. Companies like Buitoni and Perugina expanded operations to retail outlets in Paris and New York, where novelties like Buitoni's Spaghetti Bar in New York's Times Square (opened in 1939) met with great success. The companies' efforts to create a consumer base in Italy met with mixed results: domestic demand for chocolates and liquor fluctuated while the fascist regime discouraged methods of building consumer loyalty. (In 1937, for example, the Ministry of Finance banned consumer contests for prizes.) After 1945, however, food industries like Buitoni and Perugina went from companies with limited local activity and export to highly developed industrial concerns. At first, Italian consumers could not afford chocolates and other processed foods; these industries continued to export to the United States in order to stay afloat. In 1954, parliamentary debate on the Italian food industry noted how there '(e)xisted a permanent contradiction between what was offered and how much money one had to buy goods.'[59] At the time, the contradiction referred to the problem created by weak consumer demand. The situation changed rapidly as economic conditions improved throughout the country. Demand for chocolate, for example, doubled between 1953 and 1956.

Much of the food industry, organized as it was along traditional and artisanal lines, could not keep up with booming internal demand. Even as late as 1960, only 15 percent of the 25,000 flour-processing mills nationwide produced over 500 quintals per day; only 20 percent of the 1,100 pasta firms produced more than a hundred quintals per day. There were only 550 processing plants for rice, 600 firms for preserving vegetables, and 5,000 large dairy manufactures.[60] Moreover, food processing remained a regional enterprise: sweets and pasta (over 40 percent) were made in the north; olive oil, fruit preserves, and canned tomatoes were made in the south. Several companies (Barilla, Buitoni, Perugina, Ferrero, and later SME International) did achieve national, then international, prominence through programs of investment and modernization starting in the 1950s. Buitoni, for example, had formed the International Buitoni Organization, expanding into prepared *minestre*, fruit juices, and melba toast by the late 1950s. In 1969, Buitoni joined with Perugina, expanding production and markets as far away as Kenya, Mexico, and Guatemala.[61] The uneven development of the processed-food industry illustrates the specific nature of Italy's dietary progress after the war. That is, several of the larger companies diversified production, expanded markets, and achieved national recognition, but the majority of food-processing firms remained small, artisanal, and local.

Many products bearing different brand names were introduced and marketed to apprehensive consumers. No longer a luxury item, baby food helped define child-hood as a distinct stage of life. Consumers were inundated with advertising copy for Cirio jams and jellies, Buitoni pasta, Ritz crackers, Knorr soup mix, Pavesini cookies, and Simmenthal canned meats. These products were sold as part of the modern Italian lifestyle, as important to have as a Fiat refrigerator or a Siemens vacuum cleaner. In order to foster brand-name association food industries gave away small items (pins, pencils, calendars) and encouraged consumers to collect proofs of purchase (*punti*) for items like a tablecloth or a set of placemats. The popular television program *Carosello* (1957–75) reinforced the importance of brand names with short programs where brand-name goods were incorporated into story lines. *Carosello* introduced many Italian families to the world of mass consumption, becoming a national institution as millions of young children were sent to bed after the program was over. Print advertisements in magazines also directed Italian consumers toward products like Barilla pasta: 'seven boxes of seven different shapes of Barilla pasta comprise a week's meals for the entire family.'[62] Some of the foods heavily marketed under fascism were not as well advertised after the war. Although the National Rice Board still promoted rice consumption, its straightforward advertising copy ('Don't lose your head – there's always a plate of rice') paled in comparison with splashy advertisements and clever marketing techniques for processed foods.

New products were marketed first to the middle class, a population that increased steadily in size and created its own cultural and consumer ethos in the postwar era. Magazines like *La cucina italiana* and *Casabella*, roadmaps to middle-class status, displayed lavish photos of new townhouses, exotic vacation destinations, and ideal household pets. Food played a critical role in creating this new lifestyle. Culinary magazines featured sections on entertaining, including how to mix cocktails like martinis, manhattans, whiskey sours, or Italian versions like the *Negroni* (vermouth, bitters, gin, and seltzer) or the *Americano* (vermouth, bitter Campari, angostura bitters, lemon, and seltzer). Cookbooks and magazines featured more recipes for meat dishes and more recipes for international dishes – Chinese soups, French sauces, Indian curries – for family and guests. Entertaining at home was an important feature of middle-class life, as evidenced by the resurgence in popularity of books on manners (*galateo*). Such books instructed readers not to talk with their mouths full or cut bread with a knife; they also provided tips for what to serve to guests for which occasions.

The new middle class ate out. Dining out in restaurants and *trattorie* became a regular event for many Italians in the years of the economic miracle. Establishments across the country offered more sophisticated dishes made with meat and other rich ingredients. For a while, meat consumption made up for the deprivations suffered under fascism. As one food expert recently explained, meat eating became a way of exorcising, or at least making up for, 'centuries of hunger.'[63] In this respect, Italians had a lot of lost time to make up for. In Milan, patrons could order turkey stuffed with minced veal, sausage, giblets, ham, chestnuts, onions, apples, shallots, truffles, grated cheese, and chopped egg. Or they could try a dish called *Messicani*: rolls of thinly sliced veal filled with chopped veal, ham, pork, breadcrumbs and parmigiano cheese, cooked in butter and served with gravy. Restaurant menus offered a veritable orgy of meat dishes. Even the humble chicken was prepared with a flourish: at *Al Pappagallo* in Bologna, the signature dish was 'chicken, on a stuffed tomato, covered with *sauce blanche*, flavored with white truffles, and garnished with purèed potatoes, from which sprout the wings of potato chips.'

Dining out also meant the opportunity to sample Italy's regional cuisine. A variety of regional dishes became a standard offering at restaurants, so that in Syracuse, Sicily, at the *Ristorante dell'Orologio*, diners could choose from *zampone e cotecchino con lenticchie* (Modenese sausages served with lentils), *mozzarella in carrozza* (fried mozzarella cheese sandwiches from Naples), and *bistecche di manzo ai ferri* (beefsteak prepared Florentine style).[64] In the more humble *trattorie*, it was not unusual to find *pizza al forno, spaghetti al pomodoro*, or *zuppa pavese* (consommé with poached eggs, fried bread, and grated cheese) on the menu, despite the fact that the dishes represented diverse regions across Italy. Certainly, restaurateurs consciously shaped a 'national' cuisine for the enjoyment of tourists. Elizabeth David's first edition of *Italian Food* in 1954 regretted the postwar homogenization of restaurant offerings by cooks and waiters; 'So convinced are these gentlemen that foreigners will accept only spaghetti in tomato sauce, to be followed by a veal cutlet, that the traveler, unless of an unusually determined nature, gives in over and over again, and finally returns home with the conviction that there is nothing else to be had in the whole country.'[65] The universal quality of this trend, however, suggests that regional dishes were intended for tourists and Italians alike, as Italians were introduced to regional cuisine in their own neighborhoods.

After 1945, more chefs and cooks offered a tour of Italy as a menu standard: *risotto alla milanese, risi e bisi* (rice and peas from the Veneto region), *pesto* (from Liguria), *bistecca alla fiorentina, spaghetti amatriciana* (from Lazio), and *pasta al pomodoro* (from Catania). Many of the regional specialties offered at restaurants throughout Italy were simple: rice and peas, or pasta with tomato sauce. They stood in sharp contrast to – and perhaps provided the culinary antidote to – rich meat dishes offered up at fancier restaurants. The gastronomic guides published by the *Touring Club Italiano*, along with numerous published tourist guides, indicate that regional cuisine became standard after 1945 (although some restaurants offered a variety of regional dishes as early as the 1920s).[66]

Restaurant menus mixed the old and the new as well as the elegant and the austere. Italian food habits continued to reflect the contradictions of postwar prosperity long after the immediate provisioning crises were over. Consequently, consumers saw no contradiction between eating a juicy steak and sipping wine out of a recycled Nutella glass, although they would not necessarily do so at the same time. Years of going without, along with a nostalgia for an imagined past of simple abundance, influenced consumer habits. Ultimately, the past would prove difficult to discard; food habits tended to reflect a culinary conservatism. Women's magazines were full of splashy advertising copy for new products but suggested menus remained the same: *tagliatelle* in broth, meatballs, salad, cheese, fruit. Even the upscale *La cucina Italiana* carried features on shopping economically, checking market prices, using rabbit fur, and preparing tripe (*La trippa: nutriente ed economica*).[67] A popular contest from 1959 challenged women to feed a family of five for under 1,000 lire. The winning entry came in at 810 lire and consisted of grated carrots, semolina *gnocchi*, meatballs, spinach, and baked apples, along with bread and wine.[68]

Menu plans and recipes evoked conditions of austerity rather than affluence, even as late as the 1960s. Practice mirrored prescription, as social-scientific studies from the 1950s and 1960s remarked that the essential structure of meals changed little, whether consumers were *contadini* or bourgeois. One study from Padua, conducted in 1958–59, reported that rural workers consumed bread with coffee and milk every morning, and at noon, a *minestra* for the first course, followed by a meat or cheese dish and a side dish of vegetables. Dinner was a lighter version of lunch. Although the *contadini* consumed more meat, wine, and fresh vegetables than they did in the years immediately after the war, the structure of their meals remained unaltered, as did their preference for uncomplicated dishes.[69]

The decades of the 1950s and 1960s fostered seemingly contradictory trends in consumer behavior. Although there was a tremendous increase in private consumption levels as Italians tested the limits of the new consumerism, there was also heightened awareness of continuing inequalities between north and south, and between rich and poor. Italians were able to experiment with more elaborate dishes and foods, yet they also clung to the traditional *minestra* and the simple breakfast of bread and coffee. Postwar lifestyles meant freedom and excitement in the form of Vespa scooters or dining out, but they also made Italians anxious. Catholic and Marxist subcultures reasoned that the new consumerism did not solve the nation's social problems, and more broadly, Italians wondered if they were losing something by adopting such high levels of consumption.[70] Once again, Italians worked through their anxieties by talking about, preparing, and consuming food. Italians may have pieced together an eclectic acceptance of the new economy and the new consumerism, but at the same time they struggled to commemorate the foods and dishes they lost as a consequence of economic change. The word 'lost' is perhaps an inappropriate one, given the history of Italian cuisine. After all, did Italians realistically desire to go back to the traditions of the late nineteenth century or life under fascism? Undoubtedly, nostalgia for past culinary traditions was a nostalgia for an imagined past.

Redefining Italian Cuisine

In the decades after 1945, Italian consumers struggled to define and preserve the traditions and foods considered characteristically Italian. National pride in Italian cuisine was nothing new; the fascist regime made this pride the ideological foundation of its food policies. Throughout the 1950s, however, Italians turned to food as a way of understanding regional traditions and folklore. Local food festivals (the *sagra*, *fiera*, and *festa*) became extremely popular and were catalogued for tourists and gourmands in numerous guides and books. Festivals commemorating the grape and chestnut harvests were the most popular, followed by festivals for wine or some type of sweet. Even the more unusual festivals (such as the festival of trout with polenta in Bedonia or the mullet festival in Ortona) experienced a revival of interest coincident with the publication of guides to food festivals and the promotion of such festivals by citizens and local government.[71] Interest in the rustic peasant cooking of the past flourished throughout Italy. Lowly peasant dishes such as *bagna cauda* in Piedmont (an olive-oil fondue) became fashionable among the affluent; the simple dish of pasta *aglio e olio* (with garlic and oil) became a popular late-night snack. Moreover, dining clubs and societies dedicated to regional cuisine sprang up throughout the country. Food and wine societies sought to preserve the link between food consumption and conviviality. Proprietors of restaurants and *trattorie* consciously prided themselves in preserving past culinary traditions, advertising special dishes and banquets for historically minded gourmets.[72] Generally speaking, Italians were interested in the cooking of the past. Pellegrino Artusi's *L'arte di mangiar bene* and Ada Boni's *Il talismano della felicità* went through numerous reprints. After 1960, *La cucina italiana* carried the feature *La cucina di trent'anni fa* that looked back to fascism's culinary trends on a semi-regular basis.

Parliamentarians and scientists also recognized the need to preserve certain traditions. Parliamentary deputies Giuseppe Aliberti and Luigi Renato Sansone defended Italian foods and regional habits throughout the 1950s. Postwar food policies were sensitive to the traditions and experience of the Italian population and did not try to change food habits – particularly regional ones – radically.[73] Old habits from the fascist past were difficult to discard. Despite the government's orientation away from closed markets, the National Nutrition Institute worried that the influx of imported foods – South African apples, Egyptian onions, American asparagus – presented a danger to consumers because members of the Institute did not perceive these products to be as nutritious as domestic produce.[74] The Institute also upheld the nutritional value of pasta, wheat bread, and wine as the foundations of Italian diet; imported goods, particularly meat, did not receive as much scientific attention.[75] It is tempting to categorize these anxieties as oppositional responses to Americanization, but nostalgia for the cuisine of the past encompassed resistance to a variety of impulses. As much as the search for Italy's culinary past could be termed opposition, it also signified the building of a shared culture.

The term Americanization, however, was used often in discussions about Italian food after the war, although the exact nature of this anxiety is somewhat hard to define. Under fascism, the American diet was defined as inferior because it consisted mostly of canned, prepared foods. Critics of American food habits (and domestic economists in particular) worried that if Italians adopted an American lifestyle, they would not enjoy their food.[76] The standardization of products and the hurried pace of food consumption made American food habits distinctive. Thus, under fascism the criticism of Americanization was cultural, not economic, in that it focused on lifestyle choices and not the threat of competition. In the first decade after the war, Italian critics of Americanization adopted a new understanding of the process, one that acknowledged the dual nature of Americanization. In 1952, for example, Giuseppe Aliberti decried the American premium on packaged convenience foods but admired the nutritional standards set by the United States government for the food industry and consumers. Aliberti also marveled at the American method of enriching prepared foods with vitamins, and wondered if Italy might follow this example by enriching pasta.[77] Still, many Italians cast a wary eye toward American habits and production methods, worrying that the greater the degree of Americanization, the greater the risk that Italian food would lose the qualities of nutrition and taste.[78]

Concerns about the Americanization of the Italian diet were out of proportion to the exact nature of the threat if we define Americanization as a preference for convenience (prepared) foods and a distributive sector geared toward high volume and standardized products. For example, Italy lagged behind other European nations in the number of supermarkets per inhabitant: the neighborhood shop and the local food market predominated as major retail channels. In 1960, for example, 95 percent of all food purchases were made in small stores and not in supermarkets. There were only 316,000 supermarkets throughout the nation in 1951 and this number increased to 437,000 by 1965.[79] By 1970, Italy had one supermarket for every 122,461 inhabitants, compared to one for every 34,357 French consumers and one for every 31,326 West German consumers. There was, moreover, little evidence to support worries that Italians consumed too many prepared and packaged foods. Indeed, Italians consumed far less frozen and packaged foods than did their Western European counterparts: only 0.11 kilograms per person per year in 1964 and less than a half-kilogram by 1969.[80]

Certainly, some American foods (Coca-Cola, Ritz crackers) and American trends (picnics, cocktail parties) were popular in Italy, but the population was far from Americanized in terms of eating habits. Advertising for Coca-Cola was aimed almost exclusively at young Italians while Nabisco crackers were marketed as special treats for picnics or outings. We must be careful not to confuse changes in Italian food habits over the past fifty years with the process of Americanization, then. Italian food habits changed most dramatically in response to shifts in societal and family structures (smaller families, women working outside the home, more varied leisure patterns) that occurred elsewhere in Europe as well as in the United States. Anthropologist Carole Counihan's study of food habits in twentieth-century Florence reveals that women were most likely to feel the tensions between new work patterns and family expectations for meals, tensions that were sharpened further by men's unwillingness to do much of the housework.[81] Increasing numbers of women turned to prepared foods, frozen foods, and take-away items to meet the demands of family and work. Working families were also more likely to shop at supermarkets than at the traditional mom-and-pop grocery stores because supermarkets offered more convenient hours and one-stop shopping. Corresponding with new work and social rhythms, Italians ate more meals outside the home: young families went on Sunday outings instead of having lunch at their mother's house; couples dined out in restaurants; workers and students consumed lunch or a snack closer to the workplace or university.[82] These changes did not add up to the complete Americanization of food habits, however. Italians used special equipment to cook pasta while camping; a snack consumed outside the home might consist of locally produced ice cream. Italian consumers adapted to social change by combining the new with the familiar.

The Italian food industry has taken full advantage of the nostalgia for the simple tastes of Italy's past in order to sell its products. This was the case particularly during the anti-consumerist 1970s, when marketing styles associated ideas about what constituted traditional Italian cuisine with the promotion of a healthy lifestyle. Although the health-food craze was not as strong in Italy as it was in the United States, the food industry made wholesome ingredients and peasant conviviality part of its marketing campaigns to appeal to health-conscious Italians. Consciousness about health and nutrition was intensified throughout the 1970s by a series of scandals involving the food industry, all of which prompted a closer look at food adulteration and certain foods that might be harmful to consumers.[83] Partly in response to public concern about food's origins and preparation, food packaging emphasized the freshness of foods no matter how they were prepared. Words like 'all natural' and 'fresh' became standard elements in advertising and packaging. The most extreme example of this would be Genepesca, a brand of frozen fish that avoided packaging altogether so as to 'maintain the natural form of the product.'[84]

Perhaps the most successful example of nostalgic marketing was the line of Mulino Bianco (the White Mill) cookies and baked goods launched by Barilla. The products were marketed under the *colazione in campagna* (breakfast in the country) campaign, an advertising blitz that featured families enjoying cookies and cakes for breakfast. The White Mill figured prominently in all advertising, reinforcing the supposed rural origins of the baked goods. In gastronomic literature and advertising, rural cuisine was linked with wholesome ingredients and healthy food, a complete reversal from earlier scientific discussions of the rural diet. Making this association paid off for Barilla. Mulino Bianco cookies were a phenomenal success for Barilla: by 1990, one quarter of all cookies, 37 percent of all baked snacks, and half of all melba toast (*fette*) sold were under the Mulino Bianco label.[85] Indeed, popular products like Mulino Bianco cookies and Nutella quickly became part of Italy's culinary heritage, in part because marketing techniques to sell these foods drew upon recurrent themes from Italy's past. While cookies and chocolate spread seem a far cry from chestnut-flour bread and a sliced onion, all of these foods share a common history of austerity.

In the postwar decades of economic success, Italians embraced some new habits but did not dramatically change the foundation of popular diet, which continued to consist of pasta and bread supplemented by fresh produce, dairy products, and meat. For much of the nineteenth century and through the fascist years, Italian consumers fashioned a cuisine of scarcity because they had to. In the face of enormous economic, demographic, and social change after the Second World War, Italians held on to some aspects of this cuisine of scarcity by emphasizing simplicity of preparation and a minimum of ingredients. They discarded other aspects by consuming less corn and more meat, for example. Postwar consumers resembled Italian emigrants at the turn of the century, in that both populations dealt with dramatic change by seeking to reconstruct past traditions. Postwar consumers built traditions consciously by preserving the essential contours of

Italian cuisine and regarding regional practice as an important aspect of national cuisine. Postwar consumption habits, as this chapter has shown, suggest that consumers thought very consciously about the cuisine of the past in a culture of abundance.

This book has argued that politics shaped Italian consumption practices during and between the wars. After 1945, state intervention had more of an indirect influence on consumer habits through trade liberalization. The government did not attempt to dictate what consumers should eat. Still, consumers chose to uphold the Mediterranean diet and did not give in to excess or foreign influence. The roots of this culinary conservatism went back to Italy's liberal era but were reinforced powerfully by the fascist regime. Ideas about what was good to eat developed over time and were difficult to discard in the midst of consumer abundance. It also seems likely that the discovery and defense of the national cuisine was one way for Italians to adapt to rapid social and economic change after the war. Italian food became a very powerful means to anchor individuals within broader communities of region and nation. Food also provided Italian consumers with a sense of history, custom, and tradition, even though these elements may be invented or imagined. The durability of Italian consumption habits, even in the context of the economic and social changes of the postwar era, is testimony to the power of political and historical circumstance in shaping the cultural practices of food preparation and consumption in Italy.

Conclusion: A Cuisine of Scarcity

This book has examined the impact of politics on Italian consumers' food choices by highlighting the role of the national government. It is curious, perhaps, that this analysis turns on the activities of Italian government, which has not been known for exerting significant influence on people's lives – at least not until the fascist era, and even then, historians still debate the degree of fascist control. Rather, the influence of the Italian government ebbed and flowed, as did popular resistance to the very ideas of a nation-state or national identity. The Italian state was not necessarily or intentionally all-powerful when it came to influencing consumption habits. This book has highlighted numerous instances when ministries hesitated or refused to act, not to mention the instances when food policies had very unintended consequences or bureaucratic inertia prevented consumers from obtaining needed food supplies. Yet one must recognize the power of the Italian government in shaping popular consumption habits and a national cuisine of scarcity, whether measured through official food policies or less direct interventions in the economy that made a difference in what people could or could not afford. Given the history of popular diet in liberal and fascist Italy, government intervention was perhaps more important in shaping food habits than cultural traditions were. When given the opportunity, Italians were all too happy to jettison 'traditions' like chestnut bread and rancid polenta.

The purpose of this book is not so much to reexamine and rehabilitate the reputation of the Italian state but to understand more thoroughly a particular aspect of Italian statecraft: the government's changing views of the population in relationship to the nation's economic development and political status. Italy was not very different from other western European nations, which came to regard the health and stability of their populations as significant measures of national development. Thus, by the latter half of the nineteenth century, governments mobilized everything from eugenics to school lunch programs in order to raise fitter populations for empire, economic domination, and social harmony. Physiologists and social reformers in Italy were similarly concerned about popular health and diet, but the nation lacked the natural resources and was unable to fully mobilize economic resources to assist the population. Solutions to the 'problem' of popular diet remained in the discursive realm until the First World War, and even then, the task of improving national health through diet was briefly exercised, ending with

Mussolini's turn to economic self-sufficiency in the late 1920s. While Mussolini and his ministers may have seen the potential for some sort of rebirth or renewal of the population, their track record proved otherwise. Properly provisioning the population was, in essence, a good idea gone terribly wrong by the end of the fascist era.

The mild successes and dramatic failures of successive Italian governments illustrate the extent to which liberal and fascist statecraft attempted some control over the population through manipulating consumption practice. This book has demonstrated how politics affects consumption, by using Italy as a case study because of the longevity and volume of the debate over what to do about inadequate food consumption levels. The history of Italian food consumption presents us with a unique case in which various generations of political optimists – a motley crew of positivists, nationalists, fascists, and socialists – consciously set out to solve the problem of a miserable Italian diet. For politicians and scientists on the left, solutions included rural transformation, the development of cooperatives, and charity. For conservatives and fascists, Italy's low-wage, low-consumption economy was an obstacle to be overcome; controlling consumption played a significant role in surviving or transforming the economy. The public record of this ongoing discussion is copious, indicating that the concern about popular diet never abated, although various governments adopted their own tactics in managing or controlling food consumption. Italy's economic difficulties, combined with state intervention in food provisioning, created a different kind of history for consumption and consumerism. This book argues that there were, at various moments in Italy's past, limited or no choices for Italians in purchasing food. This world of limited choices seems to contradict the very nature of consumerism, with its emphasis on choice and abundance. As previous histories of Italian mass culture and consumerism have argued, however, it is difficult to speak of choice or even agency within a framework of an unevenly balanced economy where so many citizens were preoccupied by subsistence.[1]

Much of the narrative in this book also seems to contradict the idea of 'cuisine' as a developing (and increasingly sophisticated) reflection of the tastes and habits of a population. The field of food studies has presented us with dynamic histories where cuisine is the product of adaptation, choice, and change.[2] At the very least, most Italians were culinary conservatives, for much of the time because they had few options. It is therefore difficult to speak of Italian cuisine in terms of dramatic change, or the assimilation of new foods. And, as this book has argued, Italians who encountered a greater variety of foods changed their habits cautiously. Within Italy, food habits remained largely static, yet the symbolic significance of food was constantly shifting. The poor in Naples collected their neighbors' pasta water to drink, in the late nineteenth century and in the early 1950s. Matilde Serao, observing this habit in 1884, described it as a common survival tactic among the poor and a sign of their ingenuity in the face of adversity. For Danilo Dolci, however, the habit constituted a glaring signpost of residual urban poverty and persistent social inequality in Italy. Begging for pasta water was something to be pitied, not admired.

These last examples illustrate how individuals created food's meaning through everyday practice. Italian consumers developed all sorts of ways to cope with scarcity, and they participated in the shaping of a national cuisine. It is certainly difficult, almost impenetrable, for modern consumers to understand the intricacies of food preparation and consumption as they developed within a cuisine of scarcity. Franco La Cecla has rightly noted how Italian cuisine, built of scarcity and necessity, now constitutes a formalistic language where the attention to the smallest detail is mind-boggling: 'Is it not incredible that the dried pasta industry produced not two or three shapes, but six hundred? The culture of poverty in Italy is often a culture of variety, thousands of types of bread, thousands of ways to cook the same food, and thousands of shapes of pasta and types of pizza.'[3] This legacy of scarcity has meant that a rich formalism developed alongside peasant simplicity in the forging of Italian cuisine. This legacy still matters even in Italy today: a pinch of corn meal in pasta dough or a bit of lard in the *minestra* still make a difference in terms of how the dish tastes. Anyone who has tried to serve pasta shells with pesto to an Italian learns that there still exists a very formal language of meal preparation that is not based on a wide variety of foods or exquisite and rare ingredients. A legacy of scarcity, then, has had very positive effects on the national cuisine of Italy. Even today, the abstemious Mediterranean Diet and *Italianità* are linked together with positive connotations. The intricacies of a cuisine of scarcity are a source of pride for many Italians.

Although the focus of my analysis has been on the negative aspects of the link between scarcity and a national cuisine, I have also argued that contemporary Italian consumer habits have their roots in the past. At the same time that government inertia or fascist policies were the cause of real suffering and hunger among Italian consumers, they reinforced a cuisine of scarcity that, even today, appears peculiarly resistant to outside influence or change. Ironically, at the same time as Italian consumers have preserved a richly formalistic and simple national cuisine, Italian food is now popular in every corner of the world. Consumers from all walks of life and from every socio-economic background enjoy pizza and pasta; we can say that these have become truly 'universal' dishes. In the United States, consumers have created their own versions of Italian cuisine by commemorating the inventive simplicity of Italian immigrants in cookbooks, television cooking shows, glossy magazines, and in numerous restaurants, cafés, and *trattorie*. Refashioning and inventing Italian cuisine has grown from a modest effort to commemorate Italian-American ethnicity to a multi-million dollar industry aimed at an American public hungry for nostalgia and simplicity.

When we leaf through the pages of a glossy cookbook, we are told that Italian cooking is the product of traditions and recipes passed down through generations of Italian women. This book has provided ample evidence that many Italian consumers did not enjoy delicious pasta dishes, rich desserts, or hearty roasts until after the Second World War. Instead, generations of Italian consumers have struggled to make ends meet, making do or going without because of the vagaries of the market, the environment, or political regimes. Thus, the Italian traditions and recipes that we as non-Italian consumers commemorate are an invented tradition; they also constitute a particular definition of Italian cuisine, one among many competing definitions throughout the world. Given that Italian food now belongs to the world, the global consumer has modified and adapted both the food itself and the history of Italian cuisine. The arguments, ideas, and stories from this book are offered as a partial corrective to our current understanding of how Italian cuisine came to be and, more generally speaking, how the history of consumption develops historically. My intent has been to debunk ideas about long-standing traditions of abundance in Italy and to complicate our understanding of how cultures of consumption develop within national, historical, and above all political, contexts.

Scarcity, not abundance, shaped the national cuisine of Italy as well as ideas about consuming food. Thus, this book has focused less on the choices consumers made and more on the constraints and obstacles faced by consumers, experts, and the State. This has not meant, however, that the meaning of food in Italy was either insignificant or static. The social inequities attendant on industrialization, the major upheavals of the twentieth century, and the whims of dictators all highlighted the real, and even terrifying, significance of food in the modern era. Precisely because it was a scarce commodity, food carried a variety of meanings for individuals. Government ministers monitored and conserved food supplies, anxious about public welfare and afraid of Italy's dependence on other nations. Communities of experts constantly reconciled, adapted, and negotiated their own ideas about what was 'good to eat' with what food was available or with the government's attitudes toward intervention. And lastly, individuals and families struggled to make the most of what little food they had or did without, waiting for the day when they could finally eat their fill.

Epilogue: Food in Italy Today

Today, the close relationship between Italian food and Italian identity seems an unremarkable fact. Non-Italians understand Italy as the land of pasta, pizza, espresso, and ice cream and define Italians by their food habits. Contemporary articles and books about Italian life cannot discuss Italian identity without at least referencing food: 'Although cultured Italians wince at the hoary stereotype of "macaroni and mandolins," pasta is a test of collective identity for a people who until very recently had only a vague sense of nationhood.'[1] Every few months, an Internet poll or newspaper article reports that a majority of Italians would feel anxious or uncomfortable if deprived of pasta for even a few days. At the same time as we would like to believe that Italians have an especially meaningful relationship to food, we acknowledge that Italian food is for *everyone* to enjoy. The simplicity of Italian food appeals to a broad spectrum of consumers. Pizza and pasta can be dressed up or down. Inasmuch as workers enjoy a take-away slice of pizza for lunch, a bourgeois host can dress up a pizza with goat cheese and swiss chard for dinner guests. The simplicity of Italian food lends itself to adaptation by rich and poor, gourmands and fast-food addicts.

Today, simplicity has replaced austerity as the defining characteristic of Italian food. Oddly enough, many dishes and foods formerly associated with monotony and poor nutrition now provide the basis for *haute cuisine* outside Italy. For trend-conscious consumers, foods like pesto, sun-dried tomatoes, polenta, crusty bread, olive oil, and sweetbreads define authentic Italian cuisine. In the United States, 'authentic' Italian cuisine rivaled 'red-gravy' cuisine popularized by Italian-Americans in east-coast urban areas since the 1930s.[2] The American cookbook, restaurant, and travel industries seized upon the popularity of simple peasant food, excavating the regional diversity of Italian cooking and reinventing a tradition of Italian cooking for non-Italian consumers. As a consequence, many consumers who had grown up with spaghetti and meatballs traded in their cheese-coated veal parmesan for a more austere dish of semolina gnocchi. In part, the discovery of authentic Italian cuisine mirrored the touristic rediscovery of Italy in the 1980s and 1990s. By the late 1990s, Frances Mayes' memoir *Under the Tuscan Sun* demonstrated how food and Italian identity were inextricably linked. The book spawned a major boom in tourism to Italy and a minor boom in real-estate speculation by avid consumers of the authentic Italy, who were tempted by descriptions of Tuscan food and countryside. Every meal and dish was described as fabulous, gorgeous, unforgettable, from the cold-pressed olive oil to local wines; even the *mortadella* sandwich at the auto-grill on the highway elicited some praise. Eating and appreciating mostly simple 'peasant' food facilitated Mayes' transition to becoming an Italian and provided a tasty antidote to the hassles of renovating a villa in Tuscany. Mayes, along with numerous cookbook authors and chefs, celebrated Italian food because they found that, in her words, 'simplicity is liberating'.[3]

At the same time as Italian cuisine was celebrated for its simplicity, Italians threw caution to the wind and experimented with non-Italian dishes. Some even got fat, and many began to worry about the physical and moral effects of indulgence and excess. Italians now go en masse to gyms and they use sugar substitutes and other foods to help them lose weight (*dimagrire*). Italian consumers worry about the health risks of McDonald's franchises, genetically modified foods, and mad-cow disease. The classic Mediterranean diet is still popular, even if consumers have to pay more for locally produced olive oil, vegetables, and fish.[4] Yet an increasing number of Italians purchase frozen and canned foods at supermarkets. An estimated 600,000 Italians eat at McDonald's every day, and ethnic restaurants are now commonplace in most cities. It would appear that Italian consumers can no longer resist the lure and necessity of globalization. Thus, at the same time Italian food as an aspect of Italian identity is celebrated outside Italy, Italians are less than certain about what truly authentic Italian food is. Yet, politics and food *still* matter to some Italians, so much so that Italians are now mobilizing to defend themselves against the culinary effects of globalization, Americanization, and changes within Italy. As a result of this mobilization, Italian cuisine has now become the jealously guarded patrimony of all Italians, who no longer view austere peasant cooking and the mishmash of regional preparation techniques as a source of embarrassment, but one of pride.

Throughout the 1980s, indulgent food habits symbolized the best and worst in Italian society. Filippo Ceccarelli's recent book on food and politics in contemporary Italy suggests that in the 1980s and into the 1990s, individuals and parties in the Italian government reveled in excess. A new crop of political leaders emerged, a group of men who were unrepentantly fat, full of life, and proud of their success. The most famous of these new leaders was the Socialist Foreign Minister Gianni De Michelis, frequently photographed in discos, sweating up a storm on the dance floor with several women. De Michelis was legendary for having a large appetite. One anonymous woman reported that seeing De Michelis eat 'was like reading Rabelais' as he ate enough for three or four men.[5] Apparently, his left politics did not prevent him from indulging himself so publicly. Indeed, throughout the 1980s, the Socialist and Communist Parties came under increased public scrutiny for letting go and 'getting fat' (*si ingrassano*) in the context of socialism's phenomenal success and communism's rise in the wake of Enrico Berlinguer. Left politicians joined their conservative foes in dining on very un-Italian foods like champagne, caviar, sour cream, and boiled potatoes. The Communist Party's *Festa dell'Unità*, which usually showcased simple foods like wine, polenta, and tortellini, gave way in the mid-1970s to elaborate gourmet celebrations of various cuisines.[6] Rich food represented the fact that Italy had 'arrived' economically and politically, irrespective of political affiliation.

At the same time as excess consumption represented success, it also symbolized temptation and corruption. Peter Robb's travelogue of the Sicilian Mafia detailed how certain foods were associated with the big deals, power, and corrosive relationships between Mafiosi, businessmen, and politicians. One eyewitness account of a 1979 banquet hosted by Nino Salvo, famous for being an intermediary between Cosa Nostra and the Christian Democrats, provided a partial list of the food for special guest Giulio Andreotti and others: canapès of caviar and smoked salmon, Russian salad, *pasticcio*, lobsters, jumbo shrimp, suckling pig, wild boar, pheasant, veal, grilled fish, ricotta and whipped cream cakes, *profiteroles*, fresh fruit, and wine from the Salvo's estates.[7] The extravagant habits of socialist ministers and *Mafiosi* have mirrored the political corruption and greed that characterized Italy in the 1980s. In this context of excess, individuals have frequently turned back to simplicity. On the political horizon, the corruption scandals and collapse of the party system in Italy (*tangentopoli* and *mani pulite*) paved the way for nostalgia for simpler habits and tastes. The new politicians of the 1990s were not fat. Their more abstemious habits resonated with the political turn away from the flabby corruption of the 1980s and Italy's new consumption priorities, which focus more on aesthetics and health. Sporting a trim figure and a year-round tan, Prime Minister Silvio Berlusconi radiates good health. Umberto Bossi of Italy's Northern League is known for consuming only a beer and a sandwich for dinner (although he is known to have a weakness for beef).[8] High profile consumer/politicians like Berlusconi and Bossi emphasize austere consumption habits in the context of nationalism, or at the very least, feeling good about Italy in the wake of scandal. It is difficult, however, to classify their actions as constituting any sort of campaign to redefine Italian cuisine.

Yet there is an ongoing struggle within Italy to define and preserve Italian food from threats both real and abstract. Some of these threats can be grouped under the ominous category of globalization: fast food and genetically modified foods, for example, threaten to replace Italy's diverse regional tastes with food-as-standardized-product. Italians are not entirely averse to tampering with nature, standardizing foods or promoting Italian foods on the global market. Italian scientists have created genetically modified fruits and vegetables. There has been much discussion of how to guarantee the quality of Italian food sold outside Italy and pizza makers in Naples have gone so far as to obtain EU patents on their *Vera pizza napoletana* (made with fermented dough and topped with tomatoes and buffalo mozzarella).[9] The defense of Italian cuisine from globalization seems incongruous with the fact that Italian foods like pizza and pasta are consumed around the world and Italian cuisine is now one of the nation's most significant exports. Moreover, the exact nature of the threats to Italian cuisine is not clear. Unlike its European neighbors, Italy has resisted the siren call of McDonald's and other fast-food restaurants; Italy has about one-third the number of McDonald's restaurants that Britain, France, and Germany each has. Italians have preferred to shop at mom-and-pop stores rather than supermarkets, at least until very recently.[10] What exactly are Italians mobilizing to defend? Is Italian cuisine in danger?

There is no doubt that globalization and European integration have had a measurable impact on the foods Italians eat and the manner in which they eat them. In this sense, Italian consumers are no different from consumers elsewhere who now have to contend with the impact of bureaucracy, technology, and corporate consolidation on their food habits.[11] Within Italy, however, there are volatile and very public debates concerning the presence of McDonald's restaurants and the possibility of genetically modified foods in Italy. Both of these debates concern the quality and meaning of Italian food, yet these debates also resonate with broader concerns like the ongoing struggle between Italy and forms of US imperialism, or the economic position of the nation's small farmers. Widespread anxiety about the impact of globalization has instigated the defense of Italian foodways in the form of the Slow Food movement, which is fast becoming a political voice to define and defend Italian cuisine. At the same time as Italians mobilize to defend Italian foodways, they are as concerned about what food represents to Italians as they are about the food itself. Within the context of discussing the threats to Italian food, Italian consumers think about the nation's economic health and evaluate what has been lost in the blur of global markets, European integration, and the new priorities of postindustrial life.

From the very moment that McDonald's opened its first restaurant in Italy in 1985 in Bolzano, there has been controversy about the presence of McDonald's in Italy. As part of its 'Global Realization' plan, McDonald's launched 300 restaurants throughout Italy with plans to open more, mostly in the central and southern regions of the country. The number of Italian franchises and workers (approximately 10,000) is small in comparison with those in France, where McDonald's now boasts 900 restaurants and 35,000 employees.[12] Like the French, however, Italians have loudly protested McDonald's when the opportunity arises. On 16 October, World Anti-McDonald's Day, Italian consumers and McDonald's workers mobilize against the quality of fast food and the working conditions in the restaurants. Strikes and protests for other reasons frequently end up in front of a McDonald's, which functions as a lightning rod for anti-global and anti-American sentiment.[13] The protests have also been accompanied by violence. Between the years 1997 and 1999, motorcyclists damaged

McDonald's restaurants throughout Italy with Molotov cocktails. Despite the fact that McDonald's is popular with Italian children and teenagers, and despite the fact that McDonald's has conducted its standard campaign of charity and public service within Italy, the very existence of McDonald's restaurants continues to elicit disapproval and indignation.

Italian critics demonstrate obvious disdain for McDonald's food. *La Stampa*'s food writer Edoardo Raspelli recently came under fire for describing their 'rinky-dink, wilting hamburgers; those obscene French fries that taste like cardboard.'[14] There is no question that McDonald's food tastes nothing like Italian food. But the nature of Italian protest concerns more than the quality of food. More importantly, perhaps, McDonald's restaurants represent a new way to do business, without the involvement of organized labor or farmers, two groups whose political influence wanes as Italy restructures its economy toward a global, corporate model. Interestingly enough, since organized labor, farmers, and consumers have raised their voices against McDonald's, the corporation has had to adjust its business practices in order to carry out its plan for global realization in Italy. Thus, the question is not whether McDonald's is taking over Italian foodways, but rather how 'Italianized' McDonald's is willing to become in order to do business in Italy.

For McDonald's executives, good business practice has meant buying Italian. For example, the Italian operation buys most of its beef from the Cremonini Group outside of Modena and McDonald's Italy asserts that over 85 percent of the food served is produced within Italy. (Restaurants in Italy are either owned by McDonald's Italia or individual franchisees.) In addition to pacifying farmers and economic nationalists, the strategy of buying Italian has proved advantageous to the corporation's growth within Italy. In 1996, McDonald's Italy bought out the largest domestic fast-food chain, Burghy, in an agreement that enabled McDonald's to open shops in eighty locations without the hassle of obtaining permits or licenses from the Italian bureaucracy. The acquisition of Burghy was a major boost for McDonald's, as the company had only limited success in opening new restaurants in its first decade in Italy. (Between 1985 and 1994, only twenty-three restaurants were opened in Italy.) Similarly, the corporation's recent deal with AGIP service stations has been strategic, leading to the opening of twenty drive-through restaurants with more on the way. McDonald's has succeeded in its campaigns to 'buy Italian,' and now tries to 'sell Italian' as well. McDonald's has offered salads with a distinctly Mediterranean flavor (the *fiordiriso* with rice, tuna, ham, and mushrooms, or the *caprese* with tomatoes and mozzarella cheese), pizza by the slice (*pizza mia*), espresso, and ice cream.

Despite these efforts to win over Italian consumers, McDonald's Italy and individual franchisees frequently have come under fire for violating workers' rights. In October of 2000, McDonald's workers in Florence walked out to protest the 'intimidatory climate' at the restaurant. In November of 2000, Roman workers struck to protest 'inhumane working conditions.' Italian workers complain that they are not allowed sufficient break time and are reprimanded for drinking water or eating a few chocolate chips on the job.[15] Organized labor continues to criticize McDonald's for its labor practices and for hiring mostly university students on a part-time basis. In a general sense, McDonald's represents an American attitude toward labor rights, which Italians deem particularly threatening in light of Prime Minister Berlusconi's efforts to weaken the hand of organized labor. The proliferation of McDonald's restaurants, and the corporation's plans to expand, mean more competition for the proprietors of cafés and take-away food stores.

Italian defenders of McDonald's do not argue that that the food tastes good. Rather, they maintain that American business practices championed by McDonald's provide a solution to Italy's current economic problems. Young employees contend that they receive useful training in the areas of quality control, customer service, and time management.[16] Defenders also argue that McDonald's brings much-needed jobs to Italy and provides unique opportunities for entrepreneurs to open a franchise. The president of McDonald's-Italy is Mario Resca, a successful businessman, President of the American Chamber of Commerce in Italy, board member of numerous communications interests, and a very public representative of McDonald's. Indeed, only successful businessmen can afford to open a McDonald's franchise in Italy, as a minimum of 150,000 Euros is needed to start the initial investment, not to mention the charisma, perseverance, and connections one needs to obtain the appropriate licenses and permits for highly visible locations in historic city centers.[17]

The latest chapter in the McDonald's in Italy saga is the corporation's recent lawsuit slapped against Edoardo Raspelli, food critic for the newspaper *La Stampa*, for 21 million Euros, the amount equal to what McDonald's Italy spent on advertising in the nation in the year 2002. Raspelli was interviewed in December of 2002 for an article in *La Stampa* about the posted loss in profits for McDonald's. His comments resonated with what Italians already knew about McDonald's food: that the restaurants put a premium on service above all else. Although a bit harsh in his judgment of McDonald's (Raspelli likened eating at McDonald's to filling up at a petrol station), Raspelli balanced his criticism with the observation that Italian restaurateurs might be able to learn something about fast service and catering to youth from the corporation. Several months later, an astonished Raspelli was served a summons to appear in court; the amount of the lawsuit, he maintained, was intended to intimidate him, given that McDonald's did not sue the newspaper or the reporter who interviewed him.[18] Much of the controversy surrounding Raspelli's case has little to do with food, although Raspelli has made his thoughts on McDonald's food perfectly clear. Journalists and Raspelli have wondered aloud why such a wealthy corporation would use excessive force in dealing with a solitary food critic? Raspelli's case underscores Italy's concern with the disproportionate amount of power available to McDonald's and how that translates into business practice within Italy.

Another example of a current threat to Italian food that is not entirely about Italian food would be the protests against genetically modified foods. Specifically, Italian farmers have mobilized against GMOs and their struggle has made Italy into one of the most vocal opponents of GMOs in the European Union. Italian farmers have good reason to oppose trends that could threaten their livelihood. Over the last two decades, agriculture in Italy has been replaced by either agribusiness or agritourism; Paul Ginsborg has described the growth of multi-national food companies (Nestlé-Italia, Unilever-Italia, and Kraft-Italia), which control even agricultural production, as one of the most startling developments in the Italian economy in recent years.[19] Italian agriculture's transformation has left farmers in the dust, with little control over their futures. Small producers have few resources at their disposal, although they have organized through Coldiretti, the agricultural union. Coldiretti, along with Italian environmental organizations (such as Greenpeace), have waged a sustained campaign against genetically modified foods, working to prevent their entry into Italy and requesting warning labels on all genetically-modified produce or processed foods made with GMOs. Small farmers in Italy object to GMOs because of the control US-based biotechnology companies have over the market. Farmers also worry that Italian consumers may not buy genetically modified produce because of possible health risks. Further, farmers and consumers worry about the potential environmental impact of biotech innovations.

Under Giulio Amato's prime ministry, Agricultural Minister and Green Party member Pecoraro Scanio came under fire for what some called an 'extreme' anti-GMO stance. Scanio tried to protect Italian farmers, arguing that 'Italy doesn't need genetically manipulated organisms because the world image of its agricultural products is based on quality and wholesomeness.'[20] In the spring of 2001, Scanio embargoed a shipment of 500 tons of corn and soy seeds from the US company Monsanto because of suspicions that Monsanto intentionally sold genetically modified seeds to Italy. (Initial tests on a sample of seeds indicated evidence of genetic contamination.) The embargo led to a national brouhaha and an international scandal as farmers protested the disruption in their planting season. Arsonists destroyed Monsanto's grain stored in Italy, and Scanio implied that Monsanto might have set the fire in order to hide the truth. The affair ended when tests revealed the seeds in question were not genetically modified after all. In the aftermath of the scandal, then Prime Minister Giuliano Amato forced Scanio to allow the first field trials of genetically modified crops in Italy. Political candidates swore they would be less hostile to scientific interests, and, ultimately, Amato's center-left coalition was voted out of power. Critics castigated Scanio for his mishandling of the Monsanto embargo, but ultimately, Scanio's complaints about

GMOs were, and are, played out all over Europe. The European Union placed a moratorium on biotech foods in 1998 pending further research into the possible health risks of GMOs. US trade interests have opposed the ban, contending that Europe's ban constituted unfair trade practices, and filing suit with the World Trade Organization. Although the EU has recently accepted biotech foods (July 2003), such foods have to be labeled clearly, so as to allow consumers to decide for themselves. Italian farmers are still wary, but pleased, given that Coldiretti has fought for GMO-labeling.

Protests against GMOs are less about the food itself than about the plight of Italian farmers, who struggle against the European Union's Common Agricultural Policy, and their own government's position on immigrant labor, now the backbone of agricultural labor in Italy.[21] Thus, discussions and protests about food in Italy today frequently overlap with other concerns, the position of small farmers, for example, or the rights of unionized workers. As Italians struggle to defend their food and cuisine, they also struggle to guarantee that the ways in which food is produced and sold within Italy are protected and maintained, hence the drive to patent *la vera pizza napoletana* against the popularity of McDonald's *pizza mia*. It is difficult to determine, however, whether this campaign will be successful, given that the small retailers and the few farmers left in Italy have little power relative to entities like McDonald's, Monsanto, or the World Trade Organization. Once again, debates about food – in this instance its production and distribution – are also discussions about inequalities of power and their political consequences within Italy.

Yet Italian farmers, retailers, and restaurateurs have received some support from a growing consumer movement called Slow Food. The Slow Food movement was first launched in Paris in 1989, the result of numerous discussions among European critics and intellectuals regarding the presence of McDonald's in Europe. Slow Food seeks to mobilize consumers against fast food and globalization's impact on regional and local cuisine. Their manifesto against 'McDonaldization' underscores how much Slow Food members see cuisine and life as being intimately related:

> We are enslaved by speed and have all succumbed to the same insidious virus: *Fast Life*, which disrupts our habits, pervades the privacy of our homes and forces us to eat *Fast Foods* ... A firm defense of quiet material pleasure is the only way to oppose the universal folly of *Fast Life* ... our defense should begin at the table with *Slow Food*. Let us rediscover the flavors and savors of regional cooking and banish the degrading effects of fast food.[22]

For Slow Food members, the 'degrading effects' of fast food are social as much as nutritional or physiological. Slow Food's response to fast life and fast food has been the organization of *convivia*, or local societies (currently 560 societies with 65,000 members around the world) modeled on the already existing food and wine societies that emphasized the social aspect of food consumption. These societies, which have spread beyond Europe, encourage consumers to celebrate local tastes by patronizing small farmers and food merchants in their area.

Although *Slow* Food is a global movement, there is no question that Italians have been the driving force behind the organization. Slow Food started in part as a response to the construction of the McDonald's franchise in the Piazza di Spagna in Rome in 1986. Italian Carlo Petrini is the president and founder of Slow Food and many of the convivia are located in Italy. In 1996 the society began printing *Slow*, a quarterly journal published in five languages and edited by Alberto Capatti, an Italian food historian. The same year, Slow Food launched the Ark of Taste, a campaign to protect the world's diversity of tastes, cultures, and producers. Now, with organizations around the world and its own website (www.slowfood.com) and editorial house in Piedmont (Bra), the Slow Food movement has expanded its work to defend rural agriculture and artisanal food production against EU regulation and globalization.[23]

Slow Food's motives are many: members seek to protect the small producer and the educated consumer against marketing, fast-food franchising, biotechnology, and proclaimed food prejudices such as vegetarianism. The movement works toward its goals with a grass-roots effort to discover and promote the foods that are not mass-produced or marketed; consumers can find out about a certain cheese produced in Italy or grains grown by Native Americans through the work of the *convivia*, who publicize their efforts on the Internet. As medieval historian and food expert Massimo Montanari observed: 'the diffusion of "global" food models like McDonald's and its imitators has, paradoxically, stirred up a search for diversity, the reconstruction of more or less invented roots, the rediscovery or reinvention of "local" cuisine. Society has produced a formidable antidote to the danger of cultural standardization.'[24] Montanari proposes that Slow Food members put information about local food cultures (invented or discovered) on the Internet for circulation and adoption by others. Because Slow Food divides food along the lines of standardized and traditional, consumers may eat fast foods like pizza and falafel as long as they are not mass-produced. Thus, Slow Food opposes globalization but embraces a culinary global village.

The Slow Food movement is political in its opposition to the disproportionate power of the food industry over consumers and small producers. In this sense, Slow Food members object to the standardization of taste wrought by corporate capitalism and globalization. Culturally, Slow Food seeks to defend or preserve a certain way of life that is disappearing, a way of life that is readily measured by food habits. The very words Slow Food emphasize a nostalgia for food as that which builds conviviality and requires time and thought for preparation. The nostalgia is for having 'real' food that tastes good, instead of eating genetically modified super-foods or thinking about food only in terms of how it impacts one's health or appearance. Yet the nostalgia is also for having the time to eat a Sunday family dinner or the time to go around to several markets instead of doing all one's shopping at the supermarket. In this sense, the nostalgia is a response to recent changes in Italian society, particularly those involving the family (which, for good or bad, has been considered the anchor of Italian society) and attitudes toward consumption, which now prioritize a certain level of comfort for fewer members. As the Italian family grows 'long and thin' because of economic and attitudinal change, the desire for food to build communities, and perhaps rebuild families, increases.[25] Once again, food, its abundance or absence, and the rituals surrounding its preparation and consumption, bring people together.

Slow Food pays close attention to the food we eat, but members also pay careful attention to food's social context, especially methods of production and preparation. There are several reasons why food's social context would be so important in contemporary Italy. The nation's more distant culinary past was neither diverse nor enticing; it would be difficult to get nostalgic about eating polenta and onions 365 times a year. More recently, however, changes in Italian social structure coincided with the rapid development of the food industry during the 1960s and 1970s. Thus the proliferation of frozen pizzas and packaged breakfast foods appeared even more threatening in the context of economic and geographic mobility or changes in family structure. Over the last decade, as Italians sort through the rubble of political corruption, excessive consumption, and economic uncertainty, talking about and mobilizing around food is one way to redefine Italian identity. The intellectuals behind Slow Food in Italy are savvy enough to understand that much of Italy's culinary past is invented or re-invented; their goal is to protect what food *means* to producers and consumers alike.

Although Italians may decry the quickening pace and shifting structure of their lives, they have chosen to talk about their anxieties by discussing food. There are few debates about the widespread use of the *telefonino* or cell phone; Italians are not mobilizing to abolish the Internet. Today's debates about hamburgers, frozen pizza, and genetically modified soybeans highlight food's centrality as a means of discussing larger political issues within Italy. Given that this book has traced the history of a public and political discourse about food in Italy, the prominence of these current debates should come as no surprise. Italians have turned to food as a way to think about, and through, the issues of social change, economic transformation, and political crisis. When we read the 'Slow Food Manifesto', we are reminded that from the very start of Italy's existence as a nation, individuals have used food to measure the well-being of the population and define what it means to be Italian. Whereas nineteenth-century positivists worried about inadequacy, twenty-first century intellectuals worry about excess. Whereas earlier generations of experts and reformers focused on the allocation of food because it was a scarce commodity, intellectuals and critics today examine imbalances in economic and political power that have a profound influence on what Italian consumers eat.

Although there is plenty to eat in Italy, food remains a salient political issue. In part, this is due to the historical legacy of scarcity and monotony. Since Italian unification in 1861, food, its availability and allocation, have been discussed in terms of social inequality and political struggle. Similarly, the slippage between what was *said* about food and what was *eaten* highlights the political nature of food consumption. Historian Hans Teuteberg argues that food habits are inherently social by virtue of being part of the communications process.[26] It must follow, then, that food habits are also inherently political, for communications involve contests of power, meaning, and knowledge. Food habits, like the standard of living or the gross domestic product, came to symbolize Italy's political status, economic health, and aspirations for the future. They still do.

Notes

Introduction

1. See John Burnett, *Plenty and Want. A Social History of Diet in England from 1815 to the Present Day* (London: Nelson, 1966); John Burnett and Derek Oddy (eds), *The Origins and Development of Food Policies in Europe* (Leicester: Leicester University Press, 1994); Peter Scholliers (ed.), *Food, Drink and Identity: Cooking, Eating and Drinking in Europe Since the Middle Ages* (Oxford: Berg, 2001); and Hans Teuteberg (ed.), *European Food History: A Research Review* (Leicester, Leicester University Press, 1992).
2. Quoted in Charles Richards, *The New Italians* (London: Penguin, 1994), p. 79.
3. This was accompanied by a flurry of publications all referring to the alimentary problem. To name but a few: Mario Bellini, *Il problema dell'alimentazione nazionale* (Bologna: Paolo Neri, 1917); G. Consolani, *Se sia possibile risolvere in Italia il problema del pane e della carne* (Rovigo: Corriere, 1918); N.R. D'Alfonso, *Il problema dell'alimentazione come problema educativo* (Milan: Società Libraria, 1918); Luigi De Voto, *Il problema dell'alimentazione in guerra e dopo* (Rome: Bertero, 1916); Maggiorno Ferraris, *Il problema dell'ora presente: Quattro anni di lotta contro caro-viveri* (Rome: Nuova Antologia, 1919); and Giorgio Levi, *Il problema del pane* (Florence: Aldo Funghi, 1920).
4. For a history of its activities and a summary of the philosophy of Slow Food, see Carlo Petrini (ed.) *Slow Food: Collected Thoughts on Taste, Tradition, and the Honest Pleasures of Food* (White River Junction: Chelsea Green Publishing, 2001). Italy has roughly one-third the number of McDonald's restaurants that Britain, France, and Germany each has. The situation has changed in the last decade, however. Since 1985, McDonald's has opened over 240 restaurants throughout the peninsula with plans to open 200 more, mostly in the southern and central regions. Burger King is also making inroads to franchising in Italy, with plans to open at least 100 outlets over the next few years.
5. Roland Barthes, 'Toward a Psychosociology of Contemporary Food Consumption,' in Elborg Forster and Robert Forster (eds), *European Diet from*

Pre-Industrial to Modern Times (New York: Harper and Row, 1975), p. 50.

6. Two very fine studies are Alberto Capatti and Massimo Montanari, *La cucina italiana: Storia di una cultura* (Bari: Laterza, 1999); and Paolo Sorcinelli, *Gli Italiani e il cibo: Appetiti, digiuni e rinunce della realtà contadina alla società del benessere* (Bologna: CLUEB, 1992).

7. Neil McKendrick, John Brewer, and J.H. Plumb (eds), *The Birth of a Consumer Society: The Commercialization of Eighteenth Century England* (Bloomington: Indiana University Press, 1982). See also the essays by Colin Campbell, 'Understanding traditional and modern patterns of consumption in eighteenth century England: A character-action approach,' pp. 40–57 and Jan de Vries, 'Between purchasing power and the world of goods: Understanding the household economy in early modern Europe', pp. 85–132 in John Brewer and Roy Porter (eds), *Consumption and the World of Goods* (London: Routledge, 1993).

8. Erica Carter, *How German Is She? Postwar West German Reconstruction and the Consuming Woman* (Ann Arbor: University of Michigan Press, 1997); Belinda Davis, *Home Fires Burning: Food, Politics, and Everyday Life in World War I Berlin* (Chapel Hill: University of North Carolina Press, 2000); Victoria de Grazia, *How Fascism Ruled Women: Italy, 1922–45* (Berkeley: University of California, 1992); and Jurgen Kocka, *Facing Total War: German Society 1914–18* trans. Barbara Weinberger (Cambridge MA: Harvard University Press, 1984).

9. Jack Goody, *Cooking, Cuisine, and Class* (Cambridge: Cambridge University Press, 1982); Stephen Mennell, *All Manners of Food. Eating and Taste in England and France from the Middle Ages to the Present* (London: Basil Blackwell, 1985); Sidney Mintz, *Sweetness and Power: The Place of Sugar in Modern History* (New York: Viking Penguin, 1985); and H.J. Teuteberg, 'The General Relationship Between Diet and Industrialization', in Elborg and Robert Forster, *European Diet from Pre-Industrial to Modern Times*, and his edited collection, *European Food History: A Research Review*.

10. On food consumption and identity formation, see Warren Belasco, *Appetite for Change: How the Counterculture Took on the Food Industry* (Ithaca: Cornell University Press, 1993); Donna Gabaccia, *We Are What We Eat: Ethnic Food and the Making of Americans* (Cambridge MA: Harvard University Press, 1998); Jeffrey Pilcher, *Que vivan los tamales! Food and the Making of Mexican Identity* (Albuquerque: University of New Mexico Press, 1998); and Rebecca Spang, *The Invention of the Restaurant: Paris and Modern Gastronomic Culture* (Cambridge MA: Harvard University Press, 2000). On the artificial manipulation of food in the United States, see Daniel Charles, *Lords of the Harvest: Biotech, Big Money, and the Future of Food* (Cambridge MA: Perseus Publishing, 2001).

11. Arjun Appadurai, 'Gastro-Politics in Hindu South Asia', *American Ethnologist* 8, 3 (1981), p. 494.
12. Sidney Mintz, *Tasting Food, Tasting Freedom* (Boston: Beacon, 1996), p. 4.
13. In Italy, the topic of food consumption is beginning to attract attention. The most recent works in this field include Alberto Capatti, Alberto De Bernardi, and Angelo Varni (eds), *Storia d'Italia*, Annali 13: *L'alimentazione* (Turin: Giulio Einaudi, 1998); Alberto Capatti and Massimo Montanari, *La cucina italiana. Storia di una cultura*; Franco La Cecla, *La pasta e la pizza* (Bologna: Il Mulino, 1998); and Paolo Sorcinelli, *Gli Italiani e il cibo*.

Chapter 1 Unification through Monotony

1. Matilde Serao, *Ventre di Napoli*, 1884, in Pietro Pancrazi (ed.), *Serao: Romanzi e racconti Italiani dell'Ottocento,* Volume I (Milan: Garzanti, 1944), pp. 1103–4.
2. This point is made eloquently by Paolo Sorcinelli, *Gli Italiani e il cibo: Appetiti, digiuni e rinunce della realtà contadina alla società del benessere* (Bologna: CLUEB, 1992), p. 111.
3. The unrest of the 1890s pushed the issues of social inequality, and government intervention, to the forefront of a national debate. On liberal social policy see Maria Sophia Quine, *Italy's Social Revolution: Charity and Welfare from Liberalism to Fascism* (New York: Palgrave, 2002).
4. Sabino Cassese, *Lo stato introvabile: Modernità e arretrattezza delle istituzioni italiane* (Rome: Donzelli, 1998).
5. The science of nutrition created new expectations for what people should eat, whether measured in terms of calories, vitamins, nutrients, or according to the relationship between food and the body's capacity to provide labor power. On the development of the science of labor and the science of nutrition in nineteenth-century Europe, including Italy, see Anson Rabinbach, *The Human Motor: Energy, Fatigue, and the Origins of Modernity* (New York: Basic Books, 1990).
6. Vera Zamagni, *The Economic History of Italy, 1860–1990: Recovery After Decline* (Oxford: Clarendon, 1993), p. 197.
7. On Italian unification, the best English-language summary of recent historiography is Lucy Riall, *The Italian Risorgimento: State, Society and National Unification* (London: Routledge, 1994). Good overviews of Italy in the nineteenth century include John Davis (ed.), *Italy in the Nineteenth Century* (Oxford: Oxford University Press, 2000); Raffaele Romanelli, *L'Italia liberale 1861–1900* (Bologna: Il Mulino, 1979); and Christopher Seton-Watson, *Italy from Liberalism to Fascism 1870–1925* (London: Methuen, 1967).

8. The situation stood in stark contrast to that in the rest of Western Europe, where the rise of the wage economy and the industrialization of the food sectors meant more food, at cheaper prices, for more consumers. Expanded colonial production, domestic distribution systems, and modern food-processing systems made goods like tea, coffee, cocoa, and liquor commonplace. Consumers ate more fresh produce, meats, and dairy products and spent less on bread, corn, and potatoes. For an overview of nineteenth-century western European dietary trends, see H.J. Teuteberg, 'The General Relationship between Diet and Industrialization', in Elborg Forster and Robert Forster (eds), *European Diet from Pre-Industrial to Modern Times* (New York: Harper and Row, 1975), p. 79.

9. Roberto Vivarelli, 'La questione contadina nell'Italia unita,' *Rivista storica italiana* 102, 1 (April 1990), p. 117.

10. Cited in Giorgina Levi, 'L'alimentazione dei lavoratori in Piemonte nell'ultimo ventennio del secolo XIX', in Renato Allio (ed.), *Il tempo di riposo* (Milan: Feltrinelli, 1991), p. 24.

11. Inchiesta della Società Italiana di Antropologia ed Etnologia, published in *Annali di Statistica* Serie II, Vol. 8 (1879), cited in Guido Galeotti, *Condizioni ed evoluzione dei consumi alimentari in Italia* (Rome: Unione Nazionale Consumatori, 1969), p. 20. See also Costantino Felice, *Il disagio di vivere: Il cibo, la casa, le malattie in Abruzzo e Molise dall'Unità al secondo dopoguerra* (Milan: Franco Angeli, 1989), pp. 19–21.

12. Piero Bevilacqua, 'Emigrazione transoceanica e mutamenti dell'alimentazione contadina Calabrese fra Otto e Novecento,' *Quaderni storici* 6, 47 (August 1981), p. 524.

13. The poor as a social category constituted a sizable percentage of urban populations. Numbers vary, but Stuart Woolf, working with census data from Florence, estimated roughly 24 percent of the city's population to be poor, that is, in need of public assistance of some sort, on the eve of the First World War: Stuart Woolf, 'Come e che cosa mangiavano i Fiorentini cent'anni fa?' *Fiorentin mangia fagioli*, special publication of CGIL and Camera di Lavoro di Firenze, 1993, pp. 9–42.

14. Luigi Barzini, *The Italians* (New York: Atheneum, 1977), p. 21, p. 39. Disgusted reactions to Italian cuisine had a long history. For an overview of travelers' reactions in the seventeenth century, see Chloe Chard, 'The Intensification of Italy: Food, Wine and the Foreign in Seventeenth Century Travel Writing,' in Gerald Mars and Valerie Mars (eds), *Food, Culture and History* (London: London Food Seminar, 1993).

15. Dino Coltro, *La nostra polenta quotidiana: Storie di donne* (Venice: Marsilio, 1989), p. 32.

16. Paolo Mantegazza, *Quadri della natura umana*, Volume I, *Feste ed ebbrezze* (Milan: Giuseppe Bernadoni, 1871), p. 41.

17. Constantino Felice, *Il disagio di vivere*, p. 29.
18. Serao, *Ventre di Napoli*, pp. 1075–6.
19. Ibid., p. 1077.
20. Carlo Cipolla, *Storia economica dell'Europa pre-industriale* (Bologna: Il Mulino, 1980), pp. 38–9.
21. Maria Antonietta Visceglia, 'I consumi in Italia in età moderna,' in Ruggiero Romano (ed.), *Storia dell'economia italiana*, Volume II, *Verso la crisi* (Turin: Einaudi, 1991), pp. 211–41; Emilio Sereni, 'Note di storia dell'alimentazione nel Mezzogiorno: I Napolitani da "mangiafoglie" a "mangiamaccheroni",' in *Terra nuova e buoi rossi* (Turin: Einaudi, 1981).
22. Zamagni, *Economic History of Italy*, p. 58.
23. This was noticed by several social commentators; see for example Mario Alberti, 'Le statistiche dei prezzi delle derrate alimentari,' *La riforma sociale* 23, 19 (October 1912), pp. 700–14.
24. Measured in volume, exported goods decreased according to the following percentages: wine (70), rice (64), olive oil (48) and increased: eggs (106), pasta (170), citrus fruit (350), fresh produce (753), cheese (841), and flour (2,128). Imports increased for tobacco (109), preserved fish (137), wheat (193), coffee (264), and cereals (1,110). Zamagni, *Economic History of Italy*, pp. 118–19, Table 3.2.
25. And the backward status of their own profession. Historian Raymond Grew observed that nineteenth-century Italian scientists attempted to compete with their European counterparts, but a 'concern that Italy was backward acquired a lasting place in Italian national discourse.' Raymond Grew, 'Culture and Society, 1796–1896', in John Davis (ed.), *Italy in the Nineteenth Century* (Oxford: Oxford University Press, 2000), p. 217.
26. The study of statistics arose in the wake of the Napoleonic era, detailing human behaviors, especially crime and suicide. On the relation of statistics to the rise of 'objective' knowledge about natural and social processes, see Ian Hacking, *The Taming of Chance* (Cambridge: Cambridge University Press, 1990); and Theodore M. Porter, *The Rise of Statistical Thinking, 1820–1900* (Princeton University Press, 1986). On Italian food monographs, see Stefano Somogyi, 'L'alimentazione nell'Italia unita,' *Storia d'Italia* Vol. 5, Tomo 1, *I documenti* (Turin: Einaudi, 1973), p. 846. On Italian statistics see Carl Ipsen, *Dictating Demography: The Problem of Population in Fascist Italy* (Cambridge: Cambridge University Press, 1996) and Silvana Patriarca, *Numbers and Nationhood: Writing Statistics in Nineteenth-Century Italy* (Cambridge: Cambridge University Press, 1996).
27. Alberto Caracciolo, *L'inchiesta agraria Jacini* (Turin: Einaudi, 1973), p. 86.
28. On degeneration in France, see Robert Nye, *Crime, Madness and Politics in Modern France: The Medical Concept of National Decline* (Princeton:

Princeton University Press, 1984); Karen Offen, 'Depopulation, Nationalism and Feminism in *Fin-de-Siècle* France', *American Historical Review* 89, 3 (June 1984), pp. 648–76; and Rabinbach, *Human Motor*, Chapters 1 and 6. British fears of degeneration were tied more closely to the physical stature of the working classes and their military performance in the Boer War and the First World War; see for example John Burnett, *Plenty and Want: A Social History of Diet in England from 1815 to the Present Day* (London: Nelson, 1966), Chapters 8 and 11; and J.M. Winter, 'Military Fitness and Civilian Health in Britain During the First World War,' *Journal of Contemporary History* 15 (1980), pp. 211–44.

29. Consumption habits of the middle and upper classes were largely unexamined by the scientific communities, except in cases where anecdotal evidence about their food habits was used to contrast to the habits of less fortunate populations.

30. Social scientists usually distributed ledgers (*libretti*) in which families recorded consumer purchases, estimates of spending, and daily meal plans. Completed ledgers were almost always returned to the author of the study, but they did not always reveal an accurate assessment of consumption habits. Gina Lombroso noted that in her 1896 study of a suburb of Turin, housewives severely underestimated the amount of money spent on food as well as the volume of food consumed by the family, 'as if they have the intention of living on air.' Information about diet had to be gleaned from a variety of sources and scientists tended to rely more on personal observation, seeing that the data coming directly from the subjects was unreliable, even unusable. Gina Lombroso, 'Sulle condizioni sociali economiche degli operai di un sobborgo di Torino,' *La riforma sociale* 3, 6 (10 September 1896), p. 323.

31. Tammèo, *La prostituzione: Saggio di statistica morale*, published in 1890 and cited in Alfredo Niceforo, *Italiani del nord e Italiani del sud* (Turin: Fratelli Bocca, 1901), p. 178.

32. Francesco Nitti, 'L'alimentazione e la forza di lavoro dei popoli,' *La riforma sociale* 1, 2, 18, 19 (1894), p. 541.

33. There would not be an established international scientific nutritional standard for diet until the First World War, when the Interallied Scientific Commission issued a recommendation for a minimum of 145 grams of protein, 75 grams of fat, 480 grams of carbohydrates, and 3,300 calories daily for a person engaged in moderate labor. On the debate between German and American physiologists over protein and fat intake, see Avner Offer, *The First World War: An Agrarian Interpretation* (Oxford: Clarendon, 1989).

34. See, for example, Ruggero Oddi, *Gli alimenti e la loro funzione nella economia dell'organismo individuale e sociale* (Turin: Fratelli Bocca, 1902), pp. 42–3.

35. Sidney Sonnino, *Discorsi parlamentare*, 1925, cited in Roberto Vivarelli, 'La questione contadino nell'Italia unita', pp. 91–2.

36. Arsenio Brugnola, *Il bilancio nutritivo e l'alimentazione del contadino nell' Umbria come base allo studio dell'etiologia della pellagra* (Perugia: Tipografia Cooperativa, 1903), pp. 153–4.

37. Pietro Albertoni and Felice Rossi, 'Bilancio nutritivo del contadino Abruzzese e sue condizioni fisiologiche, psicologiche ed economiche', originally published in 1906 and reprinted in Commissione per lo Studio di Problemi dell'Alimentazione, *Studi sulla alimentazione di Pietro Albertoni e di Angelo Pugliese* (Naples: N. Jovene, 1937), p. 152.

38. Cited in Niceforo, *Italiani del nord e Italiani del sud*, p. 203. See also A. Zerboglio, *Le basi economiche della salute* (Alessandria: Tipografia Sociale 'La Provincia', 1897).

39. Alfredo Niceforo, *Ricerche sui contadini: Contributo allo studio antropologico ed economico delle classi povere* (Milan: Remo Sandron, 1907); and *Lo studio scientifico delle classi povere* (Trieste: Giuseppe Maylander, 1907), p. 59.

40. Maria Montessori, 'Influenza delle condizioni di famiglia sul livello intellettuale degli scolari,' *Rivista di filosofia e scienze affini* (1904), cited in Niceforo, *Forza e ricchezza: Studi sulla vita fisica ed economica delle classi sociali* (Turin: Fratelli Bocca, 1906), p. 241.

41. Francesco Nitti, 'L'alimentazione e la forza di lavoro dei popoli,' pp. 417–40, 537–56.

42. Although the framing of the Southern Problem ultimately hardened into anti-Southern prejudice and racism by the turn of the century. See Vito Teti, *La razza maledetta: Origini del pregiudizio antimeridionale* (Rome: Manifestolibri, 1993). Until recently, the 'Southern Problem' has been analyzed according to theories of economic development and modernization. The historiography of this field is simply too immense and complicated to do it justice in a footnote. An engaging summary of some of this historiography is John Davis, 'Casting off the "Southern Problem": Or the Peculiarities of the South Reconsidered,' in Jane Schneider (ed.), *Italy's 'Southern Question': Orientalism in One Country* (Oxford: Berg, 1998).

43. Achille Spatuzzi, Luigi Somma, Errico de Renzi, *Sull'alimentazione del popolo minuto in Napoli* (Naples: Stamperia della R. Universitá, 1863), pp. 105–6.

44. Sidney Sonnino, *La Sicilia nel 1876: I contadini in Sicilia* (Florence: G. Barbèra, 1877), p. 193.

45. 'Le condizioni economiche e sociali dei contadini dell'agro di Sassari,' *La riforma sociale* 16, 13 (15 April 1906), p. 279.

46. Angelo Celli, *L'alimentazione maidica e il modo di migliorarla* (Milan: Pietro Agnelli, 1897).

47. On this point see Paolo Sorcinelli, *Gli Italiani e il cibo*, p. 117.

48. Alfredo Niceforo, *Italiani del nord e italiani del sud*. Niceforo's conclusions were also cited in Guido Galeotti, *Condizioni ed evoluzione dei consumi alimentari in Italia*, p. 23. Southern Italians consumed more wheat than their Northern counterparts, but this statistic is negligible, Niceforo asserts, if we consider that overall, Northern Italians consumed more cereals and grains than did Southern Italians.

49. Alfredo Niceforo, *Italiani del nord e Italiani del sud*, p. 163.

50. Ibid., p. 183.

51. Cited in ibid., p. 203.

52. For example, the average difference in the north between the lower orders and the well off (*agiati*) was 2.1 centimeters whereas in the south it was 3.4 centimeters, and on the two islands, it was 3 centimeters. Ibid., pp. 1–5, 26–7, and 132–3.

53. Gina Lombroso, 'Sulle condizioni sociali economiche degli operai di un sobborgo di Torino,' p. 324.

54. F. Cardani, and F. Massari, *Condizioni economico-rurali del contadino Cremasco, Milanese, Pavese, Lodigiano*, cited in Stefano Somogyi, 'L'alimentazione nell'Italia unita,' p. 845.

55. Alberto Caracciolo, *L'inchiesta agraria Jacini*, p. 157.

56. Renato Allio, 'Pane e minestra – Perdrix et bécasses', *Studi Piemontesi*, 15, 2 (November 1986), pp. 359–77.

57. Ibid., p. 369. There were 443 mutual-aid societies in Italy in 1862 and this number grew to 6,535 by 1904. These societies provided sick pay, pensions, and loans, and some opened consumer cooperatives. Zamagni, *The Economic History of Italy*, p. 205.

58. Paolo Sorcinelli, *Gli Italiani e il cibo*, pp. 43–7. On the history of food taxes in liberal Italy see Giuseppe Moricola, 'Il "commensale insaziabile": fiscalità e consumi alimentari in età liberale,' in Alberto Capatti, Alberto De Bernardi, and Angelo Varni (eds), *Storia d'Italia*, Annali 13, *L'alimentazione* (Turin: Einaudi, 1998), p. 348. The work of Jonathan Morris on shopkeepers in Milan clearly demonstrates that members of the retail sector were particularly anxious about the effects of customs duties on profit margins and their ability to attract customers. Jonathan Morris, *The Political Economy of Shopkeeping in Milan, 1886–1922* (Cambridge: Cambridge University Press, 1993). See also Paolo Sorcinelli, *Gli Italiani e il cibo*, pp. 43–7.

59. Giulio Curato, 'Monografie di famiglie borghesi del comune di Troja (Provincia di Foggia)', *La riforma sociale* 21, 17 (November–December. 1910), p. 746.

60. Pietro Albertoni and Ivo Novi, 'Sul bilancio nutritivo di una famiglia borghese italiana', originally published in *Memoria di R. Accad. Di Scienze,*

Istituto di Bologna, 1896, reprinted in *Studi sulla alimentazione di Pietro Albertoni e di Angelo Pugliese*, pp. 102–3.

61. See for example Luigi Camboni, 'Monografia di famiglia agricole del Comune di Mores (Provincia di Sassari)', *Giornale degli economisti*, 30 (May–June 1905), p. 560.

62. Angelo Mosso, *La fatica* (Milan: Fratelli Treves, 1891), p. 193.

63. The history and activities of the Society are recounted in the *Bolletino della Società Italiana per lo studio della alimentazione*, Volumes 1 and 2 (Rome: Tipografia G. Ramella & Co., 1919, 1920).

64. A summary of the history of hygiene in nineteenth-century Italy can be found in Achille Sclavo, *L'igiene in Italia negli ultimi venti anni* (Siena: L. Lazzeri, 1909).

65. Piero Camporesi, 'Introduzione', in Pellegrino Artusi, *La scienza in cucina e l'arte di mangiar bene* (Turin: Einaudi, 1970), pp. x–xi.

66. Hasia Diner, *Hungering for America: Italian, Irish, and Jewish Foodways in the Age of Migration* (Cambridge MA: Harvard University Press, 2001).

67. Between 1876 and 1915, 45 percent of emigrants were from the northern regions, 20 percent came from Italy's center, and 35 percent came from the south and islands. After 1945, a little over half of Italy's emigrants would come from southern Italy. For an overview of Italy's waves of emigration, see Donna Gabaccia, *Italy's Many Diasporas* (Seattle: University of Washington Press, 2000); information on migration statistics are from page 2.

68. On return migration and emigrant remittances see Dino Cinel, *The National Integration of Italian Return Migration, 1870–1929* (Cambridge: Cambridge University Press, 1991).

69. Donna Gabaccia, *We Are What We Eat: Ethnic Food and the Making of Americans* (Cambridge MA: Harvard University Press, 1998), pp. 51–5.

70. Gabaccia, *We Are What We Eat*, Chapter Two; and Franco La Cecla, *La pasta e la pizza* (Bologna: Il Mulino, 1998). See also Diner, *Hungering for America*, Chapter 3; and Simone Cinotto, *Una famiglia che mangia insieme. Cibo ed etnicità nella comunità italoamericana di New York, 1920–1940* (Turin: Otto, 2001).

71. These observations are recorded in Piero Bevilacqua, 'Emigrazione transoceanica'.

72. Report of A. Bernandy, published in *Bolletino dell'emigrazione* 1911, cited in ibid., p. 539.

73. Peppino Ortoleva, 'La tradizione e l'abbondanza: Riflessioni sulla cucina degli italiani d'America,' *AltreItaliani* (January–June 1992), p. 47.

74. Simone Cinotto, *Una famiglia che mangia insieme*, Chapter One.

75. E. Franzina, *Merica! Merica! Emigrazione e colonizzazione nelle lettere dei contadini veneti in America Latina (1876–1902)*, cited in Paola Corti,

'Emigrazione e consuetudini alimentari', in Capatti *et al.*, *Storia d'Italia*, Annali 13, *L'alimentazione*, p. 697.

76. Emilio Sereni, *Terra nuova e buoi rossi*.

77. Franco La Cecla, *La pasta e la pizza*, pp. 60–61; Donna Gabaccia, *We Are What We Eat*, pp. 150–51.

78. United States Tariff Commission, *Italian Commercial Policy and Foreign Trade, 1922–1940* (Washington DC: Government Printing Office, 1941); Istituto Nazionale delle Conserve Alimentari. Federazione Nazionale Fascista delle Conserve Alimentari, *Annuario dell'industria delle conserve alimentari* (Rome: SAIGE, 1934).

79. Indeed, many Italian immigrants reproduced markets for the various specialties of their particular region; for example, Paola Corti found the reproduction of Piedmontese cuisine by immigrants to include dishes like *bagna cauda*, *asado*, and *salami*, yet industries producing regional prepared foods – *panforte* from Siena or *salami* from Piedmont – remained relatively small. Paola Corti, 'Emigrazione e consuetudini alimentari.'

80. It should also be pointed out that the acts of out-migration and remittance, in some areas, made for dietary improvements within Italy. Piero Bevilacqua's study of Calabria, for example, argues for a greater diffusion of meat, coffee, and tea consumption because Calabrians could afford a better diet: Bevilacqua, 'Emigrazione transoceanica.'

81. Zamagni, *Economic History of Italy*, pp. 186–9, p. 202.

82. Riccardo Bachi, *L'alimentazione e la politica annonaria in Italia* (Bari: Laterza, 1926), pp. 18–23.

83. Study conducted by the Ministero dell'Interno, Direzione Generale di Sanità, and cited in Aristide Tomiolo, 'Il problema della carne in Venezia nell'anno 1910', in Municipio di Venezia, *Relazione della Giunta al Consiglio Comunale circa le proposte presentate dalla Commissione per il Rincaro dei Viveri* (Venice: C. Ferrari, 1912), Table 2.

84. The inquest was published in eight volumes between 1909 and 1911. The scope was grand: 15,500 questionnaires were distributed, out of which 6,400 were returned, and later, the inquest delegation interviewed 3,400 respondents. *Inchiesta parliamentare sulle condizioni dei contadini nelle provincie meridionali e nella Sicilia* (Rome: Giovanni Bertero, 1909–11), Volumes I–VIII. The regions covered were Abruzzi, Molise, Campania, Puglie, Calabria, Basilicata, and Sicilia.

85. Vol. V, Tomo II, *Calabrie*, p. 480. See also Vol. VIII, *Relazione finale dal presidente*, pp. 28, 32, 43, 46–7. The exception to this was Basilicata, where observers lamented that despite improving economic conditions, the diet of the peasants remained unchanged. Vol. VIII, *Relazione finale dal presidente*, p. 39.

86. Vol. V, Tomo II, *Calabrie*, p. 476.
87. Angelo Preziotti, 'I consumi del contadino nel comune di Cannara (Provincia di Umbria)' *La riforma sociale* 16, 13 (15 August 1906), p. 647.
88. Domenico Orano, *Come vive il popolo a Roma: Saggio demografico sul quartiere Testaccio* (Pescara: Ettore Croce, 1912), p. 429. The study covered the spending and consumption habits of 1,300 families.
89. For an overview of the Italian food industry see Francesco Chiapparino, 'Tra polverizzazione e concentrazione: L'industria alimentare dall'Unità al periodo tra le due guerre,' in Capatti *et al., Storia d'Italia,* Annali 13, *L'alimentazione,* pp. 207–70.
90. Francesco Chiapparino, 'Nascita di una grande impresa: la Perugina, 1907–1923', *Proposte e ricerche* 23 (1989), p. 242.
91. Menuccio Ruini, 'The Italian Co-operative Movement,' *International Labour Review,* 5, 1 (January 1922), pp. 13–33.
92. Alberto De Bernardi, 'Pellagra, stato e scienza medica: la curabilità impossibile', in Franco Della Peruta (ed.), *Storia d'Italia,* Annali 7, *Malattìa e medicina* (Turin: Einaudi, 1984), p. 700.
93. *Inchiesta parlamentare sulle condizioni dei contadini nelle provincie meridionali e nella Sicilia,* Vol. VI, Tomo I, *Sicilia,* p. 458.

Chapter 2 The Great War and the Rise of State Intervention

1. Avner Offer, *The First World War: An Agrarian Interpretation* (Oxford: Clarendon, 1989), p. 1. In nineteenth-century Europe, government intervention usually assisted populations in need, in particular schoolchildren and the urban poor. For an overview of the historical development of food policies in Europe see John Burnett and Derek Oddy, 'Introduction' to their edited collection, *The Origins and Development of Food Policies in Europe* (Leicester: Leicester University Press, 1994).
2. According to the terms of the Pact of London (26 April 1915), Italy committed itself to the war on the side of the Entente in order to receive the Trentino, Cisalpine Tyrol, Istria, Trieste, parts of Dalmatia, and several islands on the Adriatic.
3. Antonio Gibelli's *La Grande Guerra degli Italiani* 1915–1918 (Milan: Sansoni, 1998) synthesizes many of the recent histories written on the war. Works that deal with the social and cultural aspects of the war include: Bruno Bezza and Giovanna Procacci (eds), *Stato e classe operaia in Italia durante la prima guerra mondiale* (Milan: Franco Angeli, 1983); Alessandro Camarda and Santo Peli (eds), *L'altro esercito: La classe operaia durante la prima guerra mondiale* (Milan: Feltrinelli, 1980); Mario Isenghi, *Operai e contadina nella Grande Guerra* (Bologna: Capelli, 1982); Diego Leoni and

Camillo Zadra (eds), *La Grande Guerra: Esperienza, memoria, immagini* (Bologna: Il Mulino, 1986); and Luigi Tomassini, *L'Italia nella Grande Guerra, 1915–1918* (Milan: La Fenice, 1995).

4. There is one recent study of food policy in the First World War Italy: see Maria Concetta Dentoni, *Annona e consenso in Italia 1914–1919* (Milan: Franco Angeli, 1995).

5. This was the argument made by Riccardo Bachi, *L'alimentazione e la politica annonaria in Italia* (Bari: Laterza, 1926) and Giorgio Mortara, *La salute pubblica in Italia durante e dopo la guerra* (Bari: Laterza, 1925).

6. The financial ramifications of this are discussed in Douglas Forsyth, *The Crisis of Liberal Italy: Monetary and Fiscal Policy, 1914–1922* (Cambridge: Cambridge University Press, 1993).

7. A Royal Decree Law (20 December 1914) allowed chambers of commerce and consumer cooperatives to band together for the purpose of requesting cereals from the government, through a national consortium directed by the Ministry of the Interior. Between December 1914 and June 1915, over sixty-eight provincial consortia had formed, acquiring and distributing a substantial volume of cereals, including over 2.5 million quintals of wheat. Figures from December 1914 to June 1915 include 2,537,219 million quintals of wheat; 19,163 quintals of corn; 2,401 quintals of flour; and 114,839 quintals of other cereals, all worth over ninety-one million lire. Unione delle Provincie d'Italia, *I consorzi granari provinciali e la loro opera a tutto il 30 giugno 1915: Considerazione sommarie e dati statistici* (Rome: Tipografia Cooperativa Sociale, 1915), in Archivio Centrale dello Stato (hereafter referred to as ACS), Ministero dell'Interno, Divisione per le Amministrazioni Communali e Provinciali (hereafter referred to as Comuni), 1913–15, busta 837, fascicolo 15.100.60–A, division 2, section 2.

8. The history of UTAG is faithfully recounted in Vicenzo Giuffrida, *Provital: Approvvigionamenti alimentari d'Italia durante la Grande Guerra* (Padua: CEDAM, 1936).

9. To offer a comparison, imports of other cereals averaged a 270 percent increase over the course of the war. Military provisioning also led to dramatic increases of imports for fresh and frozen meat, coffee, sugar, and cocoa. Giuffrida, *Provital*, pp. 316–17; Gaetano Pietra, 'In regime alimentare sanzionistico,' *L'economia italiana* 21, 2 (February 1936), p. 146.

10. Giorgio Mortara, *Prospettive economiche 1922* (Milan: Università Bocconi, 1922), pp. 16–17.

11. Prime Minister Antonio Salandra recognized the need for Italy to produce more wheat. Beginning in the winter of 1915, Salandra's government began tracking grain supplies and production through an annual grain census. Prefects reported adequate supplies for the winter and spring of 1915, but

declared that almost nothing was left over for emergencies or for export to other regions. Salandra's ministers also tried to boost agricultural production in 1915, offering agricultural credit, machinery and fertilizers, and offering awards to farmers with the highest yields. Lastly, the government was prepared to intervene, if necessary, in any labor disputes that might impact on production. Luigi Einaudi, *La condotta economica e gli aspetti sociali della guerra italiana* (Bari: Laterza, 1933), pp. 133–5. On the grain census, see ACS, Presidenza del Consiglio dei Ministri, Guerra Mondiale, 1915–18 (Hereafter referred to as PCM Guerra), b. 49, f.2: 'Censimento di Grano'.

12. The protests began on 10 January 1915 and continued until 21 March 1915. ACS, Ministero dell'Interno, Direzione Generale Pubblica Sicurezza, Divisione Polizia Giudiziaria (hereafter referred to as Polizia Giudiziaria), 1913–15, b. 3, f. 10071.1–10071.29.

13. ACS Polizia Giudiziaria 1913–15, b. 3, f. 10071.2: 'Ancona' and f. 10071.12: 'Brescia.'

14. Memorandum from the Minister of Agriculture to the Minister of the Interior, dated 25 August 1916. ACS Direzione Generale Sanità Pubblica, Atti Amministrativi, 1910–20, b. 584.

15. Implementation of and protest against the export bans can be found in ACS, Comuni 1913–15, b. 838, f. 15100–75, division 2a, section 2a; and Comuni, 1913–15, b. 837, f. 15100–60, division 2, section 2; and Comuni 1916–18, b. 1101. Government surveillance of potential violators of export bans can be found in ACS, Ministero dell'Interno, Polizia Giudiziaria, 1890–1919, bb. 183 and 184.

16. In Milan, price controls were instituted as early as 6 August 1914 and for most of 1914 and a few months into 1915, bread sold for 2–3 cents under the fixed price. Rome took immediate action by instituting fixed prices on bread and other items in August 1914, using municipal bakeries to set an example and pressure private bakeries into compliance. See Emilio Coldara on Milan and Saverio Benucci on Rome, in Massone *et al.*, 'La lotta contro il caro-viveri,' *Nuova Antologia* 186 (1 November 1916), pp. 97–110.

17. Reports from the Prefect of Genoa to the Minister of the Interior, ACS Polizia Giudiziaria 1913–15, b. 3, f. 10071.28: 'Genoa.'

18. Telegram from S.R., Cattolica Eraclèa, to Ministry of Interior, dated 25 July 1915. Telegram from Comune di Monterchi, Prov. Di Arezzo, to Ministry of Interior, dated 20 February 1915. ACS Comuni, b. 837, category 15.100 'Affari Vari,' division 2, section 2.

19. Report from Bologna, Memorandum from Ministry of Interior, Direzione Generale, to Divisione Quarta, Re: Bologna. ACS Polizia Giudiziaria, b. 3, f. 10071.11: 'Bologna, Rincaro Viveri.'

20. Aldo Contento, 'La guerra e l'aumento regionale dei prezzi,' *Giornale degli economisti* 56 (May 1918), p. 260; Giuffrida, *Provital*, p. 165.

21. Silvio Crespi, *La politica degli approvvigionamenti in Italia* (Rome: Tipografia del Senato, 1918), p. 11.

22. Graham Lusk, *The Elements of the Science of Nutrition* (Academic Press, 1976[1906]), pp. 75–7. See also E.H. Starling, *Report on Food Conditions in Germany* (London: HMSO, 1919). The Italian perspective on the Food Committee is recounted in Giuffrida, *Provital*, Chapters 10 and 14.

23. Paolo Sorcinelli, *Gli Italiani e il cibo: Apetiti, digiuni e rinunce della realtà contadina alla società del benessere* (Bologna: CLUEB, 1992), p. 152.

24. Almost six million men were mobilized for service over the course of the war, out of a population of thirty-six million.

25. Filippo Rho, *L'alimentazione del soldato di terra e di mare in pace e in guerra* (Milan: Rava, 1915); and 'La riforma della razione alimentare e del soldato e l'economia nazionale,' *Annali d'igiene* 27 (1917), pp. 477–87; Gaetano Zingali, *Il rifornamento dei viveri dell'esercito italiano* (Bari: Laterza, 1926).

26. Angelo Pugliese, 'L'alimentazione del nostro soldato in guerra', originally published in 1915 and reprinted in Commissione per lo Studio di Problemi dell'Alimentazione, *Studi sull'alimentazione di Pietro Albertoni and Angelo Pugliese* (Naples: N. Jovene, 1937), pp. 421–34.

27. Zingali, *Il rifornamento dei viveri dell'esercito italiano*, p. 31; Giuffrida, *Provital*, p. 262.

28. Pugliese, 'L'alimentazione del nostro soldato in guerra,' p. 427.

29. Francesco Amateis, *La lotta contro il caro vivere* (Milan: U. Hoepli, 1916), pp. 13–14.

30. Assunta Trova, 'L'approvvigionamento alimentare dell'esercito italiano dall'Unità alla Seconda Guerra Mondiale,' in Capatti *et al.* (eds), *Storia d'Italia*, Annali 13: *L'alimentazione* (Turin: Einaudi, 1998): 497–530.

31. Giovanni Giuriati, *Diario di guerra* (Scheiwiller, 1988), cited in Gibelli, *La Grande Guerra degli Italiani 1915–1918*, p. 158. Giuriati was an 18-year-old peasant from Treviso who had been captured by the Austrians. Giorgio Mortara's study of public health during the war noted that lack of food was the primary cause of death for Italians in prisoner-of-war camps. Mortara, *La salute pubblica in Italia durante e dopo la guerra*, p. 53.

32. On food preservation during the war see Guido Rovesti, *Conserve alimentari di guerra* (Casale Monferrato: Fratelli Marescalchi, 1917).

33. The scientific debate over rations and their relation to military defeat at Caporetto is discussed by Zingali, *Il rifornamento*, pp. 531–2.

34. Alessandro Lustig, 'Considerazioni personali sulla razione alimentare dei soldati,' *Bolletino della Società Italiana per lo Studio della Alimentazione* 1, 4–6 (1919), pp. 83–90.

35. Zingali, *Il rifornamento*, p. 643.
36. Benito Mussolini, *My Diary, 1915–17*, trans. Rita Wellman (Boston: Small, Maynard, 1925), p. 42.
37. Letter to the Secretary of State from the American Consulate in Florence, dated 19 September 1917. United States Department of State, *Records of the Department of State Relating to the Internal Affairs of Italy, 1910–1929*, Microfilm Series. Reel 51, Document 865.50/29.
38. Bachi, *L'alimentazione e la politica annonaria in Italia*, p. 275.
39. These requests can be found in ACS Polizia Giudiziaria 1916–18, b. 4.
40. ACS PCM Guerra, b. 142, s.f. 11: 'Restrizioni nei consumi.'
41. For example, the Convegno Nazionale dei Commercianti ed Esercenti condemned Canepa's performance at a meeting in July–September, 1917. Camera di Commercio e Industria della Provincia di Bergamo, *In merito all'Ente Nazionale dei Consumi ed ai provvedimenti economici governativi* (Bergamo: Tipografia Commerciale, 1917), p. 5.
42. Rationing for grain, flour, and bread was made obligatory. In areas where pasta, corn, corn flour, rice, rye, or barley were considered to be primary foods, those items were rationed as well. ACS PCM Guerra 1915–18, b. 142, s.f. 12.
43. U.S. observers questioned Crespi's competence at a time when Italy appeared to be on the brink of social revolution, noting that he had almost failed in the manufacture of cotton goods until he was bailed out by the Banca Commerciale Italiana. It was thought that the Banca Commerciale played a strong role in Crespi's rise to power as food undersecretary. Letter from Karl G. Macvitty, American Vice Consul for Genoa, to the U.S. Secretary of State, dated 25 September, 1918. United States Department of State, *Records of the Department of State Relating to the Internal Affairs of Italy*, 1910–29, Reel 51 Document 865.50/58.
44. Dentoni, *Annona e consenso in Italia*, p. 66.
45. Many of these arguments in the press are summarized in 'La politica degli approvvigionamenti e dei consumi', *Nuova Antologia* 187 (16 September 1917), pp. ix–xvi.
46. Umberto Ricci, *Il fallimento della politica annonaria* (Florence: La Voce, 1921), p. 193 and p. 450. Ricci was a professor of statistics at the University of Pisa.
47. Giacomo Bonomo, *Il prezzo d'impero del grano e la politica agraria ed annonaria di guerra* (Messina: D'Angelo, 1917), pp. 80–1.
48. Susan Zuccotti, 'The Wartime Experience and Politicization: Workers and Peasants in the Province of Milan, 1915–18,' Ph.D. Dissertation, Columbia University, 1979, pp. 296–300.
49. Dentoni, *Annona e consenso in Italia*, p. 121.

50. ACS Polizia Giudiziaria 1916–18, bb. 4 and 5.
51. Circular from the Prefect of Turin to all mayors, dated 18 August 1918. ACS PCM Guerra 1915–18, b. 142, f. 4.
52. Fresh and frozen meat imports increased 1,300 percent and sugar imports increased 600 percent. Giuffrida, *Provital*, p. 252.
53. Office of Labor study cited in Michele Pietravalle, *Politica annonaria di guerra* (Campobasso: Giovanni Colitti e Figlio, 1917), p. 12. Mario Balestrieri, *I consumi alimentari della popolazione italiana dal 1910 al 1921* (Padua: Metron, 1942). Balestrieri was a professor of statistics at the University of Padua.
54. United States Tariff Commission, *Italian Commercial Policy and Foreign Trade, 1922–1940*, Second Series (Washington DC: Government Printing Office, 1941), p. 75. H. Earle Russell, Consul of Rome, Italy, 'Italian Grain Production and Trade,' 28 March 1924. United States Department of State, *Records of the Department of State*, Microfilm reel 51, document 865.6131/15. These estimates were confirmed by Balestrieri, *I consumi alimentari*.
55. Luigi Einaudi, 'Il problema del riso e l'esportazione ell'estero,' pp. 243–7 in Luigi Einaudi, *Cronache economiche,* Vol. IV (1914–18) (Turin: Einaudi, 1961).
56. The Comitato Scientifico per l'Alimentazione noted the lack of wartime studies and in 1918, urged the government to better coordinate statistics and studies of food-consumption habits by instituting more grand inquiries and funding smaller scale studies. Francesco Coletti, 'Ricerche statistiche sui consumi alimentari in Italia,' *Reale Accademia dei Lincei, Comitato Scientifico per l'Alimentazione* 3 (1918), pp. 1–6.
57. Angelo Pugliese, 'Alimentazione della famiglia operaia durante la guerra,' first published in 1918, reprinted in Commissione per lo Studio di Problemi dell'Alimentazione, *Studi sulla alimentazione*, pp. 455–8, p. 475. His work on the province of Milan was published as *L'alimentazione popolare in Provincia di Milano: Se e come si può migliorare* (Milan: Grafica degli Operai, 1920).
58. Angelo Pugliese, *Brevi cenni sulle condizioni igieniche della provincia di Milano con speciale riguardo all'alcoolismo e al nicotismo degli adolescenti* (Milan: Grafica degli Operai, 1920), p. 24, pp. 36–7, p. 84.
59. Guglielmo Tagliacarne, 'La spesa per l'alimentazione in una grande città,' *Il commercio* 4, 11 (November 1931), pp. 70–6.
60. Guido Possenti, 'La finanza italiana ed i consumi voluttuari,' *Economia* 2, 10–11 (October–November 1924), pp. 240–1.
61. Einaudi, *La condotta economica*, p. 182.
62. For example, Corrado Gini, 'Prefazione', p. vii, in Mario Balestrieri, *I consumi alimentari*.

63. For example, Ettore Piccoli, *L'alimentazione dell'uomo* (Milan: R. Quintieri, 1921), p. 32; N.R. D'Alfonso, *Il problema dell'alimentazione come problema educativo* (Milan: Società Libreria, 1918), p. 28.

64. These books included the above-mentioned works by Piccoli and D'Alfonso as well as Achille Sclavo, *Sull'alimentazione umana* (Siena: Lazzeri, 1917).

65. Speech of Crespi to the Chamber of Deputies, 25 November 1918, cited in Bachi, *L'alimentazione e la politica annonaria in Italia*, p. 167.

66. See, for example, Reale Commissione d'Inchiesta sulle Violazioni del Diritto delle Genti Commesse dal Nemico, *Documenti raccolti nelle provincie invase*, Vol. VI (Milan: Bestetti and Tumminelli, 1920); and Comune di Venezia, Ufficio di Statistica, *Il censimento generale del 1 Dicembre 1921 della popolazione di Venezia* (Rome: Poligrafica Italiana, 1923).

67. Documents in ACS Polizia Giudiziaria 1916–18, b. 5.

68. See Robert Vivarelli, *Il fallimento del liberalismo. Studi sulle origini del fascismo* (Bologna: Il Mulino, 1981).

69. Adrian Lyttelton, *The Seizure of Power: Fascism in Italy 1919–1929* (Princeton: Princeton University Press, 1973), pp. 30–1.

70. Milan data reported in Bachi, *L'alimentazione e la politica annonaria in Italia*, p. 171. Wage statistics from Alberto Cova, *L'occupazione e i salari: Contribuiti per una storia del movimento sindacale in Italia* (Milan: Franco Angeli, 1977), p. 45, Table 2.10.

71. Circular from the Ministry of Interior to the Prefects, dated 28 May 1919. ACS Pubblic Sicurezza 1920, b. 70, f. C1 8, s.f.: 'Approvvigionamenti.'

72. On food riots elsewhere during the First World War, see Belinda Davis, *Home Fires Burning: Food, Politics, and Everyday Life in World War I Berlin* (Chapel Hill: University of North Carolina, 2000); and Barbara Alpern Engel, 'Not by Bread Alone: Subsistence Riots in Russia During World War I', *Journal of Modern History* 69 (December 1997), pp. 696–721.

73. Telespresso from Prefect of Vicenza to Ministry of Interior, dated 14 August 1919. ACS Pubblica Sicurezza 1919, b. 153: 'Agitazione Caroviveri'.

74. Riccardo Bachi observed erroneously that local authorities requisitioned goods without the consent of merchants, thereby lending an air of semi-legality to the riots: Bachi, *L'alimentazione e la politica annonaria in Italia*, p. 169. Archival evidence suggests that local retailers cooperated and even initiated measures to prevent looting. See for example the telegrams from the prefects to the Ministry of Interior, ACS Pubblica Sicurezza 1919, b. 153: 'Agitazione Caroviveri.'

75. Telegram from Nitti to the Prefect of Palermo, dated 8 July, 1919. ACS Pubblica Sicurezza 1920, b. 70, s.f. 'Approvvigionamenti'.

76. Camarda and Peli, *L'altro esercito*, p. 243.

77. Order of the day, sent by the General Confederation of Italian Industry to the

Prime Minister, dated 7 June 1919. ACS PCM Guerra 1915–18, b. 143, f. 24.

78. Concern that the government was not doing enough to control retail activity echoed internationally. Woodrow Wilson, in his message to the US Congress on 14 August 1919, urged European nations to continue wartime controls with particular attention accorded to the retail sector: to crack down on speculation, institute new governmental agencies to inform the public of retail price controls, and supervise interregional trafficking in foodstuffs. Telegram from New York (sender unknown) to the President of the Council of Ministries regarding President Wilson's Congressional speech on the cost of living, 14 August 1919. ACS PCM Guerra 1915–18, b. 144, f. 33.

79. Order of the Day, sent by the National Confederation of the Association of Merchants and Retailers to the Prime Minister, dated 10 May 1919. ACS PCM Guerra 1915–18, b. 143, f. 24.

80. Mortara, *Prospettive Economiche 1922*, pp. 16–17.

81. Forsyth, *Crisis of Liberal Italy*, p. 247.

82. Riccardo De Angeli, 'Il problema del prezzo del pane', *La critica sociale* 30, 21 (1–15 November 1920), p. 331.

83. Paolo Frascani, *Politica economica e finanza pubblica durante la prima dopoguerra* (Naples: Giannini e Figli, 1975), p. 154. Liberal economist Luigi Einaudi also criticized the dual price system because it would be difficult to determine who should be allowed to purchase which type of bread. Luigi Einaudi, 'I due prezzi del pane,' *Cronache economiche e politiche*, Vol. VII (1919–20) (Turin: Einaudi, 1965), p. 617.

84. Charles Maier, *Recasting Bourgeois Europe: Stabilization in France, Germany and Italy in the Decade After World War I* (Princeton: Princeton University Press, 1975), p. 173.

85. 'Contro l'aumento del prezzo del pane per i lavoratori', *Avanti!* (30 March 1920), cited in Pietro Nenni, *Storia di quattro anni, 1918–22* (Milan: SugarCo., 1976), p. 97, footnote 27.

86. Forsyth, *Crisis of Liberal Italy*, p. 235.

87. Cited in Luigi Einaudi, 'Grovigli inestricabili,' *Cronache economiche*, Vol. VII (1919–20), p. 631.

88. These foods were wheat bread, wheat flour, macaroni, beef, bacon, oil, milk, rice, and butter. Ugo Giusti, 'Methods of Recording Retail Prices and Measuring the Cost of Living in Italy,' *International Labour Review* 4, 3 (November 1921), p. 259.

89. Maier, *Recasting Bourgeois Europe*, pp. 324–5.

90. Luigi Einaudi, 'L'ostruzionismo sul pane,' *Cronache economiche,* Vol. VI (1914–18), p. 16.

91. Gaetano Rasi, 'La politica economica e i conti della nazione', *Annali*

dell'economia italiana, Vol. 6, No. 1 (1915–22) (Milan: Istituto IPSOA, 1982), p. 154.

92. Flyer attributed to the Casa del Popolo, Camera del Lavoro Confederale, Rome, undated. ACS Pubblica Sicurezza 1921, b. 61, f. 24: Prezzo del Pane.
93. Notiziario, 18 June 1921, 'Contro il caro vita – Movimento Fascista,' ACS Pubblica Sicurezza 1921, b. 61, f. 4: 'Approvvigionamento.'
94. Ugo Trevisanto, 'Sulla falsa via', *Gazzetta di Venezia*, 22 June 1921, reprinted in Trevisanto, *Libertà di commercio e politica annonaria nel dopoguerra* (Bologna: Zanichelli, 1924), p. 140.
95. Mario Bellini, *Il problema dell'alimentazione nazionale* (Bologna: Paolo Neri, 1917); G. Consolani, *Se sia possibile risolvere in Italia il problema del pane e della carne* (Rovigo: Corriere, 1918); Ignazio di Pace, *La crisi della carne* (Naples: Giannini e Figlio, 1917); Maggiorno Ferraris, *Il problema dell'ora presente* (Rome: Nuova Antologia, 1919); Arnaldo Luraschi, *Memoriale presentata alla Commissione Generali dei Consumi a Roma, 7 giugno 1917* (Milan: Società Milanese, 1917); and Antonio Puglisi, *Il problema dell'approvvigionamento carneo dal punto di vista nazionale* (Rome: Enrico Voghera, 1917).
96. Filippo Virgilii, 'Il bilancio alimentare del mondo,' *Nuova Antologia* 197 (September–October 1918), p. 301.
97. Mario Ferraguti, *Battaglia per la vittoria del grano* (Milan: Stampa Commerciale, 1929), p. 24; Sebastiano Lissone, *Perchè l'Italia abbia il suo pane: il sistema Soleri* (Turin: Grafico Moderno, 1920).
98. National patrimony did not dramatically decline on account of war, but was insufficient before, during, and after the war. Gaetano Zingali, 'Del consumo e della produzione dei bovini in Italia e del programma di ricostituzione del patrimonio bovino,' *La riforma sociale* 26, 30 (September–December 1919), pp. 449–66.
99. A prime example is Gaetano Toscano, *Verso nuove forme di assistenza sociale* (Spoleto: Panetto e Petrelli, 1918).
100. See Giovanna Procacci, 'Gli effetti della Grande Guerra sulla psicologia della popolazione civile,' *Storia e problemi contemporanei* 10 (1992), pp. 77–91.

Chapter 3 The Cooking of Consent

1. Lorenzo La Via, *Politica e tecnica fascista dei prezzi* (Rome: Arti Grafiche R. Cecconi, 1937), pp. 6–7.
2. Italian nationalists emphasized the virility and not the decline of the Italian race, denouncing emigration, clamoring for an Italian empire, and trumpeting austerity as a source of strength. On the relationship between nationalism and concepts of identity and race, see Silvio Lanaro, *Nazione e lavoro:*

Saggio sulla cultura borghese in Italia 1870–1925 (Venice: Marsilio, 1979).

3. Speech to the Confederazione Generale Fascista dell'Industrie Italiane, 1933. Confederazione Generale Fascista dell'Industrie Italiane, *Fascist Era Year XII* (Rome: Confederazione Generale Fascista dell'Industrie Italiane, 1933), p. 8.

4. Benito Mussolini, speech to the Italian Senate, Rome, 18 December 1928, 'Concerning the Economic Policy of the Regime', reprinted in *Speeches of Benito Mussolini on Italian Economic Policy During the First Decennium* (Rome: Istituto Italiano di Credito Marittimo, 1932), p. 129. Not everyone agreed with Mussolini's estimation of popular eating habits. Certainly, there were fewer complaints about dietary inadequacy, but scientists still clung to some notion of nutritional backwardness. Dr. Virgilio Ducceschi, a member of the fascist National Research Council (CNR), summed up the new scientific consensus best by asserting that Italians were 'abstemious by tradition; first by choice, a virtue of even the affluent, and next by a necessity that reflects our economic and physiological misery'. Virgilio Ducceschi, *Prime linee di una storia dell'alimentazione umana* (Milan: Poligrafica degli Operai, 1936), foreword.

5. The historiography for Italian fascism is immense. Overviews of this historiography are R.J.B. Bosworth, *The Italian Dictatorship: Problems and Perspectives in the Interpretation of Mussolini and Fascism* (London: Arnold, 1998); and A. Del Boca, M. Legnani and M. Rossi, *Regime fascista: Storia e storiografia* (Bari: Laterza, 1995).

6. Letter from Giuseppe Di Cagno to Mussolini, dated 18 January 1923. ACS Comuni 1922–24, b. 1636, f. 7/15100.50: 'Bari.'

7. Cited in Luigi Einaudi, 'Cambi, prezzi e salari,' *Cronache economiche e politiche* Vol. 10 (Turin: Einaudi, 1965), p. 41.

8. Proceedings are published in Associazione dei Comuni Italiani, *Considerazioni sul problema annonario*, relatore: Carlo Piazza, Assessore per l'Annona al Comune di Milano, Congresso dei Comuni per il Problema Annonario, Rome, 10 September 1924 (Rome: Tipografia Bianchi, 1924).

9. The transportation of foodstuffs had always been a problem in Italy. See Filippo Carli, 'Il movimento delle derrate alimentari in Italia,' *Il commercio* 4, 11 (November 1931), pp. 664–93.

10. Also, the cost of transportation in the south was higher. Camera di Commercio e Industria di Roma, *Organizzazione dei sistemi di rifornamento e di distribuzione delle principali derrate alimentari* (Rome: Tipografia della Camera dei Deputati, 1924), pp. 9–10. The same sentiments are echoed in Unione delle Camere di Commercio e Industrie Italiane, *Il problema del costo della vita. Relazione presentata al convegno delle reppresentanze degli enti*

locali e delle organizzazioni economiche tenuto a Roma il 22 Giugno 1923 (Rome: Carlo Colombo, 1923).

11. Camera Confederale del Lavoro di Roma e Provincia, *Contro il caro-vita: Relazione-programma alle organizzazioni camerali* (Rome: Farri, 1925).

12. Unione delle Camere di Commercio e Industrie Italiane, *Il problema del costo della vita*, pp. 3 and 6.

13. Telegram from Prefect of Turin to Ministry of the Interior, 23 March 1923, ACS, Comuni 1922–24, b. 1637, s.f. 63/15100–60: 'Turin.' Telegram from Prefect of Milan to Ministry of the Interior, 2 October 1924, ACS Comuni 1922–24, b. 1636, s.f. 38/15100–60: 'Milan'. Telegram from the Organization of Bakery Workers, Saronno, to the Presidenza Consiglio Ministri, 13 December 1923, ACS Comuni 1922–24, b. 1991. Open letter from the merchants of Benevento to the citizens of Benevento, ACS Comuni 1922–24, b. 1636, s.f. 9/15100–60: 'Benevento.' Memorandum from the Organization of Florentine Consumers to Giacomo Acerbo, Undersecretary of State, 18 December 1923, ACS Comuni 1922–24, b. 1636, s.f. 15100–60G: 'Florence.'

14. These commissions determined bread prices but they were not allowed to implement any price changes or other policies without permission from the Ministry of the Interior. Circular from the Minister of the National Economy to the Prefects, 19 October 1924, ACS Pubblica Sicurezza 1924, b. 47, f. 42: 'Ordine Pubblico.'

15. Giacomo Matteotti was a respected Socialist deputy in Parliament who exposed fascist violence and fraud at the voting polls. He was murdered by the fascists. The public was outraged and the press called for Mussolini's resignation.

16. ACS Pubblica Sicurezza 1925, b. 72, f. 4: 'Aumento Prezzo Pane: Deficienza Grano.' Excerpt from Mussolini's speech, 'In Defense of the Lira' (Pesaro, 18 August 1926), translated and excerpted in *Speeches of Benito Mussolini*, p. 122.

17. Memo from Minister Belluzzo to Minister Federzoni regarding bread-making, 30 July 1925, ACS Comuni 1925–27, b. 1994.

18. Telegram from the Prefect of Rome to the Ministry of the Interior, 1 August 1925, ACS Pubblica Sicurezza 1925, b. 72, f. 4: 'Aumento Prezzo Pane: Deficienza Grano.' With regard to 'anti-government bakers,' Mussolini prided himself on bringing bakers into line when he cut their wages for night work and abolished the 'quintalato,' the customary walk bakers took after baking 150 kilograms of bread. Benito Mussolini, 'In defense of the lira,' *Speeches of Benito Mussolini*, p. 123.

19. Letter from Belluzzo to Federzoni, 15 October 1926, ACS Comuni, 1925–27, b. 1991. Unione delle Camere di Commercio, *Il problema dell costo di vita*, p. 7; Camera di Commercio, Roma, *Organizzazione dei sistemi*, p. 14.

20. By July of 1927 foods with price controls included rice, pasta, frozen and fresh beef, cheese, dried cod, stockfish, tuna in oil, lard, butter, corn flour, fava beans, and dried beans.

21. Those foods demonstrating highest levels of viscosity were foods like bread, wine, coffee, and canned goods: all were foods that either involved heavy processing or were imported. Foods of lower viscosity included rice, eggs, olive oil, sugar, butter, and pasta. Giacomo Veronese, 'Il problema dei prezzi all'ingrosso e di prezzi al minuto,' *Il commercio* 3, 5 (May 1930), pp. 3–26; *Gli indici dei prezzi normali all'ingrosso ed al minuto dei generi alimentari in Italia* (Rome: Tipografia del Giornale d'Italia, 1933); 'La "vischiosità" dei prezzi dei generi alimentari in Italia', *Il commercio* 6, 7 (July 1933), pp. 271–80; 'La riduzione dei prezzi,' *Il commercio*, 7, 4 (April 1934), pp. 192–3; 'Commercianti e prezzi nella politica economica attuale', *Il commercio* 9, 1 (January 1936), pp. 26–30; and *Contributo allo studio della vischiosità dei prezzi delle merci* (Rome: Carlo Colombo, 1937).

22. Miller based his observations on readings of *Il sole*. He observed that almost half the price of sugar (sixteen out of thirty-two cents per pound) went to various government taxes. Henry Miller, *Price Control in Fascist Italy* (New York: Columbia University Press, 1938), pp. 139–40. On the effects of local taxes on family spending habits, see Filippo Clementi, 'I dazi interni nei rapporti dei prezzi di consumi,' *Il commercio* 2, 4 (April 1929), pp. 30–5; and Giacomo Veronese, 'Il problema dei prezzi all'ingrosso e dei prezzi al minuto.'

23. On rationalizing the grocery trade see Lorenzo La Via, *Politica e tecnica fascista dei prezzi*, pp. 75–7. Writings from chambers of commerce include Unione delle Camere di Commercio, *Il problema del costo della vita*; Associazione Comuni Italiani, *Considerazione sul problema annonario*; and G. Martinelli, *È possible diminuire il costo della vita?* (Arezzo: Editoriale Italiana Contemporanea, 1928).

24. Regarding Minister Rossi, see Guglielmo Tagliacarne, 'Se il numero degli esercenti di vendita al minuto influisce sugli alti prezzi,' *Economia* 9, 6 (June 1931), pp. 25–39; on European comparisons, see Federazione Internazionale del Commercio al Dettaglio di Alimentari, *I problemi del commercio alimentare* (Rome: Il Giornale del Commercio, 1933).

25. Guido Possenti, 'La finanza italiana ed i consumi voluttuari,' *Economia* 2, 10–11 (October–November 1924), pp. 239–44.

26. Vera Zamagni, *La distribuzione commerciale in Italia fra le due guerre* (Milan: Franco Angeli, 1981), pp. 11, 32–3, 71. See also the proceedings from the Sixth Congress of the Federazione Internazionale del Commercio al Dettaglio di Alimentari, published as *I problemi del commercio alimentare*, for a detailed self-examination of the Italian retail sector.

27. Results of the study were published in *Quaderni della nutrizione* Vols. I, III, and V (May 1934, March 1936, and December 1938). Regional differences were addressed in Alfredo Niceforo and Guido Galeotti, 'Tipi di alimentazione in alcune regioni d'Italia,' *Barometro economico italiano* 7 (10 January 1935), pp. 39–40. Rural workers were composed of shepherds, farmers, day laborers and sharecroppers. The middle classes consisted of large landowners, managers of commercial or industrial concerns, retail merchants and civil servants. The working class included workers in industry, artisans, tradesmen, fishermen, and workers in small industrial and retail concerns.

28. Camera di Commercio e Industria, Ufficio di Statistica, *Statistica della macellazione e consumo carneo in Italia nell'anno 1925* (Milan: Archetipografia di Milano, 1927); Ugo Giusti, 'Sul consumo di generi alimentari in alcune grandi città Italiane,' *Il commercio* 3, 1 (January 1930), pp. 15–26; and Angelo Pugliese, 'Sull'uso della carne in Italia,' originally published in 1930 and reprinted in Commissione per lo Studio di Problemi dell'Alimentazione, *Studi sulla alimentazione di Pietro Albertoni e Angelo Pugliese* (Naples: N. Jovene, 1937).

29. V. Agnello, 'L'alimentazione in Sicilia,' in *Le forze sanitarie*, 3 (1934), pp. 101–10, reviewed in *Quaderni della nutrizione* 1, 2 (June 1934), p. 163.

30. Domenico Preti, *Economia e istituzioni nello stato fascista* (Rome: Editori Riuniti, 1980), p. 71.

31. 'Average-man' statistics were popular, especially in terms of determining the number of calories available, per person, in the fascist era. Statisticians based their conclusions by taking import, export, and production levels and dividing them by the number of citizens reconfigured as 'average-man'" coefficients (men between 18 and 59 were assigned a coefficient of 1; adolescent males and adult women were given a coefficient of 0.8; younger males and female adolescents and children were weighted accordingly).

32. Giuseppe Galletti, *L'alimentazione ed il suo costo* (Milan: Cooperativa Grafica degli Operai, 1923).

33. 'Agricultural Wages in Italy,' *International Labour Review* 25, 3 (March 1932), pp. 389–93; 'Wages and Hours of Work in Italian Industries in 1925,' *International Labour Review* 15, 1 (January 1927), pp. 98–103.

34. Vera Zamagni, *An Economic History of Italy*, p. 308.

35. Giuseppe Tassinari, *Fascist Economy*, trans. Eduardo Cope (Rome: Laboremus, 1937), p. 110; United States Tariff Commission, *Italian Commercial Policy and Foreign Trade*, 1922– 1940 (Washington DC: Government Printing Office, 1941), p. 77.

36. See Mario Tambara, 'Le attrezzature degli ammassi granari,' *L'economia italiana* 22, 4 (April 1937), pp. 354–60.

37. Quoted in Giuseppe Tassinari, *Fascist Economy*, p. 106.

38. For example, 'Il Duce ha iniziato la trebbiatura del grano di Sabaudia', *Agricoltura fascista* 7 (30 June 1935), p. 1.

39. On European agricultural policies during the war, see Rondo Cameron, *A Concise Economic History of the World*, 2nd edn (Oxford: Oxford University Press, 1993), pp. 347–59; and Charles P. Kindleberger, *A Financial History of Western Europe*, 2nd edn (Oxford: Oxford University Press, 1993), Chapters 20 and 21.

40. As Anthony Cardoza's study of Bologna points out, local agricultural assistance in the postwar period was unevenly distributed. The agrarian leaders in the Po valley and Bologna achieved growth by accommodating the interests of large commercial farmers, through mechanization, marketing, and export campaigns. Little was done to help small-scale farmers. Anthony Cardoza, *Agricultural Elites and Italian Fascism* (Princeton: Princeton University Press, 1982), p. 252.

41. Carl T. Schmidt, *The Plough and the Sword* (New York: Columbia University Press, 1938), p. 45; Luigi Messadaglia, *Per la storia dell'agricoltura e dell'alimentazione* (Piacenza: Federazione Italiana dei Consorzi Agrari, 1932), p. 151.

42. Royal Institute for International Affairs, Information Department, *The Economic and Financial Position of Italy* (London: Oxford University Press, 1935).

43. The figures factor in population increase and wheat used for seeding. Statistics from Istituto Centrale di Statistica, *Sommario di statistiche storiche dell'Italia, 1861–1942* (Rome: Istituto Poligrafico dello Stato, 1968), pp. 10, 62; and Benedetto Barberi, *Le disponibilità alimentari della popolazione italiana dal 1910 al 1942* (Rome: Istituto Poligrafico dello Stato, 1946), p. 5.

44. 'Mentre il Duce indice l'XI concorso nazionale per la vittoria del grano', *La voce del consumatore* 4, 7 (15 July 1933), p. 3.

45. Stefano Camilla, *La massima, più razionale e pratica utilizzazione del frumento colla produzione industriale della farina 'scia'. Conferenze tenuta 21 Dicembre 1922, Società Piemontese di igiene, Torino* (Turin: Enrico Schioppo, 1923).

46. For example, B. Cusimano, 'Il pane e la razza,' *L'alimentazione italiana* 5, 1–2 (31 October–15 November 1938), p. 3. Giuseppe Tallarico, *Grano e pane* (Rome: Editoriale degli Agricoltori, 1933); *La vita degli alimenti* (Florence: Sansoni, 1934); *Lo stato biologico degli alimenti e lo sviluppo* (Rome: R. Garroni, 1930); 'L'alimentazione e la prolificità umana,' *Razza e civiltà* 2, 2 (March 1941), pp. 81–91.

47. For example, Sabato Visco, 'Alcuni risultati di un'indagine sulla panificazione nella provincia di Sassari,' *Quaderni della nutrizione* 3, 3–4 (July

1936), pp. 157–70: Angelo Maioli, *Il problema nazionale della distribuzione del pane in base ad una inchiesta statistica* (Rome: Biblioteca Federale di Studi e di Propaganda, 1935).

48. The study surveyed the habits of 112 rural families over an extended period of time. Despite an experienced directive committee, however, the INEA study was idiosyncratic at best. In terms of geographical distribution, a disproportionate number of families (31) were from Tuscany while only one family was from the Lazio region. The president of the directive committee was Arrigo Serpieri, Minister of Agriculture, Parliamentary Deputy, Professor of Rural Economy and Director of the *Reale Istituto Superiore Agrario e Forestale* of Florence. Committee members also included Professor Francesco Coletti, Professor of Statistics and Demography at the University of Pavia and veteran of the *Inchiesta Faina*; and Ugo Giusti, docent in Demography at the University of Rome. Istituto Nazionale di Economia Agraria, Studi e monografie: *Monografie di famiglie agricole. I. Mezzadri di Val di Pesa e del Chianti* (Milan-Rome: Società Anonima Treves, 1931–33), p. 39. See also Alfonso Ciuffolini, *Indagine sulle condizioni di vita dei contadini* (Rome: Tipografia Luzzatti, 1930).

49. Ignazio Silone, *Vino e pane* (Milan: Mondadori, 1982), p. 114.

50. Carlo Levi, *Christ Stopped at Eboli* trans. Frances Frenaye (New York: Noonday, 1998), p. 21.

51. Out of 110 families responding, twenty-five families spent 50 percent or less of their total income on food, fifty-three families spent 66–75 percent, and thirty-two families spent more than 75 percent. Reported in Ugo Giusti, 'La monografia di famiglia,' in Società Italiana di Demografia e Statistica, *Atti della V Riunione* (Florence: Tipografia Unione Arti Grafiche, 1940), p. 186.

52. The 'Manifesto of Futurist Cooking' was first published in the *Gazzetta del Popolo* in Turin on 28 December 1930. F.T. Marinetti and Fillìa, *La cucina futurista* (Milan: Longanesi, 1986).

53. Letter from Marco Rampereti to Marinetti, Ibid., p. 42.

54. There was of course some regional variation, with northern Italians consuming 9–10 kilograms per year compared to 1 or 2 kilograms that southern Italians consumed. 'I pregi di un prodotto italiano,' *La voce del consumatore*, 3, 1 (15 January 1932), p. 11. On regional variation see Istituto Nazionale di Economia Agraria, Studi e Monografie, *Caratteri e problemi della risicoltura italiana* (Rome: Mario Bondini, 1935).

55. For example, 'Un problema nazionale: il riso,' *La voce del consumatore* 4, 7 (15 July 1933), p. 14; 'Il riso: elisir di lunga vita in cicchi,' *Casa e lavoro* 4, 7 (July 1932), p. 223; Erminia de Benedetteni *Il nostro nido: Consigli sul buon governo della casa*, 5th edn (Palermo: Società Anonima, 1938), pp. 101–4; Luigi De Voto, 'La difesa del riso italiano: Per parte medici,' *Il*

cittadino (23 January 1930), article held in ACS, Consiglio Nazionale delle Ricerche, b. 232, f. 1930. On the *Ente Nazionale Risi*, 'La propaganda per un maggiore consumo del riso e la fervida azione del Comitato Nazionale,' *Il giornale del commercio* (10 March 1934), p. 2; 'I risultati dell'autotreno del riso,' *Agricoltura fascista* 7 (3 February 1935), p. 2; and 'La difesa del consumatore,' *La voce del consumatore* 5, 6 (15 June 1934), p. 6.

56. ACS, Pubblicca Sicurezza 1928, b. 167, f. 'Affari Generale', s.f. 1: 'Giornata Nazionale di Propaganda di Riso.' Confederazione Fascista dei Lavoratori dell' Agricoltura, *Campagna monda del riso* (Rome: Arte della Stampa, 1938).

57. Marescalchi's writings include *L'esportazione del vino italiano* (Casale Monferrato: Fratelli Marescalchi, 1925); *Politica del vino* (Casale Monferrato: Fratelli Marescalchi, 1924); *I vini e gli alberghi* (Florence: Casa Vinicola Barone Ricasoli, 1934); *I vini tipici d'Italia* (Casale Monferrato: Fratelli Marescalchi, 1924); and *Vino* (Turin: Tipografia Autarchia Nazionale, 1938). On the activities of the *autotreni*, see 'L'autotreno di vino a Roma,' *Agricoltura fascista* 7 (3 February 1935), p. 2.

58. On the contradictions faced by the Italian middle class confronting mass consumption under fascism, see Victoria de Grazia, *The Culture of Consent: Mass Organization of Leisure in Fascist Italy* (Cambridge: Cambridge University Press, 1981) and *How Fascism Ruled Women: Italy, 1922–45* (Berkeley: University of California Press, 1992). An anecdotal history of everyday life under fascism is Gian Franco Venè, *Mille lire al mese: Vita quotidiana della famiglia nell'Italia fascista* (Milan: Mondadori, 1988).

59. These goods were rare for economic reasons. A washing machine, for example, cost 10,000 lire, almost a year's salary for a middle-class family. Vittorio Gregotti, *Il disegno del prodotto industriale, Italia 1860–1980* (Milan: Electa, 1998), pp. 197–199.

60. Alberto De Bernardi, 'Modernizzazione e consumi nell'Italia fascista,' *Il Risorgimento* 2 (1992), p. 421.

61. Because Italy's middle class was so small for much of the nineteenth and early twentieth centuries, there were very few cookbooks or magazines published, at least not in comparison with numbers of publications in the United States and Great Britain, where this literature prescribed female middle-class norms. Culinary literature of the early twentieth century was aimed at the upper middle classes and was dominated by male gourmands.

62. Lucia Pagano, *Economia domestica* (Palermo: Industrie Riunite Editoriali Siciliane, 1934), p. 192.

63. Piero Meldini, 'La cucina della famiglia fascista,' introduction to the 1977 reprint of Zia Carolina, *Cucina pratica* (Milan: Guaraldi, 1977), p. xx.

64. For an overview of culinary literature in the late nineteenth and twentieth centuries see Maria Paola Moroni Salvatori, 'Ragguaglio bibliografico sui

ricettari del primo Novecento,' in A. Capatti, A. De Bernardi, and A. Varni (eds), *Storia d'Italia*, Annali 13, *L'alimentazione* (Turin: G. Einaudi, 1998), pp. 889–925.

65. See for example 'Cucina in 10 minuti o cucina preparata lungamente?' *Casa e lavoro* 3, 2 (Februrary 1931), p. 61; 'La frutta: gioia della gioventù e conforto della vecchiaia,' *Casa e lavoro* 4, 12 (December 1932), p. 357; Mario Stelvio, 'Le moderne teorie sull'alimentazione,' *La cucina italiana* 5, 7 (15 July 1933), p. 8; 'Le arancie,' *La cucina italiana* 5, 2 (15 February 1933), p. 3.

66. Fernanda Momigliano, *Vivere bene in tempi difficili* (Milan: U. Hoepli, 1933). See also Paola Alferazzi Benedettini, *Consigli di economia domestica* (Florence: Stianti, 1936); and Ettore Piccoli, *L'alimentazione dell'uomo* (Milan: R. Quintieri, 1921).

67. Benedettini, *Consigli di economia domestica*, p. 71; Lidia Morelli, *Massaie di domani* (Turin: S. Lattes, 1938), pp. 225–39.

68. Dario Fornari, *Il cuciniere militare* (Novara: Tipografia Cattaneo, 1932), part II.

69. Ines Bergamo and Mimy Bergamo, *A tavola! Menus stagionali relative ricette* (Milan: U. Hoepli, 1936), p. xiii; Petronilla, *Ricette di Petronilla* (Milan: Olivini, 1935), p. 18.

70. One example is Benedettini, *Consigli di economia domestica.*

71. Chiara Bellati, *La nostra casa* (Milan: Vita e Pensiero, 1929); Scuola Serale 'Buona Massaia' di S. Giovanni, Brescia, *La buona massaia* (Brescia: Istituto Figli di Maria Immacolata, 1928).

72. Maria Diez Gasca, *Cucine di ieri e cucine di domani* (Rome: Tipografia delle Teme, 1928), p. 130.

73. Momigliano, *Vivere bene in tempi difficili*, pp. 17–24, 93–6.

74. Touring Club Italiano, *Guida gastronomica d'Italia* (Milan: TCI, 1931). See also La Federazione Nazionale Fascista Pubblici Esercizi, *Ristoranti d'Italia* (Rome: Società Anonima Editrice, 1938), which recommended restaurants and hotels that honored the art of cooking.

75. Gasca, *Cucine di ieri e cucine di domani*, p. 132.

76. 'Abbasso con il cosmopolitanismo gastronomico,' *La cucina italiana* 5, 4 (15 April 1933); 'Fuori i barbari,' *La cucina italiana* 5, 6 (15 June 1933).

77. Bergamo and Bergamo, *A tavola!*, p. xvi.

78. Lidia Morelli's work includes *La casa che vorrei avere* (Milan: U. Hoepli, 1933); *Come sistemare e governare la mia casa* (Milan: U. Hoepli, 1938); *L'arte più difficile* (Milan: Garzanti, 1940); *Massaie di domani*; and *Nuovo ricettario domestico* (Milan: U. Hoepli, 1941). See also Gasca, *Cucina di ieri e cucina di domani.*

79. Consumer practice as experienced by Italian housewives was limited to small purchases of the right kinds of foods. Domestic literature stressed an

emerging brand loyalty among female consumers by suggesting that certain products were reliable or hygienic. The budding food industry also did its share to promote brand-consciousness. Maggi meat extracts, a company founded in 1900 by a Swiss emigrant, published numerous cookbooks and pamphlets for women, instructing them on how to use liquid extract, bullion cubes, and freeze-dried soups. Cirio tomato products also published cookbooks based on recipe contests, which were popular among readers. Brand loyalty was still a somewhat limited practice, considering that nationally recognized name brands were small in number: Maggi, Cirio, Arrigoni, Perugina, and Buitoni.

80. *Per mangiar bene: 600 ricette* (Milan: Società Italiana dei Prodotti Maggi, 1928); Società Generale delle Conserve Alimentari 'Cirio', *Nuove orizzonti per la vostra mensa* (Portici: E. della Torre, 1936); *100 maniere per contentare il marito: 100 maniere per contentare la moglie* (Giuntera, 1930).
81. *La cucina italiana* 8, 2 (1 February 1936), p. 7. The editors of *La cucina italiana* changed the format of the magazine after the death of founder Delia Notari at the end of 1943, soliciting more reader input and sponsoring more contests.
82. Quoted in Gian Franco Venè, *Mille lire al mese*, p. 77.

Chapter 4 Austerity and Decline

1. 'Vibrante entusiasmo popolare nella celebrazione della VI Festa Nazionale dell'Uva,' *L'alimentazione italiana* 1, 9 (30 September 1935), pp. 4–5.
2. On fascist theories of consumption, see Attilio Racheli, 'Il consumatore e il commercio,' *Il commercio* 9, 7 (July 1936), pp. 396–8; and 'L'intervento statale nel consumo,' *Il commercio* 9, 9 (September 1936), pp. 501–2.
3. 'La nostra produzione alimentare,' *L'alimentazione italiana* 1, 9 (15 October 1935), p. 1.
4. Rina Simonetta, 'Donne d'Italia, in cucina!' *La cucina italiana* 5, 12 (December 1935), p. 15. During sanctions, in journals like *La cucina italiana* and *L'alimentazione Italiana*, there was much criticism of the British, who supported sanctions and who allegedly consumed five or six meals a day.
5. For example, the volume of tomato paste and canned tomatoes produced in Italy reached almost 300 million pounds in 1937, making Italy second only to the United States in volume produced. Although the regime promised to reserve the domestic supply of food for Italians in order to make economic self-sufficiency work, over 85 percent of canned tomatoes and over 34 percent of tomato paste were exported that year, primarily to the United States and to the United Kingdom. United States Tariff Commission, *Italian Commercial Policy and Foreign Trade*, 1922–1940 (Washington DC: Government Printing Office, 1941), pp. 147–8.

6. Prefects reported little or no trouble implementing and enforcing these price reductions. ACS, Comuni, 1934–36, b. 2454, f. 15100–60: 'Affari Generali.'

7. Report from PNF Secretary, dated 14 September 1935, ACS, PNF, Situazione politica e economica delle provincie, b. 7: 'Milan', f.: 'Varie.' Price controls continued through 1937. The first aim was of course political: price controls prevented consumer runs on goods during the invasion and later, in the wake of devaluation of the lira (October 1936), controlled the cost of living and facilitated exports. Initially, with the formation of the central *Comitato Permanente per la Vigilanza sui Prezzi* (Permanent Committee to Control Prices, decreed by D.L. 5 October 1936, no. 1746), the regime vowed to lessen the slippage, or viscosity, between wholesale and retail prices. 'Il partito per i prezzi', *L'alimentazione italiana* 2, 21–22 (15 November 1936), p. 1; and Diego De Castro, *Prezzi e politica dei prezzi in Italia, Germania e Francia nell'ultimo quadriennio* (Turin: Collegio Artigianelli, 1939). The Permanent Committee was disbanded in favor of a Central Guild Committee on Prices, whose primary objective appeared to be freezing prices and permitting slight increases by official decree; the prices for wheat, rice, and olive oil, for example, were fixed for periods of up to a year.

8. 'Grido la giustizia, Grido di vittoria', *Il giornale del commercio* (5 October 1935), p. 1. On the survival of retail merchants under fascist policies, see Jonathan Morris, 'The Fascist "Disciplining" of the Italian Retail Sector, 1922–40', *Business History* 40 (1998), pp. 138–64.

9. Henry Miller, *Price Control in Fascist Italy* (New York: Columbia University Press, 1938), pp. 75, 90, 110. Information on regional increases in prices in the period 1936–38 from Giacomo Veronese, *Contributo allo studio della vischiosità dei prezzi delle merci* (Rome: Carlo Colombo, 1937), p. 171.

10. Food imports accounted for 32 percent of all imports when Mussolini assumed power in 1922. Throughout the 1920s, food imports held steady at an average of 25 percent of total imports, dropping down to 15 percent in 1933 and averaging this amount until 1938. Food exports rose from 23 percent of total goods exported to an average of 33 percent of the total in the years 1935–38. US Tariff Commission, *Italian Commercial Policy and Foreign Trade*, p. 88.

11. Wheat imports for 1924 cost 2,051 million lire in 1924 and 310 million lire in 1936; these values were converted into 1927 gold-standard lire for purposes of comparison. William G. Welk, *Fascist Economic Policy: An Analysis of Italy's Economic Experiment* (Cambridge MA: Harvard University Press, 1938), p. 167.

12. On criticisms of Battle for Grain, see Vera Zamagni, *The Economic History of Italy 1860–1990* (Oxford: Clarendon, 1993), p. 259; and the Royal Institute for International Affairs, *The Economic and Financial Position of Italy* (London:

Oxford University Press, 1935). On corn production, see 'Disciplina del mercato del granoturco,' *Il commercio* 11, 10 (October 1938), p. 51.

13. Francesco Bocca di Fuoco and Ugo Cavallazzi, 'Organizzazione e tecnica dell'esportazione italiana,' *Il commercio* 11, 10 (October 1938), pp. 32–5. See also 'Vita corporativa, L'orto-frutticoltura,' in *Il commercio* 9, 10 (October 1936), pp. 544–5; and Istituto Nazionale per l'Esportazione, *Dati statistici sulle esportazioni italiane e sulle corrispondenti principali importazioni estere nel quinquennio 1927–31* (Rome: Castaldi, 1932).

14. Benedetto Barberi, *Le disponibilità alimentari della popolazione italiana dal 1910 al 1942* (Rome: Istituto Poligrafico dello Stato, 1948), p. 5.

15. 'Dichiarazioni dell'On. Tassinari,' *L'alimentazione italiana* 2, 23–24 (15–31 December 1936), p. 5. On the impact of the Battle for Grain on livestock production see Carlo Piazza, *La vita della nazione* (Milan: Editori Associati, 1939), p. 24; Arrigo Serpieri, 'Il fascismo per l'agricoltura,' in Amelio Dupont (ed.), *Realizzazioni fasciste nella vita italiana* (Rome: Tipografia del Senato, 1932), p. 101; and Carl T. Schmidt, *The Plough and the Sword* (New York: Columbia University Press, 1938), chapter IV.

16. Sabato Visco, 'Autarchia alimentare,' *Autarchia alimentare* 1, 5 (October 1938), p. 4.

17. ACS, Consiglio Nazionale delle Ricerche, Comitato Agricoltura, bb. 144,146, and 148; Confederazione Fascista degli Industriali, *L'industria in A.O.I.* (Rome: L'organizzazione industriale, 1939).

18. On Ethiopian agricultural campaigns see Angelo Ferrari, *Il problema dei commestibili e l'Etiopia* (Lodi: G. Biancardi, 1937); Sabato Visco, 'L'alimentazione nelle colonie e ne possedenti' and Edgardo Taschdjian, 'Sguardo sulle possibilità agricole dell'Abissinia,' *L'agricoltura coloniale* 30 (1936). Numerous articles on the nutritional value of Ethiopian produce were published in the *Quaderni della nutrizione*. On the marketing of products from Ethiopia, see Karen Pinkus, *Bodily Regimes: Italian Advertising Under Fascism* (Minneapolis: University of Minnesota Press, 1995).

19. Vera Zamagni, *La distribuzione commerciale in Italia fra le due guerre* (Milan: Franco Angeli, 1981), pp. 32–3.

20. See for example the letter from M.A. to Mussolini, 20 August 1936, reprinted in Teresa Maria Mazzatosta and Claudio Volpi (eds), *L'Italietta fascista (lettere al potere 1936–1943)* (Bologna: Capelli, 1980), pp. 121–2.

21. The actual figure was 2,888,000 in 1934, up from 2,328,924 in 1933. On the work of the Ente Opere Assistenziali, see Giuseppe De Michelis, *Alimentazione e giustizia sociale* (Rome: Istituto Nazionale di Cultura Fascista, 1937), pp. 46–55.

22. David Horn, 'Welfare, the Social and the Individual,' *Cultural Anthropology* 3 (November 1988), p. 400; see also his *Social Bodies: Science, Repro-*

duction, and Italian Modernity (Princeton: Princeton University Press, 1994) for a more detailed explanation of fascist social policies. See Sophia Maria Quine, *Italy's Social Revolution: Charity and Welfare from Liberalism to Fascism* (New York: Palgrave, 2002) for a history of fascist charity.

23. Simona Colarizi, *L'opinione degli Italiani sotto il Regime, 1929–43* (Bari: Laterza, 1991), p. 91.

24. Miller, *Price Control in Fascist Italy*, p. 140.

25. 'La Mostra dei Rifiuti,' *Profamilia* 39, 23 (5 June 1938), p. 338.

26. Ferrucio Lantini, 'La reazione alle sanzioni e il nuovo equilibrio economico,' *Il commercio* 8, 12 (December 1935), p. 767; see also Lantini, *La famiglia nella resistenza alle sanzioni* (Rome: Società Editrice Novissima, 1936) and *La donna nella resistenza economica della nazione* (Rome: Istituto Nazionale Fascista di Cultura, 1936). A similar argument was made by Angela Zucconi, 'La donna e l'independenza economica,' *Il commercio* 10, 3 (March 1937), pp. 39–41.

27. 'Per una carta d'alimentazione,' *L'alimentazione italiana* 3, 9–10 (15–30 July 1937), p. 1; Luisa Passerini, *Mussolini immaginario* (Bari: Laterza, 1991), p. 123. Mussolini's austere habits failed to guarantee good health, given that he suffered from chronic abdominal discomfort.

28. Rina Peloggio, 'Nozioni di economia domestica,' P.N.F., Federazione dei Fasci Femminili, *Corso preparatorio per visitatrici fasciste* (Novara: Cattaneo, 1940), p. 71.

29. Lina Ferrini, *Economia in cucina senza sacrificio a tavola* (Milan: Gino Conte, 1939). See also Mara, *Per mangiar bene...e spender poco* (Milan: SADEL, 1936).

30. Lidia Morelli, *Le massaie contro le sanzioni* (Turin: S. Lattes and Company, 1935); on the use of lemons, see p. 20.

31. Bottazzi cited in Confederazione Fascista dei Lavoratori dell'Agricoltura, *L'alimentazione dei lavoratori agricoli in Italia* (Rome: Arte della Stampa, 1936), pp. 3–4.

32. Cited in Derek J. Oddy, 'Food, Drink and Nutrition,' in F.M.L. Thompson (ed.), *The Cambridge Social History of Nutrition*, Vol. 2 (Cambridge: Cambridge University Press, 1990), pp. 273–4.

33. Alfredo Niceforo, *Bilanci alimentari delle nostre vecchie plebi rurali* (Naples: SIEM, 1937), pp. 12–19. Alfredo Niceforo, 'Dati statistici sull'alimentazione della popolazione italiana,' in Bottazzi, *et al.*, *Documenti per lo studio della alimentazione della popolazione italiana nell'ultimo cinquantennio* (Naples: N. Jovene, 1933).

34. Carlo Foà, 'Alimentazione e sanzioni,' in Federazione Provinciale Fascista Milanese, *Corso di preparazione politica per i giovani* Volume 3 (Milan: Popolo d'Italia, 1936), pp. 25–61. For a summary of caloric recommendations

for Italian workers, see Rosario Sottilaro, 'Indagini sulle condizioni di vita e sull'alimentazione dei lavoratori,' *Rivista del lavoro* 5 (May 1937), pp. 39–45.

35. Filippo Bottazzi, opening address, Reale Accademia d'Italia, Atti dei Convegni 7. Convegno di Scienze Fisiche, Matematiche e Naturali, 26 Settembre–2 Ottobre, 1937, *Lo stato attuale delle conoscenze sulla nutrizione* (Rome: Reale Accademia d'Italia, 1938), pp. 20–1.

36. 'Can Italy Feed Herself?' *The Economist* (18 June 1938), p. 644.

37. Vera Cao-Pinna, 'Inchieste statistiche sul regime alimentare di 11 famiglie di artigiani e 10 famiglie agiate, nella città di Cagliari,' *Quaderni della nutrizione* 2, 1 (July 1935), p. 2.

38. Ugo Giusti, 'Sul consumo di generi alimentari in alcune grandi città italiane,' *Il commercio* 3, 1 (January 1930), pp. 15–26.

39. Alessandro Costanzo, 'Risultati di un'inchiesta sui bilanci di 744 famiglie operaie italiane,' in Società Italiana di Demografia e Statistica, *Atti della V Riunione* (Florence: Unione Arti Grafiche, 1940), pp. 229–65.

40. Angelo Pugliese, 'Alimentazione ed evoluzione sociale', in Pietro Albertoni and Angelo Pugliese (eds), *Studi sulla alimentazione*, pp. 611–15. See also Carlo Foà, 'La fisiologia dell'alimentazione,' in Federazione Provinciale Fascista Milanese, *Corso di preparazione politica per i giovani*, Vol. 2.

41. For example, Pietro Silvio Rivetta (Pseudonym: Toddi), *Preferite i prodotti nazionali!* (Milan: Ceschina, 1938); Arturo Marescalchi, *Storia della alimentazione e dei piaceri della tavola* (Milan: Garzanti, 1942) provides an exhaustive regional breakdown of cuisine.

42. Henry Aimes Abot, *Eating My Way Through Italy* (San Francisco: Golden State Company, 1939).

43. See Virgilio Ducceschi, *Prime linee di una storia dell'alimentazione umana* (Milan: Poligrafica degli Operai, 1936).

44. Oddone Fantini, 'Autarchia economica e politica alimentare,' in R. Università di Firenze, Facoltà di Scienze Politiche, *Studi in memoria di Giovanni Dettori*, Vol. I (Florence: Carlo Cya, 1941): p. 180, pp. 188–9.

45. Anti-Semitic legislation was first passed in September 1938 and prevented foreign Jews from entering Italy, and banned Jews from teaching and secondary education. In November, intermarriage between Jews and non-Jews was banned, and Jews were excluded from jobs in the army and the bureaucracy.

46. 'Can Italy Feed Herself?' *The Economist* (18 June 1938), p. 645.

47. According to Ronchi's memoirs. Vittorio Ronchi, *Guerra e crisi alimentare in Italia, 1940–1950* (Rome: Edizioni Agricole, 1977), p. 32.

48. See 'Pane e disciplina corporative,' *Il commercio* 11, 5–6 (May–June 1938), pp. 2–3.

49. Vittorio Ronchi, *Guerra e crisi alimentare in Italia*, pp. 32–33.

50. Ugo Angellili, 'Memento alimentare,' *L'alimentazione italiana*, 6, 5 (15–29 February 1940), p. 1; Mussolini quoted in 'Il Duce ai veliti del grano,' *L'alimentazione italiana* 6, 5 (15–29 February 1940), p. 1.

51. Ernesto Bertarelli, 'Periodici bellici e parsimonie alimentari,' *Sapere* 5, 10 (15 October 1939), pp. 288–9. On wartime restrictions see Luigi Fontana Russo, *Preparazione e condotta economica della guerra* (Rome: Cremonese, 1942).

52. ACS, Ministero dell'Interno, Direzione Generale di Pubblica Sicurezza (hereafter referred to as Pubblica Sicurezza), Divizione Affari Generali e Riservati, II Guerra Mondiale A5G, b. 25, f. 10 'Spirito Pubblico.'

53. General production estimates from Shephard B. Clough, *The Economic History of Modern Italy* (New York: Columbia University Press, 1964), p. 277. Wheat yields cited in Nicola Gallerano, Luigi Ganapini, Massimo Legnani, and Mariuccia Salvati, 'Crisi di regime e crisi sociale,' in Gianfranco Bertolo (ed.), *Operai e contadini nella crisi italiana del 1943–1944* (Milan: Feltrinelli, 1974), p. 7.

54. See Simona Colarizi, 'Vita alimentare degli Italiani e razionamento (1941),' in Commissione Italiana di Storia Militare, *L'Italia in guerra: Il secondo anno 1941* (Gaeta: Grafico Militare, 1992), pp. 279–89; and Vittorio Ronchi, *Guerra e crisi alimentare in Italia*.

55. Correspondence in ACS, Ministero dell'Agricoltura e Foreste, Direzione Generale Alimentazione, b. 43, s.f. 'Richieste di nuovi riconoscimenti.'

56. Urgentissima raccomandata, from Marziali, prefect of Milan, to the Ministry of Interior, Public Security, Police Division, 17 July 1940, in ACS, Pubblica Sicurezza, Affari Generali e Riservati, II Guerra Mondiale A5G, b. 104, f. 46 'Incetta Rialzo Prezzi' Cat A5G N. 46, S.N. 48, Ins. 8, 'Milano.'

57. Riccardo Mariani, *Borsari neri in Roma, città aperta* (Rome: NES, 1989), p. 27.

58. Vittorio Ronchi, *Guerra e crisi alimentare in Italia*, pp. 51–2, pp. 63–4.

59. Simona Colarizi, 'Vita alimentare degli Italiani e razionamento (1941),' p. 287.

60. Report from informer dated 20 June 1942, cited in Angelo Imbriani, *Gli Italiani e il Duce: Il mito e l'immagine di Mussolini negli ultimi anni del fascismo (1938–1943)* (Naples: Liguori, 1992), pp. 136–68.

61. Rosetta Loy, *First Words: A Childhood in Fascist Italy*, Trans. Gregory Conti (New York: Henry Holt, 2000), p. 137.

62. Correspondence regarding these requests can be found in ACS, Ministero dell'Agricoltura e Foreste, Direzione Generale Alimentazione, Serie V, b. 72.

63. Lutz Klinkhammer, *L'occupazione tedesca in Italia. 1943–1945* (Turin: Bollati Boringhieri, 1993), pp. 186–7.

64. Vittorio Ronchi, *Guerra e crisi alimentare in Italia*, pp. 115–17.

65. Under allied occupation, the black market filled with allied goods. See Luigi Ceccarelli, *Roma alleata* (Rome: Rendina, 1994) and Paolo De Marco,

Polvere di piselli: La vita quotidiana a Napoli durante l'occupazione alleata 1943–44 (Naples: Liguori, 1996).

66. Report from Prefecture of Milan to Ministry of the Interior, 'Applicazione e inconvenienti del bolletino del Commissariato dei Prezzi per i generi ortofrutticoli,' 10 February 1944, p. 2. ACS, Repubblica Sociale Italiana, Segretaria Particolare Duce (hereafter referred to as RSI, SPD), Carteggio Riservato (1943–45), b. 17, f. 92, s.f. 1.

67. Interviews conducted with Italian citizens in spring of 1942. Pier Paolo Luzzatto-Fegiz, *Alimentazione e prezzi in tempo di guerra* (Trieste: Editrice Università di Trieste, 1948), pp. 115–16. See also Mario Pinotti, 'Pesaro tra la linea gotica e il pane difficile,' in Giorgio Rochat *et al*. (eds), *Linea Gotica 1944: eserciti, popolazioni, partigiani* (Milan: Franco Angeli, 1986), pp. 223–61.

68. *Che si mangia domani?* (V. Ferri, 1941).

69. Oral testimonies are from Sandra Lotti, 'Donne nella guerra: strategie di sopravvivenza tra permanenze e mutamenti,' in Rochat *et al*., *Linea gotica 1944*, pp. 225–7.

70. Norman Lewis, *Naples, '44* (New York: Henry Holt, 1994), p. 31.

71. Pier Paolo Luzzatto-Fegiz, 'Nuove ricerche sui bilanci familiari,' *Giornale degli economisti e annali di economia* 5, 3–4 (March–April 1946), pp. 197–207; and *Alimentazione e prezzi in tempo di guerra*.

72. Luigi Cavazzoli, *La gente e la Guerra: La vita quotidiana del 'fronte interno.' Mantova 1940–45* (Milan: Franco Angeli, 1989), p. 94.

73. Luzzatto-Fegiz, *Alimentazione e prezzi in tempo di guerra*, p. 183, Table 23.

74. Klinkhammer, *L'occupazione tedesca in Italia*; Cinzia Spigola, 'Crisi alimentare e problemi di ordine pubblico in Sicilia nel secondo dopoguerra,' in Nicola Gallerano (ed.), *L'altro dopoguerra: Roma e il sud* (Milan: Franco Angeli, 1986), pp. 341–54.

75. Claudio Dellavalle, 'Lotte operaie, Torino,' in Bertolo, *Operai e contadini nella crisi italiana del 1943–1944*, pp. 192–253.

76. Agostino Giovagnoli's study of charity in Rome indicates that the numbers of meals served in soup kitchens increased dramatically over the period 1943–45 as charities were swamped with the new poor. The soup kitchen at the Circolo di San Pietro, one of the largest operations in the city, reported an all-time record of serving 1,800,000 meals for the month of May, 1944. Agostino Giovagnoli, 'Chiesa, assistenza, e società a Roma tra il 1943 e il 1945,' in Gallerano, *L'altro dopoguerra: Roma e il sud*, pp. 217–18.

77. David W. Ellwood, *Italy 1943–45* (New York: Holmes & Meier, 1985), p. 130.

78. Interception #15811, Rome, 23 March 1944, 10 a.m., and Interception #12009, Rome, 6 March 1944, 2:40 p.m. ACS Ministero dell'Interno, Pubblica Sicurezza, Ispettorato Generale di Pubblica Sicurezza, Servizi Annonari, b. 17, f. 1.

79. Minister of Agriculture Moroni quoted in Klinkhammer, *L'occupazione tedesca in Italia*, p. 248.

80. Undated document 'Per la approvvigionamento della città di Roma' and letter from Moroni to Ministry of the Interior, dated 18 November 1943. ACS, Pubblica Sicurezza, Segretaria Del Capo della Polizia RSI, 1943–45, b. 33, s.f. 53.

81. Correspondence dated 16 April and 23 May 1944, ACS, RSI SPD, Carteggio Riservato (1943–45), b. 23, f. 164 'Commissariato Nazionale dei Prezzi' s.f. 'Visione per il Duce.'

82. Klinkhammer, *L'occupazione tedesca in Italia*, p. 194, p. 180.

83. Commissariato Staordinario del Governo per il Piemonte, 'Appunto per il Duce, No. 1635' dated 28 December 1944. ACS, RSI SPD, Carteggio Riservato, b. 23, f. 164 'Commissariato Nazionale dei Prezzi' s.f. 6, 'Provvedimenti e disposizioni relative alla questione dei prezzi.'

84. Letter from Alleanza Nazionale delle Cooperative, to Mussolini, 2 January 1945, 'Osservazioni e proposte sul progettato provvedimento di requisizione dei magazzini e negozi dei commercianti privati,' ACS, RSI SPD, Carteggio Riservato b. 23, f. 164 'Commissariato Nazionale dei Prezzi' s.f. 4 'Varia.'

85. See correspondence of Moroni in ACS, Presidenza PCM RSI, Segretario Particolare del Sottosegretario Barracu (1943–45), b. 17, f. 166. Memorandum from Ministero dell'Agricoltura ai Capi delle Provincie, dated 21 December, 1944, Oggetto: Situazione alimentare politica annonaria. ACS, RSI, Segretario Particolare Duce, Carteggio Riservato (1943–45), b. 80, f. 650.

86. See reports from Capo della Provincia, Milan, dated 21 December 1944, 19 February and 4 March 1945. ACS, RSI SPD, Carteggio Riservato (1943–45), b. 17, f. 92, s.f. 1.

87. See report from Colonel F. Collu, 'Situazione politico-economico di Alessandria e Provincia' 21 March 1945; also, reports on political and economic situation in provinces, ACS, PCM RSI, Segretario Sottosegretario Barracu, b. 1, f. 63 'Alessandria' f. 57 'Como' and f. 32 'Milano.'

88. Letter from SEPRAL office in Agrigento to Commissario Generale dell'Alimentazione, dated 15 March 1944. ACS Ministero dell'Agricoltura e Foreste, Direzione Generale Alimentazione, Serie V, b. 80, s.f. 22, 'Disciplina Alimentare.'

89. Cited in Ellwood, *Italy 1943–45*, p. 49.

90. De Marco, *Polvere di piselli*; Ellwood, *Italy 1943–45*, p. 64.

91. ACS, Ministero Agricoltura e Foreste, Direzione Generale Alimentazione, Serie V, b. 80.

92. UNRRA, Italian Mission, *Conferenze sull'alimentazione per le assistenti sanitarie del Veneto, Forlì, Ferrara e Ravenna* (Venice: Carlo Ferrari, 1946).

93. Martin Clark, *Modern Italy 1871–1995* 2nd edn (London: Longman, 1996), p. 290.

94. Ronchi, *Guerra e crisi alimentare in Italia*, pp. 112–13.

95. Interview published in Luzzatto-Fegiz, *Alimentazione e prezzi in tempo di guerra*, p. 67.

96. However, the tremendous historical interest in the Holocaust has encouraged Italian historians to examine native anti-Semitism. Several recent studies have demonstrated the culpability of the scientific profession, the involvement of the Catholic Church, and the centrality of anti-Semitism to fascism's rule from 1930 onward. These studies have challenged previously held notions that the growing isolation of Italian Jews from political and civic life was merely a tragic consequence of the military alliance with Nazi Germany. On the scientific profession see, Giorgio Israel and Pietro Nastasi, *Scienza e razza nell'Italia fascista* (Bologna: Il Mulino, 1998); on fascist years, see relevant essays in Alberto Burgio, *Nel nome della razza* (Bologna: Il Mulino, 1999).

97. On this point see Victoria de Grazia, 'Die Radikalisierung der Bevolkerungs-politik im Faschistischen Italien: Mussolini's "Rassenstat",' *Geschichte und Gesellschaft* 26 (2000), pp. 219–54. De Grazia's theorizing of fascist population policies informs this interpretation of fascist food policy. On racial theory during the fascist era, and in particular the racial theories stressing Italian adaptability, see Aaron Gillette, *Racial Theories in Fascist Italy* (New York: Routledge, 2002), Chapter 5.

98. See, for example, the essays printed in *Popolazione e fascismo* (Ernesto della Torre, 1933); Giorgio Mortara, 'Costo e rendimento economico dell'uomo,' in *Atti dell'Istituto Nazionale delle Assicurazioni* Vol. 6 (Rome: Tipografia Del Senato, 1934).

99. 'From a biological perspective a reduction in the consumption of these goods is neither advisable nor a good sign: these foods are indispensable for the physiological alimentary economy of the race. For this reason we should ener-getically avoid any tendency to reduce their consumption.' Sabato Visco, 'Il fabbisogno alimentare del popolo italiano,' in Luigi Lojacono, *L'independenza economica italiana* (Milan: U. Hoepli, 1937): 107; 'Autarchia alimentare,' *Autarchia alimentare* 1, 5 (October 1938), pp. 3–12.

100. Regarding Corrado Gini's professional relationships, see Israel and Nastasi, *Scienza e razza nell'Italia fascista*, pp. 106–48.

101. For example, the periodical *L'alimentazione italiana* published a few articles linking food and character and several pieces linking the consumption of certain foods with certain races. Based on findings of the CNR's Food and Agriculture Committees, these articles ranked African races as most inferior because of their consumption of grains like millet and sorghum; Asian races in the middle because of their consumption of rice; and European races as

superior because of their consumption of wheat and rye. See for example 'Il pane e la razza,' *L'alimentazione italiana* 5, 12 (31 October–15 November 1938), p. 3.

102. Tallarico's work includes *Lo stato biologico degli alimenti e lo sviluppo* (Rome: R. Garroni, 1930); *Grano e pane* (Rome: Ramo Editoriale degli Agricoltori, 1933); *La vita degli alimenti* (Florence: Sansoni, 1934); *Le sanzioni e gli alimenti solari* (Rome: Istituto Nazionale Fascista di Cultura, 1936); and *L'alimento e la prolificità umana* (Rome: Tipografa "Europa," 1941).

103. These included Giorgio Mortara, professor of statistics at the University of Milan; Carlo Foà, professor of human physiology at the University of Milan; Amedeo Herlitzka, Professor of Human Physiology at the University of Turin; and Riccardo Bachi, Department of Political Economy, University of Rome.

104. In 1885, the Ministry of the Interior, in collaboration with the General Office of Statistics, surveyed foodstuffs available for consumption, but did so without distinguishing between the use of foods for human consumption and for other reasons, like for use in animal fodder. The same General Office of Statistics kept track of several basic food items. During the First World War, the government sponsored several national inquiries, beginning with the *Inchiesta Granaria* of 1914–15; also, the General Office of Statistics and the Ministry of the Interior solicited reports from prefects and chambers of commerce regarding food availability throughout the war. See Benedetto Barberi, *Indagine statistica sulle disponibilità alimentari della popolazione italiana dal 1922 al 1937* (Rome: Tipografia Failli, 1939), p. 8.

105. Lorenzo Spina, 'I consumi alimentari della popolazione italiana nell' anteguerra (1910–14) e negli ultimi anni (1926–30),' in Comitato Italiano per lo Studio dei Problemi della Popolazione,' *Atti del Congresso Internazionale per gli studi sulla popolazione*, Vol. 2 (Rome: Istituto Poligrafico dello Stato, 1934), pp. 455–96; see also Guido Galeotti's summary of Spina's work, Guido Galeotti, 'Le disponibilità dei generi alimentari in Italia nel 1910–14 e nel 1928–32,' *Quaderni della nutrizione* 1, 4 (August 1934), pp. 340–2. Barberi, *Le disponibilità alimentari della popolazione italiana dal 1910 al 1942*. Spina and Barberi, as well as many other statisticians and scientists, determined average caloric availability, per person, based on the availability of food in Italy. In work based on average-man coefficients, scientists offered differing estimates of caloric availability, per person. Spina was the most generous in his estimates: caloric availability, per person, rose from 3,080 calories during war to 3,340 in the immediate postwar years, 3,477 in 1925–30 and 3,690 during sanctions. Barberi's 1939 study of the fascist years offered a more conservative estimate, rising from 3,177 calories in 1922 to a high of 3,554 calories in 1926 then declining slowly to a low of

2,977 calories in 1936. Lorenzo Spina's estimates cited in Arturo Marescalchi, *Storia della alimentazione e dei piaceri della tavola*, p. 99; Barberi's estimates are from his 'Indagine sulle disponibilità alimentari delle popolazioni italiani,' *Annuali di statistica* 7 (1939), p. 69.

106. Corrado Gini, 'Prefazione' in Mario Balestrieri, *I consumi alimentari della popolazione italiana dal 1910 al 1921* (Padua: Metron, 1925); Sabato Visco, 'Autarchia alimentare,' p. 6.

107. Carlo Foà, 'Il problema nazionale dell'alimentazione,' pp. 93–8.

108. During the war, workers did receive supplementary rations, but they were more likely to receive bread or cornmeal instead of milk and meat. Increased milk consumption might have been the most efficient way for workers to get more fats, proteins, and vitamins, but Italy was no closer to realizing a plan like this in 1939 than it was in 1914. Istituto Nazionale dei Biologia, Consiglio Nazionale delle Ricerche, undated report, 'Breve relazione sulla esigenze alimentari della popolazione civile,' 18 pages. ACS, Ministero dell'Agricoltura e delle Foreste, Direzione Generale Alimentazione, b. 62, s.f. 31 'Fabbisogni.'

109. See Appunto per il Duce, from Ministero dell'Agricoltura e delle Foreste, 15 November, 1941, in ACS Ministero dell'Agricoltura e Foreste, Direzione Generale Alimentazione, Serie V, 1939–57, b. 23, s.f. IV/12, 'Varie, 1941.'

110. The Rome-Berlin axis led to the adoption of anti-Semitic legislation in Italy in November of 1938, but the alliance also sanctioned the Nazi racial classi-fication of Italians, ranked somewhere below the rest of western Europe but somewhere above eastern Europe and the Soviet Union.

111. Katherine Duff, 'Economic Relations Between Germany and Italy, 1940–43,' in Arnold Toynbee and Veronica Toynbee (eds), *Hitler's Europe* (Oxford: Oxford University Press, 1954), pp. 317–24; Brunello Mantelli, *Camerati del lavoro: I lavoratori italiani emigrati nel Terzo Reich nel periodo dell'asse 1938–43* (Florence: La Nuova Italia, 1992). Spanish workers contracted to work in Germany also experienced discrimination in terms of work conditions and food rations. See Wayne H. Bowen, *Spaniards and Nazi Germany: Collaboration in the New Order* (Columbia MO: University of Missouri Press, 2000), p. 187.

112. Mantelli, *Camerati del lavoro*, p. 317.

113. Letter from Il Comandante Germanico di Roma, Esercito Tedesco in Italia, to Ministero dell'Interno, Roma, dated 23 February 1944. ACS, RSI, Pubblica Sicurezza, Capo della Polizia RSI- Chierici (1943–45), b. 35, f. 56 'Trattamento preferenziale circa generi alimentari, ai lavoratori e famiglie.'

114. Letter dated 27 April 1944, from 'Un'Italiano dela (*sic*) povera affamata Roma' to Mussolini, ACS, RSI, SPD, Carteggio Riservato (1943–45), b. 18, s.f. 1, 'Situazione locale, varia.'

115. Gallerano *et al.*, 'Crisi di regime e crisi sociale,' pp. 50–1. See also Angela Raspin, *The Italian War Economy 1940–43* (New York: Garland, 1986).
116. Interview with teacher from Abruzzo, Luzzatto-Fegiz, *Alimentazione e prezzi in tempo di guerra*, p. 85. See also the interviews on page 101.
117. Letter, from 'Gruppo di ex-combattenti, 1915–1918' to Mussolini, dated 7 April 1944. ACS, RSI SPD, Carteggio Riservato, 1943–45, b. 17, f. 92, s.f. 7.
118. According to statistics compiled by the Food and Agriculture Organization (FAO) after the war. See Cavazzoli, *La gente e la guerra*, pp. 53–5.
119. Capo della Provincia, Milan, 'Appunto per il Duce: Relazioni mensili comunali mese di dicembre' dated 19 February 1945. ACS, SPD Carteggio Riservato (1943–45), B. 17, F. 92, S.F. 1.
120. Ministero dell'Agricoltura e delle Foreste, Report on food availability, 1944, 35 pp.; 'Situazione Alimentare, Appunto per il Duce,' 28 July 1944; and 'Importazioni dalla Germania, Appunto per il Duce,' 24 October 1944. ACS, RSI SPD, Carteggio Riservato (1943–45), b. 82, f. 653.
121. Ministero dell'Agricoltura e delle Foreste, 'Limiti e carattere dell'ingerenza germanica, nei suoi eccessi: Appunto per il Duce,' 27 May 1944. ACS, RSI SPD, Carteggio Riservato (1943–45), b. 82, f. 653.
122. Mantelli, *Camerati del lavoro*, p. 343, pp. 377–80.
123. Goebbels cited in F. W. Deakin, *The Brutal Friendship: Mussolini, Hitler, and the Fall of Italian Fascism* (New York: Harper and Row, 1962), p. 557.
124. Mussolini quoted in Macgregor Knox, *Mussolini Unleashed 1939–1941: Politics and Strategy in Fascist Italy's Last War* (Cambridge: Cambridge University Press, 1982), p. 13.
125. Mussolini's speech of 17 April 1943, cited in Deakin, *The Brutal Friendship*, p. 319.
126. Letter from Ambassador Rahn to Mussolini, 19 April 1944. ACS, RSI SPD, Carteggio Riservato (1943–45), b. 23, f. 164.

Chapter 5 The Challenge of Abundance

1. The Alto Commissariato went through several name changes during the war, from the Commissariato Generale dell'Alimentazione in 1943 (RD 28 December 1943, n. 30B), to the Alto Commissariato dell'Alimentazione in 1944 (RD 13 December 1944, n. 1944), to the Ministero dell'Alimentazione in 1945 (DL 21 June 1945, n. 349), and back to the Alto Commissariato dell'Alimentazione at the end of 1945 (DLL 22 December 1945, n. 838).
2. Contact between the Commissariat and the Allied Military Government (AMGOT) was constant, as Vittorio Ronchi recalled, 'We always found the British functionaries to be precise and persevering, this was less the case with the Americans, due in part to the rapid turnover of their personnel. In any

case, given our country's situation, in spite of our best efforts to recover, there is no doubt that without the help of the Americans, days of hunger and revolution would have consumed our country.' Vittorio Ronchi, *Guerra e crisi alimentare in Italia* (Rome: Edizioni Agricole, 1977), p. 231. On relations between the United States and Italy see John Harper, *America and the Reconstruction of Italy, 1945–1948* (Cambridge: Cambridge University Press, 1986) and James Miller, *The United States and Italy, 1940–1950: The Politics and Diplomacy of Stabilization* (Chapel Hill: University of North Carolina Press, 1986).

3. Vera Cao Pinna, 'I risultati di un'indagine sui consume e sulle spese alimentari di 65 famiglie nella città di Roma (gennaio–febraio 1947),' published in *Quaderni della nutrizione* (May 1948) and cited in Stefano Somogyi, 'L'alimentazione nell'Italia unita,' *Storia d'Italia*, Vol. 5, *I Documenti* (Turin: Einaudi, 1973), pp. 870–71.

4. For example, unemployment dropped from two to one-half million between 1950 and 1963; the gross domestic product doubled in the same period; and Italy ranked third (after West Germany and Japan) in industrial growth. Martin Clark, *Modern Italy*, 2nd edn (London: Longman, 1996), pp. 349–53.

5. Vera Zamagni, *The Economic History of Italy, 1860–1990* (Oxford: Clarendon, 1993), pp. 346–49.

6. Overviews of contemporary Italian history include Zygmunt Baranski and Robert Lumley (eds), *Culture and Conflict in Postwar Italy* (New York: St. Martin's, 1990); Paul Ginsborg *A History of Contemporary Italy: Society and Politics, 1943–1988* (London: Penguin, 1990); Norman Kogan, *A Political History of Italy: The Postwar Years* (New York: Praeger, 1983); Silvio Lanaro, *Storia dell'Italia repubblicana* (Venice: Marsilio, 1992); Aurelio Lepre, *Storia della prima repubblica: L'Italia dal 1942 al 1992* (Bologna: Il Mulino, 1993); Donald Sassoon, *Contemporary Italy* 2nd edn (Harlow: Longmans, 1997); Stuart Woolf (ed.), *The Rebirth of Italy* (London: Longman, 1972).

7. These requests and others can be found in ACS Ministero dell' Agricoltura e delle Foreste, Direzione Generale Alimentazione Serie V, b. 46, s.f. 'Assegnazioni generi Pasqua Ebraica' and s.f. 'Assegnazioni speciali generi alimentari.' The Alto Comissariato's responses are held in b. 57 and b. 58.

8. Centro di Azione Latina, *Italy's Economy 1961* (Milan: Giuffrè, 1961), p. 56.

9. ACS Ministero dell' Agricoltura e delle Foreste, Direzione Generale Alimentazione, b. 61, 'AVISS' (Assegnazione viveri integrazione salari stipendi).

10. On the activities of the IRO in Italy after the war, ACS Ministero dell' Agricoltura e delle Foreste, Direzione Generale Alimentazione, Serie V, b. 81 'Servizio Razionamento Tesseramento' s.f. 'IRO' and b. 83.

11. Quoted in Filippo Ceccarelli, *Lo stomaco della Repubblica: Cibo e potere in Italia dal 1945 al 2000* (Milan: Longanesi, 2000), p. 26.
12. ACS Ministero dell' Agricoltura e delle Foreste, Direzione Generale Alimentazione, bb. 18 and 19.
13. Giuseppe Aliberti, *Per una nuova fisiologia sociale dell'alimentazione* (Rome: Istituto di Medicina Sociale, 1952), pp. 92–3.
14. Many of the early school cafeterias (*refettori scolastici*) were set up and organized through a joint effort by UNRRA's AAI (the *Amministrazione per le Attività Assistenziali Italiane e Internazionale*), the Food and Agriculture Organization (FAO) of the UN, and Italy's *Istituto Nazionale della Nutrizione*. The impact of these feedings are summarized in Giuseppina Pastori, *Mangiare per vivere: Le razione alimentare* (Brescia: La Scuola Editrice, 1953). In 1946, an UNRRA study argued that supplemental feedings for children flattened out regional differences in consumption patterns with regard to protein and fat consumption. However, there were still striking differences between regions in terms of carbohydrate and calorie intake, even with the supplemental feedings:

	North	*Center*	*South/Islands*
Cereal	474	437	384 grams
Meat	22.8	21.1	21.4 grams
Fats	16	19	17 grams
Milk	261	188	222 grams
Vegetables	62	78	113 grams
Sugar	11	13	9 grams
Calories	2,055	1,948	1,792

UNRRA provided an average of 412 extra calories per day for over two million Italian children in 1945–46; this amount accounted for an average of 21 percent of the total calories consumed by most children. Delegazione del Governo Italiano per i rapporti con l'UNRRA, *I risultati di una inchiesta sui consumi alimentari nelle convivenze assistite dall'UNRRA* (Rome: United Nations, 1947).
15. Cited in Ginsborg, *History of Contemporary Italy*, p. 117.
16. Filippo Ceccarelli, *Lo stomaco della Repubblica*, p. 36.
17. Camera dei Deputati. *Atti della Commissione Parlamentare di Inchiesta sulla miseria in Italia e sui mezzi per combatterla*, Vo. I, *Relazione Generale* (Milan: Istituto Editoriale Italiano, 1953), p. 27. For a summary of the inquiry see Paolo Braghin (ed.), *Inchiesta sulla miseria in Italia* (Turin: Einaudi, 1978).

18. The Ministry of Justice, for example, increased rations for prisoners and juvenile offenders, including 100 grams of canned meat per week (200 grams per week for sick prisoners). ACS Ministero dell' Agricoltura e delle Foreste, Direzione Generale Alimentazione Serie V, b. 55 'Razionamenti speciali'. Local SEPRAL organizations were charged with assessing whether prisoners received adequate rations during and after the war.

19. These included the Clinica Pediatrica at the University of Rome, the Istituto Fisiologico at the University of Naples; the Clinica Medica at the University of Bari; and the Istituto di Medicina del lavoro at the University of Palermo. For a listing of the studies see Francesco Mancini, 'Attuali conoscenze sull'alimentazione e sullo stato di nutrizione degli Italiani,' in Istituto Nazionale della Nutrizione, *Alimenti ed alimentazione* (Istituto Nazionale della Nutrizione, 1970), pp. 105–47.

20. In the early 1950s, international organizations (FAO, the OECE) highlighted Italy's backward nutritional status by comparing national data to those in other European countries. A 1951 survey by the European Economic Community, for example, ranked Italy and Greece lowest in terms of calories, fats, meat, milk, and sugar consumed (compared to England, France, West Germany, Norway, Sweden, Holland, and Belgium). OECE, *Niveaux de consommation alimentaire dans le Pays de l'OECE*, cited in Bruno Rossi Ragazzi, 'Situazione e prospettive dall'alimentazione popolare secondo i rilievi statistici,' in Ufficio Attività Culturali delle Democrazia Cristiana, *Alimentazione popolare* (Rome: Libertas, 1953), p. 42.

21. Other markers included living in dwellings with more than four persons per room and having no or inappropriate shoes to wear. Camera dei Deputati, *Atti della Commissione Parlamentare di Inchiesta sulla miseria*, Vol. 2, *Indagini Techniche*, Maria Cao Pinna, 'Le classi povere,' p. 41.

22. Camera dei Deputati, *Atti della Commissione Parlamentare*, Vol. 1, *Relazione Generale*. Data on household budget from p. 85, data on consumption of meat, sugar, and wine from Tables 23, 24, and 25, pp. 70–2.

23. For a detailed analysis of class-based consumption habits in the 1950s and 1960s, see Paolo Braghin, *Le diseguaglianze sociali* (Milan: Sapre, 1973), Chapter 4.

24. Camera dei Deputati, *Atti della Commissione Parlamentare di Inchiesta sulla miseria*, Vol. 14, *Inchiesta a carattere comunitario, risultati e orientamenti relazione*, p. 93, table 37.

25. About 1.75 million left the south between 1951 and 1961, about 10 percent of the national population in 1951. Another 2.3 million left between 1961 and 1971. Martin Clark, *Modern Italy*, p. 357–60.

26. At the end of the war, there were several surveys that argued for a monotonous and inadequate diet in both the north and south. See Ugo Giusti,

Armonie e contrasti di ambiente e di vita in Italia (Rome: Migliaresi, 1945).
27. Camera dei Deputati, *Atti della Commissione Parlamentare di Inchiesta sulla miseria*, Vol. 7, *Indagini delle delegazioni parlamentari. La miseria in alcune zone depresse*, p. 96, p. 351.
28. Braghin, *Le diseguaglianze sociali*, pp. 212–16.
29. Sabato Visco, 'Nuovi indirizzi della alimentazione e l'agricoltura italiana,' *Alimentazione italiana* 3, 3 (March 1957), pp. 7–11.
30. 'L'indagine statistica sui bilanci di famiglie non agricole negli anni 1953–54,' *Annali di statistica* 8, 9 (1960), cited in Somogyi, 'L'alimentazione nell'Italia unita,' pp. 872–3.
31. Danilo Dolci, *To Feed the Hungry: Enquiry into Palermo*, trans. P.D. Cummins (London: Macgibbon and Kee, 1959), pp. 171–80, 245–6.
32. Comment by Domenico Miraglia, in Ufficio Attività Culturali delle Democrazia Cristiana, *Alimentazione Popolare*, pp. 202–6.
33. ISTAT results summarized in Somogyi, 'L'alimentazione nell'Italia unita,' pp. 874–6.
34. For 15 percent of the families, nutritional intake was sufficient, and for 35 percent of the families, it was considered good. Of the families, 40 percent consumed meat once a week, and 40 percent of the families consumed meat once or twice a month. Study conducted by Istituto di Scienze Demografiche at the University of Palermo, conducted under the auspices of the Consiglio Nazionale delle Ricerche in 1966, cited in Somogyi, 'L'alimentazione nell'Italia unita,' p. 887.
35. The study was conducted by the Ministry of Health in 1965. Nutritional levels were determined in terms of caloric intake and vitamins consumed. Regions with good nutrition levels were located mostly in the north: Milan, Pavia, Turin, Genoa, Reggio Emilia, Bologna, Savona, Rome, Umbria. The worst nutritional levels were found in the south: Basilicata, Puglia, Calabria, Sicilia, Sardegna. Results reported in 'Sopratutto la tutela igienica degli alimenti,' *Alimentazione italiana* 12, 1 (January 1966), pp. 5–6.
36. Study conducted and published by G. Ferro-Luzzi and E. Sofia, published in *Quaderni della nutrizione*, cited in Mancini, 'Attuali conoscenze', p. 142.
37. Carmela D'Apice, *L'arcipelago dei consumi* (Bari: De Donato, 1981), pp. 122–24.
38. Quote is from Clemente Maglietta, *L'industria alimentare in Italia: Discorso pronunciato alla Camera dei Deputati nella seduta del 23 Giugno, 1954* (Rome: Tipografia della Camera dei Deputati, 1954), p. 13.
39. Agricultural expert Giovanni Merlini, at a 1952 conference on food policy sponsored by the Christian Democratic party, equated policies that prioritized the production of all crops with the 'resurrection of an autarkic direction' for the state. Such a move would be a dangerous error, as 'many Italian workers

are more or less sick of autarky.' Giovanni Merlini, 'Alimentazione e produttività dell'agricoltura' in Ufficio Attività Culturali delle Democrazia Cristiana, *Alimentazione popolare*, pp. 70–1.

40. Even though the left advocated greater protection for Italian agriculture, there was not much of an official discussion about boosting agricultural production as there had been in years past. Agricultural policy in the 1950s consisted of a series of temporary measures mostly to address the problem of peasant land occupations and even these piecemeal measures failed to satisfy rural Italians. From the end of the war into the 1990s, the exodus of persons out of rural Italy meant a drop in the number of people employed in agriculture (from 8.6 million in 1945 to 2.5 million in the early 1990s). Official concern about rural Italy focused on ways to alleviate misery in these areas and not necessarily on ways to improve agricultural production. Zamagni, *Economic History of Italy 1860–1990*, p. 346–7.

41. As outlined in September 1951 by Roberto Lucifredi, Undersecretary of State, 'La pubblica amministrazione e l'alimentazione popolare,' in *Alimentazione popolare*, p. 179.

42. 'La politica alimentare d'oggi,' *Alimentazione italiana* 7, 12 (December 1961), pp. 5–9. Miraglia also mentioned agricultural production, but this assumed secondary importance to issues of consumption and distribution.

43. During this time, the production of automobiles increased from 369,000 per year to over one million; refrigerator production increased from 500,000 to over two million, and the production of washing machines increased from 100,000 to over one million. M.R. Storchi, *Il poco e il tanto: Condizioni e modi di vita degli Italiani dall'unificazione a oggi* (Naples: Liguori, 1999), p. 165; Paolo Sorcinelli, *Gli Italiani e il cibo* (Bologna: CLUEB, 1992), p. 221.

44. Paolo Quirino's estimates of food expenditures chart a decrease from 62.8 percent of the total budget in 1926 to 43.5 percent in 1961 to 34.6 percent in 1971. Paolo Quirino, 'I consumi in Italia dall'Unità ad oggi,' in Ruggiero Romano (ed.), *Storia dell'economia italiana*, Vol. 3: *L'età contemporanea: un paese nuovo* (Turin: Einaudi, 1991), p. 247.

45. National production of meat, for beef and veal, measured in thousands of quintals, increased from 2,323 in 1948 to 4,802 in 1959; for chicken, 495 in 1948 to 1,329 in 1959. Centro di Azione Latina, *Italy's Economy 1961*, p. 79.

46. Figures are from ISTAT, cited in D'Apice, *L'arcipelago dei consumi*, Table 2, p. 144, and Table 6, p. 150.

47. Braghin, *Le diseguaglianze sociali*, p. 180.

48. According to statistician Guglielmo Tagliacarne, the salaries of agricultural workers increased 880 percent, for industrial workers 567 percent, for service workers 475 percent, averaging a 520 percent increase for workers generally. The cost of living only increased by 152 percent. Guglielmo Tagliacarne, *Il*

bilancio degli Italiani. Il conto economico ed il conto sociale (Novara: Edipem, 1970), p. 17.

49. ISTAT figures cited in Anna Bartolini, *Gli alimenti tra salute e portafoglio* (Milan: Nicola Teti, 1979), p. 8.

50. Guido Galeotti's calculations indicate that protein comprised 11.9 percent of all calories consumed in the period 1961–66; down from 14.3 percent in the period 1920–39 and 12.1 percent in the period 1951–60. Fat consumption comprised 26.6 percent of calories consumed in 1961–66, up from 21 percent in 1920–39 and 22.7 percent in 1951–60. Guido Galeotti, *Condizioni ed evoluzione dei consumi alimentari in Italia* (Rome: Unione Nazionale Consumatori, 1969), p. 53.

51. 2,000–2,400 calories per day were recommended for persons with a sedentary lifestyle, 2,400–3,000 calories per day for persons performing moderate labor, and 3,000–4,500 for persons engaged in heavy labor. Bruno Rossi Ragazzi, 'Situazione e prospettive dell'alimentazione popolare secondo i rilievi statistici,' in *Alimentazione popolare*, pp. 36–8, 42; and Giuseppe Aliberti, *Per una nuova fisiologia sociale dell'alimentazione* (Rome: Istituto di Medicina Sociale, 1962), p. 78.

52. Ancel Keys and Margaret Keys, *Eat Well and Stay Well* (Garden City NY: Doubleday 1963).

53. Giuseppe Aliberti, *Alimentazione umana* (Milan: Garzanti, 1954), p. 91; Gino Bergami, *Imparare a nutrirsi* (Turin: ILTE, 1957); and Giulio Buogo, *L'alimentazione e la salute nelle ricerche biochimiche e nella igiene sociale* (Milan: De Kaan, 1963), p. 36.

54. Giulia Lazzari Turco, *Il piccolo focolare: Ricette di cucina per la massaia economa*, 3rd edn (Trento: GB Monauni, 1947).

55. Terzilio Borghesi, *Per voi donne! Vivere sane, vivere belle: Alimentazione, ginnastica, massaggio, igiene* (Florence: Macrì, 1953), p. 29.

56. Rinaldo Nanni, *L'arte e la tecnica della cucina italiana: Tratte dalle esperienze praticate nel cinquantennio delle mie peregrinazione nelle varie cucine regionali italiane ed estere* (Bologna: Compositori, 1956).

57. Ginsborg, *History of Contemporary Italy*, p. 183.

58. Gigi Padovani, *Gnam! Storia sociale della Nutella* (Rome: Castelvecchi, 2000).

59. *L'industria alimentare in Italia*, p. 4.

60. Figures are from Centro di Azione Latina, *Italy's Economy 1961*, pp. 171–9.

61. Renato Covino, 'Dalla ricostruzione agli anni ottanta,' in Giampaolo Gallo (ed.), *Sulla bocca di tutti: Buitoni e Perugina, una storia in breve* (Perugia: Electa, 1990).

62. Albino Ivardi Ganapini and Giancarlo Gonizzi, *Barilla. Cento anni di pubblicità e comunicazione* (Parma: Archivio Storico Barilla, 1994).

63. Marco Riva, 'Foto di gruppo a tavola,' in Cesare Colombo and Alberto Terzi (eds), *Tra sogno e bisogno: 306 fotografie e 13 saggi sull'evoluzione dei consumi in Italia, 1940–1986* (Milan: Sipiel, 1986), p. 246.

64. Richard Hammond and George Martin, *Eating in Italy* (New York: Charles Scribner's Sons, 1957), pp. 40–1, 71, 110.

65. Elizabeth David, preface to the first edition of *Italian Food*, reprinted in Elizabeth David, *Italian Food* (London: Penguin, 1989), p. xv.

66. Regional guides include Giuseppe Cavazzana, *Itinerario gastronomico ed enologico d'Italia* (Milan: Banco Ambrosiano, 1949) and in English, Hammond and Martin, *Eating in Italy*. Ugo Giusti chronicled consumption habits for all the regions at the end of the Second World War, see Ugo Giusti, *Armonie e contrasti di ambiente e di vita in Italia* (Rome: Migliaresi, 1945).

67. 'La trippa: nutriente ed economica,' *La cucina italiana* 6, 10 (October 1957), pp. 804–5.

68. *La cucina italiana* 8, 6 (June 1959), pp. 520–1.

69. Daily intake varied by season. Thirteen out of sixty-two families studied did not reach sufficient calories-per-day intake in terms of food (that is, minus the wine). Giulio Bussadori, *Inchiesta alimentare in due comuni della provincia di Padova* (Padua: Nicoletti, 1962).

70. For a history of postwar models of consumption and consumerism see Vanni Codeluppi, *I consumatori: Storia, tendenze, modelli* (Milan: Franco Angeli, 1992).

71. The majority of the festivals described in Marianna Caroselli's *Usi e costumi d'Italia* (Milan: Gastaldi, 1962), focus on food or drink.

72. Occasionally, male cookbook authors and gourmands blamed Italian women for destroying the simplicity of Italian cuisine by adding too many rich ingredients or too much seasoning. Male-operated restaurants and *trattorie* were seen as the last defense against the bastardization of Italian cuisine. See for example Nanni, *L'arte della cucina italiana*.

73. Luigi Renato Sansone, *Agricoltura ed alimentazione* (Rome: Tipografia Camera dei Deputati, 1954), p. 17; Aliberti, *Per una nuova fisiologia sociale dell'alimentazione*, p. 63.

74. Many of these fears are articulated in a special issue of the periodical *Alimentazione*, issue dedicated to the First National Convention on the Problems of Alimentation, *Alimentazione* 1, 6–7 (June–July 1954).

75. See for example the collected essays in Istituto Nazionale della Nutrizione, *Alimenti ed alimentazione* (Rome: Istituto Nazionale della Nutrizione, 1970).

76. Ines Bergamo and Mimi Bergamo, *A tavola!* 2nd edn (U Hoepli, 1936); and Irene Brin, *Usi e costumi 1920–40* (Rome: Donatella De Luigi, 1944).

77. Aliberti, *Per una nuova fisiologia sociale dell'alimentazione*, pp. 99–146.

Many social scientific studies used FAO figures or standards from the US National Research Council's Food and Nutrition Board.

78. Italian gastronomic literature is rife with references to the decreasing quality of Italian foods. A prime example is the introduction to the writings of Luciano Voegelin, a gastronome killed in the bombardment of Treviso on 7 April 1944: 'More and more, our food is becoming artificial. It is more likely to come from a chemical laboratory than from the earth. Man can go to the moon, but he will never become used to adulterated food.' See Alberto Voegelin, 'Introduzione,' Luciano Voegelin, *La scienza in cucina e nel ristorante (Quel che si mangia: Manuale di arte e scienza gastronomica)* Vol. 1 (Trento: Temi, 1966), p. 9.

79. Luca Vercelloni, 'La modernità alimentare,' in Capatti *et al.*, *Storia d'Italia*, Annali 13, *L'alimentazione*, p. 958.

80 'Sempre la falsa riforma del commercio,' *Alimentazione italiana* 16, 7 (July 1970), pp. 24–25; 'I consumi italiani di surgelati nel 1969,' *Alimentazione italiana* 16, 8 (August 1970), p. 11.

81. Carole Counihan, *Around the Tuscan Table: Food, Family and Gender in Twentieth Century Florence* (New York: Routledge, 2004). One 1988–89 survey of Italian families with children found women spent an average of 5.5 hours per day on household tasks while men spent only 48 minutes per day. The proportion did not vary much if the woman held a job outside the home. Cited in Paul Ginsborg, *Italy and its Discontents. Family, Civil Society, State: 1980–2001* (New York: Palgrave, 2003), p. 80.

82. On this point see Marco Riva, 'Foto di gruppo a tavola,' in Columbo and Terzi, *Tra sogno e bisogno*, p. 247.

83. Throughout the 1960s, food experts affiliated with the National Institute for Nutrition or the Ministry of Agriculture raised concerns that food laws were outdated and the public was ignorant of food adulteration. The emphasis on quality control for the food industry intensified throughout the 1960s, and by 1969 there was widespread concern that Italian food products measure up to the standards set by the European Community. See for example 'Chiamolo "Ministro dell'Agricoltura della Alimentazione e delle Foreste" Convegno sulla Alimentazione a Napoli, Giugno 1966', *Alimentazione italiana* 12, 6 (July 1966), p. 4.

84. In 1974, several scandals in the food industry occurred, one involving the use of common wheat instead of durum wheat to make pasta as a way of keeping prices down and the other involving the use of rapeseed oil (a highly toxic substance) in combination with other oils. Later in the 1970s, there were controversies over the use of hormones in livestock production as well as over the use of coloring agents and synthetic flavors. 'The Food Industry,' in Omar Calabrese (ed.), *Modern Italy: Images and History of a*

National Identity, Vol. 4, *The Difficult Democracy* (Milan: Electa, 1985), pp. 339–46.

85. See Ganapini and Gonizzi, *Barilla: Cento anni di pubblicità e comunicazione*.

Conclusion

1. In particular, the work of Victoria de Grazia for the fascist period illustrates the rise of mass consumption in the midst of a low-wage economy. Italians, in particular Italian women, felt the contradictions between living under a presumably modernizing regime during the rise of mass consumerism, and being unable to obtain access to such a world. Victoria de Grazia, *The Culture of Consent: The Mass Organization of Leisure in Fascist Italy* (Cambridge: Cambridge University Press, 1981) and *How Fascism Ruled Women, Italy 1922–45* (Berkeley: University of California Press), 1992.

2. Insightful examples of these types of study include Donna Gabbaccia, *We Are What We Eat: Ethnic Food and the Making of Americans* (Cambridge MA: Harvard University Press, 1998); Stephen Mennell, *All Manners of Food: Eating and Taste in England and France from the Middle Ages to the Present* (University of Illinois Press, 1996 [1985]); and Jeffrey Pilcher, *Que vivan los tamales! Food and the Making of Mexican Identity* (Albuquerque: University of New Mexico Press, 1998).

3. Franco La Cecla, *La pasta e la pizza* (Bologna: Il Mulino, 1998), p. 99.

Epilogue

1. Paul Hoffman, *That Fine Italian Hand* (New York: Henry Holt, 1990), p. 26.

2. Italian-Americans began selling pizza to their neighbors in the 1930s. Red-gravy restaurants followed, serving a variety of Italian-American versions of southern Italian foods (spaghetti and meatballs, lasagna, veal parmesan, pizza), mostly in areas with high concentrations of Italian-Americans in the northeastern United States.

3. Frances Mayes, *Under the Tuscan Sun. At Home in Italy* (New York: Broadway Books, 1997), p. 124.

4. Studies of consumer habit reveal that throughout the 1980s and 1990s, Italian consumers ate mostly carbohydrates, supplemented by meat, dairy products, and fats. The classic Mediterranean Diet is most popular in the south. Francesco G. Leone, 'The Structure of Food Consumption in the Mezzogiorno of Italy,' *Rivista di Antropologia* 76 supplement (1998), pp. 293–300.

5. Filippo Ceccarelli, *Lo stomaco della Repubblica: Cibo e potere in Italia dal 1945 al 2000* (Milan: Longanesi, 2000), p. 25.

6. The *Festa* has since gone back to emphasizing authentically Italian cuisine, but the food remains of very high quality.

7. Peter Robb, *Midnight in Sicily* (New York: Vintage Books, 1999), p. 250.

8. Ceccarelli, *Lo stomaco della Repubblica*, p. 269. Bossi's 'Made in Padania' campaign conjures up memories of Mussolini's autarkic policies, and the *Festa Padana* features only northern gastronomic specialties.

9. Daniel Williams, 'Venice Gets its Tomatoes Fresh, and in a Stew,' *The Washington Post* (2 June 2003), on-line edn.

10. The number of supermarkets in Italy has increased from 3,696 in 1996 to 6,413 in 2000. The number of small food shops has decreased from 254,000 in 1991 to 193,000 in 2001. 'Italy Losing Mom-and-Pop Shops' (15 February 2003), published on-line at www.cnn.com.

11. An engaging case study of the United States is Marion Nestle, *Food Politics: How the Food Industry Influences Nutrition and Health* (Berkeley: University of California Press, 2002).

12. Numbers are from the McDonald's websites, www.mcdonalds.com and www.mcdonalds.it.

13. Strikes in October of 2002 in defense of article 18 of Italy's labor law coincided with world anti-McDonald's day; therefore some of the protests against McDonald's also touched on Italian labor issues and anti-Berlusconi sentiment. Farmers protesting EU and Italian agricultural policies in December of 2000 protested at McDonald's. Environmentalists opposing genetically modified foods protested at McDonald's (as they did in Genoa in May of 2000 for example), even though McDonald's halted the purchase of genetically modified foods.

14. Raspelli was sued for his comments, see below; the interview was published in *La Stampa* in 2002 as a sidebar to a larger story about how McDonald's was losing profits and closing down restaurants. The quote is from Edoardo Raspelli, 'Arch Enemies,' *The Guardian Unlimited* (4 June 2003), on-line edn.

15. Italian McDonald's workers have used the Internet to vent their frustrations with their employer; their complaints can be found on www.chainworker.org.

16. Alessandra Retico, 'Fritture e tabelle orarie, una giornata da McDonald's,' *La Repubblica* (11 May 2003), on-line edn.

17. The Italian bureaucracy is not for the faint of heart. In the walled city of Lucca, for example, a franchisee was denied permission to set up a McDonald's within the city limits; he retaliated by building a 'real full blown Texas size, free-standing' McDonald's at Lucca's exit off the *autostrada*. Raymond Role, 'In the Shadow of the Golden Arches: Adventures in a Post-Contadino Society,' *The Informer* July 2001, Issue 162, 'Understanding Italy,' on-line edn (www.informer.it).

18. Raspelli, 'Arch Enemies;' '"Ha diffamato l'hamburger:" McDonald's contro Raspelli,' *La Stampa* (27 May 2003), on-line edn.

19. Paul Ginsborg, *Italy and its Discontents: Family, Civil Society, State: 1980–2001* (New York: Palgrave, 2003), p. 20.

20. 'Italy: A GMO-free Country?' *The Scientist* (21 November 2000), on-line version.

21. The most popular agricultural concerns in Italy are specialized crops like fruit, grapes, and nurseries, which receive little or no funding from EU agricultural policies.

22. Manifesto of the International Movement for the Defense of and the Right to Pleasure, Paris, 9 November, 1989, www.slowfood.com.

23. A collection of writing from members of the movement worldwide is available in English, Carlo Petrini (ed.), *Slow Food: Collected Thoughts on Taste, Tradition, and the Honest Pleasures of Food* (White River Junction: Chelsea Green, 2001).

24. Massimo Montanari, 'The Faithless Hamburger,' *Slow* Year IV, No. 21 (April–June 2001), on-line edn.

25. Italian demographers characterize families as 'long and thin' because adult children are staying longer in the home and because reproduction rates are declining.

26. Hans Teuteberg, 'Agenda for a Comparative History of Diet,' in H.J. Teuteberg (ed.), *European Food History: A Research Review* (Leicester: Leicester University Press, 1992), p. 4.

Bibliography

Archival Sources

Archivio Centrale dello Stato (ACS), Rome, Italy
   Consiglio Nazionale delle Ricerche
     Comitato Agricoltura
   Direzione Generale Sanità Pubblica
   Ministero di dell'Agricoltura e delle Foreste
     Direzione Generale Alimentazione
   Ministero dell'Interno
     Divizione per le Amministrazioni Communali e Provinciali
     Divizione Generale Pubbblica Sicurezza
       Divizione Polizia Giudiziaria
       Divizione Generale Affari Generali e Riservati
       Divizione Generale di Pubblica Sicurezza
       Divizione del Capo della Polizia RSI
   Partito Nazionale Fascista
     Situazione Politica e Economia delle Provincie
   Presidenza del Consiglio dei Ministri
     Guerra Mondiale
   Repubblica Sociale Italiana
     Segretaria Particolare Duce
     Segretaria Particolare del Sottosegretario Barracu
     Pubblica Sicurezza, Capo della Polizia RSI-Chierici
United States Department of State, *Records of the Department of State Relating to the Internal Affairs of Italy, 1910–29*, Microfilm Series.

Periodicals

Agricultura coloniale
Agricoltura fascista
Alimentazione
Alimentazione italiana
Annali d'igiene

Annali di statistica
Autarchia alimentare
Barometro economico italiano
Bolletino della Società Italiana per lo Studio della Alimentazione
Casa e lavoro
Il commercio
La critica sociale
La cucina italiana
Economia
L'economia italiana
The Economist
Il giornale del commercio
Giornale degli economisti
International Labour Review
Nuova Antologia
Profamilia
Quaderni della nutrizione
La riforma sociale
Rivista del lavoro
Slow
La voce del consumatore

Primary Sources

Abot, H., *Eating My Way Through Italy*, San Francisco: Golden State Company, 1939.
Alberti, M., 'Le statistiche dei prezzi delle derrate alimentari,' *La riforma sociale* 23, 19 (October 1912), pp. 700–14.
Aliberti, G., *Per una nuova fisiologia sociale dell'alimentazione*, Rome: Istituto di Medicina Sociale, 1952.
——, *Alimentazione umana*, Milan: Garzanti, 1954.
Amateis, F., *La lotta contro il caro vivere*, Milan: U. Hoepli, 1916.
Angello, V., 'L'alimentazione in Sicilia,' in *Le forze sanitarie*, 3 (1934), pp. 101–10.
Artusi, P. *La scienza in cucina e l'arte di mangiar bene*, reprint, Turin: Einaudi, 1970.
Associazione dei Comuni Italiani, *Considerazioni sul problema annonario*, Rome: Bianchi, 1924.
Bachi, Riccardo, *L'alimentazione e la politica annonaria in Italia*, Bari: Laterza, 1926.
Balestrieri, M., *I consumi alimentari della popolazione italiana dal 1910 al 1921*, Padua: Metron, 1925.
——, *Indagine statistica sulle disponibilità alimentari della popolazione italiana dal 1922 al 1937*, Rome: Tipografia Failli, 1939.

Barberi, B., *Le disponibilità alimentari della popolazione italiana dal 1910 al 1942*, Rome: Istituto Poligrafico dello Stato, 1946.

Bartolini, A., *Gli alimenti tra salute e portafoglio*, Milan: Nicola Teti, 1979.

Bellati, C., *La nostra casa*, Milan: Vita e Pensiero, 1929.

Bellini, M., *Il problema dell'alimentazione nazionale*, Bologna: Paolo Neri, 1917.

Benedettini, P., *Consigli di economia domestica*, Florence: Stianti, 1936.

Bergami, G., *Imparare a nutrirsi*, Turin: ILTE, 1957.

Bergamo, M., and Bergamo, I., *A tavola! Menus stagionali relative ricette*, 2nd edn, Milan: U. Hoepli, 1936.

Bonomo, G., *Il prezzo d'impero del grano e la politica agraria ed annonaria di guerra*, Messina: D'Angelo, 1917.

Borghesi, T., *Per voi donne! Vivere sane, vivere belle: Alimentazione, ginnastica, massaggio, igiene*, Florence: Macrì, 1953.

Bottazzi, F., Niceforo, A., and Quagliariello, G. (eds), *Documenti per lo studio della alimentazione della popolazione italiana nell'ultimo cinquantennio*, Naples: N. Jovene, 1933.

Brin, I., *Usi e costumi, 1920–1940*, Rome: Donatella De Luigi, 1944.

Brugnola, A., *Il bilancio nutritivo e l'alimentazione del contadino nell'Umbria come base allo studio dell'etiologia della pellagra*, Perugia: Unione Tipografia Cooperativa, 1903.

Buogo, G., *L'alimentazione e la salute nelle ricerche biochimiche e nella igiene sociale*, Milan: De Kaan, 1963.

Bussadori, G., *Inchiesta alimentare in due comuni della provincia di Padova*, Padua: Nicoletti, 1962.

Camboni, L., 'Monografia di famiglia agricole del Comune di Mores (Provincia di Sassari),' *Giornale degli economisti* 30 (May–June 1905), pp. 475–571.

Camera Confederale del Lavoro di Roma e Provincia, *Contro il caro-vita: Relazione – programma alle organizzazioni camerali*, Rome: Farri, 1925.

Camera dei Deputati, Parliamento, *Atti della Commissione Parlamentare di Inchiesta sulla miseria in Italia e sui mezzi per combatterla*, 14 volumes, Milan: Istituto Editoriale Italiano, 1953.

Camera di Commercio e Industria, Ufficio di Statistica, *Statistica della macellazione e consumo carneo in Italia nell'anno 1925*, Milan: Archetipografia di Milano, 1927.

Camera di Commercio e Industria della Provincia di Bergamo, *In merito all'Ente Nazionale dei Consumi ed ai provvedimenti economici governativi*, Bergamo: Società Editrice Commerciale, 1917.

Camera di Commercio e Industria di Roma, *Organizzazione dei sistemi di rifornamento e di distribuzione delle principali derrate alimentari*, Rome: Tipografia della Camera dei Deputati, 1924.

Camilla, S., *La massima, più razionale e pratica utilizzazione del frumento colla produzione industriale della farina 'scia,'* Turin: Enrico Schioppo, 1923.

Cao-Pinna, V., 'Inchieste statistiche sul regime alimentare di 11 famiglie di artigiani e 10 famiglie agiate, nella città di Cagliari,' *Quaderni della nutrizione* 2 (July and August 1935), pp. 1–60, pp. 109–64.

Carli, F., 'Il movimento delle derrate alimentari in Italia,' *Il commercio* 4, 11 (November 1931), pp. 664–93.

Caroselli, M., *Usi e costumi d'Italia*, Milan: Gastaldi, 1962.

Cavazzana, G., *Itinerario gastronomico ed enologico d'Italia*, Milan: Banco Ambrosiano, 1949.

Celli, A., *L'alimentazione maidica e il modo di migliorarla*, Milan: Pietro Agnelli, 1897.

Centro di Azione Latina, *Italy's Economy 1961*, Milan: Giuffrè, 1961.

Ciuffolini, A., *Indagine sulle condizioni di vita dei contadini*, Rome: Luzzatti, 1930.

Clementi, F., 'I dazi interni nei rapporti dei prezzi di consumi,' *Il commercio* 2, 4 (April 1929), pp. 30–5.

Coletti, F., 'Ricerche statistiche sui consumi alimentari in Italia,' *Reale Accademia dei Lincei, Comitato Scientifico per L'Alimentazione* 3 (1918), pp. 1–6.

Comitato Italiano per lo Studio dei Problemi della Popolazione, *Atti del Congresso Internationale per gli studi sulla popolazione*, Vol. 2, Rome: Istituto Poligrafico dello Stato, 1934.

Commissione per lo Studio dei Problemi dell'Alimentazione, *Studi sulla alimentazione di Pietro Albertoni e Angelo Pugliese*, Naples: N. Jovene, 1937.

Comune di Venezia, Ufficio di Statistica, *Il censimento generale del 1 Dicembre 1921 della popolazione di Venezia*, Rome: Poligrafica Italiana, 1923.

Confederazione Fascista degli Industriali, *L'industria in A.O.I.*, Rome: Società Editoriale de 'L'Organizzazione Industriale,' 1939.

Confederazione Fascista dei Lavoratori dell'Agricoltura, *L'alimentazione dei lavoratori agricoli in Italia*, Rome: Arte della Stampa, 1936.

——, *Campagna monda del riso*, Rome: Arte della Stampa, 1938.

Confederazione Generale Fascista dell'Industrie Italiane, *Fascist Era Year XII*, Rome: Confederazione Generale Fascista dell'Industrie Italiane, 1933.

Consolani, G., *Se sia possibile risolvere in Italia il problema del pane e della carne*, Rovigo: Corriere, 1918.

Contento, A., 'La guerra e l'aumento regionale dei prezzi,' *Giornale degli economisti* 56 (May 1918), pp. 256–67.

Crespi, S., *La politica degli approvvigionamenti in Italia*, Rome: Tipografia del Senato, 1918.

Curato, G., 'Monografie di famiglie borghesi del comune di Troja (Provincia di Foggia),' *La riforma sociale* 21 (November-December 1910), pp. 736–79.

D'Alfonso, N.R., *Il problema dell'alimentazione come problema educativo*, Milan: Società Editrice Libraria, 1918.

David, E., *Italian Food*, reprint, London: Penguin, 1989.

De Angeli, R., 'Il problema del prezzo del pane,' *La critica sociale* 30, 21 (1–15 November 1920), pp. 328–32.

De Brun, A., *Le cucine economiche*, Turin: Unione Torinese, 1914.

De Castro, D., *Prezzi e politica dei prezzi in Italia, Germania e Francia nell'ultimo quadriennio*, Turin: Collegio Artigianelli, 1939.

Delegazione del Governo Italiano per i rapporti con l'UNRRA, *I risultati di una inchiesta sui consumi alimentari nelle convivenze assistite dall'UNRRA*, Rome: United Nations, 1947.

De Michelis, G., *Alimentazione e giustizia sociale*, Rome: Istituto Nazionale di Cultura Fascista, 1937.

De Voto, L., *Il problema dell'alimentazione in guerra e dopo*, Rome: Bertero, 1916.

di Pace, I., *La crisi della carne*, Naples: Giannini e Figlio, 1917.

Dolci, D., *To Feed the Hungry: Enquiry into Palermo*, trans. P.D. Cummins, London: Macgibbon and Kee, 1959.

Ducceschi, V., *Prime linee di una storia dell'alimentazione umana*, Milan: Poligrafica degli Operai, 1936.

Dupont, A., *Realizzazioni fasciste nella vita italiana*, Rome: Tipografia del Senato, 1932.

Einaudi, L., *La condotta economica e gli aspetti sociali della guerra italiana*, Bari: Laterza, 1933.

——, *Cronache economiche e politiche*, Volume IV (1914–18), Turin: Einaudi, 1961; and Volumes VI, VII (1919–20), and X, Turin: Einaudi, 1965.

Federazione dei Fasci Femminili, *Corse preparatorio per visitatrici fasciste*, Novara: Cattaneo, 1940.

Federazione Internazionale del Commercio al Dettaglio di Alimentari, *I problemi del commercio alimentare*, Rome: Il Giornale del Commercio, 1933.

Federazione Nazionale Fascista Pubblici Esercizi, *Ristoranti d'Italia*, Rome: Società Anonima Editrice, 1938.

Federazione Provinciale Fascista Milanese, *Corso di preparazione politica per i giovani*, Volumes 2 and 3, Milan: Popolo d'Italia, 1935, 1936.

Ferraguti, M., *Battaglia per la vittoria del grano*, Milan: Stampa Commerciale, 1929.

Ferrari, A., *Il problema dei commestibili e l'Etiopia*, Lodi: G. Biancardi, 1937.

Ferraris, M., *Il problema dell'ora presente: Quattro anni di lotta contro caroviveri*, Rome: Nuova Antologia, 1919.

Ferrini, L., *Economia in cucina senza sacrificio a tavola*, Milan: Gino Conte, 1939.

Finer, H., *Mussolini's Italy*, London: Victor Golancz, 1935.

Fornari, D., *Il cuciniere militare*, Novara: Cattaneo, 1932.

Galeotti, G., *Condizioni ed evoluzione dei consumi alimentari in Italia*, Rome: Unione Nazionale Consumatori, 1969.

Galletti, G., *L'alimentazione ed il suo costo*, Milan: Cooperativa Grafica degli Operai, 1923.

Gasca, M., *Cucina di ieri e cucina di domani*, Rome: Tipografia delle Teme, 1928.

Giuffrida, V., *Provital: Approvvigionamenti alimentari d'Italia durante la Grande Guerra*, Padua: CEDAM, 1936.

Giusti, U., 'Methods of Recording Retail Prices and Measuring the Cost of Living in Italy,' *International Labour Review* 4, 3 (November 1921), pp. 257–74.

——, 'Sul consumo di generi alimentari in alcune grandi città Italiane,' *Il commercio* 3, 1 (January 1930), pp. 15–26.

——, *Armonie e contrasti di ambiente e di vita in Italia*, Rome: Migliaresi, 1945.

Hammond, R., and Martin, G., *Eating in Italy*, New York: Charles Scribner's Sons, 1957.

Inchiesta parlamentare sulle condizioni dei contadini nelle provincie meridionali e nella Sicilia, 8 volumes, Rome: Giovanni Bertero, 1909–11.

Istituto Nazionale della Nutrizione, *Alimenti ed alimentazione*, Rome: Istituto Nazionale della Nutrizione, 1970.

Istituto Nazionale delle Conserve Alimentari, Federazione Nazionale Fascista delle Conserve Alimentari, *Annuario dell'industria delle conserve alimentari*, Rome: SAIGE, 1934.

Istituto Nazionale di Economia Agraria, Studi e monografie. *Monografie di famiglie agricole*, 6 volumes, Milan-Rome: Società Anonima Treves, 1931–33.

——, *Caratteri e problemi della risicoltura italiana*, Rome: Mario Bondini, 1935.

Istituto Nazionale per l'Esportazione, *Dati statistici sulle esportazioni italiane e sulle corrispondenti principali importazioni estere nel quinquennio 1927–31*, Rome: Castaldi, 1932.

Keys, A. and Keys, M., *Eat Well and Stay Well*, Garden City, NY: Doubleday, 1963.

Lantini, F., 'La reazione alle sanzioni e il nuovo equilibrio economico,' *Il commercio* 8, 12 (December 1935), pp. 765–9.

——, *La donna nella resistenza economica della nazione*, Rome: Istituto Nazionale Fascista di Cultura, 1936.

——, *La famiglia nella resistenza alle sanzioni*, Rome: Società Editrice Novissima, 1936.

La Via, L., *Politica e tecnica fascista dei prezzi*, Rome: Arti Grafiche R. Cecconi, 1937.

Levi, C., *Christ Stopped at Eboli*, trans. Frances Frenaye, New York: Noonday, 1998.

Levi, G., *Il problema del pane*, Florence: Aldo Funghi, 1920.

Lewis, N., *Naples, '44*, New York: Henry Holt, 1994.

Lissone, S., *Perchè l'Italia abbia il suo pane: il sistema Soleri*, Turin: Grafico Moderno, 1920.

Lojacono, L., *L'independenza economica italiana*, Milan: U. Hoepli, 1937.

Lombroso, G., 'Sulle condizioni sociali economiche degli operai di un sobborgo di Torino,' *La riforma sociale* 3, 6 (10 September 1896), pp. 310–30.

Luraschi, A., *Memoriale presentata alla Commissione Generali dei Consumi a Roma, 7 guigno 1917*, Milan: Società Milanese, 1917.

Lusk, G., *The Elements of the Science of Nutrition*, reprint, New York: Academic Press, 1976 [1906].

Lustig, A., 'Considerazioni personali sulla razione alimentare dei soldati,' *Bolletino della Società Italiana per lo Studio della Alimentazione*, 1, 4–6 (1919), pp. 83–90.

Luzzatto-Fegiz, P., 'Nuove ricerche sui bilanci familiari,' *Giornale degli economisti e annali di economia* 5, 3–4 (March–April 1946), pp. 197–207.

——, *Alimentazione e prezzi in tempo di guerra*, Trieste: Università di Trieste, 1948.

Maglietta, C., *L'industria alimentare in Italia. Discorso pronunciato alla Camera dei Deputati nella seduta del 23 giugno 1954*, Rome: Tipografia della Camera dei Deputati, 1954.

Maioli, A., *Il problema nazionale della distribuzione del pane in base ad una inchiesta statistica*, Rome: Biblioteca Federale di Studi e di Propaganda, 1935.

Mantegazza, P., *Quadri della natura umana*, Volume I: *Feste ed ebbrezze*, Milan: Giuseppe Bernadoni, 1871.

Mara, *Per mangiar bene ... e spender poco*, Milan: SADEL, 1936.

Marescalchi, A., *Politica del vino*, Casale Monferrato: Fratelli Marescalchi, 1924.

——, *I vini tipici d'Italia*, Casale Monferrato: Fratelli Marescalchi, 1924.

——, *L'esportazione del vino italiano*, Casale Monferrato: Fratelli Marescalchi, 1925.

——, *I vini e gli alberghi*, Florence: Casa Vinicola Barone Ricasoli, 1934.

——, *Vino*, Turin: Tipografia Autarchia Nazionale, 1938.

——, *Storia della alimentazione e dei piaceri della tavola*, Milan: Garzanti, 1942.

Marinetti, F.T., and Fillìa, *La cucina futurista*, reprint, Milan: Longanesi, 1986.

Martinelli, G., *È possibile diminuire il costo della vita?* Arezzo: Editoriale Italiana Contemporanea, 1928.

Massone, E., Caldara, E., and Benucci, S., 'La lotta contro il caro-viveri,' *Nuova Antologia* 186 (1 November 1916), pp. 97–110.

McGuire, C., *Italy's International Economic Position*, New York: Macmillan, 1926.

Messadaglia, L., *Per la storia dell'agricoltura e dell'alimentazione*, Piacenza: Federazione Italiana dei Consorzi Agrari, 1932.

Miller, H., *Price Control in Fascist Italy*, New York: Columbia University Press, 1938.

Ministero di Agricoltura, Industria, e Commercio, Udine, *La cucina popolare di Udine nei suoi 25 anni di vita*, Udine: Fratelli Tovolini, 1912.

Momigliano, F., *Vivere bene in tempi difficili*, Milan: U. Hoepli, 1933.

Morelli, L., *La casa che vorrei avere*, Milan: U. Hoepli, 1933.

——, *Le massaie contro le sanzioni*, Turin: S. Lattes, 1935.

——, *Come sistemare e governare mia casa*, Milan: U. Hoepli, 1938.

——, *Massaie di domani*, Turin: S. Lattes, 1938.

——, *L'arte più difficile*, Milan: Garzanti, 1940.

——, *Nuovo ricettario domestico*, Milan: U. Hoepli, 1941.

Mortara, G., *Prospettive economiche 1922*, Milan: Università Bocconi, 1922.

——, *La salute pubblica in Italia durante e dopo la guerra*, Bari: Laterza, 1925.

——, 'Costo e rendimento economico dell'uomo,' in *Atti dell'Istituto Nazionale delle Assicurazioni*, Volume 6, Rome: Tipografia del Senato, 1934.

Mosso, A., *La fatica*, Milan: Fratelli Treves, 1891.

Municipio di Venezia, *Relazione della Giunta al Consiglio Comunale circa le proposte presentate dalla Commissione per il Rincaro dei Viveri*, Venice: C. Ferrari, 1912.

Mussolini, B., *My Diary, 1915–17*, trans. Rita Wellman, Boston: Small, Maynard, 1925.

——, *Speeches of Benito Mussolini on Italian Economic Policy During the First Decennium*, Rome: Istituto Italiano di Credito Marittimo, 1932.

Nanni, R., *L'arte e la tecnica della cucina italiana. Tratte dalle esperienze praticate nel cinquantennio delle mie peregrinazione nelle varie cucine regionali italiane ed estere*, Bologna: Compositori, 1956.

Niceforo, A., *Italiani del nord e Italiani del sud*, Turin: Fratelli Bocca, 1901.

——, *Forza e ricchezza. Studi sulla vita fisica ed economica delle classi sociali*, Turin: Fratelli Bocca, 1906.

——, *Ricerche sui contadini: Contributo allo studio antropologico ed economico delle classi povere*, Milan: Remo Sandron, 1907.

——, *Lo studio scientifico delle classi povere*, Trieste: Giuseppe Maylander, 1907.

——, *Bilanci alimentari delle nostre vecchie plebi rurali*, Naples: SIEM, 1937.

——, and Galeotti, G., 'Tipi di alimentazione in alcune regioni d'Italia,' *Barometro economico italiano* 7 (10 January 1935), pp. 39–40.

Nitti, F., 'L'alimentazione e la forza di lavoro dei popoli,' *La riforma sociale* 1 (1894), pp. 417–40, pp. 537–56.

Oddi, R., *Gli alimenti e la loro funzione nella economia dell'organismo individuale e sociale*, Turin: Fratelli Bocca, 1902.

Orano, D., *Come vive il popolo a Roma: Saggio demografico sul quartiere Testaccio*, Pescara: Ettore Croce, 1912.

Pagano, L., *Economia domestica*, Palermo: Industrie Riunite Editoriali Siciliane, 1934.

Pancrazi, P., *Serao: Romanzi e racconti Italiani dell'Ottocento*, Milan: Garzanti, 1944.

Partito Nazionale Fascista, Federazione dei Fasci Femminili, Novara, *Corso preparatorio per visitatrici fasciste*, Novara: Cattaneo, 1940.

Pastori, G., *Mangiare per vivere: Le razione alimentare*, Brescia: La Scuola Editrice, 1953.

Petronilla, *Ricette di Petronilla*, Milan: Olivini, 1935.

Piazza, C., *La vita della nazione*, Milan: Editori Associati, 1939.

Piccoli, E., *L'alimentazione dell'uomo*, Milan: Quintieri, 1921.

Pietra, G., 'In regime alimentare sanzionistico,' *L'economia italiana* 21, 2 (February 1936), pp. 144–52.

Pietravalle, M., *Politica annonaria di guerra*, Campobasso: Giovanni Colitti e Figlio, 1917.

Possenti, G., 'La finanza italiana ed i consumi voluttuari,' *Economia* 2, 10–11 (October-November 1924), pp. 239–44.

Preziotti, A., 'I consumi del contadino nel comune di Cannara (Provincia di Umbria),' *La riforma sociale* 16, 13 (15 August 1906), pp. 636–47.

Pugliese, A. *L'alimentazione popolare in Provincia di Milano: Se e come si può migliorare*, Milan: Cooperativa Grafica degli Operai, 1920.

——, *Brevi cenni sulle condizioni igieniche della provincia di Milano con speciale riguardo all'alcoolismo e al nicotismo degli adolescenti*, Milan: Cooperativa Grafica degli Operai, 1920.

Puglisi, A., *Il problema dell'approvvigionamento carneo dal punto di vista nazionale*, Rome: Enrico Voghera, 1917.

Reale Accademia d'Italia. Convegno di Scienze Fisiche, Matematiche e Naturali, 26 settembre-2 ottobre, 1937, *Lo stato attuale delle conoscenze sulla nutrizione*, Rome: Reale Accademia d'Italia, 1938.

Reale Commissione d'Inchiesta sulle Violazioni del Diritto delle Genti Commesse dal Nemico, *Documenti raccolti nelle provincie invase*, Volume VI, Milan: Bestetti e Tumminelli, 1920.

Reale Università di Firenze, Facoltà di Scienze Politiche, *Studi in memoria di Giovanni Dettori*, Volume I, Florence: Carlo Cya, 1941.

Rho, F., *L'alimentazione del soldato di terra e di mare in pace e in guerra*, Milan: Rava, 1915.

——, 'La riforma della razione alimentare e del soldato e l'economia nazionale,' *Annali d'igiene* 27 (1917), pp. 477–87.

Ricci, U., *Il fallimento della politica annonaria*, Florence: La Voce, 1921.

Ronchi, V., *Guerra e crisi alimentare in Italia, 1940–1950, Ricordi e esperienze*, Rome: Edizioni Agricole, 1977.

Rovesti, G., *Conserve alimentari di guerra*, Casale Monferrato: Fratelli Marescalchi, 1917.

Royal Institute for International Affairs, Information Department, *The Economic and Financial Position of Italy*, London: Oxford University Press, 1935.

Ruini, M., 'The Italian Co-operative Movement,' *International Labour Review* 5, 1 (January 1922), pp. 13–33.

Russo, L., *Preparazione e condotta economica della guerra*, Rome: Cremonese, 1942.

Sansone, L., *Agricoltura ed alimentazione*, Rome: Tipografia della Camera dei Deputati, 1954.

Schmidt, C., *The Plough and the Sword*, New York: Columbia University Press, 1938.

Sclavo, A., *L'igiene in Italia negli ultimi venti anni*, Siena: L. Lazzeri, 1909.

——, *Sull'alimentazione umana*, Siena: L. Lazzeri, 1917.

Scuola Serale 'Buona Massaia' di S. Giovanni, Brescia, *La buona massaia*, Brescia: Istituto Figli di Maria Immacolata, 1928.

Sigurini, G., *Per l'istituzione di una cucina economica*, Udine: Fratelli Tovolini e G. Jacob, 1902.

Silone, I., *Vino e pane*, reprint, Milan: Mondadori, 1982.

Società Generale delle Conserve Alimentari 'Cirio,' *Nuove orizzonti per la vostra mensa*, Portici: E. della Torre, 1936.

Società Italiana dei Prodotti Maggi, *Per mangiar bene: 600 ricette*, Milan: Società Italiana dei Prodotti Maggi, 1928.

Società Italiana di Demografia e Statistica, *Atti della V Riunione*, Florence: Tipografia Unione Arti Grafiche, 1940.

Sonnino, S., *La Sicilia nel 1876: I contadini in Sicilia*, Florence: G. Barbèra, 1877.

Sottilaro, R., 'Indagini sulle condizioni di vita e sull'alimentazione dei lavoratori,' *Rivista del lavoro* 5 (May 1937), pp. 39–45.

Spatuzzi, A., Somma, L., and de Renzi, E., *Sull'alimentazione del popolo minuto in Napoli*, Naples: Stamperia della R. Università, 1863.

Starling, E., *Report on Food Conditions in Germany*, London: HMSO, 1919.

Tagliacarne, G., 'Se il numero degli esercenti di vendita al minuto influisce sugli alti prezzi,' *Economia* 9, 6 (June 1931), pp. 25–39.

——, 'La spesa per l'alimentazione in una grande città,' *Il commercio* 4 (November 1931), pp. 70–6.

——, *Il bilancio degli Italiani: Il conto economico ed il conto sociale*, Novara: Edipem, 1970.

Tallarico, G., *Lo stato biologico degli alimenti e lo sviluppo*, Rome: R. Garroni, 1930.

——, *Grano e pane*, Rome: Editoriale degli Agricoltori, 1933.

——, *La vita degli alimenti*, Florence: Sansoni, 1934.

——, *Le sanzioni e gli alimenti solari*, Rome: Istituto Nazionale Fascista di Cultura, 1936.

——, *L'alimento e la prolificità umana*, Rome: Tipografia Europa, 1941.

Tambara, M., 'Le attrezzature degli ammassi granari,' *L'economia italiana* 22, 4 (April 1937), pp. 354–60.

Tassinari, G., *Fascist Economy*, trans. Eduardo Cope, Rome: Laboremus, 1937.

Toddi (Rivetta, P.S.), *Preferite i prodotti nazionali!* Milan: Ceschina, 1938.

Toscano, G., *Verso nuove forme di assistenza sociale*, Spoleto: Panetto e Petrelli, 1918.

Touring Club Italiano, *Guida gastronomica d'Italia*, Milan: TCI, 1931.

Trevisanto, U., *Libertà di commercio e politica annonaria nel dopoguerra*, Bologna: Zanichelli, 1924.

Turco, G., *Il piccolo focolare. Ricette di cucina per la massaia economa*, 3rd edn, Trento: GB Monauni, 1947.

Ufficio Attività Culturali delle Democrazia Cristiana, *Alimentazione popolare*, Rome: Libertas, 1953.

Unione delle Camere di Commercio e Industria Italiane, *Il problema del costo della vita*, Rome: Carlo Colombo, 1923.

Unione delle Provincie d'Italia, *I consorzi granari provinciali e la loro opera a tutto il 30 giugno 1915: Considerazione sommarie e dati statistici*, Rome: Sociale, 1915.

United Nations Relief and Rehabilitation Administration, Italian Mission, *Conferenze sull'alimentazione per le assistenti sanitarie del Veneto, Forlì, Ferrara e Ravenna*, Venice: Carlo Ferrari, 1946.

United States Immigration Commission, Reports of the Immigration Commission, *Emigration Conditions in Europe*, Washington, D.C.: Government Printing Office, 1911.

United States Tariff Commission, *Italian Commercial Policy and Foreign Trade, 1922–1940*, Washington, D.C.: Government Printing Office, 1941.

Veronese, G., 'Il problema dei prezzi all'ingrosso e di prezzi al minuto,' *Il commercio* 3, 5 (May 1930), pp. 3–26.

——, *Gli indici dei prezzi normali all'ingrosso ed al minuto dei generi alimentari in Italia*, Rome: Tipografia del Giornale d'Italia, 1933.

——, 'La "vischiosità" dei prezzi dei generi alimentari in Italia,' *Il commercio* 6, 7 (July 1933), pp. 271–80.

——, 'La riduzione dei prezzi,' *Il commercio* 7, 4 (April 1934), pp. 192–3.

——, 'Commercianti e prezzi nella politica economica attuale,' *Il commercio* 9, 1 (January 1936), pp. 26–30.

——, *Contributo allo studio della vischiosità dei prezzi delle merci*, Rome: Carlo Colombo, 1937.

Virgilii, F., 'Il bilancio alimentare del mondo,' *Nuova Antologia* 197 (September–October 1918), pp. 297–301.

Visco, S., 'Alcuni risultati di un'indagine sulla panificazione nella provincia di Sassari,' *Quaderni della nutrizione* 3, 3–4 (July 1936), pp. 157–70.

Voegelin, L., *La scienza in cucina e nel ristorante (Quel che si mangia: Manuale di arte e scienza gastronomica)*, Trento: Temi, 1966.

Welk, W., *Fascist Economic Policy: An Analysis of Italy's Economic Experiment*, Cambridge MA: Harvard University Press, 1938.

Zerboglio, A., *Le basi economiche della salute*, Alessandria: La Provincia, 1897.

Zingali, G., 'Del consumo e della produzione dei bovini in Italia e del programma di ricostituzione del patrimonio bovino,' *La riforma sociale* 26, 30 (September–December 1919), pp. 449–66.

——, *Il rifornamento dei viveri dell'esercito italiano*, Bari: Laterza, 1926.

Zucconi, A., 'La donna e l'independenza economica,' *Il commercio* 10, 3 (March 1937), pp. 39–41.

Secondary Works

Allio, R., 'Pane e minestra – Perdrix et bécasses,' *Studi Piemontesi* 15, 2 (November 1986), pp. 359–77.

——, *Il tempo di riposo: Squarci di vita sociale del proletariato torinese di fine secolo*, Milan: Feltrinelli, 1991.

Appadurai, A., 'Gastro-Politics in Hindu South Asia,' *American Ethnologist* 8, 3 (1981), pp. 494–511.

Baranski, Z. and Lumley, R. (eds), *Culture and Conflict in Postwar Italy*, New York: St Martin's, 1990.

Barzini, L., *The Italians*, New York: Atheneum, 1977.

Belasco, W., *Appetite for Change: How the Counterculture Took on the Food Industry*, Ithaca: Cornell University Press, 1993.

Bertolo, G. (ed.), *Operai e contadini nella crisi italiana del 1943–1944*, Milan: Feltrinelli, 1974.

Bevilacqua, P., 'Emigrazione transoceanica e mutamenti dell'alimentazione contadina Calabrese fra Otto e Novecento,' *Quaderni Storici* 6, 47 (August 1981), pp. 520–55.

Bezza, B. and Procacci, G. (eds), *Stato e classe operaia in Italia durante la prima guerra mondiale*, Milan: Angeli, 1983.

Bosworth, R., *The Italian Dictatorship: Problems and Perspectives in the Interpretation of Mussolini and Fascism*, London: Arnold, 1998.

Bowen, W., *Spaniards and Nazi Germany: Collaboration in the New Order*, Columbia, MO: University of Missouri Press, 2000.

Braghin, P., *Le diseguaglianze sociali*, Milan: Sapre, 1973.

——, (ed.), *Inchiesta sulla miseria in Italia*, Turin: Einaudi, 1978.

Brewer, J. and Porter, R. (eds), *Consumption and the World of Goods*, London: Routledge, 1993.

Burgio, A. (ed.), *Nel nome della razza*, Bologna; Il Mulino, 1999.

Burnett, J., *Plenty and Want: A Social History of Diet in England from 1815 to the Present Day*, London: Nelson, 1966.

——, and Oddy, D. (eds), *The Origins and Development of Food Policies in Europe*, Leicester: Leicester University Press, 1994.

Calabrese, O. (ed.), *Modern Italy: Images and History of a National Identity*, vol. 4, *The Difficult Democracy*, Milan: Electra, 1985.

Camarda, A. and Peli, S. (eds), *L'altro esercito: La classe operaia durante la prima guerra mondiale*, Milan: Feltrinelli, 1980.

Cameron, R., *A Concise Economic History of the World*, 2nd edn, Oxford: Oxford University Press, 1993.

Capatti, A. and Montanari, M., *La cucina italiana. Storia di una cultura*, Bari: Laterza, 1999.

Capatti, A., De Bernardi, A., and Varni, A. (eds), *Storia d'Italia*, Annali 13, *L'alimentazione*, Turin: G. Einaudi, 1998.

Caracciolo, A., *L'inchiesta agraria Jacini*, Turin: Einaudi, 1973.

Cardoza, A., *Agricultural Elites and Italian Fascism*, Princeton: Princeton University Press, 1982.

Carter, E., *How German is She? Postwar West German Reconstruction and the Consuming Woman*, Ann Arbor: University of Michigan Press, 1997.

Cassese, S., *Lo stato introvabile: Modernità e arretrattezza delle istituzioni italiane*, Rome: Donzelli, 1998.

Cavazzoli, L., *La gente e la guerra: La vita quotidiana del 'fronte interno' Mantova*, 1940–45, Milan: Franco Angeli, 1989.

Ceccarelli, F., *Lo stomaco della repubblica. Cibo e potere in Italia dal 1945 al 2000*, Milan: Longanesi, 2000.

Ceccarelli, L., *Roma alleata*, Rome: Rendina, 1994.

Charles, D. *Lords of the Harvest: Biotech, Big Money, and the Future of Foods*, Cambridge MA: Perseus, 2001.

Chiapparino, F., 'Nascita di una grande impresa: la Perugina, 1907–1923,' *Proposte e ricerche* 23 (1989), pp. 235–50.

Cinel, D., *The National Integration of Italian Return Migration, 1870–1929*, Cambridge: Cambridge University Press, 1991.

Cinotto, S., *Una famiglia che mangia insieme: Cibo ed etnicità nella comunità italoamericana di New York, 1920–1940*, Turin: Otto, 2001.

Cipolla, C., *Storia economica dell'Europa pre-industriale*, Bologna: Il Mulino, 1980.

Clark, M., *Modern Italy 1871–1995*, 2nd edn, London: Longman, 1996.

Clough, S., *The Economic History of Modern Italy*, New York: Columbia University Press, 1964.

Codeluppi, V., *I consumatori: Storia, tendenze, modelli*, Milan: Franco Angeli, 1992.

Colarizi, S., *L'opinione degli Italiani sotto il Regime, 1929–43*, Bari: Laterza, 1991.

——, 'Vita alimentare degli Italiani e razionamento (1941),' in Commissione Italiana di Storia Militare, *L'Italia in guerra: Il secondo anno 1941*, Gaeta: Grafico Militare, 1992.

Colombo, C., and Terzi, A. (eds), *Tra sogno e bisogno: 306 fotografie e 13 saggi sull'evoluzione dei consumi in Italia, 1940–1986*, Milan: Sipiel, 1986.

Coltro, D., *La nostra polenta quotidiana: Storie di donne*, Venice: Marsilio, 1989.

Counihan, C., *Around the Tuscan Table: Food, Family and Gender in Twentieth Century Florence*, New York: Routledge, 2004.

Cova, A., *L'occupazione e i salari: Contributi per una storia del movimento sindicale in Italia*, Milan: Franco Angeli, 1977.

D'Apice, C., *L'arcipelago dei consumi*, Bari: De Donato, 1981.

Davis, B., *Home Fires Burning: Food, Politics, and Everyday Life in World War I Berlin*, Chapel Hill: University of North Carolina Press, 2000.

Davis, J. (ed.), *Italy in the Nineteenth Century*, Oxford: Oxford University Press, 2000.

Deakin, F.W., *The Brutal Friendship: Mussolini, Hitler and the Fall of Italian Fascism*, New York: Harper and Row, 1962.

De Bernardi, A., 'Pellagra, stato e scienza medica: la curabilità impossibile,' in F. Della Peruta (ed.), *Storia d'Italia*, Annali 7, *Malattìa e medicina*, Turin: Einaudi, 1984.

——, 'Modernizzazione e consumi nell'Italia fascista,' *Il Risorgimento* 2 (1992), pp. 417–26.

de Grazia, V., *The Culture of Consent: Mass Organization of Leisure in Fascist Italy*, Cambridge: Cambridge University Press, 1981.

——, *How Fascism Ruled Women, Italy 1922–45*, Berkeley: University of California Press, 1992.

——, 'Die Radikalisierung der Bevolkerungspolitik im Faschistischen Italien: Mussolini's "Rassenstat",' *Geschichte und Gesellschaft* 26 (2000), pp. 219–54.

Del Boca, A., Legnani, M., and Rossi, M., *Regime fascista: Storia e storiografia*, Bari: Laterza, 1995.

De Marco, P., *Polvere di piselli: La vita quotidiana a Napoli durante l'occupazione alleata, 1943–44*, Naples: Liguori, 1996.

Dentoni, M., *Annona e consenso in Italia, 1914–1919*, Milan: Franco Angeli, 1995.

Diner, H., *Hungering for America: Italian, Irish, and Jewish Foodways in the Age of Migration*, Cambridge MA: Harvard University Press, 2001.

Duff, K., 'Economic Relations Between Germany and Italy, 1940–43,' in A. Toynbee and V. Toynbee, (eds), *Hitler's Europe*, Oxford: Oxford University Press, 1954.

Ellwood, D., *Italy 1943–45*, New York: Holmes & Meier, 1985.

Engel, B., 'Not by Bread Alone: Subsistence Riots in Russia During World War I,' *Journal of Modern History* 69 (December 1997), pp. 696–721.

Felice, C., *Il disagio di vivere. Il cibo, la casa, la malattie in Abruzzo e Molise dall'Unità al secondo dopoguerra*, Milan: Franco Angeli, 1989.

Forster, E. and Forster, R. (eds), *European Diet from Pre-Industrial to Modern Times*, New York: Harper and Row, 1975.

Forsyth, D., *The Crisis of Liberal Italy, Monetary and Fiscal Policy, 1914–1922*, Cambridge MA: Cambridge University Press, 1993.

Frascani, P., *Politica economica e finanza pubblica durante la prima dopoguerra*, Naples: Giannini e Figli, 1975.

Gabaccia, D., *We Are What We Eat: Ethnic Food and the Making of Americans*, Cambridge MA: Harvard University Press, 1998.

——, *Italy's Many Diasporas*, Seattle: University of Washington Press, 2000.

Gallerano, N. (ed.), *L'altro dopoguerra: Roma e il sud*, Milan: Franco Angeli, 1986.

Gallo, G. (ed.), *Sulla bocca di tutti: Buitoni e Perugina, una storia in breve*, Perugia: Electa, 1990.

Ganapini, A. and Gonizzi, G., *Barilla: Cento anni di pubblicità e comunicazione*, Parma: Archivio Storico Barilla, 1994.

Gianetti, A. and Rustichini, R., 'Consumi operai e salari negli anni 20 in Italia,' *Movimento operaio e socialista* (October-December 1978), pp. 347–72.

Gibelli, A., *La Grande Guerra degli Italiani (1915–1918)*, Milan: Sansoni, 1998.

Gillette, A., *Racial Theories in Fascist Italy*, New York: Routledge, 2002.

Ginsborg, P., *A History of Contemporary Italy: Society and Politics, 1943–1988*, London: Penguin, 1990.

——, *Italy and its Discontents: Family, Civil Society, State: 1980–2001*, New York: Palgrave, 2003.

Goody, J., *Cooking, Cuisine, and Class*, Cambridge: Cambridge University Press, 1982.

Gregotti, V., *Il disegno del prodotto industriale, Italia 1860–1980*, Milan: Electa, 1998.

Hacking, I., *The Taming of Chance*, Cambridge: Cambridge University Press, 1990.

Harper, J., *America and the Reconstruction of Italy, 1945–1948*, Cambridge: Cambridge University Press, 1986.

Hoffman, P., *That Fine Italian Hand*, New York: Henry Holt, 1990.

Horn, D., 'Welfare, the Social and the Individual,' *Cultural Anthropology* 3 (November 1988), pp. 395–407.

——, *Social Bodies: Science, Reproduction, and Italian Modernity*, Princeton: Princeton University Press, 1994.

Imbriani, A., *Gli Italiani e il Duce: Il mito e l'immagine di Mussolini negli ultimi anni del fascismo (1938–1943)*, Naples: Liguori, 1992.

Ipsen, C., *Dictating Demography: The Problem of Population in Fascist Italy*, Cambridge: Cambridge University Press, 1996.

Isnenghi, M., *Operai e contadina nella Grande Guerra*, Bologna: Capelli, 1982.

Israel, G. and Nastasi, P., *Scienza e razza nell'Italia fascista*, Bologna: Il Mulino, 1998.

Istituto Centrale di Statistica, *Sommario di statistiche storiche dell'Italia, 1861–1942*, Rome: Istituto Poligrafico dello Stato, 1968.

Kindleberger, C., *A Financial History of Western Europe*, 2nd edn, Oxford: Oxford University Press, 1993.

Klinkhammer, L., *L'occupazione tedesca in Italia, 1943–1945*, Turin: Bollati Boringhieri, 1993.

Knox, M., *Mussolini Unleashed 1939–1941: Politics and Strategy in Fascist Italy's Last War*, Cambridge: Cambridge University Press, 1982.

Kocka, J., *Facing Total War: German Society 1914–18*, trans. B. Weinberger, Cambridge MA: Harvard University Press, 1984.

Kogan, N., *A Political History of Italy: The Postwar Years*, New York: Praeger, 1983.

La Cecla, F., *La pasta e la pizza*, Bologna: Il Mulino, 1998.

Lanaro, S., *Nazione e lavoro: Saggio sulla cultura borghese in Italia, 1870–1925*, Venice: Marsilio, 1979.

——, *Storia dell'Italia repubblicana*, Venice: Marsilio, 1992.

Leone, F., 'The Structure of Food Consumption in the Mezzogiorno of Italy,' *Rivista di Antropologia* 76 Supplement (1998), pp. 293–300.

Leoni, D., and Zadra, C. (eds), *La Grande Guerra: Esperienza, memoria, immagini*, Bologna: Il Mulino, 1986.

Lepre, A., *Storia della prima repubblica: L'Italia dal 1942 al 1992*, Bologna: Il Mulino, 1993.

Loy, R., *First Words: A Childhood in Fascist Italy*, Trans. G. Conti, New York: Henry Holt, 2000.

Lyttelton, A., *The Seizure of Power: Fascism in Italy, 1919–1929*, Princeton: Princeton University Press, 1973.

Maier, C., *Recasting Bourgeois Europe: Stabilization in France, Germany and Italy in the Decade After World War I*, Princeton: Princeton University Press, 1975.

Mantelli, B., *Camerati del lavoro: I lavoratori italiani emigrati nel Terzo Reich nel periodo dell'asse 1938–43*, Florence: La Nuova Italia, 1992.

Mariani, R., *Borsari neri in Roma, città aperta*, Rome: NES, 1989.

Mars, V. and Mars, G. (eds), *Food, Culture, and History*, London: The London Food Seminar, 1993.

Mayes, F., *Under the Tuscan Sun: At Home in Italy*, New York: Broadway Books, 1997.

Mazzatosta, T. and Volpi, C. (eds), *L'Italietta fascista (lettere al potere 1936–1943)*, Bologna: Capelli, 1980.

McKendrick, N., Brewer, J., and Plumb, J.H. (eds), *The Birth of a Consumer Society: The Commercialization of Eighteenth Century England*, Bloomington: Indiana University Press, 1982.

Meldini, P., 'La cucina della famiglia fascista,' in Zia Carolina, *Cucina pratica*, reprint, Milan: Guaraldi, 1977.

Mennell, S., *All Manners of Food: Eating and Taste in England and France from the Middle Ages to the Present*, London: Basil Blackwell, 1985.

Miller, J., *The United States and Italy, 1940–1950: The Politics and Diplomacy of Stabilization*, Chapel Hill: University of North Carolina Press, 1986.

Mintz, S., *Sweetness and Power: The Place of Sugar in Modern History*, New York: Viking Penguin, 1985.

——, *Tasting Food, Tasting Freedom*, Boston: Beacon Press, 1996.

Morris, J., *The Political Economy of Shopkeeping in Milan, 1886–1922*, Cambridge: Cambridge University Press, 1993.

——, 'The Fascist "Disciplining" of the Italian Retail Sector 1922–40,' *Business History* 40 (1998), pp. 138–64.

Nenni, P., *Storia di quattro anni, 1918–22*, Milan: SugarCo, 1976.

Nestle, M., *Food Politics: How the Food Industry Influences Nutrition and Health*, Berkeley: University of California Press, 2002.

Nye, R., *Crime, Madness, and Politics in Modern France: The Medical Concept of National Decline*, Princeton: Princeton University Press, 1984.

Oddy, D., 'Food, Drink and Nutrition,' in F.M.L. Thompson, (ed.), *The Cambridge Social History of Nutrition*, Vol. 2 Cambridge: Cambridge University Press, 1990.

Offen, K., 'Depopulation, Nationalism and Feminism in *Fin-de-Siècle* France,' *American Historical Review* 89, 3 (June 1984), pp. 648–76.

Offer, A., *The First World War: An Agrarian Interpretation*, Oxford: Clarendon, 1989.

Ortoleva, P., 'La tradizione e l'abbondanza. Riflessioni sulla cucina degli italiani d'America,' *AltreItaliani* (January–June 1992), pp. 31–52.

Padovani, G., *Gnam! Storia sociale della Nutella*, Rome: Castelvecchi, 2000.

Passerini, L., *Mussolini immaginario*, Bari: Laterza, 1991.

Patriarca, S., *Numbers and Nationhood: Writing Statistics in Nineteenth-Century Italy*, Cambridge: Cambridge University Press, 1996.

Petrini, C., *Slow Food: Collected Thoughts on Taste, Tradition and the Honest Pleasures of Food*, White River Junction: Chelsea Green, 2001.

Pilcher, J., *¡Que vivan los tamales! Food and the Making of Mexican Identity*, Albuquerque: University of New Mexico Press, 1998.

Pinkus, K., *Bodily Regimes: Italian Advertising Under Fascism*, Minneapolis: University of Minnesota Press, 1995.

Porter, T., *The Rise of Statistical Thinking, 1820–1900*, Princeton: Princeton University Press, 1986.

Preti, D., *Economia e istituzioni nello stato fascista*, Rome: Riuniti, 1980.

Procacci, G., 'Gli effetti della Grande Guerra sulla psicologia della popolazione civile,' *Storia e problemi contemporanei* 10 (1992), pp. 77–91.

Quine, M., *Italy's Social Revolution: Charity and Welfare from Liberalism to Fascism*, New York: Palgrave, 2002.

Quirino, P., 'I consumi in Italia dall'Unità ad oggi,' in R. Romano, (ed.), *Storia dell'economia italiana*, Vol. 3, *L'età contemporanea: un paese nuovo*, Turin: Einaudi, 1991.

Rabinbach, A., *The Human Motor: Energy, Fatigue, and the Origins of Modernity*, New York: Basic Books, 1990.

Rasi, G., 'La politica economica e i conti della nazione,' in *Annali dell'economia italiana*, Vol. 6, No. 1, Milan: IPSOA, 1982.

Raspin, A., *The Italian War Economy 1940–43*, New York: Garland, 1986.

Riall, L., *The Italian Risorgimento: State, Society and National Unification*, London: Routledge, 1994.

Richards, C., *The New Italians*, London: Penguin, 1994.

Robb, P., *Midnight in Sicily*, New York: Vintage Books, 1999.

Rochat, G., Santarelli, E., and Sorcinelli, P. (eds), *Linea Gotica 1944: eserciti, popolazioni, partigiani*, Milan: Franco Angeli, 1986.

Sassoon, D., *Contemporary Italy*, 2nd edn, Harlow: Longman, 1997.

Romanelli, R., *L'Italia liberale 1861–1900*, Bologna: Il Mulino, 1979.

Schneider, J. (ed.), *Italy's 'Southern Question': Orientalism in One Country*, Oxford: Berg, 1998.

Scholliers, P. (ed.), *Food, Drink and Identity: Cooking, Eating and Drinking in Europe since the Middle Ages*, Oxford: Berg, 2001.

Sereni, E., *Terra nuova e buoi rossi*, Turin: Einaudi, 1981.

Seton-Watson, C., *Italy from Liberalism to Fascism, 1870–1925*, London: Methuen, 1967.

Somogyi, S., 'L'alimentazione nell'Italia unita,' in *Storia d'Italia*, Volume 5, Tomo 1, *I documenti*, Turin: Einaudi, 1973.

Sorcinelli, P., *Gli Italiani e il cibo: Appetiti, digiuni e rinunce della realtà contadina alla società del benessere*, Bologna: CLUEB, 1992.

Spang, R., *The Invention of the Restaurant. Paris and Modern Gastronomic*

Culture, Cambridge MA: Harvard University Press, 2000.

Storchi, M., *Il poco e il tanto: Condizioni e modi di vita degli Italiani dall'unificazione a oggi*, Naples: Liguori, 1999.

Teti, V., *La razza maledetta: Origini del pregiudizio antimeridionale*, Rome: Manifestolibri, 1993.

Teuteberg, H. (ed.), *European Food History: A Research Review*, Leicester: Leicester University Press, 1992.

Tomassini, L., *L'Italia nella Grande Guerra, 1915–18*, Milan: Fenice, 1995.

Venè, G.F., *Mille lire al mese: Vita quotidiana della famiglia nell'Italia fascista*, Milan: Mondadori, 1988.

Visceglia, M., 'I consumi in Italia in età moderna,' in R. Romano (ed.), *Storia dell'economia italiana*, Volume II, *Verso la crisi*, Turin: Einaudi, 1991.

Vivarelli, R., *Il fallimento del liberalismo: Studi sulle origini del fascismo*, Bologna: Il Mulino, 1981.

——, 'La questione contadina nell'Italia unita,' *Rivista storica italiana*, 102, 1 (April 1990), pp. 87–165.

Winter, J., 'Military Fitness and Civilian Health in Britain During the First World War,' *Journal of Contemporary History* 15 (1980), pp. 211–44.

Woolf, S. (ed.), *The Rebirth of Italy*, London: Longman, 1972.

——, 'Come e che cosa mangiavano i Fiorentini cent'anni fa?' *Fiorentin mangiafagioli*, special publication of CGIL and Camera di Lavoro di Firenze, 1993, pp. 9–42.

Zamagni, V., *La distribuzione commerciale in Italia fra le due guerre*, Milan: Franco Angeli, 1981.

——, *The Economic History of Italy, 1860–1990: Recovery After Decline*, Oxford: Clarendon Press, 1993.

Zuccotti, S., 'The Wartime Experience and Politicization: Workers and Peasants in the Province of Milan, 1915–18,' Ph.D. Dissertation, Columbia University, 1979.

Index

238 · *Index*

Bonomi, Ivanoe, 58
Bossi, Umberto, 157
Bottazzi, Filippo, 72, 100–2, 119
brand names, 32, 35, 141–3, 149, 193–4n79
bread
    as a status indicator, 11, 14, 34
    containing non-wheat flours, 105
    festivals, 77
    fixed prices, 56, 68–9
    nutritional value, 77, 147
    pane comune, 69
    pane integrale, 77
        fertility and, 119
    rationing, 109, 114
    tipo unico laws, 42–3, 47–8, 58, 105
    wheat bread as a staple, 1, 3, 16, 34, 40, 50
    wood pulp in, 109
bread commissions, 69
bread-making industry,
    government assistance, 69
bread subsidies, 3–4, 40, 50, 52, 55–9
British Medical Association, Nutrition Committee, 101
Brugnola, Arsenio, 20–1
Buitoni (brand name), 35, 143
Buitoni's Spaghetti Bar, 142
Burger King, 167n4

C
Caffarel (brand name), 35
calorie consumption, 72–3, 126–7, 132, 134–5
    dietary recommendations, 45–6, 101–2, 120, 139–40, 211n51
        international standards, 172n33
    physiological requirements, 120
    ration card allowances, 4, 111, 120
    regional differences, 102, 134–6
    study of, 26
calories available per person, 72, 203–4n105
Camporesi, Piero, 27
Canepa, Luigi, 47
Cao-Pinna, Vera, 102
Capatti, Alberto, 163
carbohydrates
    dietary recommendations, 73, 101–2, 139–40, 172n33
    diet based on, 17, 63, 84, 136
Carolina, Zia,
    Cucina pratica, 83, 86
Carosello (television program), 143
Casa e lavoro, 83
Catholic Church
    approval of social-scientific investigation, 18
    food assistance, 131–2
Ceccarelli, Filippo, 156

Central Institute of Statistics (Istituto Centrale di Statistica or ISTAT), 72, 118, 120, 122, 133–5, 139
Central Office of Demography and Race (Demorazza), 118–19
charity
    administered through the National Fascist Party, 97
    as a stigma, 36–7
    food assistance, 131–2
Chef Boy-Ar-Dee (brand name), 32
Chiapparino, Francesco, 35
children,
    food programs, 131–2, 207n14
chocolate, 35, 111–12, 141–2
Christian Democratic Party, 128–9
    food policies, 132–3, 136–7
Christ Stopped at Eboli (Levi), 78
Ciano, Galeazzo, 104
Cinotto, Simone, 30
Cirio (brand name), 32, 35, 143
CNR (Consiglio Nazionale delle Ricerche) (National Research Council), 72, 74, 92, 96, 102
coal subsidy, 53
cocktails, 87, 127, 138, 144
Colarizi, Simona, 97, 107
Coldiretti (agricultural union), 161–2
Commissariato Generale de Consumi Alimentari (General Commissariat for Food Consumption), 47
Commissione per lo Studio dei Problemi dell'Alimentazione (Committee for the Study of Alimentary Problems), 72–4
Common Agricultural Policy, 162
Communist Party, 128–9, 156–7
companatico, 1, 16, 24, 34, 78
conservation as national policy, 41–3, 47, 74, 77
Consiglio Nazionale delle Ricerche (National Research Council) (CNR), 72, 74, 92, 96, 102
consumer cooperatives, 48, 178n7
consumer education, 137
consumer ethic, 8–9, 12
    emphasis on austerity, 46, 49, 85, 141
consumerism, 8–9, 146
consumer/merchant conflicts, 42–3, 69–70
consumption, ethic of, 8–9, 12
    emphasis on austerity, 46, 49, 85, 141
consumption habits
    as a measure of national development, 129
    as a political problem, 59–61, 117
    as a symbol of national resistance, 98, 103, 105
    changes in, 13, 33–8, 40, 50–1, 120
    control of, 4–5, 63–6, 141–2

nutritional standards, international, 20, 73,
  101–2, 172n33
nutritionists, 19–20

O
obesity, 156–7
Offer, Avner, 39
Office of Propaganda to Discipline
  Consumption, 45–6
Operation Barbarossa, 108
Orano, Domenico, 34
Orlando, Vittorio Emanuele, 52

P
Pact of Steel, 65, 122
pane comune, 69
pane integrale, 77
  fertility and, 119
Passerini, Luisa, 99
pasta
  as a staple, 3, 15–16, 33, 84–5, 155
  external markets for, 32
  Futurist battle against, 78–9
  history of, 29, 31–2
  Italian identity and, 155
  nutritional value of, 147
  price of, 57, 69, 111
  rations, 106, 109–10, 114, 116
pasta industry, 32, 35, 153
pasta water, 11, 135, 152–3
peasant diet, 22–3
pellagra (niacin deficiency disease), 23, 36
Peloggio, Rina, 99
Perugina (brand name), 35, 143
Petrini, Carlo, 163
physical development
  divergence between rich and poor, 19–23,
    26–7, 119, 151
pizza
  as a staple, 1, 16, 33, 153, 159, 164
  history of, 29
  Italian identity and, 155
  patents, 157, 162
PNF (National Fascist Party), 59
  charity administered through, 97
polenta, 1, 16, 22–3, 34, 84, 151
politicians, indulgent food habits, 156–7
the poor, 170n13
  diet of, 133–5, 152–3
poor and rich
  divergence between consumption habits, 17,
    24–5, 134
  divergence in physical development, 19–23,
    26–7, 119, 151
population
  as a managed national resource, 93, 118–20,
    124

as a measure of national development, 151
  fascist policies, 64, 93, 118–19
  food as a measure of well-being, 164
  Italian, as backward and inadequate, 19
pork consumption, 50
post-First World War era
  agricultural production, 60
  consumption habits, 51–9
  state intervention, 51–9
post-Second World War era
  affluence, 127–9, 138–46
  agricultural production, 128, 137
  consumption habits, 126–7, 129, 138, 145,
    148–50
  diet, 5, 145
  food policies, 129–37, 147
  Italian cuisine, 149–50
  Italian identity, 129, 151
  lifestyle, 128–30, 143–4, 146
  nutrition studies, 133–6
  shortages of food, 127, 130
  state intervention, 130, 150
potato production, 76
poverty, 133, 136, 138, 153
power, inequality in the food industry, 162–3
pre-industrial diet, 3
Preti, Domenico, 73
Price Control in Fascist Italy (Miller), 97
price controls, 53–4, 195n7
  citizen participation in, 44
  enforcement of, 95, 107
  fascist, 53–4, 65, 70, 74, 106
    failure of, 116–17
    for staple foods, 94–5
  grain consortia and, 41
  under Italian Social Republic (RSI), 113–15
  municipal governments and, 36, 42–4
  unintended consequences of, 48, 71
price policies, national, 55
prices
  divergence in, 68
  lower, 137
  versus wages, 53, 55, 58, 94
  wholesale, 68
price subsidies, 3–4, 40, 50
price viscosity, 71
price/wage imbalance, 53, 94
prisoners of war, provisions for, 46
production costs, fixed prices and, 55
profits, control of, 70
proof of purchase, redemption for items, 142–3
propaganda
  about food, 65
  austerity and, 125
  encouraging rice consumption, 79
  promoting an ideal diet, 98, 105
  women as the audience for, 99

prosperity, 127
protein consumption, 50, 72, 84–7, 134–5, 211n50
  dietary recommendations, 20, 45, 73, 93, 101–2, 139–40
  international standards, 172n33
  high-fat, high-protein diet, 139
  inadequate, 21–3, 25, 111, 119, 132
  physiological requirements, 99, 119
  pre-industrial diet, 3
  substitutes for, 80
  see also meat consumption
protest
  anti-American, 158
  anti-global, 158
  anti-McDonald's, 215n13
  as unpatriotic, 69
  consumer/merchant conflicts, 42–3, 69–70
  cost-of-living riots, 52–4, 57, 59
  fascist control of, 65
  food policies and, 97, 116
  food shortages and, 41–2, 44, 47, 49, 107–8, 113
  social justice and, 58
Provincial Association of Farmworkers and Merchants, 91
Provisioning and Consumption, Ministry for, 49
public discourse about food, 5
  nineteenth century food consumption, 12, 37
Pugliese, Angelo, 45, 50, 103

Q
Quaderni della nutrizione, 75

R
race, 118
  food and, 202–3n101
  racial classifications, 204n110
  racial degeneration, 118–19
racism, 64, 124
Rahn, Rudolf von, 113, 125
Raspelli, Edoardo, 159–60
rationing
  bread, 109
  caloric intake and, 111
  extra rations
    for Italians who worked for the Wehrmacht, 121
  requests for, 106, 115–16, 130
  German rules for, 122
  mandatory, 47–8
  per capita levels, 123
  Second World War, 4, 81, 91, 104–6
  voluntary, 47
ration tickets, food supplies and, 109

Reale Accademia d'Italia (Royal Academy of Italy), 101
reconstruction, 127
regional diversity
  as the foundation of Italian cuisine, 86, 103, 125, 128, 144–6, 155
  in consumption levels, 134–6
relief organizations, 131
renunciation
  as a cultural value, 2
  as a national virtue, 64, 127
  see also austerity
Resca, Mario, 160
Resistance, anti-fascist forces, 108
restaurants, featuring regional cuisine, 144–6
retail merchants
  campaign against, 65–8, 70–1
  price controls and, 94–5
  speculation and, 96
retail prices, wholesale prices and, 71
Rho, Filippo, 45
Ricci, Umberto, 48
rice consumption, 85, 109, 143
  as a substitute for pasta, 79
rice production, 76
rich and poor
  divergence between consumption habits, 17, 24–5, 134, 146
  divergence in physical development, 19–23, 26–7, 119, 151
Riforma Sociale, La, 22
rights
  of women, 128
  of workers, 159–60
Risorgimento (national unification), 11, 13–14, 18
Robb, Peter, 157
Ronchi, Vittorio, 104, 107, 116
Rossi, Cesare, 71
Rossi, Felice, 21
Royal Academy of Italy (Reale Accademia d'Italia), 101
Royal Institute for International Affairs, 76
RSI (Italian Social Republic), 108, 112–15
rural workers, 188–9n27

S
saccharine, 51
salaries
  average, 133
  versus cost of living, 55, 57–8, 67, 94, 111, 125
  increasing, 137–8, 210–11n48
Salvo, Nino, 157
Sansone, Luigi Renato, 147
sayings about food, 15
Scanio, Pecoraro, 161